Geoff Hamilton
organic
GARDENING

THIS BOOK IS A GIFT
OF FRIENDS
OF THE ORINDA LIBRARY

WITHDRAWN

D1441721

Geoff Hamilton
organic
GARDENING

LONDON, NEW YORK, MUNICH, MELBOURNE, DELHI

New edition, 2011
Revised and updated by Nick Hamilton

DK Publishing
SENIOR EDITOR Helen Fewster
SENIOR ART EDITOR Lucy Parissi
MANAGING EDITOR Esther Ripley
MANAGING ART EDITOR Alison Donovan
PRODUCTION EDITOR Joanna Byrne
PRODUCTION CONTROLLER Erika Pepe
JACKET DESIGNER Mark Cavanagh
DK PICTURE LIBRARY Lucy Claxton, Jenny Baskaya
ASSOCIATE PUBLISHER Liz Wheeler
ART DIRECTOR Peter Luff
PUBLISHER Jonathan Metcalf

US CONSULTANT Lori Spencer
AMERICANIZER Kate Johnsen
US EDITOR Liza Kaplan

DK India
SENIOR EDITOR Rukmini Chawla Kumar
EDITOR Nidhilekha Mathur
ART EDITORS Mahua Mandal, Nitu Singh,
Nishesh Bhatnagar
MANAGING EDITOR Suchismita Banerjee
MANAGING ART EDITOR Romi Chakraborty
PICTURE RESEARCHER Jyoti Sachdev
DTP MANAGER Sunil Sharma
DTP DESIGNERS Manish Chandra Upreti, Jagtar Singh

First edition, 1987
SENIOR EDITOR Jemima Dunne
SENIOR ART EDITOR Neville Graham
EDITORS Sophie Mitchell, Tim Hammond
ART EDITOR Derek Coombes
DESIGNER Joanna Martin
MANAGING EDITOR Daphne Razazan

Revised edition, 2008
Additional text: Ian Spence
Additional design: Nicola Liddiard

First American Edition, 1993
This American Edition, 2011

Published in the United States by
DK Publishing
375 Hudson Street
New York, New York 10014

11 12 13 14 15   10 9 8 7 6 5 4 3 2 1

001—179523—February/2011

Copyright © 1987, 2008, 2011 Dorling Kindersley
Limited
All rights reserved

Without limiting the rights under copyright reserved
above, no part of this publication may be reproduced,
stored in or introduced into a retrieval system, or
transmitted, in any form, or by any means (electronic,
mechanical, photocopying, recording, or otherwise),
without the prior written permission of both the
copyright owner and the above publisher of this book.

Published in Great Britain by Dorling Kindersley
Limited.

A catalog record for this book is available from the
Library of Congress.

ISBN 978-0-7566-7179-2

DK books are available at special discounts when
purchased in bulk for sales promotions, premiums,
fund-raising, or educational use. For details, contact:
DK Publishing Special Markets, 375 Hudson Street,
New York, New York 10014 or SpecialSales@dk.com.

Discover more at
www.dk.com

CONTENTS

NB *Latin plant names are given
throughout the book where they differ
from the common names*

INTRODUCTION

❝My father wrote this book more than 20 years ago and re-reading it to update this new edition has reaffirmed what a great gardener he really was. His knowledge, innovative methods, and easy-to-follow instructions make this book as invaluable to gardeners today as it was in 1987.❞

– Nick Hamilton, September 2010

ORGANIC GARDENING is a divisive subject. There are those who think that organic methods of cultivation are the only remaining way to save the planet and, at the other extreme, those who think that organic gardening is only carried out by rabid, environmentally obsessed loonies. I believe neither. Fortunately, many millions of gardeners all over the world are now beginning to consider organic gardening methods and to evaluate them rationally. Even the long-skeptical scientists are having second thoughts as the public demand for chemical-free food and a safer environment increases.

I have been a professional gardener for 30 years and I have to admit that, up to 10 years ago, I too was skeptical about organic gardening. Of course, it's hard to argue with the developments resulting from modern research: agricultural and horticultural science has increased yields dramatically, which has kept food prices stable for years and increased the general well-being of the population of the Western world a thousandfold. Indeed it would be foolish to deny that science has made, and is still making, a tremendous contribution to the art of growing both productive and ornamental plants. However perfect nature's methods may be, it was

never intended that the land should be as productive as we now demand. While nature may have intended one scraggy little wild carrot in every yard, we demand a big fat juicy carrot every few inches. So we have needed all our ingenuity to improve on nature's methods.

Research has helped in a variety of ways that are more than acceptable to the organic gardener: varieties of both productive and ornamental plants have been improved almost beyond recognition; quality has been enhanced by finding ways of protecting our plants against the worst of weather; yields have been improved by extending harvesting periods using glass and plastic. And, as a result of research into plants and the way in which they grow, cultivation techniques have been developed to such an extent that the Western world's pantry is full to overflowing.

THE MISTAKES OF MODERN TECHNOLOGY

Modern technology has its uses and cannot be broadly condemned, but there have been many mistakes. The dramatic turnaround from scarcity to plenty over the past century has been achieved at the expense of a massive and ever-increasing input of chemicals and with little thought for tomorrow.

▲ **A source of water** *A pool, however small, will attract all kinds of insects and small mammals.*

◄ **Mixed planting scheme** *Mixing flowers and vegetables in the same bed can look very attractive.*

Where corn has proven more profitable than cows, the practice of replacing organic matter on the land has died out. The result is that soils are becoming lifeless and, in many instances, simply disappearing into the sea. Larger agricultural machines have demanded larger fields and, as a result, trees and shrubbery have disappeared taking their dependent wildlife with them.

Plants need a certain level of nutrients for healthy growth so, in order to maintain these levels, more and more chemical fertilizers are poured on to the land year after year, filling the plants we eat with alien chemicals and polluting our waterways.

The traditional practice of mixing and rotating crops has been abandoned for short-term profit with the result that pests and diseases build up to uncontrollable proportions. Killing them with poison sprays becomes essential and, as resistant strains of both pests and diseases develop, more powerful chemicals have to be used. It is this aspect that is most troubling to us, the consumers of food produced in this way.

Every year, some chemical previously thought to have been safe is banned somewhere in the world. One of the early cases was the insecticide DDT. There is no doubt that it saved many thousands of lives by killing malaria-carrying mosquitoes, but it was also found to build up in the bodies of animals and birds, causing untold losses of wildlife; it was banned in most Western countries before it caused any deaths in humans. This was followed by the soil insecticide dieldrin, the selective weedkiller loxynil, suspected of causing birth defects, and, in most Western countries, the herbicide, trichlorophenoxy-acetic acid, or 2,4,5-T, which has been linked with cancer. Not only have these chemicals been shown to cause untold damage to wildlife, but some have also been found in alarming quantities in food, even after processing and cooking.

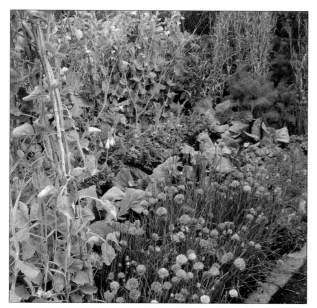

▲ **A variety of vegetables** *Planting a wide range of vegetables not only produces a varied crop, but also reduces the risk of pest and disease attack.*

WHAT IS THE SOLUTION?

For anyone with a garden, the solution seems simple: grow your own produce. But the chemical industry is big business, so gardeners have, over the years, been persuaded that they too can "benefit" from research carried out by the commercial growers and farmers. After all, what is good for the professional must be good for amateurs—but nothing is further from the truth.

While we can certainly benefit in some ways from research, there is absolutely no need for the home gardener to follow commercial practices blindly. Remember the professional grows on a large scale for profit, while we do so on a small scale for pleasure. He needs all his harvest to be ready at the same time, while we want to stagger it. What's more, there is no need to sacrifice anything in terms of yield and quality. Let me give you an example.

If a farmer has 20 acres of cabbages, he can almost certainly expect an attack of cabbage white butterfly; no self-respecting butterfly could miss such an opportunity. So, to avoid the hungry caterpillars devouring the entire crop, the farmer may have no alternative but to spray. The gardener, on the other hand, has perhaps only ten or a dozen plants. And, if he is an organic gardener, they'll be interplanted with other crops and so effectively camouflaged from the butterflies, who recognize them by sight and perhaps smell. The chances are the cabbages will be missed altogether but, if a butterfly does see them and lay her eggs, there is still no need to reach for a spray. All you need to do is walk down the row occasionally, pick off the offending caterpillars, and drop them into a jar of paraffin. You will get one hundred percent control and it will cost you nothing. What's more, your cabbages will be perfectly clean and healthy. Even better, if you grow the right kind of plants in the ornamental borders and among the vegetables, the birds and the ground beetles will do the job for you.

PEAT-FREE DEVELOPMENT

There is increasing concern about the use of peat as a growing medium. Peat is a dwindling natural resource, and excavating peat bogs on an industrial scale to supply gardens not only destroys unique habitats but is damaging to the wider environment.

There are many alternatives available that are either completely free of peat or have a reduced peat content. The majority are made from bark, coir, or wood chips, with some even incorporating the material produced from green recycling centers.

These products work well, with coir the preferred choice for propagation while the others are more suited for growing plants. The move toward peat-free gardening has gained momentum. Many amateur gardeners are already following the lead taken by professional growers and choosing, wherever possible, a peat-free alternative.

The same philosophy applies to fertilizers. In a natural soil there are millions of microorganisms munching away on our behalf, producing the nutrients that plants need for healthy growth. Look after them by feeding the soil (rather than applying chemical fertilizers to feed the plants) and they'll repay you a thousandfold. They'll not thank you for a daily dose of paraquat.

MY EXPERIMENTS

Let's look at the other side of the coin for a moment. Ever since I started gardening, I have come across some extraordinary and imaginative remedies for plant ills and some cultivation techniques that stretch credibility well beyond its breaking point. Moreover, organic gardening does have more than its fair share of eccentrics. And that can be disconcerting. On the other hand, Christopher Columbus was held to be eccentric for saying that the world was round until he actually proved it. And that has been my solution.

Over the past 10 years I have been conducting various experiments. I've tried to keep an open mind (and that has not always been easy). However outlandish the theory seemed, I've tried it under as near scientifically experimental conditions as possible. It's important to set up proper trials because, in many cases, when an organic gardener has reported complete success with a pest or disease control, he has not grown a control plot at the same time. The gardener may think, for example, that carrot fly was defeated by surrounding the rows with creosoted string, but how does anyone know that there would have been an attack in the first place? Unless a nearby row is attacked, the experiment proves nothing. I have tried the creosoted string method and it didn't work.

I set up trials to test the many suggested organic controls for cabbage root fly. I grew one row with a bit of rhubarb stem underneath the plants, one row with a few mothballs, one with a layer of comfrey spread over the soil, and another watered with extract of nettle leaves. In order to be as comprehensive as possible, I grew other rows treated with the chemical insecticides dianzon and bromophos. Most outlandish of all, I surrounded each plant in one of the rows with a bit of carpet pad. And, of course, I grew a control row with no treatment at all.

The cabbage root fly did attack and the rows with rhubarb, mothballs, comfrey, and nettles all suffered, as did the control row. Those that were treated with soil insecticides were about 80 percent free, but the row with the carpet pad was completely unscathed. I use it every year now and it doesn't cost me anything.

I now have a row of four identical plots about 15 × 20ft (5 × 6.5m), each growing identical plants, ranging from apple trees and fruit bushes down to cauliflower, cabbages, carrots, and other vegetables. One plot is treated organically, one inorganically, one traditionally using a mixture of the two methods and, of course, there is the obligatory control plot, which gets no added organic matter or chemicals at all. I thought at first that the experiments would be invalidated by having the plots so close together: wouldn't their close proximity mean that the insects would simply hop from one plot to another, that weeds could creep under the fences, and microbes move through the soil?

Well, of course, that may be so, but I realized that this was the way it had to be. If the experiment was to benefit the average gardener, the organic plot would have to be able to cope with the ills sent from next door. After all, few of us are lucky enough to be completely isolated, and converting the entire street to organic gardening would take much more than gardening skills.

But, amazingly, I found not the slightest problem. Weeds tried to creep in from the next plot but I dealt with those by installing a plastic barrier beneath the fence. Most marvelous of all, the hoverflies attracted by the marigolds in the organic plot, ate the greenfly in the next door plot as well, and the frogs hopped in and took care of their slugs too.

THE AIM OF THIS BOOK

So, this book is the result of 30 years gardening and 10 years of organic trials. I don't claim that you'll find every organic remedy you've ever heard of and you won't find any magic or mysterious folklore.

What you will discover is a mixture of traditional gardening and modern technology, all of which has been tried and tested over the years in my own garden and proven to be effective. My aim is to make a productive, beautiful, interesting, and enjoyable garden that provides an alternative habitat for wildlife of all kinds; gives me a happy, healthy, and absorbing occupation; and provides me with food that tastes like nature intended and that I know is free from pollution. I'd like to share that with you.

THE ORGANIC WAY

THERE IS NOTHING MYSTICAL or magical about organic gardening. It is simply a way of working with nature rather than against it, of recycling natural materials to maintain soil fertility, and of encouraging natural methods of pest and disease control, rather than relying on chemicals. It is in fact far less involved than the methods employed by the chemical grower.

Organic gardening is much more than just a way of growing plants without chemical sprays and artificial fertilizers. It recognizes that the complex workings of nature have been successful in sustaining life over hundreds of millions of years, so the basic organic cultivation principles closely follow those found in the natural world. Don't be misled into thinking that these principles will have a detrimental effect on yield or quality. In fact, you are much more likely to increase both and, in doing so, you will be providing an alternative habitat for wildlife, while being certain that the fruit and vegetables produced in your garden are safe, flavorful, and chemical-free.

THE CHEMICAL GARDENER

The purely chemical gardener uses his soil simply as a means of anchoring plant roots and of holding artificial fertilizers to provide plant nutrients. This approach does have excellent results, in the short term.

In the long term, however, it has two disastrous consequences. Because organic matter is not replaced, the soil organisms die out; without them the soil structure breaks down and the soil becomes hard, airless, and unproductive. Attempts at "force-feeding" the plants result in soft, sappy growth, which is prone to attack by all manner of pests and diseases. In order to control them, chemical pesticides are used, often with short-term success. But, in killing the pest, they also kill its natural predators so, eventually, the problem gets worse. Stronger and more poisonous pesticides have to be resorted to, and so it goes on. It is a vicious circle that, once started, is difficult to break.

THE ORGANIC GARDENER

The organic gardener has a more constructive approach based on an awareness that there is a fine balance in the natural world which allows all the species to coexist without anyone gaining dominance.

By growing a wide diversity of plants, the organic gardener will attract and build up a miniature ecosystem of pests and predators so that, provided the balance isn't upset by killing them with chemicals, no species will be allowed to build up to an unacceptable level.

The soil is teeming with millions of microorganisms which, in the course of their lives, will release those nutrients required for healthy plant growth from organic matter. So, rather than feeding the plants, the organic way is to feed the soil with natural materials and allow the plants to draw on that reservoir of nutrients as and when they want them. Plants grown this way will be stronger and more able to resist attacks by pests and diseases.

Improving on nature

Natural methods of sustaining plant growth were never intended to support the kinds of demands we make on our gardens. The technique itself is perfect, but, to produce a good crop, we have to intensify it.

The main ways of doing this are quite simple: feeding the soil and improving its texture; protecting seeds during germination; making sure that the plants have adequate water; and being vigilant in controlling pests and diseases.

LOOKING AFTER THE SOIL

In nature, for example, soil fertility is maintained by recycling organic matter (see next page). Gardeners, on the other hand, remove much of the organic material from the productive garden in the form of fruit and vegetables, and from the ornamental garden by weeding, pruning, mowing, and cutting flowers. This organic matter has to be replaced through the compost heap, animal manure, and green-manure crops. Even then, our intensive methods may need further inputs of concentrated animal and plant residues.

In nature, soil texture, aeration, and drainage is maintained by the action of burrowing animals such as worms and insects. Gardeners can improve on this by digging regularly.

SEEDING AND WATERING
In nature, many of the seeds produced never germinate due to adverse conditions or predation, while in the garden, this no longer has to be haphazard. We can ensure that seeds and mature plants are protected and that the right amount of water is supplied in dry weather.

CONTROLLING PESTS AND DISEASES
We can improve on natural methods of pest and disease control too. We can deliberately fill our gardens with a wide diversity of plants that we know will attract and encourage the predators of the pests that threaten our cultivated plants.

THE FINAL CROP
Our plant breeders have produced varieties that are resistant to pests and diseases and that will give us bigger crops and more beautiful flowers, while thousands of years of growing experience have enabled us to come up with techniques that will outcrop nature many times over.

But, if we are to continue our success, we must stick to the rules. We may be able to manipulate nature in the short term by using chemical methods but it is folly to think that we can ever assume complete control.

GARDENING WITH NATURE

ENRICHING THE SOIL
In nature, dead or rotting vegetation and animal manure provide adequate nourishment for the soil. As man removes the crops he grows, he must add compost and manure to improve the soil.

Nature Man

DIGGING
Despite the activity of burrowing animals and penetrating plant roots, untended soil is still relatively hard and compacted. Man can improve the texture by digging to allow air and water through the soil.

Nature Man

SEEDING
In nature, relatively few seeds germinate because of competition from other plants and poor conditions. In the garden, most seeds will germinate as they can be given optimum conditions and spacings.

Nature Man

WATERING
Plants are dependent on water for their survival. While adequate rainfall cannot be guaranteed in nature, in the garden, additional water can be given to the plants in very dry weather.

Nature Man

PEST CONTROL
Nature maintains its delicate balance by ensuring that pests and predators control each other's numbers. Man can encourage and assist this process while also protecting his plants using artificial means.

Nature Man

THE FINAL CROP
Left to its own devices, nature would not produce a very abundant harvest, either in terms of quantity or the size of the individual foods. The harvest from cultivated ground is richer and far more varied.

Nature Man

Worms pull plant remains into the upper layers of the soil. Worm casts are a valuable fertilizer.

The soil feeds the plants

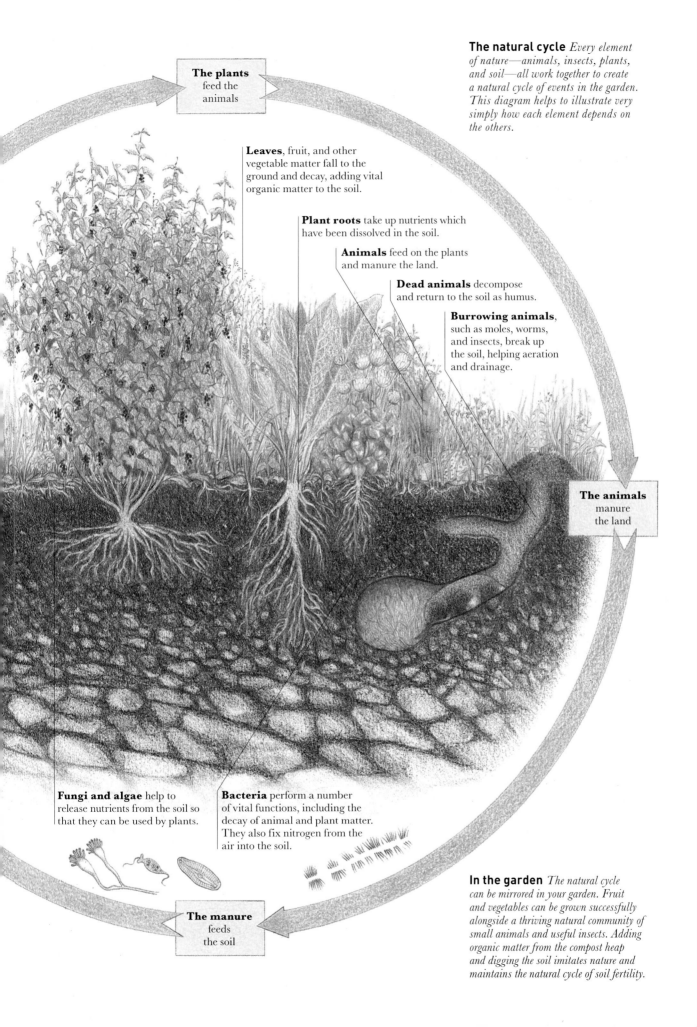

The plants feed the animals

Leaves, fruit, and other vegetable matter fall to the ground and decay, adding vital organic matter to the soil.

Plant roots take up nutrients which have been dissolved in the soil.

Animals feed on the plants and manure the land.

Dead animals decompose and return to the soil as humus.

Burrowing animals, such as moles, worms, and insects, break up the soil, helping aeration and drainage.

The natural cycle *Every element of nature—animals, insects, plants, and soil—all work together to create a natural cycle of events in the garden. This diagram helps to illustrate very simply how each element depends on the others.*

The animals manure the land

Fungi and algae help to release nutrients from the soil so that they can be used by plants.

Bacteria perform a number of vital functions, including the decay of animal and plant matter. They also fix nitrogen from the air into the soil.

The manure feeds the soil

In the garden *The natural cycle can be mirrored in your garden. Fruit and vegetables can be grown successfully alongside a thriving natural community of small animals and useful insects. Adding organic matter from the compost heap and digging the soil imitates nature and maintains the natural cycle of soil fertility.*

THE SOIL

THE SOIL IS THE BASIC RAW MATERIAL of the gardener's art. It should never be dismissed as a mere collection of mineral particles used to anchor roots, or worse still as "dirt." It is much more than that.

Certainly, its basic structure consists of rock particles broken down by frost and thaw action, wind and river flow, to produce the different textures that give us soil "types" (*see p. 14*). However, a large part of its makeup is organic matter—vegetable and animal remains in various stages of decay—along with air and water, which are all essential for the support of plant and animal life. All of this provides a home for millions and millions of living organisms such as soil fungi, algae, bacteria, insects, and worms, which work to provide just the right conditions for healthy plant growth. These organisms provide the plants with food in a form they can ingest and improve the structure of the soil by breaking it up and allowing more air to circulate.

It is perhaps in the treatment of soil, more than anywhere, that organic gardening differs from other gardening methods. The very first principle of organic gardening is to nurture and encourage this subterranean life so that it can support a much larger plant population than nature ever intended (*see also* Soil Improvement *and* Fertilizers, *pp. 18–42*).

THE FORMATION OF SOIL

Soil is formed over millions of years by the physical or chemical weathering of rock. Clay soils are formed by chemical weathering, where the mineral composition of the rock is changed usually by the action of weak acids. Other types of soil are the result of physical weathering, which does not involve any change in the chemical content of the rock, but gradually erodes it mechanically. This physical weathering may happen within the rock or externally.

In hot climates, such as those which prevail in desert areas, the widely fluctuating temperatures of day and night cause rocks to expand and contract regularly. Over a period of time the stress caused by the continual expansion and contraction leads to the physical disintegration of the rock and the formation of soil particles.

In colder conditions, like those that affected much of the world during the last Ice Age, rocks are broken down by the action of water entering cracks in the rock and freezing. As it freezes, the water expands, forcing the rock to split open. The movement of giant glaciers was responsible for the formation of soil as it wore away fragments of the rock below, and the action of streams and rivers also serves to wear away rocks to form soil.

What is soil?

The soil in your garden is a very complex structure and its cultivation depends on many different elements. There are several different soil types that all have advantages and disadvantages. For example, the soil may be acid or alkaline; it may be heavy or light; it may drain well or badly; it may be very rocky.

SOIL PROFILE

What you see in your garden is simply the surface of the soil. Soil is made up of three layers: topsoil, subsoil, and the soil parent matter. Topsoil is formed over the years by the addition of organic matter that follows the decomposition of dead plants or animals (*see p. 11*). It is inhabited by a wide range of living organisms, and it is in this layer that the majority of the feeding roots of plants exist. Topsoils can be improved and deepened by the regular addition of organic matter (*see pp. 18–34*).

The second layer is the subsoil, which is low in nutrients, generally contains few or no microorganisms, and is therefore inhospitable to roots. Thus, when digging deeply, it is advisable to bring to the surface only very small amounts of subsoil; these can be mixed with organic matter and will, eventually, turn into topsoil. Double digging breaks up subsoil and improves drainage without bringing the subsoil to the surface (*see* Basic Techniques, *p. 264*).

The nature of the subsoil has a profound effect on the water-holding capacity of the soil in general. If you have light sand or chalk subsoil, which drains very freely, you will need to increase the bulky organic matter content (*see pp. 16–17*), and thus the water-holding capacity, of the topsoil. On the other hand, heavy clay subsoil, which drains poorly, may necessitate the installation of an artificial drainage system (*see Basic Techniques, p. 262*).

The third layer—the parent material—is the original mineral from which the soil was formed. This layer is normally deep enough not to concern the gardener, but may, on high ground, be comparatively near the surface. If this is the case, try to increase the depth of the topsoil by adding organic matter to the top layer.

SOIL TYPES

There are five main soil types: clay, sand, silt, chalk, and peat. Generally, it is the nature of the original rock and the size of the mineral fragments that determine the soil type (*see p. 14*). It is important to know what kind of soil you are dealing with in your garden because the way in which you manage it, the timing of cultivations, and the plants you grow will depend to a large extent on the nature of the soil.

However, having said this, most soils contain a mixture of minerals. If a soil is referred to as, for example, "clay," then this indicates its major constituent. Soil mixtures are known as loams; for example, a soil made up of 50 percent clay and silt and 50 percent sand is a "medium loam." Similarly, a soil which contains a high proportion of sand might be described as a "sandy loam," while one which contains a relatively large amount of clay might be described as a "heavy loam."

PRACTICAL CHARACTERISTICS

Soils can also be heavy or light. A heavy soil contains a much higher proportion of clay. This type of soil has very small particles that tend to pack together, preventing free passage of water. Heavy soil is often very difficult to work initially because it tends to be either very wet and sticky or very dry and hard. Eventually though, when it has been ameliorated by the natural drainage afforded by plant roots and the addition of organic matter, heavy soil becomes an excellent moisture- and nutrient-retaining medium. Light soils, on the other hand, are easy to dig and warm up quickly in the spring but allow very free drainage, which has its own problems. Water and nutrients disappear through the topsoil, go into the subsoil, and eventually out the drainage system. Light soils require constant additions of organic matter to form a topsoil that retains moisture and generally need more applications of fertilizers than heavy soils.

ACIDITY AND ALKALINITY

Soil may also contain lime, which will cause it to be either "acid" or "alkaline," depending on the amount. The lime content will make a considerable difference to the fertility of the soil and will govern the range of plants you can grow because it has the ability to make some nutrients unavailable to plants (*see pp. 38–39*). For a straightforward test to determine the amount of lime in the soil, see p. 36.

ROCKS

The proportion of rocks or gravel in your soil does not influence its texture classification, but may affect its fertility and drainage. Rocky soil has the advantages and disadvantages of a free-draining soil (*see pp. 16–17*) and it may need regular applications of bulky organic matter to improve water retention. If you are lucky enough to have a heavy topsoil and a very rocky subsoil, you have the best of both worlds, with surface moisture and nutrient retention, plus good drainage of excess water.

IDENTIFYING SOIL LAYERS

If you dig a deep hole in the garden, the varying color and textures make it easy to identify the different layers. This is a valuable exercise because it enables you to understand the nature of your soil and therefore gives you a clue as to the best way to work it. The depth of each layer will vary considerably from one area to the next.

Topsoil This is the darkest layer of soil. It contains the organic matter, fungi, bacteria, insects, and worms necessary for healthy plant growth. The depth of the topsoil can range from 2in (5cm) to 6ft (2m). The deeper this layer, the better, because plant roots have more space to grow and take up nutrients.

Depth of root growth

Subsoil Lighter in color than topsoil because it contains no humus, this layer is largely devoid of plant nutrients. The structure of subsoil affects the drainage of the soil.

Parent matter This consists mostly of unaltered rock. It is the area least affected by any cultivation of topsoil. The depth at which this level starts depends on the underlying rock and the height of the piece of land.

Soil types

When seen together the five soil types—clay, sand, silt, peat, and chalk—look very different. Remember that many soils are a mixture of minerals; the soils illustrated here are as near to the pure mineral as possible. Each soil type has advantages and disadvantages, so each needs a slightly different management technique and supports different types of plants. This is discussed in more detail in *The Ornamental Garden* (*see pp. 74–125*) and *The Vegetable Garden* (*see pp. 132–201*).

CLAY

This is a heavy, cold soil which feels sticky when moist and hard and compacted when dry. The minute particles are less than 0.002mm in size. This means that clay does not drain easily and is difficult to work in wet conditions. However, it is possible to turn it into a very workable fertile soil (*see opposite*). Clay soils are normally well supplied with plant foods and are capable of supporting a wide variety of plants. *See p. 92 for a list of plants for clay soil.*

SAND

This is a dry, light soil, which will feel gritty if rubbed between your fingers. Sand particles range in size from 0.2mm, for the very finest sand, to 2mm for the coarsest. Sandy soil is easy to work and particularly good because it warms up quickly in the spring and can therefore be cultivated earlier than most soils. Because it is free-draining, nutrients tend to be lost easily so it will need to be supplemented with a great deal of organic matter as well as extra fertilizer. *See p. 92 for a list of plants for sandy soil.*

CHALK

A pale, very "hungry-looking" soil, chalk often contains a high proportion of rocks and flints. The large particles make it free-draining and very quick to lose nutrients and water. Often, the topsoil is rather shallow, making it unsuitable for plants with deep roots. Worse still, chalk is very alkaline; in other words it contains a great deal of lime, making it inhospitable to many plants. *See p. 93 for a list of plants for chalky soil.*

SILT

This type of soil is neither gritty nor sticky. The soil particles are small—between 0.002mm and 0.02mm, making silt smooth and silky to the touch. When wet, it has a tendency to pack down, leaving the soil cold, heavy, and badly drained, like clay. However, it is possible to improve the texture of the soil by applying liberal quantities of well-rotted compost or manure. Silt soils support the same range of plants as clay. *See p. 92 for a list of plants for silt soil.*

PEAT

Peat is a distinctive dark brown or gray color, and has a spongy texture. It is rich in decomposed organic matter and therefore requires little additional compost or manure. The younger brown peat is much easier to work and more fertile than the heavier, black, boglike type. All peaty soils tend to become waterlogged, so need to be drained artificially. Peat is usually acid and therefore will need to have lime added to increase the range of plants that can be cultivated. *See p. 93 for a list of plants for acid soil.*

Soil management

The ideal soil has a good crumbly structure, is rich in organic matter, drains well enough to prevent the topsoil becoming waterlogged in heavy rain, and is capable of providing the nutrients needed for healthy plant growth. The various soil types described on the left all have their own advantages and disadvantages. Each type is in fact a mixture of different particles in varying proportions, and a short period of observation and a test will soon establish which mineral predominates. You can then use one of the following management techniques to get the best from your particular soil.

Identifying your soil type *Take a handful of soil from your garden and rub a little between your finger and thumb. Clay feels sticky and will roll into a ball that simply changes shape when pressed. Sand is coarse and gritty, while silt feels silky smooth. Chalk has a dry, crumbly feel and a grayish-white color, while peat is just the reverse—black and moist.*

Clay

While clay is beset with problems initially, a little work and sound management can produce excellent results. It is certainly true that, in the early stages of cultivation, clay is not nearly as convenient to work as a light soil such as sand. When it is wet, it rapidly becomes a soggy mess of mud and, when it dries out, it sets like concrete.

Clay is a badly drained, cold, and heavy soil because the spaces between each particle are too small to allow free passage of water and air, so the soil is always in danger of settling down to form a solid, airless mass. Improving the soil structure can take a few years, but a good clay soil is capable of growing far better crops than a sandy soil ever could.

DIGGING

It is best, if you can, to dig a clay soil during the fall *(see p. 263)*, either at a time when there has been a little rain to soften the hard-baked soil, or when it is drying out after being soaked, but before it is hard again. In temperate climates, these times are fairly frequent, but in drier climates it calls for good organization and rapid action when the weather changes.

When heavy soil gets wet and dries out again, it expands and contracts, causing the mass of soil to crack into innumerable small clods. If water then gets into these cracks and freezes, it will force them further apart, breaking the soil down to a sowable tillage. So dig clay soils in the fall, leaving the surface rough and uneven through the winter to expose the maximum amount of soil surface to the elements. At the same time, you can work the organic material into the upper levels.

DRAINAGE

Because clay was broken down chemically, it's also possible to combine the particles chemically by a process known as "flocculation." If sufficient lime is added to the soil, the tiny particles of clay will bind together to form much larger crumbs, through which air, water, and plant roots can freely pass. Check the requirements of the plants you want to grow and use as much lime as you can without making conditions intolerable for them (see p. 35). In addition, if your soil is very heavy, dig coarse sand into the soil—approximately one to two bucketfuls every square yard/meter (see p. 75).

Raising a section of soil above its immediate surroundings will improve drainage considerably, helping the soil dry out and warm up; raise your ornamental beds slightly (see p. 75) and grow your vegetables on the deep bed system (see p. 135). The important thing with clay is that you should never walk on it when it is wet or you'll destroy years of work. If you have to walk on it, lay boards down first.

ORGANIC MATTER

Adding plenty of bulky organic matter to a clay soil will hold the particles apart so that roots and water can pass through. After a few years, when the level of organic matter is satisfactory and the soil is filled with the roots of previous crops, clay becomes much easier to work. In fact, every plant you grow plays its part in improving the soil for the next plant generation.

Silt

The main problem with a silt soil, as with clay, is one of drainage. Of all the soils formed by grinding, silt has the smallest particles. Only the particles of clay are smaller, but they were formed by chemical action.

The size of the particles means that they tend to pack together very closely when wet, preventing the free passage of water and air through the soil. So drainage is poor and there is a danger of the

soil settling down to form an airless mass. However, if you never walk on the soil when it is wet (use boards) and condition it as recommended here, silt is perfectly manageable and will produce satisfactory results.

DIGGING

Silt soil should be cultivated only when it is dry enough not to stick to your boots. Conditions underfoot permitting, aim to dig silt during the fall to take advantage of weather which will help break the soil down to a sowable tillage. Like clay, when silt gets wet and dries out again, it expands and contracts, causing the mass of soil to crack into small clods. If water then gets into these cracks and freezes, it will force them further apart, breaking the soil down even more. So by digging silt over in the fall, you expose the maximum amount of the soil surface to the elements and work the organic material into the topsoil at the same time.

DRAINAGE

In order to improve drainage, the soil particles have to be forced apart physically to allow free passage of air, water, and plant roots. Do this by digging one or two bucketfuls of coarse sand into the soil every square yard/meter (see p. 75) when you dig in the organic matter. Raising your ornamental beds slightly and growing vegetables on the deep bed system will improve drainage, helping the soil dry out and warm up.

ORGANIC MATTER

The structure of silt soils benefits greatly from the addition of liberal quantities of well-rotted compost or manure. Adding plenty of bulky organic matter to the soil will hold the particles apart so that roots and water can pass through more easily. If possible, keep the soil covered with a green-manure crop in order to add organic matter and remove surface water (see p. 32).

Sand

A very light soil, sand tends to drain easily and can therefore be cultivated when other soils are lying sodden and unworkable. As it also warms up quickly, it is an ideal soil for raising early crops. However, sand is also hungry and very demanding. So the price of having an easy soil to work is the need to apply extra organic matter and plant food, in the form of fertilizers (see pp. 35–42), because nutrients, as well as water, will drain away.

DIGGING

When you cultivate sand is relatively unimportant. It is not necessary to leave a sandy soil rough during the winter months for the frost and rain to break down. The large particles make it very easy to cultivate to a fine tillage anyway, so it is best to dig it in the spring a short while before you intend to sow or plant. If you never venture on the soil when it is so wet that it sticks to your boots, you will not go far wrong.

DRAINAGE

During the year, sandy soil will tend to lose water, both through surface evaporation and free-draining, and this could be detrimental to the plants. To reduce the problem, spread organic matter, or mulch, over the beds between plants as often as you can (*see p.20*). This lowers the evaporation rate and improves the soil structure.

ORGANIC MATTER

It is very important to improve sandy soils by adding substantial amounts of bulky organic material each year. Because of the quick-draining nature of the soil, the organic matter will work down into the subsoil very quickly so, to save work and to put it in the root zone, dig the organic matter into the top few inches or spread it over the surface.

Try to maintain a cover of vegetation over the surface more or less all the time, and certainly in the winter, when the "leaching" of nutrients is at its most rapid. In the vegetable garden, it is a good idea to grow a green-manure crop during the winter when the beds are empty and to dig it in during the spring (*see p.32*). This will not only hold many of the nutrients in the soil during the winter, but will also add large quantities of organic matter.

Chalk

There are two big disadvantages with chalk soils. Firstly, they are thin, dry, and "hungry." This is because the particles are very large, like those in sandy soil, so water drains through rapidly, taking plant nutrients with it. Plant nutrients, in the form of organic fertilizers, will therefore need to be added to the soil. Secondly, perhaps even worse, chalk is a very alkaline soil, and so unsuitable for many plants (*see p.35*).

DIGGING

Generally there is no need to worry too much about the timing of cultivations. Like sand, chalk soils are normally dry enough to work, even in the depths of winter. It is not necessary to leave a chalky soil rough during the winter months for the frost and rain to break down. Instead dig it in the spring a few weeks before sowing. Because the topsoil is usually not very deep, digging should be kept shallow and, if the area is fairly small, it could be worthwhile adding a layer of topsoil to the surface.

DRAINAGE

Generally, drainage on chalk soil is too good and the need is to retain water and nutrients. This can be done by adding bulky organic matter that will also help to acidify the soil.

ORGANIC MATTER

On chalk, more than any other type of soil, it is important to try and keep the soil surface covered. Grow a crop of green manure during the winter and dig it in during the spring (*see p.32*). During the growing season, it is even worth sowing a fast-growing green-manure crop between vegetables, just to keep the soil covered.

Mulching, or spreading organic material on top of the soil between plants, is also important during the growing season. You should use acid materials, such as peat, grass cuttings, compost, or manure, in order to counteract the alkalinity of the soil.

Peat

If you are lucky enough to be growing on peaty soil, grow as intensively as you can, as it is always potentially very fertile and usually easy to work. You'll find it easy to produce bumper crops and beautiful flowers year after year. Properly managed, a peat soil is superb but, like other soils, it does have its problems. Most importantly, peat soils are liable to be acidic and will therefore need generous applications of lime to restore the pH balance in the fruit and vegetable plots (*see p.36*). In the ornamental garden, provided you choose the correct plants, this should not be necessary (*see p.93*).

Furthermore, when they are drained, peat soils tend to dry out quite rapidly in hot weather. If they are allowed to dry out completely, they will shrink and may be difficult to get wet again. To prevent this, some hand watering may be necessary in dry weather.

DIGGING

The timing of cultivation is not critical. It is not necessary to leave peat rough during the winter.

DRAINAGE

Moorland and fenland peats are often badly drained so you may need to install a drainage system (*see p.262*).

ORGANIC MATTER

A major advantage of peat is that it is not normally necessary to add any humus-making materials. Peat, unlike the other soils, is largely made up of decomposed matter. It therefore has a low mineral content but contains an excess of organic matter. However, the soil is likely to be low in nutrients to start with so you may need to add fertilizers (*see p.35*).

SOIL IMPROVEMENT

THERE ARE VARIOUS CULTIVATION TECHNIQUES that you can employ to improve your particular soil; these are discussed in the previous chapter. All soil types will benefit from the addition of bulky organic matter in the form of compost or manure or some other soil conditioner. This is the key to soil fertility, and a healthy, fertile soil is the basis of the organic approach to gardening. In fact it is the basis of good gardening, whether you are committed to organic principles or not. Organic matter will improve the drainage or increase the water-holding capacity of your soil (*see pp. 17–19*). It will also, over a period of time, increase the depth of usable topsoil.

I have a perfect example of the value of organic matter in my own garden. My soil is a rich, dark brown color, fibrous and full of worms, a reliable indicator of the presence of healthy numbers of other less obvious life. Everything I plant seems to thrive, and the soil is a pleasure to work. This is because it gets the benefit of hefty doses of manure and compost every year.

Yet I need to walk only a few feet to the cornfield next door, which never sees any organic matter from one year to the next, to find a soil that is hard, compacted, and airless. It's difficult to force a fork through the top layer of soil and, when you do, there's not a worm to be seen. Granted, there are monoculture farmers like my neighbor who still grow very good crops of wheat, year after year, without the soil ever seeing a forkful of manure. With no cattle on their farms it would be difficult to supply the manure and, in the interests of convenience and economy, they even burn the straw after the harvest. However, they do so at the cost of enormous inputs of chemicals and of a steadily deteriorating soil.

WHAT SHOULD YOU USE TO IMPROVE YOUR SOIL?

There is no doubt at all that, if you put on sufficient well-rotted manure every year, your soil will remain fertile and your plants will prosper. But where is all the manure to come from, particularly if you live in a city? The days are long gone when you could follow the horse and cart with a shovel and bucket. And, if you live in the country, particularly if it is a corn-growing area, the farmer's children don't even know what cows look like.

So the gardener's alternative is compost. But is that being realistic? Certainly it looks good during the early summer when you start to fill your compost container with grass cuttings. After a couple of mowings, it fills up to overflowing and you have to start another. Yet by the time it has rotted down completely, it has shrunk to no more than a few bucketfuls.

USING STORE-BOUGHT MATERIAL

In fact a normal-sized garden with a productive vegetable plot will simply not produce enough compost. You will have to buy some form of organic matter, and be constantly on the lookout for suitable composting material. Naturally, the more you can gather, the better, because you will have to buy less. Even if you live in a city there are ways and means of doing this (*see p. 26*).

Unfortunately it is almost impossible to garden totally organically, because virtually everything that you might use is polluted with some chemical or other. Straw has been sprayed with weedkiller, fungicide, and insecticide; the cows have been force-fed with growth-promoting hormones; even the leaves swept from the pavements are polluted with lead from gasoline. So, if you are a purist—and I am—you may feel safer if you compost all imported material for at least a year in the hope that the toxins will be leached out.

FEEDING THE SOIL

Plants need certain nutrients in specific proportions to be present in the soil (*see p. 39*). These nutrients will be supplied by the addition of sufficient compost or manure (*see p. 20*), but you may have to use organic fertilizers as well to achieve the required balance. The techniques of feeding and the type of fertilizer you use to feed the soil will vary depending on your soil type, where you are, and how much organic matter is available to you. In addition, the degree of acidity or alkalinity, or pH, of your soil will affect the availability of some of these nutrients (*see p. 35*). So, you may find that, having established the pH level and taken measures to adjust it if necessary, you release more nutrients, therefore increasing the fertility of your soil.

The four phases of soil management

I divide soil management into four phases: the first phase is testing the soil; the second involves the general soil conditioning and replacement of nutrients with organic matter; phase three involves the application of fertilizer; the fourth phase covers more specialized application of fertilizers for specific plant needs.

If you have moved into an established garden that is obviously growing good crops, or if you have decided to convert to organic methods and there are no nutrient deficiencies showing up in your garden (*see pp. 38–39*), start with the second phase. However, unless you know the acidity or alkalinity, or pH value, of your soil, you should test it before you start (*see p. 36*).

1 Analyzing your soil

If you are starting out, especially on virgin soil, it is a good idea to have it tested at the outset so that you know where you stand. Soils that have been uncultivated for many years are often grossly deficient in one or other of the elements necessary for healthy plant growth (*see pp. 38–39*). Chemical growers would then repeat this soil test every year using sophisticated equipment to ascertain the exact requirements of the next crop. I have never believed that gardeners, however diligent, need to get involved in this. Once you know what you are working with, I don't think that it is necessary; annual home pH testing is sufficient (*see p. 36*).

It is best to send a sample of your soil away for professional analysis. The kits for testing nutrient levels in soil that are available to amateur gardeners are not accurate enough to be worthwhile. Used regularly, they will indicate a trend but no more than that. There are plenty of reputable companies who will analyze your soil. You will find them advertised in gardening magazines. They will be able to tell you the exact chemical makeup of your soil and, if there is a deficiency, exactly how much fertilizer you need to use to correct it. Remember, though, when you send the sample, to ask them to recommend organic fertilizers.

2 Using soil conditioners

This stage deals with the general soil improvement and replacement of plant nutrients removed by previous crops. It is here that there will be variation because it depends on how much, and what type, of organic material you have available to you.

First of all, it should be taken as given that all organic material not actually used in the kitchen is returned to the soil as compost, and that this should be supplemented by manure (*see p. 27*) or some other purchased soil conditioner (*see p. 29*), as necessary. Organic matter should be dug in during the fall and spread over the soil as a mulch in the growing season (*see p. 20*). This will increase the water-holding capacity of light soils and open up very heavy soils, as well as supplying all the nutrients. If you can put sufficient organic matter on to the soil, there may be no need to add any concentrated fertilizers. However, it is difficult to define "sufficient" because the amount needed depends entirely on your soil, the weather, the plants you wish to grow, and so on. You need to have a great deal of compost and/or manure if you are going to avoid using concentrated fertilizers completely (*see next page*).

3 Adding general fertilizer

Not everyone can get sufficient supplies of manure or compost. This is, therefore, where concentrated fertilizers come in. If, for any reason, the manuring falls below the recommended levels, you will have to make up the nutrients "out of the bag." Use a general fertilizer such as blood, fish, and bone meal or pelleted chicken manure. The application rates vary according to the soil and the plants you want to grow, so I have made recommendations in the relevant sections of the book. In fact some crops, for example peas, can generally grow quite well without the addition of fertilizer, so there is no need to apply it. Others, such as potatoes, will need extra. Most fruit trees and bushes will need fertilizer in the spring whether or not they are mulched with manure or compost, as will the ornamental garden (*see pp. 74–125*).

Where any trace element deficiencies have occurred in the past, I recommend that you give the soil a light application of kelp meal or calcified kelp pellets at the beginning of each season to make sure it does not happen again.

4 Using specific fertilizers

Some crops always need special treatment even when the manure and fertilizer levels are sufficient to start with. If, for example, you are growing tomatoes in the greenhouse, they will benefit from extra feeding and a potash fertilizer to encourage flower and fruit formation. Leafy plants that remain in the ground for a long time, like spring cabbage, may need some extra nitrogen fertilizer towards the end of the winter. Plants such as raspberries are particularly prone to iron deficiencies when grown in chalky soil; this can be corrected by spraying and liquid feeding with kelp (seaweed) fertilizer. It is a good idea to apply extra phosphorus, or phosphate, before planting trees or sowing, to encourage root growth. Again, all of these recommendations are discussed in more detail in the relevant chapters of the book: *The Ornamental Garden, The Vegetable Garden,* and *The Fruit Garden.*

SUMMARY

Your soil management regime should be:
• Test the soil pH and, if starting a new garden, have your soil tested. Make up deficiencies.
• Use heavy applications of manure or compost wherever possible (*see below*).
• If organic matter is not available in sufficient quantities, feed with a concentrated general organic fertilizer (*see pp. 35–42*).
• Give extra feeds for especially demanding plants or where specific deficiencies are noticed (*see pp. 38–39*).

Applying soil conditioners

The best materials to use to condition your soil are manure and compost; they will improve drainage or water-holding capacity and provide nutrients, but you do need a great deal to maintain soil fertility levels. Well-rotted animal manure is the very best material to use but it can be difficult to obtain. Compost can be used as a substitute for manure but, if it is to be dug into the ground, it *must* be well-rotted. The alternative soil conditioners mentioned on pp. 29–31, such as spent mushroom compost, green compost, and spent hops, while they are superb soil conditioners, they should not be looked upon as sources of plant nutrients.

Dig your compost or manure into the top layers of soil during the fall and use it as mulch during the growing season (*see below*). If it is spread over the surface of the soil between growing plants in thick layers, it acts as a weed suppressant (*see p. 58*) and will eventually be worked into the soil.

The amounts of organic matter required, and the method by which it is applied—either digging in or mulching—will vary slightly depending on your soil, the time of year, and the plants you want to grow. Ideally, you will need to use at least two 2 gallon (9 liter) buckets of well-rotted compost or animal manure for every square yard/meter of soil in the vegetable garden. Use one bucket per square yard/meter as a mulch around trees and shrubs, or in the ornamental borders; this should also be sufficient for fruit trees and bushes.

The quantities suggested are only a guide, if you can afford to use more, do not be afraid to do so. And you can always supplement your compost or manure with green-manure crops whenever the beds are empty for any length of time (*see p. 32*). If you are unable to apply organic matter in sufficient quantities, you may have to use fertilizers as well. This is discussed in the next chapter (*see pp. 35–42*).

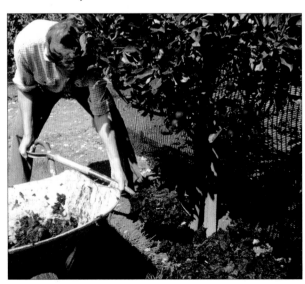

Mulching *This involves spreading a layer of organic matter over the soil where it cannot be dug into the ground because plants cannot be disturbed. Mulching is normally carried out in spring. Make sure the soil is moist before you apply the mulch because it will absorb surface water.*

Digging in manure *The most effective way to incorporate organic material into the soil is to dig it in during the fall. Dig out a trench, taking the soil to the end of the plot. Put a layer of manure in the bottom of the trench, then half fill it with soil dug from the next trench. Add more manure, then fill the trench.*

Compost

Every garden must have a compost heap. This is the ideal way to return as much organic matter as possible to the soil, following nature's example. Decomposing vegetation provides a home for millions of soil organisms, it opens up the soil, improving drainage and easing the way for root growth, and it helps over-drained soils hold water and therefore nutrients (*see p. 16*).

The plant remains that you gather from the garden in the form of waste leaves, stems from vegetables, grass cuttings, and annual flowers at the end of the season, all contain a great deal in the way of plant food and should not be wasted. However, dug in immediately, this material would initially do more harm than good.

The problem is that the rotting process is carried out by bacteria. Millions and millions of them begin to feed on anything that has just been removed from the soil. In order to carry on the decomposition, these bacteria need nitrogen, a very important plant food (*see p. 38*). If the garden waste is dug in "green," or in an unrotted state, the bacteria will draw the nitrogen from the soil for their own use, leaving growing plants desperately short of food. If the plant material is turned into compost before it reaches the soil, it will actually add nitrogen. This is because, after the initial rotting, a species of bacteria known as *Azotobacter* is attracted by the resulting conditions. These useful microorganisms can "fix" the nitrogen from the air—that is, they take it and convert it into a form that can be used by plants. So good compost, though not especially high in nitrogen, will at least not take any nitrogen from the soil.

The rotting, or composting, process takes time and a successful, well-planned organic garden should therefore have at least two compost heaps. That way, the contents of one heap can be left to rot down properly, while the other is being filled up.

Conditions necessary for good composting

Obviously, the first requirement is something to compost. Then the pile needs air, nitrogen, water, bacteria, and sometimes lime.

There are a great many old wives' tales about what can and cannot be used, but the rule is, in fact, very simple: anything that is entirely organic in origin can be composted, except for a few things that common sense tells you should be left out, such as some diseased material, cooked kitchen scraps, and so on (*see below*).

The list of organic material that can be used is endless—you should never waste anything that will rot. Do not just throw things onto the heap, but mix different materials together to make sure that air can circulate through the heap—even if that means storing some material beside the pile until you have something else to add to it. Grass cuttings, for example, if put on the heap in thick layers, will form an airless mass and turn into slime.

AIR CIRCULATION

Air is of vital importance in the compost heap. Without it the material is worked on by a different group of microorganisms, known as anaerobic bacteria. If allowed to develop, they turn grass cuttings and any other material into a stinking slime that is worse than useless on the garden.

The container should have air circulating through it and a good variety of material will create plenty of natural air spaces, so never pack down the contents too much. This can also be improved by mixing the fine material such as grass cuttings and small weeds with larger weeds, shredded newspaper, or straw.

WHAT NOT TO INCLUDE IN THE COMPOST HEAP

- Any material infected with a persistent disease, such as clubroot or blight—this should always be burned.
- The top growth of main crop potatoes. These should be burned after digging the potatoes because they may infect the heap with potato blight spores—a completely clean crop is rare.
- Prunings from woody plants, because they take too long to rot.
- Cooked kitchen scraps; they often putrefy and will attract vermin.
- Roots of pernicious weeds such as couch grass (*Agropyron repens*), ground elder (*Aegopodium podagraria*), bindweed (*Convolvulus arvensis*), and creeping buttercup (*Ranunculus repens*). These must be burned immediately as they will only multiply in the compost heap (*see p. 60*).
- Any weed seeds. You will often read that the heat of the compost heap will "cook" all the weed seeds rendering them unviable. This is true only if the heap reaches a very high temperature. In fact, a heap will only get hot enough to kill most pests and diseases but not seeds. They remain dormant until the compost is spread and end up high enough in the soil to be able to germinate. However, weeds pulled up before they seed, or even flower, should be added to the heap.

NITROGEN

Because the bacteria in the compost heap require nitrogen as a fuel, you must add a certain amount to the heap. Ideally, use animal manure as your source. I keep hens in a movable henhouse with a run that is moved around the vegetable plot whenever space becomes available. I use the droppings from the henhouse to provide the additional nitrogen for my compost heap. But I am lucky to be able to do this.

If animal manure is unavailable, you can buy organic compost fuels, or activators, in most garden stores. Alternatively, dried sewage sludge can often be obtained from the local sewage company—this is ideal not only for the compost heap but also for use as a fertilizer. Kelp (seaweed) meal is excellent and dried blood, the best form of nitrogen fertilizer, makes a very good, if slightly expensive, compost activator (*see* Organic fertilizers, *pp. 40–41*).

Whatever you use, you don't actually need very much—and not as much as the manufacturers would have you believe. A fine dusting every 12in (30cm) of compost is sufficient.

LIME

Adding lime will keep the compost "sweet"—that is, it will help neutralize the acidity. However, adding a good mixture of material will create a sweet heap without the need to add lime.

If you have chalky soil, you may feel that it would be better to omit the lime and use very acid compost to adjust the balance, and you can do this. However, the bacteria involved in rotting the compost material actually prefer conditions that are not too acid so, if

you do not add lime, the rotting process takes longer. All in all it is best to use it.

You should apply a slightly heavier dusting of lime than of the nitrogen activator every 12in (30cm) (*see p. 25*)

WATER

This is an essential ingredient of any compost heap. Generally, there will already be enough in the green material you put on the compost heap. This is certainly the case if you use grass cuttings. However, it is possible, in a hot summer, for the edges to dry out, and then you may need to apply extra water. The same may be true if you have used straw in the heap. Straw makes an excellent aerating material, especially when used with grass cuttings, and it composts well, but you need to wet it first. I have composted straw on its own, but I found that I needed to put the sprinkler on the heap for half an hour at a time to wet it sufficiently.

You may need to cover the compost heap with plastic sheeting in the winter, not only to keep the heat in, but also to prevent the compost from getting too wet (*see below*).

HEAT

Although perhaps not absolutely necessary, there is no doubt that decomposition is much faster when the material is warm. In the summer you'll have usable compost in only two or three months where, in the winter, the process slows down considerably and the compost will not be usable until the spring.

You can cover the heap with black plastic weighted at the edges; this will keep the heat in and prevent it becoming too wet, which can be a problem, particularly in winter (*see p. 25*). I prefer to place a piece of old carpet over the heap; it does not need weighting down and also "breathes," allowing more air into the heap.

BACTERIA

Finally, you need the bacteria themselves. This is the easiest job of all. There are millions in just one piece of soil, so there should be plenty in the clumps of earth that cling to the roots of the weeds you put in the heap. Some people recommend that you add layers of soil throughout the heap. In fact, this is completely unnecessary: not only is it hard work, but it also makes the compost less concentrated.

COMPOSTING HARD MATERIALS

Woody material, such as prunings from shrubs and trees, should not be composted on the main heap because it takes a long time to decompose. This is because bark contains a substance called lignin, which is difficult for bacteria to break down. The rotting of lignin is primarily carried out by fungi, rather than bacteria. These are also present in the compost heap, but their action is much slower. While the fungi do not require as much air as bacteria, they do need more light.

You can speed up the process dramatically by chopping your prunings into smaller pieces that are more readily rotted by the fungi. You can buy domestic chipping machines. They are small and do take quite a long time to produce an appreciable number of chippings but, if you can afford the time and the initial cost, they are worth the effort. The wood chippings can also be used as a mulch in ornamental flower beds to help retain moisture and to suppress weeds (*see p. 59*).

Compost containers

Although it is not essential to make your compost in a container—you can simply pile it up in the corner of the garden—the advantage of a container is that the compost rots right up to the edges of the pile. In an open heap, the edges dry out so the whole thing has to be turned two or three times during the rotting process to push the unrotted material into the center.

The size of your compost container will depend on the size of your garden. There are plenty of containers available at garden centers, many designed with the smaller garden in mind—some even suggest that it is possible to compost by adding material to the top while shoveling out the well-rotted compost at the bottom. Frankly, this is not realistic; you need two containers, one that can be left to rot down while the other is being filled up. The most useful is a solid-sided wooden box (*see below*). You can easily add more sections onto the side.

It is not difficult to make your own compost container. Again wooden ones are the best, they look good and they are cheap and easy to make (*see next page*). You can also make compost bins from bricks, plastic barrels, or stakes and wire (*see below*).

TYPES OF COMPOST CONTAINER

Compost containers are useful not only because they keep the compost moist right up to the edges but also because they keep it tidy. Whether you build your own bin or buy one, make sure that it enables you to get to the compost easily when it comes to putting it on the garden.

Manufactured compost containers

◀ Wooden compost bin
Commercial wooden bins normally come in kit form and you assemble them. Stacking bins, like this beehive model, enable you to build the heap gradually one section at a time and allow easy access to the compost.

▶ Plastic compost bin
This type of bin is useful in a small garden. A small amount of air is allowed in through the bottom and a lid keeps the contents dry and the heat in.

Homemade compost containers

▼ Wire-and-post container
This method is suitable only if you can put the compost heap somewhere it can't be seen. Hammer four stakes into the ground to make a 3ft (1m) square. Staple about 12ft (4m) of wire mesh, 3ft (1m) deep, to the outside of the stakes. Tie large pieces of cardboard to the inside of the wire.

◀ Plastic barrel container
Large plastic barrels used for fruit concentrates make ideal compost containers. Cut off the top and bottom with a sharp knife. Keep one of the cut ends and use it as a lid. Drill 1in (2.5cm) holes around the barrel—about one hole every 1sq ft (30sq cm).

▼ Brick-built compost bin
This method is suitable only if you are never going to move the heap. Stagger the bricks so that air can get into the compost heap. The front should be made of wooden slats like for the homemade wooden bin on the next page. Fix wood shims down the inside of the walls and slide the slats in.

MAKING A WOODEN COMPOST CONTAINER

This is a very simple procedure and one possible by even the most reluctant DIYer. The most important factor to consider when making this type of compost bin is to take the time to be precise, as the bin looks good enough to admire and not hide away. Make sure you buy rough sawn lumber as this will be cheaper and look perfectly fine. A pristine, smooth finish to the bin is not essential. It is still possible to buy suitable lumber from a demolition contractor, which can be half the price of new, but be careful not to slip into the minefield that is reclaimed lumber as this is often much higher in value. I have to say that my favorite are old floorboards, which are particularly good for the sides, while 3 × 4in (7.5 × 10cm) floor joists make ideal corner supports.

You need:

- 4 × 3ft (1m) lengths of 2 × 4in (5 × 10cm) wood for the uprights
- 19 × 3ft (1m) lengths of wood for the sides
- 5 × 2ft 6in (75cm) lengths of wood for the front panels (You may need to check this measurement when you have completed the main part of the bin.)
- 4 × 2ft 6in (75cm) wood shims
- 2 small pieces of wood
- Strong nails, about four per panel

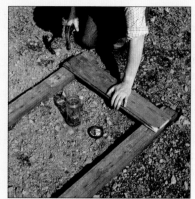

1 Place two of the uprights on the ground so that they are lying parallel to each other and 2ft 6in (75cm) apart. Place one of the side planks across them 3in (7.5cm) from the bottom of each post and nail it into position. Nail five more planks between the uprights, ensuring they all butt up against each other, and then make another wall to match.

2 Stand the two walls up parallel to each other and at right angles to a wall. Nail a piece of wood to the top of each upright to hold them in position. Working from the bottom upward, nail six pieces of wood across the back, level with those on each side.

3 Remove the support panel. Then turn the box around so that you can make the front wall. Nail a board across the front of the uprights 3in (7.5cm) from the bottom.

4 Nail two shims onto the side edge of each upright, making sure that they are far enough apart to slide the front panels between them. Nail a small piece of wood across the bottom of them to prevent the front panels from sliding out when filling the bin.

5 Slide all the front panels into the bin to make sure they fit; cut down as necessary.

6 Paint the entire container, including the cut edges and the front panels, with a water-based wood preservative. Let air dry.

7 Slide all the front panels into position. Tie a piece of string across the top of the container to prevent the sides from bulging outward when you fill it.

Managing your compost

Really good compost is supposedly brown and crumbly with the sweetest of smells, like the woods in fall. In fact it very rarely is. If you have a really big heap and a supply of only the very best organic material to rot down, you should be able to achieve that ideal during spring and summer. If your heap is small and you're using any organic material you can find, it often won't live up to that ideal. Generally, while some material is in an advanced stage of decomposition, other material will not have rotted down nearly as much. The compost is more likely to be very variable, with a lot of semi-rotted fibrous material. But that doesn't matter. It will still improve the soil and certainly do no harm; it will just take a bit longer for it to become "humus."

Getting good quality compost takes care, and each composting material needs different treatment. For example, grass cuttings should always be mixed thoroughly with some coarser material such as larger weeds, shredded newspaper, or straw, before they are added to the heap to prevent them from turning to slime (*see p. 22*).

Straw is a particularly good material to mix with grass cuttings and, if you have the space, it is well worth keeping a bale beside the heap just for that purpose. A word of warning though; straw is very dry, so it is very important to soak it thoroughly in a container of water for an hour or so before adding it to the heap.

Newspaper can be difficult to break down but it is worth using, particularly when mixed with grass cuttings. As a rough guide use about one part newspaper to four parts grass cuttings. Never put it on the heap folded into a thick wad because there won't be enough air in it and it won't rot. I cut it up into 1in (2.5cm) strips and keep it in a plastic bag until needed. Then, before use, I put it in a bucket of diluted seaweed (*see p. 41*). However, I use only a small amount and use the pages from glossy magazines in smaller pieces so that it rots down better, now that they use inks that do not contain lead. When I put kitchen scraps on the heap, I make sure there is nothing cooked on them to avoid attracting vermin. If there are any large pieces of root vegetable, I cut them into smaller pieces. I then cover the layer with grass cuttings or weeds to keep the rats and mice away. Potato peelings often cause problems because those tiny "eyes" will develop into potato plants either in the heap or when the compost is spread. But they're not difficult to pull up and provide that much more material for the next heap. Any old clothes made of natural fiber can be put on the heap as well. If you cut them into strips beforehand, they will rot down faster.

The amount of compost you can make in a year depends heavily on the type of material you use but even more on the weather. From each bin you should, in a hot year, get two good binfuls in the summer—one in early summer and another in late fall—and another in the spring if you're lucky.

BUILDING UP A COMPOST HEAP

Stand the compost container on a level surface, preferably soil. Start the heap off with a 6in (15cm) layer of coarse material such as horse manure, straw, or large weeds to make sure there is a free flow of air at the bottom. Then add more material until you have a layer 6in (15cm) deep. Sprinkle some compost activator or nitrogen fertilizer (*see p. 40*) over this layer, or add another layer of horse manure; the nitrogen in it will act as a compost activator. Add another 6in (15cm) layer of material, then cover with a dusting of lime, and so on. When you have finished filling the bin always cover it with a piece of carpet or its lid to keep it dry. Compost rots down and shrinks quickly so that which seems like a finished heap one week still has room for more the next week.

Lime

Grass cuttings

Horse manure or straw then compost activator

Lime

Leaves from vegetable garden mixed with grass cuttings

Horse manure or straw then compost activator

Grass cuttings

Horse manure

ALTERNATIVE SOURCES OF MATERIAL FOR COMPOSTING

Few gardens can produce enough waste organic material to be self-sufficient in compost. But a remarkable amount of good stuff that is thrown away can be "harvested" by the organic gardener. The local supermarket or farmers' market is an excellent source of green stuff. See if you can arrange to visit the shop or market after closing time on Saturdays to take any trash. A local sports field or golf club is also worth investigating. They often have no means of disposing of massive amounts of grass cuttings and would be glad to have them cleared away.

If you live in the country, in an area where farmers burn straw rather than bale it, it is well worth asking if you can gather some straw before the rest is disposed of. As the farmers are no longer able to burn their straw and stubble, whatever is left after harvest is plowed back into the ground. Some may spray the straw before this happens so it is important that you check this has not happened before collecting it.

The best source of free soil conditioner I have ever found was a tomato grower that used grow bags. At the end of the season they were faced with an unwanted mountain of used bags. The compost inside them was once-used and full of tomato roots but still a perfect soil conditioner, even without composting. I did, in fact, stack them for a year to ensure that any traces of chemicals had dissipated, because the nursery did not grow organically.

Leaf mold

Leaves are slow to rot because they contain lignin (*see p. 22*). Be prepared to wait at least a year, and possibly even two or three years, before you have a good, crumbly compost that is ready to use. When the leaves do rot down, however, they prove well worth waiting for. Leaf mold is really much too good to use for mulching or for digging in. Use it as a potting or seed-sowing compost (*see p. 252*).

The decaying process is very different from compost making. While green compost is rotted predominantly by bacteria, leaves are broken down by fungi which need more light and less air than the bacteria (*see p. 22*). So build the container in a corner of the garden where it can be left undisturbed.

You will need at least two heaps because it may be two to three years before the leaf mold is ready. You do not need elaborate containers, you can make them out of stakes and wire netting (*see above*). Pile the leaves into the container as you collect them, pressing down each time you add more. The leaves may need a little water in a dry summer, otherwise, you can leave them to their own devices.

Building a leaf-mold container *You need four wooden stakes that are at least 3ft (1m) tall, and about 12ft (4m) of wire mesh. Drive the stakes into the ground to make a 3ft (1m) square and staple the wire netting around the outside.*

The local government is often a good source of leaves. The leaves may be "polluted" with cigarette packs or other trash but these are easy to remove as you stack them. More concerning is the fact that they could contain lead from car exhaust emission, but all you can do is hope that it is reduced to an acceptable level, if not leached out entirely, by composting.

Sheet composting

Making good compost takes time and trouble—time that some busy gardeners might find difficult to spare. Nonetheless, as organic matter should never be thrown away, you may find it more convenient to "sheet compost" it.

This technique simply involves spreading a thin layer of organic matter on the soil between rows of vegetables or on a vacant area, and allowing it to rot down where it is. Naturally this method is useful only in productive parts of the garden where aesthetics are not important. Sheet compost can be particularly useful on areas where you walk regularly, like paths between rows, or it can be used as a mulch around fruit trees.

If you are using weeds, it's important to ensure that they have wilted beyond the recovery point before you spread them, or you may find them re-rooting and growing away in your carefully tended vegetable patch. As with weeds for the compost heap, you should ensure that they are not about to shed seeds. Grass cuttings are ideal for sheet composting, but you are almost certain to find annual meadow grass seeds in any sample cut during the summer, so watch out for unwanted sprouts.

Whatever organic matter you use as sheet compost, it will rot down into the soil much more slowly than well-rotted garden compost. There is also a danger of it causing nitrogen deficiency in the soil (*see p. 21*), so you may need to add a little nitrogen fertilizer before spreading the sheet compost.

An alternative method, which will certainly speed up the decomposition process, is to dig the sheet compost into the top inch or so. If you have a rotary cultivator, even better, because this will chop it up, after which earthworms will take care of it. In this case though, extra nitrogen will definitely be necessary. As a preventive measure, before cultivating or digging in sheet compost in this way, sprinkle a handful of dried blood over each square yard/meter of soil (*see p. 40*).

Spreading sheet compost *Sprinkle dried blood over the soil—one handful per square yard/ meter—then spread an even layer of the green material over the soil. Leave it to rot down.*

Animal manure

Animal manures are the very best sources of organic matter you could wish for on your soil, so they are worth getting, even though they are more difficult to obtain than compost. Manure can be used on any soil, not only to improve its condition, but also to feed it with nutrients. Some, like poultry manure, have to be used with care because of their high nitrogen content.

Unfortunately, much commercial animal manure is likely to be adulterated with hormone fatteners, herbicides, insecticides, and fungicides. However, if it is stacked for at least a year, there is little evidence to show that these chemicals pollute the soil or make their way into our vegetables and fruit when they are harvested. Leaving the manure for a year does mean that some of the nutrients are lost, but this can always be made up in the soil in other ways. One day, the organic movement will be powerful enough to persuade all farmers to produce healthy, unadulterated food. In the meantime, we simply have to use what is available. There is little point in trying to beg manure from organic farmers because they need it for themselves.

USING MANURE

All manure is used at full strength unless otherwise specified—although you should avoid putting it on young shoots because it will scorch them. General manure levels are given with each description; recommendations for specific plant needs are described in the relevant chapters.

COW MANURE

Many beef cattle are kept in the cruellest of living conditions where they never move around or see daylight. Their droppings are washed away through the slatted floors and disposed of as slurry. It is still sometimes possible, however, to find a farmer who grazes cattle outside some of the time and brings them into yards in the winter. So if you live in the country, cow manure can sometimes be obtained after the cows have been turned out for the summer. Compared with other forms of organic material, it's very cheap and excellent as a soil conditioner and source of nutrients. But it should be stored for 12 months before use to leach out impurities and prevent scorching of roots.

On the face of it, cow manure doesn't contain a very high percentage of plant nutrients (*see below*), when compared with an inorganic fertilizer. But you will be using a far greater volume of manure than you would of an inorganic fertilizer, so the mineral concentration is less significant. Moreover, manure will hold water and maintain that high level of fertility that organic growers continually try to achieve.

NUTRIENT CONTENT			
Nitrogen	*0.6 percent*	Potassium	*0.3–0.5 percent*
Phosphorus	*0.2–0.3 percent*	Trace elements	*Full range*
Coverage *20–30lb (9–15kg) per sq yard/meter*			

HORSE MANURE

An excellent source of organic matter, horse manure is often more readily available near urban areas. Large stables generally have a contract with commercial mushroom growers to remove manure. But there are plenty of smaller stables who are pleased to sell manure. You should use manure only from stables where straw or peat is used as bedding; wood shavings may be a source of plant disease.

Fresh horse manure must not be used directly around plants since it can cause scorching of the leaves and stems. Also, if put on the soil in an unrotted state, much of the nutrient value will be lost and the straw mixed in with the manure will take a long time to decompose. There are two alternatives. If you have access only to small quantities of manure, they are best put on the compost heap where the high nitrogen content will assist the decomposition. Large quantities are best stacked, if possible on a concrete base, and, since there is a lot of air space in the straw, and thus a danger of it drying out, you should mash down your pile as you stack it. In winter, cover the heap with plastic to protect it from excess rain. Horse manure will be ready for use in a couple of months unless you are concerned that any straw may be contaminated with pesticides, in which case leave it for a year before using it.

NUTRIENT CONTENT			
Nitrogen	0.6 percent	Potassium	0.4 percent
Phosphorus	0.6 percent	Trace elements	Full range
Coverage 20–30lb (9–15kg) per sq yard/meter			

PIG MANURE

Somewhat colder and wetter than horse or cow manure, but certainly not to be discounted for that, pig manure has a very high nutrient content. It should be treated in the same way as horse manure but, since it is heavier, there is generally no need to mash it down.

NUTRIENT CONTENT			
Nitrogen	0.6 percent	Potassium	0.4 percent
Phosphorus	0.6 percent	Trace elements	Full range
Coverage 20–30lb (9–15kg) per sq yard/meter			

SHEEP MANURE

Because sheep are not normally stabled, you don't get a mixture of straw and muck in the way you do with cow, horse, and pig manure. However, the manure itself is so high in nutrients that it is well worth going around the fields collecting it. Half a sackful will provide enough liquid manure to last the average-sized garden a whole year (see p. 42).

NUTRIENT CONTENT			
Nitrogen	0.8 percent	Potassium	0.4 percent
Phosphorus	0.5 percent	Trace elements	Full range
Use as liquid manure (see p. 42)			

CHICKEN MANURE

This is very powerful manure. It has an extremely high nitrogen content, and so should not be used undiluted. If you can find a farmer who keeps hens in an old-fashioned deep-litter house, where the hens are housed on straw, take as much manure as you can get and stack it as described for horse manure, above. If you

CHICKENS AS SOIL IMPROVERS

If you live in the country, you may find it advantageous to keep small livestock in the vegetable garden. Half a dozen chickens, for example, require only a small amount of space and will easily keep a small family in eggs throughout the year.

To fit chickens into the vegetable-growing system, house them in a small, portable house with a movable wire-mesh run to restrict them to the area. As a crop finishes, move the hens onto the space, and they will devour all the green matter there, recycling it in the form of a high-nitrogen fertilizer. They will also peck out any old seeds and soil pests that may be lurking near the surface.

have your own hens, use the manure as a source of nitrogen for the compost heap.

Chicken manure from a commercial grower can be used to compost straw. Put a layer of straw in the bottom of a compost container, soak it with water, then cover with a sprinkling of manure. Add more straw, water it, then cover with manure. Continue in this way until the bin is full, ending with a layer of manure. Leave this type of compost to rot for at least a year because the manure will contain hormones that are fed to commercially-grown chickens.

NUTRIENT CONTENT			
Fresh, wet chicken manure			
Nitrogen	1.5 percent	Potassium	0.5 percent
Phosphorus	1.5 percent	Trace elements	Full range
Coverage 7–10lb (3.25–4.5kg) per sq yard/meter			
Dry			
Nitrogen	4 percent	Potassium	1.5 percent
Phosphorus	4 percent	Trace elements	Full range
Coverage 8–12oz (20–30g) per sq yard/meter			

OTHER MANURES

Pigeon droppings contain even higher concentrations of nitrogen than chicken manure, so it is worth contacting local pigeon-racing enthusiasts. The manure can be used in the same way as chicken manure.

Rabbit manure is also ideal, though likely to be available in only small quantities. Use it in the same way as chicken manure.

Goat manure is similar to horse manure, but of better quality. If you can find any, or better still if you keep a goat yourself, compost the manure and use it in exactly the same way as horse manure (see above).

Before leaving manures, I have one suggestion that is not as crazy as it sounds. When the circus leaves town, it is often left with a manure problem, so it could be worth contacting it as soon as it arrives. I have actually used two trailer loads of elephant manure that the circus delivered free of charge.

Alternative soil conditioners

Apart from compost and manure, there are many other organic materials that can be dug into your soil or used as a mulch to help improve drainage or water-holding capacity, depending on the soil type. These materials should be looked upon only as soil conditioners; although some contain plant nutrients, they are not present in large enough quantities.

SPENT MUSHROOM COMPOST

A mixture of horse manure, peat, and chalk prepared by commercial mushroom growers. A very useful, if slightly alkaline, soil conditioner. Don't use it on acid-loving plants.

NUTRIENT CONTENT	
Nitrogen	0.71 percent
Phosphorus	0.3 percent
Potassium	0.26 percent
Trace elements	Full range

WOOL SHODDY

This is a waste material from the cleaning processes that a fleece goes through while being prepared for spinning and dyeing. The nutrient content can vary considerably.

NUTRIENT CONTENT	
Nitrogen	3–15 percent
Phosphorus	0.5–10 percent
Potassium	0.1–12 percent
Trace elements	—

KELP

This is an excellent soil conditioner because its alginate content helps bind soil particles together, thus improving structure. Kelp is particularly rich in trace elements.

NUTRIENT CONTENT	
Nitrogen	0.3 percent
Phosphorus	0.1 percent
Potassium	1.0 percent
Trace elements	Full range

COMPOSTED PINE BARK

This is normally sold partly composted and contains virtually no nutrients. It is best used as mulch, because it can cause a severe nitrogen deficiency in the soil if dug in.

NUTRIENT CONTENT	
Nitrogen	—
Phosphorus	—
Potassium	—
Trace elements	—

SPENT HOPS

If you have a brewery nearby, try to buy "spent" hops to use as a mulch or to dig in—they add organic matter as well as a small amount of nutrients.

NUTRIENT CONTENT	
Nitrogen	0.5 percent
Phosphorus	1–2 percent
Potassium	0.5 percent
Trace elements	Full range

GREEN COMPOST

Useful for adding organic matter, green compost has little nutrient value but is useful for improving soil structure and its water-holding capacity.

NUTRIENT CONTENT	
Nitrogen	—
Phosphorus	—
Potassium	—
Trace elements	—

SPENT MUSHROOM COMPOST

The waste product of the mushroom-growing industry, this can be used instead of manure, provided its limitations are kept in mind. Mushroom compost starts as fresh horse manure that is stacked so that it heats up. It is then sown with mushrooms and, finally, covered with a mixture of peat, or peat substitute, and chalk. After the crop of mushrooms has been picked, the compost is thrown away or sold either loose at the farm or packed into bales and sold at garden centers. By the time it has had a crop grown in it, the compost is quite well rotted. Nonetheless, it's still worth leaving mushroom compost for at least a year before use to leach out the chemical insecticides used by the growers and to help get rid of the pests it may harbor, such as fungus gnats. After a year it should have the consistency of coarse peat.

Mushroom compost can be put directly onto the soil around plants, but you should use it very sparingly because it can badly scorch young shoots. Remember too that, because it contains ground chalk, it will be very alkaline (see p. 35). Never use it on acid-loving plants such as rhododendrons, azaleas or heathers (Erica sp.), and some trees (see p. 82).

Before using the compost, mushroom growers normally add gypsum to it; when added to soil, this helps to bind clay particles together. So, coupled with the natural "opening" effect of the organic matter, mushroom compost is ideal for use on heavy clay soils.
Coverage: 2–3lbs (1–1.5kg) per sq yard/meter.

KELP

If you live near the ocean, the kelp washed up on the beach can be a valuable source of organic material for the soil. Kelp, or seaweed, contains a wide range of the trace elements that plants need for growth as well as small and variable amounts of the major plant foods, in particular potassium (see pp. 38–39). Recent research has shown that seaweed also contains growth-promoting hormones, which can be absorbed through leaves to improve plant health and growth. In the soil, kelp can release certain nutrients otherwise unavailable to plants, and its alginate content binds soil particles together, improving soil structure (see p. 16).

Kelp is most effective if composted for awhile, although, because it will rot down very quickly, some gardeners prefer to dig it in fresh. The fronds contain alginic acid, which is very attractive to the bacteria required on the compost heap. So, apart from its soil-conditioning value, kelp can also be used as a compost activator (see p. 22). If you can get ahold of only small quantities of kelp, this is certainly the best use for it.
Coverage: 2–3lbs (1–1.5kg) per sq yard/meter.

SPENT HOPS

The residue from the brewing industry, spent hops have a distinctive strong smell, although this soon disappears when the hops are left out in the open.

They make an excellent soil conditioner and are particularly good for mulching. The problem is that they are very difficult to get, as many breweries now sell on a contract basis to farmers. However, it is worth calling a local brewery and asking for a few bags. If bought directly from the brewery, spent hops will be wet and can either be dug in fresh or spread over the surface. They can be composted but it is not necessary. If you use them fresh, keep them away from the stems and leaves of young plants to avoid scorching them.

It is possible to buy spent hops dry but, in this form, they are really more of a fertilizer that is high in nitrogen—about 2.5–3.5 percent.
Coverage: 2–3lbs (1–1.5kg) per sq yard/meter.

WOOL SHODDY

Made up of bits of fluffy wool, this is a waste product of the clothing industry and is sometimes available in wool-processing areas. It is an excellent soil conditioner and is best used undiluted and dug in wet in the fall.
Coverage: ½–1lb (0.25–0.5kg) per sq yard/meter.

COMPOSTED PINE BARK

The timber and tobacco industries strip off hundreds of tons of bark from pine logs every year. It is chipped and sometimes partially composted before being sold.

Chipped bark makes an excellent mulch for organic weed control (see p. 59). However, it has no nutrient value, and two big disadvantages as a soil conditioner. Firstly, it is very expensive. Secondly, and perhaps more importantly, it is a very hard material in a virtually unrotted state. The lignin in bark takes a long time to break down so the bacteria use even more nitrogen in the rotting process (see p. 22). Unless you are prepared to add large amounts of nitrogen fertilizer to your soil, it is better to use another material as a soil conditioner and bark only as a mulch.
Coverage: 2–3in (5–7 cm) layer if using it as weed suppressant in ornamental borders.

GREEN COMPOST

This is produced from waste taken away in your green recycling bin and makes an excellent soil conditioner. The problem associated with it is that you do not know what may be lurking in the compost, such as pernicious weed roots or a debilitating disease. For these reasons, if possible, it is always better to make your own garden compost.
Coverage: 2–3lbs (1–1.5kg) per sq yard/meter.

PEAT SUBSTITUTES

Over the last few years there has been growing concern about the use of peat. It is extracted from peat bogs that have formed over thousands, if not millions, of years, and as the peat is used up, we destroy valuable sites for rare flora and fauna. The peat will eventually reform, but this will take many, many years and in the meantime species that depend on peat bogs for their existence may become extinct.

However, peat does not need to be used as a soil improver because there are plenty of substitutes available, most of which have already been described. There are also more peat-free composts available for seed sowing and for growing on plants in containers. Some are made from coir and others from various materials such as composted waste from municipal recycling centers or composted bark with a combination of other materials.

Some of these products will be variable in their quality (peat is consistent, which is why it has been so popular), but with a little care you will come to manage these newer products easily. The main point is to get your watering and feeding regimes right, which will come with experience. Other soil-conditioning products can be dug into the soil or used as a mulch on the soil surface. They will improve the soil structure, help retain moisture in the soil, and keep down weeds. Using such products is also less damaging to the environment: the waste would go directly to landfill sites where it would decompose or be burnt, giving off harmful greenhouse gases.

Worm-worked compost and manure

From research carried out recently on the effects of earthworms on waste materials, it's clear that worms can be put to work by the organic gardener in the soil, compost, or manure with some highly beneficial effects.

THE EFFECTS OF WORMS ON THE SOIL

Worms feed mainly on organic matter and, in the process of feeding, they break the waste down and eject it in the form of pellets. These small pellets are coated with a gel which holds them together. The resulting crumb structure helps to improve soil drainage and aeration and therefore provides a superior environment for root growth. The pellets not only change the nutrients in the organic matter into a form that is readily available to plant roots, but also convert it into a form that is released slowly, as it is required by the plants. This prevents any short-term toxicity that could otherwise develop. At the same time the water-holding capacity of soil is increased considerably, which is of great benefit.

Equally important is the way in which worms break down the organic matter into smaller granules, enabling the soil microbes to work on a greater surface area. They also produce a range of enzymes that enable the bacteria to work more efficiently. In other words, the presence of worms in the organic matter accelerates the process of decomposition.

By introducing worms into the manure or compost heap, you can dramatically speed up the rate at which it decomposes and produce an end product that is far superior for soil conditioning and feeding.

ADDING WORMS TO THE SOIL

This is not quite as easy as it sounds and a certain amount of management is required. First of all, you will need to build a wormery to provide the environment; secondly, it is important to use the right variety of worm. The worms you need are commonly known as a "nightcrawler" or "red worms;" they are used in many parts of the world by fishermen as bait. The Latin name for it is *Lumbricus terrestrisis*. These worms do not live for long in soil, but they can be found generally in manure or compost heaps, where they multiply very quickly. If you can't find any in your compost heap, buy some from a fishing tackle shop or a specialist supplier (*see p. 283*).

The worm has the convenient habit of working upward. Once it has digested one layer of organic matter, it will move up to the next layer. You can take advantage of this when building a wormery by designing it so that you can take the worm-worked material out of the bottom of the box. This leaves the worms inside to continue working on the upper layers of material in the wormery (*see next page*).

The most useful task performed by the worms is the breaking down of compost. They work through almost anything from grass cuttings to kitchen scraps and even soaked newspapers, provided they are used in moderation. In the same way as in the compost heap, it is not a good idea to use too much of anything on its own—you should mix everything together as before—and never put more than an inch of material onto the heap in a week (*see next page*). You can, however, put animal manure in the wormery on its own.

The wormery should be placed in a sunny, sheltered part of the garden because the worms will not work if the temperature is lower than about 45°F (7°C)—in freezing weather they will die. The optimum temperature for the worms is 68–75°F (20–24°C). In cold weather, cover the wormery with a piece of old carpet to keep as much heat in as possible. In very hot weather it may be necessary to water the material. It is much better for it to be too wet than too dry.

MAKING A WORMERY

First, make a wooden box that is at least 2ft (60cm) high and about 2ft (60cm) by 3ft (90cm)—the important thing is that it is slightly wider and longer than your wheelbarrow. Secondly, support the box on legs so that you can push your wheelbarrow underneath. Staple a piece of strong mesh across the bottom of the box; the mesh should be about 2in (5cm) across. Finally, make two holes in one side of the box and slide two lengths of wood in through these holes. Fix pieces of metal or wood on the ends to make the scrapers.

When the box is complete, lay a sheet of newspaper over the mesh floor and soak it with water. Cover this with a layer of old compost, or manure if you have it, and a handful of nightcrawlers. Put a thin layer of uncomposted material over the top and cover it with old carpet or insulated packaging. Build the wormery up slowly, putting no more than 3in (7cm) of material into the box each week. If you have a regular supply, this may mean that you'll have to leave it beside the container until the previous layer has been worked down.

3ft (90cm)

2ft (60cm)

2ft (60cm)

4ft 6in (1.5m) legs

18in (45cm)

9in (22.5cm)

2ft 6in (75cm)

Hole in side-wall for scraper

Handle

Scraper

2 × 2in (5 × 5cm) mesh floor

Red worm

USING WORM-CAST COMPOST

The resulting material is high in nutrients and microorganisms and should be used sparingly. It makes an admirable and easily handled mulch for use around ornamental plants, fruit trees or bushes, or between rows of vegetables. Sprinkle a little into your seed row before sowing, especially if the soil is very dry. Worm-cast compost can also be raked into the top inch or so of soil in a seedbed to help provide a good crumbly surface structure, and add vital nutrients to the soil.

You can also use it to make seed compost by mixing one part worm-cast compost and two parts peat, or potting compost using equal parts of peat and worm-cast compost.

Green manure

This is a crop grown to add organic matter to beds that are empty for a period of time. It is sown with the specific intention of digging it into the soil to provide organic matter and plant food. It is perhaps of more value to the large-scale farmer than the gardener, but there are sometimes situations when a green-manure crop is useful, even in the small garden.

The biggest problem is that green manure takes up growing space. In most gardens, there's no room for the luxury of leaving an area fallow, so manure crops have to fit in with cultivated ones. However, if your soil is particularly light (sand or chalk), it is advisable to keep it covered with something if it is likely to be vacant for any length of time. This would generally mean sowing a winter crop in the late summer or early fall and digging it in before planting or sowing vegetables the following spring. Some green-manure crops are fast-growing enough to allow sowing between crops in the growing season (*see below*). There may also be times when, for example, you are waiting to plant an ornamental border in the fall and can get a summer crop in.

The most obvious value of green manure is in providing organic matter. However, the soft green material quickly rots down, leaving a small amount of stable organic matter in the soil. Nonetheless, on soils short of organic matter, anything must be a bonus. This addition of organic matter also increases the amount of biological activity in the soil and the roots serve to break it up and improve drainage.

The greater value of green manure is in its ability to make plant nutrients available. If the crop is deep rooting, it can take up minerals from the lower levels of the soil—red clover and lupins, for example, will root down over 7ft (2m)—so that when they are dug into the soil again, these nutrients are nearer the surface and more readily available to the next crop of vegetables or flowers.

In addition, leguminous plants like beans and lupins have the ability to "fix" the nitrogen in the soil through bacteria living in tiny nodules in their roots. They remove nitrogen from the air and, when the plant is dug in, the nitrogen becomes available to the next crop.

On light soils in particular, the biggest loss of nutrients occurs in the winter through leaching or drainage during wet weather (*see pp. 16–17*). A crop of green manure in the winter will prevent this, and is therefore very valuable.

Green-manure crops also serve to suppress weeds. They generally cover the ground well, providing shade and competition for water and soil nutrients that will discourage all but the most tenacious weeds (*see p. 58*). The manure crops themselves are chosen so that they will not cause a nuisance by regrowing after they have been dug in.

SOWING CROPS FOR GREEN MANURE

Choose a plant that will mature in the time available (*see next page*), and preferably one that is unlike either the crop you have just harvested or the one you intend to sow the following season. For example, it is unwise to sow another brassica, such as mustard, after cabbages, because of the risk of perpetuating associated pests and diseases (*see p. 134*).

The soil needs to be in good condition if the crop is to be successful. If it is low in nutrients, it may be necessary to apply a fertilizer before sowing. Pre-sowing cultivation should be as thorough as for any other crop and the seedbed should be firmed up by walking before sowing. Small seeds can be sown in rows about 6in (15cm) apart or scattered by hand and raked into the top inch of soil, while large seed is sown in rows about 1ft (30cm) apart.

PLANTING AND DIGGING IN A MUSTARD CROP

Mustard is a fast- and low-growing crop. It is an ideal way to cover a piece of land that is empty for a few weeks during the growing period. As with any green-manure crop it should not be allowed to get too woody and should be cut down and worked into the soil before it flowers.

1 *Prepare the soil for sowing (see above), then scatter the seeds across the plot. Alternatively, sow thinly in seed rows about ½in (1cm) deep and 6in (15cm) apart. Most of the seeds will germinate.*

2 *When the seedlings are about 6–9in (15–20cm) tall and before they flower, they are ready for digging in. Cut plants down at the base with a spade and leave the green manure on the ground for awhile to wilt.*

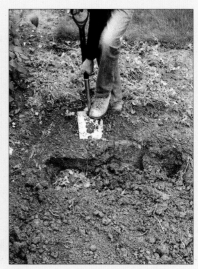

3 *Scrape back the green manure to expose a 12in (30cm) strip of soil at one end of the plot. Dig a shallow trench and scrape some green manure into it. Refill the trench. Continue until all the green manure is worked into the soil.*

WORKING GREEN MANURE INTO SOIL

Incorporating the green manure into the soil must be done in the right way if the maximum benefit is to be obtained.

Do not let the crop become too woody before you dig it in or the rotting process will take nitrogen from the soil. If the crop is fairly large, it may be best to cut it up finely before cultivating the soil. This can be done with a rotary mower or, with lower-growing crops like mustard, even a cylinder mower. Whichever way, allow a period of wilting before digging the material under. Low-growing crops can simply be cut down with a spade and allowed to wilt for a few days, then dug in, while taller plants can be worked into the surface with a rotary cultivator and then, after a few days, cultivated more deeply.

When digging in the green manure, don't bury the material deeper than about 6in (15cm). If you have allowed the crop to become hard and woody, it may be necessary to apply liquid fertilizer to assist with the rotting. Watering over with liquid seaweed or animal manure would suffice.

TYPES OF GREEN-MANURE CROPS

There are several types of green manure you can grow. The one you choose will depend mainly on the nature of your soil and the length of time the ground is to be fallow. The main distinction made here is between nitrogen-fixing crops and those that do not fix nitrogen.

Green-manure plants that act as nitrogen fixers

Alfalfa (Lucerne) *Medicago sativa*
A deep-rooted, tall perennial, alfalfa is extremely useful in the garden as long as you have enough space to let it grow for a whole season. If you have, it provides plenty of green matter, is very deep rooting and, being a legume, adds nitrogen. Sow at ½oz (15g) per sq yard/meter in the spring, then dig in fall; alternatively, sow in late summer and dig in during the spring.

Broad or fava bean *Vicia faba*
This is an excellent green-manure crop in every way. It will withstand the winter almost everywhere, it produces plenty of organic matter, it is a nitrogen-fixer, and the beans can be harvested and eaten. Sow in fall or early summer. Space out the seeds every 4in (10cm) in rows 12in (30cm) apart, if you want to harvest the beans as well. In any case, it is just as well to allow a row or two to produce beans because they can be used for seed for later crops of green manure.

Red clover *Trifolium pratense*
A low-growing nitrogen-fixer with an extensive root system that will supply plenty of organic matter, red clover is best sown in spring or late summer, but always before fall. Scatter the seeds at 1oz (30g) per sq yard/meter, in rows 6in (15cm) apart and dig in when the land is needed.

Lupin *Lupinus angustifolius*
Deep-rooting tall legume that will add nitrogen and large amounts of phosphates to the soil. Sow in spring in rows about 6in (15cm) apart, with about 3in (7cm) between each seed—1oz (30g) of seed will sow 70yd (70m) of row. Cut down and dig in in summer. A second crop can then be sown and dug in eight weeks later.

Winter tare *Vicia villosa*
Another tall plant, this is one of the most useful crops because it grows during the winter when land is vacant. Sow in rows, as for lupins, during late summer and dig them in during early spring. It can also be sown during spring and summer if land is vacant; 3oz (80g) will sow a 100yd (100m) row. Winter tare produces a large amount of green matter, has an extensive root system, and fixes nitrogen.

Green-manure plants that do not fix nitrogen

Buckwheat *Fagopyrum esculentum*
Useful only where space is available for the whole summer. Sow when the weather is warm, in spring or summer, and dig in during the fall. Sow in rows about 6in (15cm) apart, or scatter at 1oz (30g) per 7sq yard/meter. Buckwheat is tall and has a very extensive root system. It has plenty of organic matter but does not fix nitrogen. It also has the advantage that it attracts hoverflies, which eat greenfly by the thousand (*see p. 46*).

Rye *Secale cereale*
A non-legume that has an extensive root system and produces a useful amount of green material to dig in. Sow the perennial variety in late summer or fall and dig it in during the spring. Sow in rows 9in (23cm) apart or scatter at 1oz (30g) per sq yard/meter. Rather than cutting the whole crop, leave a few plants to mature in the summer and save the seed for sowing the next crop.

Phacelia *Phacelia tanacetifolia*
One of the best of all green-manure crops in spite of the fact that it does not fix nitrogen and has roots of only medium strength. It is fast growing and, if dug in when still soft, will not rob the soil of nitrogen. It does not withstand cold, so sow it after the threat of frost has passed and dig it in after about eight weeks. Scatter at about 1oz (30g) per 4sq yard/meter.

Mustard *Sinapsis alba*
A quick-growing, short and shallow-rooting crop that will make plenty of organic matter for digging in, and a good weed suppressor. Used widely in gardens where land cannot be spared for long. Sow in spring and summer and dig in before flowering. It has the big disadvantage that it is a member of the cabbage family, so it could harbor clubroot. Scatter seeds at 1oz (30g) per 4 sq yard/meter, or in rows 6in (15cm) apart (*see p. 33*).

Italian ryegrass *Lolium multiflorum*
Fast-growing and bulky, this is a good crop for sowing early in the spring. It will germinate quickly, even in cold soils, and it can be dug in before the ground has warmed up sufficiently to plant tender vegetables. It is essential to ensure that you use the *annual* strain called "Westerwolds" rather than the perennial or biennial ryegrass, which will cause endless problems by regrowing, and that you dig it in before it produces seed. Scatter about 1oz (30g) of seeds per 4sq yard/meter.

FERTILIZERS

THE USE OF CONCENTRATED FERTILIZER is probably one of the most controversial areas in organic gardening. Opinions vary: some gardeners claim that additional fertilizer is unnecessary if the correct cultivation methods are observed, where others employ methods that appear to be identical to the chemical grower except that the products used are organic in origin.

Plants need a wide and varied range of nutrients to be present in the soil for normal healthy growth. All the nutrients will be added to your soil if you follow the general soil management techniques discussed in the previous chapters.

Chemical growers assess the nutrient needs of each plant every year and supply those needs in the form of a fertilizer that is immediately available to the plants. They simply use the soil to hold the plant nutrients. But the result of using fertilizer as an alternative to organic matter is that the soil becomes an inert medium, devoid of life, and the lost nutrients have to be replaced every year.

The principle of organic gardening is to feed the soil rather than the plants growing in it. If high soil-fertility levels are maintained by regular additions of organic matter (see pp. 16–20), the plants can simply draw on the material as it is required. There is no danger of an overdose and a steady supply is ensured by the activity of all the various organisms in the soil (see p. 11).

WHY USE FERTILIZERS?

For many crops, very acceptable yields can be obtained without the addition of fertilizers, but you have to be realistic. Fertilizers are normally required for several reasons. First, you may not be able to supply your soil with all the manure or compost needed to provide the necessary nutrients. Second, you may find that your soil is grossly deficient in one or more of the essential nutrients. To correct this by adding bulky organic material can take several years; it is more realistic to add concentrated organic fertilizer as well as the organic material. Third, many gardeners wish to make much higher demands on their soil than even the hardest-working colony of bacteria and fungi could provide in the time.

So there are always occasions when fertilizers are required. What you must do is ensure that they are compatible with the requirements not only of the plants but also of the organisms in the soil. The beauty of organic gardening is that, provided you supply nature with the tools of the trade, she will do the rest.

Acidity and alkalinity

Before deciding on a soil-feeding regime, you must first discover whether the soil is acid or alkaline. This will have a major effect not only on your cultivation technique but also on the plants you choose to grow.

Acidity or alkalinity of soil is determined by its lime content. So it is obvious that you must ascertain this before you do anything else. This can be measured in units using a pH test. Simply put, pH is measured in units on a scale of 1 to 14: neutral soil has a pH of 7; anything above that is alkaline and anything below it, acid. Testing the lime content of your soil is very simple and can be done at home (see next page).

In the ornamental garden it is best to grow plants that thrive in the soil you have, rather than trying to change the pH level. There is a wide range of lime-loving plants, as well as those that prefer acid soil and many that tolerate both (see pp. 92–93). In the vegetable garden, however, most plants thrive in a pH of about 6.5, so you may have to take steps to alter the lime content (see pp. 36–37).

It is easier to make an acid soil more alkaline by adding lime than the other way round. Lime has other advantages too. Adding it to heavy clay soils, for example, will help bind the particles together (see p. 16). However, too much lime can chemically "lock up" some of the plant nutrients, particularly trace elements, so that they are unavailable to the plant roots. This will result in nutrient deficiencies.

TESTING YOUR SOIL pH

There are several
different types of kits
available for testing
soil pH that all work
on the same principle.
All are simple to use
and accurate enough
for home use. You
should always conduct
a pH test when you
take over a new garden
and it is a good idea to
repeat the test every
year, particularly if you
are trying to alter the
pH level of the soil.

Testing the soil *Test kits use a chemical solution that changes color when mixed with soil in a test tube. A yellow or orange color indicates acid soil; a dark green solution shows you have alkaline soil, while bright green means the soil has a neutral pH.*

Using a color chart *Many soils fall between the extremes—either slightly acidic, or on the alkaline side of neutral. Matching the sample against a color chart may provide a more precise idea of your soil's pH.*

Raising soil pH

This is not a complicated procedure; you can make an acid soil more alkaline simply by adding lime, but do not expect dramatic changes overnight. The effect is slow, and it is not a good practice to smother the land with lime because excessive quantities will scorch the plant roots. You should apply small amounts regularly. Bear in mind that, like other chemicals, lime will gradually be washed through the soil into the drainage system and the applications of manure and compost will have an acidifying effect on the soil.

TYPES OF LIME

Lime is available in several different forms. On the whole, the more expensive varieties last longer in the soil.

Slaked lime (*calcium oxide*) This is probably the most readily available. It is sometimes sold as "garden lime." This is better than builder's lime (hydrated lime) because it lasts longer in the soil.

Hydrated lime Builder's lime, commonly sold for use with cement, works perfectly well for garden use but must be replaced at least annually.

Ground limestone Often known as "Dolomite lime," this is the best type to use. It is more expensive than hydrated or slaked lime but it will last in the soil for several years and it contains magnesium.

Calcified seaweed It is now illegal to harvest this type of coral, so it has been replaced by a similar material, calcified seaweed. It contains several plant foods as well as lime and lasts in the soil for two to three years and is reasonably priced.

WHEN TO APPLY LIME

Apply lime several weeks before sowing or planting. Ideally, dig manure into the soil in the fall and apply lime in the spring. Never apply lime to soil that has just been manured because it will combine to form ammonia gas, which releases nitrogen into the air.

HOW MUCH LIME?

The amount of lime you use will depend to some degree on your soil type. Heavy clay soils need more than light sandy ones. As a rough guide, to increase the pH of a sandy soil by one unit, apply 2lb (1kg) lime every 100 square yards/meters. A sandy loam will need 4lb (2kg) for the same area, a medium loam about 6lb (3kg), and a heavy clay roughly 8lb (4kg). In practice, the pH level is not so critical that your plants are going to die if you do not get it exactly right. The pH levels recommended for specific plants in later chapters are intended only as a guide.

Lowering soil pH

Few garden soils are likely to be so limy that they will not grow vegetables at all. In most cases the liberal doses of compost and manure applied by organic gardeners will lower the pH sufficiently.

However, a very chalky soil can cause problems because there may be nutrient deficiencies associated with the excess lime (*see pp. 38–39*). In this case you should grow your vegetables on the deep-bed system (*see p. 136*). This technique raises the growing area slightly, preventing the surrounding alkaline water from draining into it. Then, by treating beds with heavy spreadings of organic matter—digging in manure or compost annually and applying regular mulches (*see p. 20*)—you will make the soil more acid. The same principle applies in the ornamental garden: raise the border above the level of the lawns or paths, preferably by using lots of organic matter, when you prepare the soil for planting (*see p. 75*).

BUILDING A RAISED BED FOR ACID-LOVING PLANTS

If your soil is very chalky, or alkaline, and you want to grow acid-loving plants such as rhododendrons, azaleas, or the pieris, the only way to include them in the garden is by growing them in pots, or by building a raised bed, ideally out of new railroad ties. Fill it with an acid soil mixture such as lime-free compost and sharp sand. *See p. 93 for a list of suitable plants.*

Making a raised bed out of railroad ties *This method is more suitable for a large raised bed because railroad ties are very difficult to cut. Mark out the area for the bed and lay one row of ties on their sides along the edge. Hammer stakes into the ground at the corners, and at points where two railroad ties meet, and nail them to the ties (see right); the wall can be one or two railroad ties high. Fill the bed with a mixture of half acid soil and half peat-substitute, or a mixture of three parts peat-substitute to one part sharp sand. Plant as described for shrubs (see p. 112). You can spread chipped pine bark around the bed to hide the base of the sleepers and provide extra interest.*

Acid-loving plants

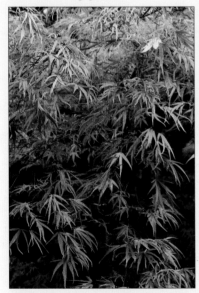

***Acer palmatum* "Linearilobum"**
This small tree has beautifully dissected foliage which turns yellow in the fall. Place in a sheltered spot where cold winds cannot scorch the delicate foliage.

Camellia reticulata
A camellia in full flower is a sight to behold. This one has handsome dark green foliage with stunning rose-red flowers in spring. Position camellias away from early morning sun, which can damage the flowers on frosty mornings.

Vaccinium corymbosum
In spring the blueberry produces pendent white flowers, sometimes tinged with pink, and in fall these are followed by blue, edible fruits. The leaves turn yellow or red in the fall.

The need for nutrients

All plants need oxygen, carbon, and hydrogen, which they get from the air, sunlight, and water. However, just as important for healthy plant growth is the presence of a range of chemical elements in the soil. These are divided into the major elements (nitrogen, phosphorus, potassium, magnesium, calcium, and sulfur) and trace elements (those needed in very small amounts but nonetheless essential). Oxygen, hydrogen, and carbon are needed in very large quantities (see opposite). By comparison, the other nutrients are needed in much smaller amounts. However, they are still needed in specific proportions, as too much of one can inactivate another. For example, too much potassium can inactivate magnesium (see below).

MAJOR ELEMENTS

Nitrogen (N), phosphorus (P), and potassium (K) are the major elements needed in the largest quantities. These are present in all general fertilizers, some of which also contain magnesium (Mg). Most soils have adequate levels of calcium and sulfur that can be retained by regular additions of organic matter and by using good cultivation techniques.

NITROGEN

One of the most important plant foods, this is a component of chlorophyll— the pigment that gives plants their green color—and a vital part of the structure of plant protein. It is the element in the soil responsible for the vegetative growth of the shoots and leaves of a plant.

Deficiency is not unusual because nitrogen is easily lost by leaching in open soils (see p. 13) and can be depleted by digging in unrotted material (see p. 21). If your soil contains insufficient nitrogen, plant leaves will become yellowed, particularly the older ones, and the plants will be stunted. Too much, on the other hand, will cause the plants to grow too quickly. There will be an abundance of "soft" leaves and these may be a darker green than normal. The softer growth will be subject to attack by insects and by frost.

Treating a nitrogen deficiency
Apply a high-nitrogen fertilizer such as dried blood (see p. 40).

PHOSPHORUS

The next most important element after nitrogen, phosphorus is needed in smaller quantities (only about one-tenth of the amount). Phosphorus, or phosphate, is mainly responsible for good root growth, so a deficiency causes slight stunting of the plant. It can be diagnosed by a distinct blue color, which affects the older leaves first. Sometimes the leaves darken and develop a blue/green tinge. In addition, the plants' root system is likely to be underdeveloped.

Treating a phosphorus deficiency
Use an application of bone meal fertilizer (see p. 41).

POTASSIUM

Also known as potash, this is required in the same quantities as nitrogen. It affects the size and quality of flowers and fruit, and is essential for the synthesis of protein and carbohydrates. Potassium deficiency results in small, inferior flowers and fruit. The plants themselves will also be stunted. It shows up in older leaves particularly, as a yellowing around the edge of the leaves, followed by a brown scorching. Alternatively, the leaves may become bluish and eventually bronzed all over. An excess can result in plants not being able to take up magnesium (see below) and could cause an imbalance with other elements.

Treating a potassium deficiency
Use an application of rock potash (see p. 41).

MAGNESIUM

Another element needed in much larger quantities than many gardeners realize, magnesium should be present in about the same quantities as phosphorus (see left). It is also a component of chlorophyll so a deficiency causes yellowing, which starts between the veins of the leaves. The deficiency generally affects older leaves first.

A magnesium deficiency is sometimes caused by plants not being able to absorb the magnesium in the soil, perhaps because there is too much potassium present. This can also happen if the soil structure is poor or if there is insufficient organic matter in the soil (see Soil Improvement, pp. 18–34).

Treating a magnesium deficiency
Apply a dose of kelp meal, liquid kelp, or liquid animal manure (see p. 40).

CALCIUM

Another element required in relatively large amounts, calcium neutralizes certain acids formed in plants and helps in the manufacture of protein. Deficiency is rare in a well-managed organic garden, but plants sometimes develop an inability to distribute calcium through their systems, though no one really knows why this occurs. The classic example is blossom-end rot in tomatoes, when the tip of the fruit blackens and rots. Lack of calcium also causes tip-burn on lettuce, black heart in celery, and browning in the centers of Brussels sprouts (see pp. 146–197). Deficiency will be most pronounced in young plant tissue.

Treating a calcium deficiency
There is no specific cure for calcium deficiency. The only treatment is by correct cultivation methods, incorporating plenty of manure or compost, aimed at building up a balanced nutrient level in the soil (see also Soil Improvement, pp. 18–34).

SULFUR

This is sometimes classified as a trace element, although sulfur is in fact needed in fairly large quantities. It forms part of many plant proteins and is involved in the formation of chlorophyll. Sulfur deficiency causes stunting and yellowing of the plant. However, the problem is rare since there is generally enough sulfur in organic soils because of the regular applications of compost and manure.

Treating a sulfur deficiency
As soon as you notice a sulfur deficiency, apply a very light dusting of calcium sulfate (gypsum) over the surface of the soil.

PROPORTIONS OF ELEMENTS REQUIRED FOR HEALTHY PLANT GROWTH

Of the elements required for healthy plant growth, oxygen, carbon, and hydrogen account for 96 percent—45 percent oxygen, 45 percent carbon, and 6 percent hydrogen. The nutrients described opposite and below, and some unspecified trace elements, make up the rest.

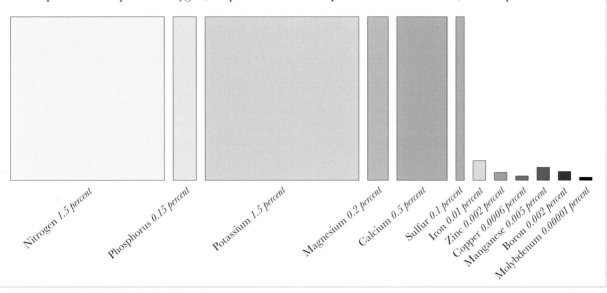

Nitrogen 1.5 percent · Phosphorus 0.15 percent · Potassium 1.5 percent · Magnesium 0.2 percent · Calcium 0.5 percent · Sulfur 0.1 percent · Iron 0.01 percent · Zinc 0.002 percent · Copper 0.0006 percent · Manganese 0.005 percent · Boron 0.002 percent · Molybdenum 0.00001 percent

TRACE ELEMENTS

So-called because they are needed in very small quantities, these elements are nonetheless vital to plant growth. There are generally considered to be six of major importance: iron, zinc, copper, manganese, boron, and molybdenum.

In a properly managed organic garden, deficiencies are extremely rare because all the trace elements are present in manure, compost, and the other bulky organic matter that the organic gardener uses. However, problems can occur when the action of trace elements such as iron, manganese, and boron is inhibited by alkaline, or limy, soil. This shows as a yellowing of rhododendron leaves and other acid-loving ornamental plants (*see p. 93*). Raspberries too are particularly susceptible to iron deficiencies, which show up as yellowing between the veins of the leaves (*see p. 228*).

It's worth stressing that the best treatment for trace-element deficiencies is to prevent them from occurring in the first place. This is normally very easily achieved in the organic garden by the continued use of bulky organic matter. Where deficiencies have occured in your garden, take the precaution of treating the soil with kelp meal fertilizer annually.

IRON
Small quantities of iron are required in the formation of chlorophyll. Symptoms of deficiency include yellowing between the veins of the leaves, especially the younger ones. It is more likely on alkaline soils and is sometimes confused with magnesium deficiency.
Treating an iron deficiency *Spray with liquid kelp then apply a measure of kelp meal and/or manure.*

ZINC AND COPPER
Both zinc and copper are enzyme activators, and a deficiency of either will have the same symptoms. Younger leaves in particular are mottled yellow, and citrus trees develop a condition known as "little leaf" that is self-explanatory.
Treating a zinc and copper deficiency *Apply kelp meal, well-rotted manure, or compost.*

MANGANESE
This is necessary for the formation of chlorophyll and protein. Deficiencies are more likely to occur in alkaline soils, and will show up as a stunting of the younger leaves and yellowing—especially between the veins.
Treating a manganese deficiency *If rapid action is required, spray with liquid kelp then apply kelp meal, manure, or compost.*

BORON
This element is important to the growing tissue of all parts of the plant. Deficiencies are more likely to occur on alkaline soils and lead to a tissue breakdown. This causes internal "corkiness," especially in apples and many root crops, and brown heart in celery and brassicas such as broccoli, cauliflower, and calabrese (*see* Pests and diseases of vegetables, *pp. 198–201*).

Treating a boron deficiency *Boron deficiency must be prevented because, if deficiencies become apparent in a crop, it is too late to save it. Apply kelp meal, manure, or compost to ensure that the next crop will not suffer from the same problem.*

MOLYBDENUM
A deficiency of this mineral, which is instrumental in the production of protein, will show up in deformed growth. It causes a condition called "whiptail" that affects the cabbage (*Brassica*) family, and results in their leaves becoming thin and straplike (*see p. 195*). Deficiency is generally due to acid soil conditions (*see p. 35*).
Treating a molybdenum deficiency *Add lime to raise the pH of acid soil (see p. 36). Spray the plants with liquid kelp fertilizer and apply kelp meal and/or manure or compost to the soil.*

Organic fertilizers

Scientists will tell you that there is no evidence to suggest that yields will be significantly heavier or that fruit and vegetables will actually taste any better if the plants are fed with organic nutrients instead of inorganic ones. And of course, they are right.

What they do not tell you is that the reason there is no evidence is that, so far, there has been no research. I have no facilities to test scientifically for taste, but I can assure any scientist that he or she will certainly notice a difference in the taste of my early potatoes compared to the inorganically grown potatoes you can buy.

Plants will take their nutrients in the form of the same chemical elements whether they are organically or inorganically derived. Organic gardeners do not suggest that plants actually take in different chemicals if they are grown naturally. What is true is that the chemicals in organic fertilizers will not harm the soil or its many inhabitants; the inorganic ones will. Indeed, organic feeding actually benefits soil microorganisms as well as plants.

There are several compound fertilizers that are described as "semi-organic" or "organically based." These may be more powerful than the completely inorganic equivalent but they are *not* the real thing. The main difference is generally in the potash content, which, in "semi-organic" fertilizers is sometimes supplemented with potassium sulfate. The following products will provide all that is necessary.

BLOOD, FISH, AND BONE MEAL

A general compound fertilizer, this is the basis of my recommended nutrition plan. Regular applications should maintain nutrient levels in all soils. The nitrogen contained in this fertilizer, however, is fairly quickly released so blood, fish, and bone meal should not be spread more than two weeks before the crops are sown or planted.

NUTRIENT CONTENT	
Nitrogen	3.5 percent
Phosphorus	8 percent
Potassium	0.5 percent
Trace elements	—

KELP MEAL

An alternative to blood, fish, and bone meal but more expensive. It is, however, better balanced and its nutrients are in a slow-release form. It contains 60 to 70 different chemical elements, including the complete range of trace elements. It can be raked into the soil before sowing or planting but its cost means that it is generally used as a compost activator and to supply trace elements (*see p. 39*). Kelp meal can be applied at any time, but it is best used when the soil is warm to enable the bacteria to break it down, making the nutrients available to plants.

NUTRIENT CONTENT	
Nitrogen	2.8 percent
Phosphorus	0.2 percent
Potassium	2.3 percent
Trace elements	Full range

HOOF AND HORN

One of the best sources of slow-release nitrogen. The ground hooves and horns are heated to 140°F (60°C) before being packed so it is very safe to use. It has to be broken down by bacteria before it becomes available to plant roots, so it must be applied a good two weeks before its effect is needed. Thereafter it will remain in the soil for some time.

Use hoof and horn fertilizer for a quick boost to overwintered plants, such as cabbages, in the spring or for any plants that appear to have stopped growing. It is not as fast-acting as dried blood (*see below*), which is used to provide a quick short-term boost.

NUTRIENT CONTENT	
Nitrogen	13 percent
Phosphorus	—
Potassium	—
Trace elements	—

DRIED BLOOD

A very fast-acting nitrogen fertilizer. Use it where a rapid nitrogen "jolt" is required, but not later than the end of the summer or it will be washed into the subsoil. If you get frosts in your garden, do not apply dried blood later than midsummer to avoid encouraging soft foliage that would be damaged by frost.

NUTRIENT CONTENT	
Nitrogen	12–14 percent
Phosphorus	Small amount
Potassium	—
Trace elements	—

FISH MEAL

A useful fertilizer that contains nitrogen and phosphate (phosphorus). Some manufacturers add potash inorganically, hence it can be sold as "semi-organic."

NUTRIENT CONTENT	
Nitrogen	*9 percent*
Phosphorus	*2.5 percent*
Potassium	—
Trace elements	—

BONE MEAL

This popular phosphate fertilizer is used for activating root growth. Buy bone meal that is clearly marked "steamed." In its raw form it can carry anthrax—but it is safe if steam treated. Even so, many gardeners wear gloves when spreading it, as a precaution.

NUTRIENT CONTENT	
Nitrogen	*3.5 percent*
Phosphorus	*22 percent*
Potassium	—
Trace elements	—

ROCK POTASH

An invaluable source of potassium—the element missing from many organic fertilizers. Rock potash is insoluble and remains in the soil for long periods, enabling plants to take it up as required.

NUTRIENT CONTENT	
Nitrogen	—
Phosphorus	—
Potassium	*10.5 percent*
Trace elements	—

WOOD ASH

A useful source of potassium and a small amount of phosphate. Put twigs and prunings, which contain useful quantities of minerals, through a shredder and use the chippings as a mulch (*see p. 59*). Alternatively, burn them and put the ash on the compost heap.

NUTRIENT CONTENT		
Nitrogen		*Varies*
Phosphorus		*according to*
Potassium		*material*
Trace elements		*burned*

DRIED ANIMAL MANURES

These contain only small amounts of the major nutrients but are rich in trace elements. Mix them with peat or mushroom compost if you cannot get bulky manures.

NUTRIENT CONTENT	
Nitrogen	*1 percent*
Phosphorus	*1 percent*
Potassium	*1.5 percent*
Trace elements	*Full range*

PELLETED CHICKEN MANURE

This general compound fertilizer has been composted and then pelleted for ease of use. It also contains some trace elements. This is a slow release fertilizer that will usually last the length of an average crop, but for longer term crops further applications would be beneficial.

NUTRIENT CONTENT	
Nitrogen	*4 percent*
Phosphorus	*2.5 percent.*
Potassium	*2.5 percent*
Trace elements	—

LIQUID KELP

There are a number of liquid kelp products available. They contain nitrogen, potash, and phosphate as well as the entire range of trace elements. They also contain growth hormones called cytokinins, which help increase the efficiency of photosynthesis and the production of protein. They are invaluable as a means of correcting deficiencies quickly.

Liquid kelp is also said to help reduce attack by fungus diseases and to protect plants from frost.

NUTRIENT CONTENT	
Nitrogen	*1.5 percent*
Phosphorus	*Min. amount*
Potassium	*2.5 percent*
Trace elements	*Full range*

LIQUID ANIMAL MANURES

These contain all the major nutrients in small quantities, but are rich in trace elements and very useful for treating trace element deficiencies.

NUTRIENT CONTENT	
Nitrogen	*1 percent*
Phosphorus	*1 percent*
Potassium	*1.5 percent*
Trace elements	*Full range*

Liquid seaweed

Liquid animal manure

HOMEMADE LIQUID FERTILIZER

It is very easy to make your own liquid manure that will be as nutritious as any you can buy. All you need is a large metal or plastic drum that holds water, a burlap sack, and some animal manure.

Sheep manure is the best because it is particularly high in nutrients (*see p. 28*), but cow, pig, horse, or goat manure can be used. About half a sackful will give a year's supply.

This method can also be used to produce a high nitrogen feed using nettles and a high potash feed using comfrey leaves.

Homemade liquid manure can be used undiluted, provided the soil has first been watered. To use it as a spray, dilute the liquid with equal parts water.

1 *Fill the drum with water. Collect up half a sackful of animal droppings. Tie up the top of the sack with a double loop of string.*

2 *Put a strong stake across the top of the drum and loop the string over it so that the sack is suspended in the water. Leave it for about two weeks, until the water is a rich, dark brown color. Remove the sack and leave the drum covered.*

Applying fertilizers

The application of organic fertilizers does not need to be quite as precise as the application of inorganic compounds. Most release their nutrients slowly so there is little chance of them scorching young plants, although you must keep granular fertilizers off the foliage.

It is impossible to give precise instructions as to how much fertilizer to apply because so much depends on your soil, the weather, and the plants you wish to grow. The only way to find out is to use the "rule-of-thumb" method of simply adding general fertilizer if growth is unsatisfactory and specific fertilizers if deficiencies show up on the plants. In addition, use an annual application on the ornamental garden and on the vegetables as directed in the relevant chapters (*see pp. 74–125 and 132–201*).

APPLYING GRANULAR FERTILIZERS

Granular fertilizers should always be used to provide general nutrients as a supplement to compost and manure. It is usually applied in the spring or before planting. Sprinkle the fertilizer over the soil as recommended, being very careful to avoid it touching the foliage, then rake it into the soil.

The application of granular fertilizers is normally recommended in "handfuls per square yard/meter." If the recommendation is to spread the fertilizer down a row of fruit or vegetables, you will need to convert the square yard/meter measurement to a linear one. This is not difficult: if the rows are 12in (30cm) apart, spread the amount of fertilizer recommended for a square yard/meter along 10ft (3m) of the row. If they are 6in (15cm) apart, it is 20ft (6m) along the row and so on. In this way, the correct distribution of fertilizer can be maintained.

APPLYING LIQUID FERTILIZERS

These are easy to put on. Dilute the liquid according to the manufacturer's instructions and simply pour it on. But the golden rule when liquid feeding is never to do so when the soil is bone dry—you may scorch the roots. Water with clear water first and let it drain away, then add the liquid fertilizer.

If you are feeding plants growing in pots, simply fill up to the rim of the pot. If they are growing in soil, water in the fertilizer generously in a fairly wide area around the plants, until the top of the soil is saturated. For plants, such as greenhouse tomatoes, that are regularly fed in this way, it is a good idea to bury a flower pot in the soil near the plant and fill that. If you use this method, the fertilizer gets deeper into the soil and you also know exactly how much you are giving the plant every time.

The advantage of liquid feeding is that, since plants can only take up nutrients in liquid form, the nutrients are available immediately; granular fertilizer has to be dissolved first. The disadvantage is that liquid fertilizer does not remain effective for as long as granular fertilizer and is leached into the subsoil fairly quickly. Liquid feeding is used to supply short-term nutrients to hungry plants and to correct deficiencies; it should *not* be considered as an alternative to solid feeding.

FOLIAR FEEDING

This method involves spraying the leaves of the plant. It is faster acting but shorter lived than other methods so is really only of value for rapid remedial action when deficiencies are seen. Liquid seaweed sprayed onto leaves, for example, is something of a "miracle cure" for trace element deficiencies. However, it should always be supplemented by feeding the soil with seaweed meal fertilizer as well.

ORGANIC PEST AND DISEASE CONTROL

OVER THE LAST CENTURY, gardening practices have closely followed those of the commercial grower and even the farmer. New methods of cultivation that improve yields or that reduce losses from pests and diseases have been discovered, and these have been translated into gardening terms. A great deal of research has also been directed at finding new methods of growing plants commercially. There is no doubt that much of the information that has come from this research has benefited the gardener, but it would be a mistake to fall into the trap of following the commercial grower automatically. Nowhere has the mimicry of the professional been more evident than in the field of pest and disease control. Just as soon as a new chemical has been produced for commercial use, so a slightly diluted version of the chemical appears in the garden shops and centers, accompanied by seductive claims that it has proved to be more effective than its competitors.

You have to remember that your requirements are very different. The farmer or commercial grower is constantly on the lookout for higher yielding, larger, and therefore more profitable varieties of plants, while you are after fruit and vegetables with flavor, which are not contaminated with chemicals. In addition, he or she may have many acres of, for example, cabbages, that are infested with caterpillars, and so have no alternative but to spray them. If you have only one or two rows of cabbages, you do not need to cover them with chemicals. Instead, walk down the rows two or three evenings a week, pick off the offending creatures, and drop them into a jar of paraffin. Likewise, a few well-directed squirts of soapy water will wash any aphids off your couple of dozen rose bushes in next to no time.

The plain fact is that, by cultivating a natural organic garden, you simply will not come across the pest and disease problems that can face the monoculture grower. Where large acreages of one crop are grown year after year, a rapid build-up of pests and diseases can easily occur. They have a plentiful supply of food and virtually no competition.

In the organic garden where there is a great diversity of planting (see p. 71), you will attract the complete spectrum of wildlife—insects, birds, and small mammals—that will create a natural balance. The result is that the larvae of hoverflies and ladybugs eat the greenfly, and the birds eat the caterpillars, and so on—no insect pest, fungus disease, or bacterium will ever have it all its own way, so there will never be an unnatural build-up of one species. But, if you start to think that all the insects are friendly and all the fungi benign, be warned that pests and diseases will rear their heads just as surely as they will anywhere else. Prevention is the best approach and there are many physical ways of doing this. Although it would be a foolish overreaction to think that you can do without pesticides completely, you should only resort to the few organic pesticides available when all else fails.

WHAT YOU CAN DO TO AVOID PESTS AND DISEASES

Start by growing strong, healthy plants that will have the ability to resist attacks from pests and diseases. Always plant into fertile soil and make sure the plants never go short of water and food. Rely as much as you can on physical methods of pest and disease prevention and control and constant vigilance, as outlined on the next few pages, and you will cut down the need for chemicals. Nature will do the rest for you.

Nature has worked out the most complex "balance of power" that makes modern international politics look like a child's game. Build up as diverse a collection of plants as you can, including as many native flowers, trees, and shrubs as possible, especially those that grow in your own locality, and provide a small area of water. By doing this you will build up a varied colony of useful insects and birds and thus keep problems to a minimum.

On the following pages I describe ways of preventing and controlling general garden pests and diseases. Treatment for pests or diseases that affect specific plants, such as greenfly on roses, blight on potatoes, or scab on fruit trees, are dealt with in the relevant chapters later in the book.

Maintaining a healthy garden

The very first rule is to adopt good cultivation practices. The organic approach to gardening—feeding the soil instead of the plant—produces much stronger growth that is, first, not as attractive to pests and diseases as the soft lushness of a force-fed plant and, second, able to cope with an attack if it does occur.

Keep the garden as clean and neat as possible. Never leave trash around. If you've been weeding, put the waste on the compost heap right away. If you've been thinning seedlings, this is even more important because insect pests are often attracted by the smell of the bruised stems.

Any plant material can be put on to the compost heap, except for ones infected with diseases such as blight, clubroot, and onion mildew. I very rarely compost the top growth of my main crop potatoes after digging, for example, because of the risk of inoculating the compost heap with spores of the potato blight; a completely clean crop is very rare (see p. 200). Recent trials have shown that the majority of disease spores and pest eggs are killed in a well-managed compost heap.

Use only pots and seed trays that have been thoroughly cleaned and, if possible, sterilized with boiling water or environmentally friendly bleach. Keep your greenhouse clean too and, if you see a sign of a pest or a fungus on a leaf, pick it off right away and get rid of it, preferably by burning it.

DAILY VIGILANCE

Make a habit, especially in the summer, when pests and diseases are most likely to appear, of walking around the garden at least once a day. Take a hoe and a plastic bag with you. Remove any weeds with the hoe, but above all, keep an eye open for the first signs of attack from pests and diseases. If you see signs of mildew or you find a caterpillar—pick it off immediately, put it into the plastic bag, and later into the trash can. The first attack of greenfly can often be removed by simply rubbing the stem of the attacked plants with your finger to squash them.

BUYING HEALTHY PLANTS

It is of vital importance to ensure that your plants are healthy when you first buy them. It is only too easy to buy in a load of trouble in the form of virus or fungus diseases, or even pests or their eggs. Some plants are covered by federal regulations, however this only applies to plant material obtained from outside the US. Free movement of plants within the United States is the likely cause of new pests and diseases being found in your area such as emerald ash borer. In many places it is possible to ask for a certificate to show that the plant you are buying is free from disease. Many fruit trees and seed potatoes come this way.

Check ornamental trees, shrubs, herbaceous perennials, and even annuals carefully before buying them; reject anything that shows the slightest sign of disease or pest attack, or of physical damage.

Examine bulbs, corms, and tubers closely. They should be firm all over and the skins should be fairly well intact. A loose skin can often mean that the bulb has become shriveled (see p. 117).

In some cases you should consider replacing your stock with new plants after a few years. Strawberries, for example, will lose their vigor after a while. This is often a sign that they have become infected with virus diseases and anything you propagate from them will also be infected. Potatoes too can become infected with virus diseases spread by aphids. The seed potatoes you buy are generally grown in areas where aphid attack is rare, so they are likely to be free from virus. So, unless you can be quite sure that your crop has not been attacked by aphids, it is worthwhile to buy new potato tubers every year.

Different varieties of the same plants may have varying degrees of resistance to pests and disease. Some varieties of potato, for example, are less susceptible to slug damage, while others show resistance to potato eelworm. There is quite a distinct variation in resistance to fungus diseases. I would not, for example, recommend growing America's favorite apple, Jonathan, or the rose variety Joseph's Coat, in an organic garden because both are very susceptible to mildew fungus. Mildew can be serious because, once it is established on one variety, it moves on to other plants.

Plant breeders are constantly trying to breed pest- and disease-resistant plants, so it is worthwhile checking the current position on new varieties before buying anything that is notoriously disease-prone. There are, for example, several varieties of snapdragon (*Antirrhinum* sp.) that have been bred specifically to resist rust fungus, there are eelworm-resistant *Phlox* and virus-resistant varieties of many plants including potatoes, strawberries, and tomatoes.

Where it is difficult to breed in resistance, it is sometimes possible to have the best of both worlds by grafting the required variety onto a resistant rootstock (see p. 277).

RAISING HEALTHY PLANTS

Of course, you should also employ the same safeguards with plants you have raised yourself, though here it's much more difficult to be ruthless about weeding out the weaklings. But bear in mind that a young plant that has been infected with a

COPING WITH CLUBROOT

Clubroot is a crippling fungus disease, which causes distortion and swelling of the roots of all members of the cabbage family and several ornamental plants too. Once the roots cease to function properly, the tops wilt and will not produce a satisfactory harvest. There is no cure for clubroot and, worse still, once it invades the soil, it is there forever whether or not you grow any host plants.

Once your soil has clubroot, I would not recommend growing cauliflower, but you can get an acceptable crop of cabbage, kale, and Brussels sprouts by sowing them in trays, then transferring them to pots until they establish a good root system. Even though the seedlings will still be affected by the disease when planted, they will then be strong and healthy enough to shrug it off. Adding lime to the soil before planting also seems to help.

1 *Sow the seed in a seed tray (see p. 271). When the seedlings are 1½ in (4cm) tall, transfer each one to a 4in (10cm) pot.*

2 *Grow the plants until the roots fill the pot— up to about 6 weeks—then plant them outside. Water well after planting.*

disease or attacked by a pest is at a disadvantage right from the start. Throw it away to avoid infecting other plants.

Keep your greenhouse scrupulously clean. Use plastic seed trays and pots for raising seeds and pot plants because they are easier to sterilize; wooden seed trays and clay pots are porous so can harbor pests (*see p. 271*).

Time your spring sowing so that plants do not have to remain in the greenhouse getting leggy and pot-bound because the weather is too cold for them to be planted outside. The real secret is to get young plants growing and then to keep them growing steadily. In some cases, this is all you need to control even the most virulent and damaging of diseases (*see above*).

One final point to bear in mind when buying or raising plants from seed is that *F1* hybrid varieties have much more vigor than those raised from open-pollinated seed. An *F1* hybrid is the result of a first-generation cross between two selected parents. These first generations always have much more vigor, which will help to tide them over in an early attack.

Companion planting

This is a technique practiced by many organic gardeners. The theory behind companion planting is that plants have specific likes and dislikes concerning their close companions in the garden and will do better if planted in close proximity to the correct plant. Similarly, by planting a particular species in the garden you can reduce the number of weeds or attract certain pest predators.

Many of the recommendations for companion planting are based on folklore and, as with many of these tales, there is some truth in them. There is a well-known theory that, because carrot fly are attracted by smell, they can be prevented by planting carrots between rows of onions, so the smell of the carrots is disguised. I have experimented with this theory over several years in carefully controlled trials but without any success. In fact an independent trial discovered that at least 10 rows of onions per row of carrots were required for the onions to have any effect. On the other hand, the cabbage white butterfly is attracted to its host plant by smell and it can be fooled by planting the highly aromatic French marigold (*Tagetes*) between the rows of cabbages. Many

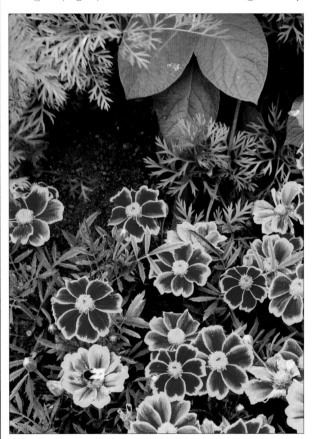

Ornamental pest control *Hoverflies, which are predators of aphids, can be attracted into the garden by planting flat, open flowers such as these French marigolds (*Tagetes*).*

scientifically controlled trials have been conducted which indicate a reduction in attack when this was done. Many gardeners have also reported similar results with eelworms, soil pests that attack potatoes in particular, where French marigolds are grown. Scientific research has confirmed that this is indeed due to a secretion from the roots of the marigolds. French marigolds are also said to help kill weeds, in particular couch grass (*Agropyron repens*), but I have not been able to test this theory in my garden.

COMPANION PLANTING TO REDUCE APHIDS

There is absolutely no doubt that marigolds (*Tagetes* and *Calendula*), planted near tomatoes or roses, for example, greatly reduce the frequency of attack by aphids—the most persistent of all garden pests. This is simply because they attract hoverflies whose larvae devour greenfly by the thousand. Hoverflies are the most valuable pest predators in the garden and there are different species all over the world. Before laying her eggs, the female needs protein, which she gets from pollen. She then lays individual eggs on colonies of aphids so that the larvae have a readily available source of food when they hatch. The hoverfly has a short feeding tube so needs to feed from an open-structured flower where the pollen is easily accessible. Therefore by planting marigolds (*Tagetes* and *Calendula*), poppies (*Papaver* sp.), nasturtiums (*Tropaeolum*),

or dwarf morning glory (*Convolvulus tricolor*) between plants, you minimize aphid attack.

I have grown garlic under rose bushes as a control for greenfly, and savory next to beans for the same purpose—all to no avail. I have tried other combinations but, as of yet, I have not achieved success. More research is needed.

ENCOURAGING OTHER PEST PREDATORS

It is more difficult to attract some of the other predators because they do not necessarily feed on flowers. Some, such as ladybugs, lacewings, and several species of wasps that feed on and lay their eggs inside aphids and other soft-bellied pests including caterpillars, can be encouraged by providing as varied a collection of plant life as possible.

It has also been found that some pests are attracted to their host plants by sight. By mixing ornamental plants and vegetables in an ornamental border, you can camouflage the host plants, which deters the pests. There is also evidence that vegetable plots that are left weed infested suffer less than clean ones. However, the yields are also lower because the weeds compete for the same light, nutrients, and water.

Some of the good results reported by many organic gardeners are, I am sure, due to companion planting. By careful consideration of which plants are cultivated together, you can promote healthy growth and utilize a completely natural form of pest control.

Controlling birds and animals

The most destructive pests in gardens are the larger ones—birds, deer, rabbits, moles, mice, and so on. There is no doubt that the most effective control for this type of pest is to prevent them from reaching the crops by physical means.

Birds

There is no really effective bird deterrent available. Scarecrows are reasonably effective for a day or two but, after a short while, the birds get used to them and take no notice. This is even true with the more elaborate electric scarecrows that have waving arms, flashing lights, and screaming sirens or blazing shotguns. If moved around constantly, they have some effect but, in the end, they are more likely to frighten your neighbors than the birds! If a scarecrow is combined with regular shooting, it will be more effective. I have found free CDs that hang from a pole and spin quite effective, and inexpensive!

PROTECTING THE PRODUCTIVE GARDEN

The only really effective control for birds is netting and that is not nearly as expensive as it may seem. Plastic netting is relatively cheap and will last a very long time if it is used carefully.

The ideal is to build yourself a fruit cage to cover the entire productive garden. Support the netting on strong posts and wires and secure it at the edges with short wire staples.

If you do not wish to go to that kind of extreme, cover only the rows of vulnerable crops. You can place a row of small wire hoops along the beds of low plants and drape nets over the top (*see opposite*). Alternatively, with crops such as strawberries or rows of fruit bushes, you can simply drape the netting over the row. If there is a danger of plants growing through the netting, as with peas for example, it is better to support the net on stakes so that it is higher than the plants. Otherwise you will damage the plant when you remove the netting.

Unlike most of the insect pests, birds generally cause the most damage during the winter, when there is little else around for them to eat. They will attack the fattening buds of fruit—particularly black currants. The cabbage (*Brassica*) family are also greatly at risk, especially when it snows, because they are often the only edible plants visible, so will attract all the birds in the area. The answer is to drive in a few short posts along the row, put a jelly jar on the top of each post, and drape the netting over the top. This can be a nuisance when you want to cut a cabbage from the middle of the row, but at least you will have some left to harvest! Ensure that the netting is firmly secured at ground level or birds may still get under the netting and could be injured trying to get out.

PROTECTING THE ORNAMENTAL GARDEN
This is more difficult because plastic netting will do nothing for the appearance of the flower borders.

And some birds particularly like to remove buds from all kinds of plants, especially burgeoning crocuses in the spring. It's odd but, with crocuses, they seem to go mainly for the yellow ones so they are to be avoided if birds are a problem. The rest can be protected by stringing black cotton thread over the top (*see below*). The birds do not see the cotton strands and, if they touch them, they will panic and fly off.

New grass seed is extremely vulnerable to attack by birds. Obviously it is impossible to rake in all the seed, so the birds are immediately attracted. Again, they can be deterred by black thread, but this is not practical over large areas. A more effective method is to cover the seeded area with perforated plastic. This can be found at most garden centers, sold as "floating cloches," for use in the vegetable garden. It has the great advantage that it not only keeps the birds away but it also encourages germination by warming the soil (*see p. 140*).

DETERRING BIRDS

Birds can be a tremendous asset in the garden as pest controllers and they are welcomed for their aesthetic value as well. However, they also cause a great deal of damage, so vulnerable plants must be protected. Fruit and vegetable plants are especially at risk, particularly in the winter or early spring when food is scarce. Some ornamental plants are also susceptible, especially early spring bulbs. The only really effective way to protect these plants is by physical means.

◀ **Protecting crops**
Place stakes along the rows of vegetables and put jelly jars over the top of each stake to protect the netting. Leaving enough netting at the edges to reach the ground, stretch it over the stakes.

▶ **Protecting fruit bushes**
Birds attack the young shoots and the fruit. Low-growing bushes can be protected by draping netting over the top. Secure the netting at one end with bricks, pull it over the bush; anchor the edges.

◀ **Protecting seedlings**
Rows of vegetable seedlings seem to be particularly at risk from bird damage and are best covered with netting supported on wire hoops. You can make the hoops by bending 12-gauge wire or use the hoops supplied with small cloches. The netting can normally be removed once the seedlings are established.

Protecting crocus buds

Obviously, it is not practical to cover the ornamental garden with netting, but some plants need protecting because they are particularly susceptible. Crocuses are often the only colorful plants in the garden in the early spring so regularly have their buds removed. To prevent this, put some small sticks into the ground around the buds and loop black thread around them and across the middle so that it forms an invisible covering. Birds will still try to attack the crocus buds because they cannot see the thread and will fly off when they touch it.

Animals

Animals such as hedgehogs, frogs, and toads should be encouraged in any garden because they feed on garden pests. However, others such as deer, rabbits, moles, or mice, must be kept out of the garden because they either feed on the plants or undermine them. Good fencing will deter deer and rabbits, but the only solution for mice and moles is to trap them.

DEER

If you live in the country near woodland, deer can be quite a problem because they eat most vegetation and strip bark from trees in winter.

Deer can jump a 10ft (3m) fence, so building one tall enough to keep them out is expensive. An alternative is to use an electric fence powered by a car battery or through a transformer run from your electrical panel. It is important to get an expert to install this type of fencing, so seek the advice of an agricultural specialist.

RABBITS

Rabbits are a problem in many rural gardens because they eat almost anything.

There is only one way to control them effectively. No amount of shooting, trapping, or ferreting will keep their numbers down; they have to be fenced out with wire netting. It is important to use 1in (2.5cm) mesh netting and to bury it at least 6in (15cm) in the ground, with 2ft 6in (75cm) above the ground (*see below*).

Erecting rabbit fencing
Hammer fencing posts into the ground around the productive garden and string two pieces of wire between them, one about a third of the way up the posts, the other near the top. Fix wire netting to the strands, burying the bottom 6–8in (15–20cm) in a trench so that it curves away from the base of the fence.

2in (5cm)

4in (10cm)

MICE

Mice are not usually a serious problem. However, if entire rows of larger seeds such as peas or beans simply disappear from your vegetable garden, suspect mice. They dig them out and carry them away, and rarely leave a visible trace.

To prevent them, you can either trap them with a conventional mousetrap or buy a cat.

MOLES

These animals can be a particular problem because not only do they damage plant roots when they burrow underground—sometimes even leaving the roots suspended in mid-air—but they also eat large numbers of worms. They undermine lawns and borders as well, leaving large mounds of earth and uneven soil sinkage.

Moles are almost impossible to keep out of the garden. My own experience is that smoke drives them off only temporarily, and the trick of making the tunnels uncomfortable by filling them with holly leaves simply makes them dig another tunnel elsewhere.

If all else fails, the only reasonably effective method is to trap them, though it goes against the grain because they are very attractive creatures.

Barrel traps are the most effective and the moles are at least killed instantly. These are set in the main runs and covered with a small amount of loose soil to keep the light out of the run. Mark the position of the barrel traps with a stick or colored marker so that you do not forget where they are, and dig them up daily.

Setting mole traps
Mole traps are set in the mole runs. To find a run, follow a straight line between two mole hills and dig down into the soil. Prepare the trap and put it into the mole run. Cover it with some loose soil and mark the position with a stick. Check the traps for moles every day.

Controlling soil pests and insects

Soil pests and insects have always proved to be a great headache for organic gardeners because there is no suitable organic chemical with which to treat them. Three soil pests that cause great problems, especially on newly dug land, are wireworms, cutworms, and leatherjackets, because they eat the roots of almost anything. One way of reducing all soil pests is to hoe between plants regularly (*see p. 57*). This brings them to the surface, where the birds will find them.

There are, however, some very effective physical controls for some of the most troublesome pests, and many natural predators can be encouraged into the garden to help get rid of them. Insects can also be controlled without resorting to chemicals. Many insects, and methods of controlling them, are specific to certain plants, so they are dealt with in the relevant chapter. Those discussed here attack a range of plants.

PHYSICAL TREATMENT FOR SOIL PESTS AND INSECTS

CATERPILLARS

The larvae of moths and butterflies are common garden pests. Some live in the soil and feed on plant roots, others may attack plant stems or fruit, but the majority live on leaves. The most seriously affected plants are those of the cabbage (*Brassica*) family, and a severe attack can completely strip crops of their foliage.
WHAT TO DO If you can spot the small clusters of tiny eggs, which moths and butterflies lay directly on the plants, simply remove them. Caterpillars themselves are usually easy to spot. Pick them off crops and drop them into a jar of paraffin.

LEATHERJACKETS

These are unmistakable in their appearance. They are white, fat, and very ugly. Leatherjackets are, in fact, the larvae of the crane fly and can be found just below the surface of the soil, nibbling away at the roots of just about anything. They sometimes come to the surface on a warm night when they may completely eat through the stem of a plant at ground level.
WHAT TO DO You will generally find leatherjackets when you are digging or hoeing. Because of their color, they are easy to see and squash, and this action is normally all that is needed to control their numbers. Ground beetles eat them, so should be encouraged by growing ground cover plants.

WIREWORMS

The larvae of the click beetle, these are thin, shiny worms with yellowish skins. They make very characteristic small holes in potatoes and carrots which can be mistaken for damage caused by slugs. Wireworms can attack any plant, but particularly favor those with fleshy roots, and here is the key to their control.

WHAT TO DO In the first year or two of cultivating newly turned soil, grow a row of wheat between the crops at intervals over the plot. The wireworms will be attracted to the wheat, which can be dug up and put on a bonfire.

You can also use old potatoes or carrots to trap the wireworms. These can be spitted on a stick and buried, so that you know where the trap is and can easily remove it for burning. Alternatively, trap them by splitting an old cabbage stalk and pushing it 2–3in (5–7cm) into the ground near the affected plants. As with the potatoes they should be dug up periodically and the worms removed and destroyed.

CUTWORMS

Perhaps even more troublesome than wireworms or leatherjackets, cutworms live just below the surface of the soil. They feed at the base of plants during the day, cutting them off at soil level.
WHAT TO DO If you find plants that have keeled over, search the soil just below the surface. Hoe an area up to about one yard/ meter away from the affected plant to expose the grubs; destroy any you find, either by squashing, burning, or drowning them in paraffin. Again, attract ground beetles.

ANTS

Ants rarely do harm to growing plants directly. The major problem is that ants carry aphids from one plant to another and protect them against attack from ladybugs and hoverfly larvae. This is because the ants feed on the sticky honeydew substance excreted by the feeding aphids.
WHAT TO DO It is often enough to control the aphids (*see next page*). However, if the ants become a real nuisance, they can be killed with a mixture of equal parts powdered sugar and borax. Put some down, on a piece of wood or stone, near to where there is ant activity and cover it to protect it from rain. The ants have a craving for sweet things and will devour the bait. The poison will then be carried into the ant nest and, as ants also eat their own droppings, it will not be long before the entire colony is destroyed.

ORGANIC PEST AND DISEASE CONTROL

PHYSICAL TREATMENT FOR SOIL PESTS AND INSECTS

SLUGS

There are several types of slugs—some more destructive than others. The very large ones live on fungi and dead organic matter and will not harm plants. The ones to worry about are the small brown or black slugs, some of which live underground and are very difficult to catch. These slugs only come to the surface in midsummer, and this is the time to attack them.

WHAT TO DO The traditional methods are still some of the most effective. One involves going out into the garden at night when the slugs are feeding and simply picking them up and dropping them into a jar of paraffin. In this way, even the underground dwellers can be greatly reduced in number. Another trick is to surround the plants most vulnerable to attack with lime, soot, or wood ash. The slugs don't like crawling through any of these, so they generally avoid the plant. The addition of a thin covering of lime will not radically alter the pH of the soil, but avoid spreading it around acid-loving plants. Spreading a mulch of ornamental pine bark is also effective.

There is another very effective solution. While I would not suggest the whole garden could be protected in the early spring, seedlings or the shoots of young herbaceous plants can simply be surrounded with plastic bottles which have been cut off at the bottom. These make ideal slug deterrents (*see above*). Large plants can be protected by removing the top and bottom of a plastic can and placing it over them. It is generally only necessary to protect plants in the early stages, since larger ones can withstand a bit of slug damage and show little ill effect. Try to attract hedgehogs to the garden, since they eat hundreds of slugs. Birds, frogs, and toads also feed on slugs so should be encouraged.

EARWIGS

These can cause problems, particularly in the ornamental garden, but they can be trapped easily. Earwigs tend to crawl to the tip of plants just as they are coming into bud and then nibble the embryo flower; they also attack leaves. The damage is often only slight, but it is enough to distort the flower and spoil the plant. Chrysanthemums and dahlias are particularly at risk.

WHAT TO DO Put a flower pot upside down on the top of a pole near the flower heads. Fill the pot with dried grass or leaves and, because they don't like daylight, the earwigs will crawl into it during the day. About once a week, simply remove the pot and burn the grass. If they are still a problem, smear grease on the stems just below the blooms.

APHIDS

These are among the most common and troublesome of garden pests, and include those species known as greenfly and blackfly. All suck the sap of plants, causing distortion and particularly attacking the young growing tips. Aphids excrete sticky honeydew on which sooty mold can grow, and transmit virus diseases.

WHAT TO DO Fortunately, there are a number of predators, such as ladybugs and hoverflies that eat aphids by the thousand. You can attract these by planting French marigolds (*Tagetes*), see *Companion planting*, p. 45. You can also rub the insects off with your fingers or hose them off with a powerful spray of water. Spray badly infested plants with insecticidal soap (*see p. 53*).

FLEA BEETLES

My favorite physical control of all is the one employed against the flea beetle. These are tiny beetles that make hundreds of small "shot holes" in the leaves of seedlings, particularly those of the cabbage (*Brassica*) family. Sometimes, in good growing weather, the seedlings will overcome it and suffer only a minor setback. In a bad growing year, when the weather is cold and constantly wet, the damage caused by the beetle can set them back weeks and may even kill them off completely, so it is best to control them.

WHAT TO DO These insects are called flea beetles because they jump sharply into the air when approached, just like a flea. Control them as described below.

1 *Use a piece of wood which measures about 1ft × 6in (30 × 15cm). Coat one side of it with heavy grease—old engine grease is ideal.*

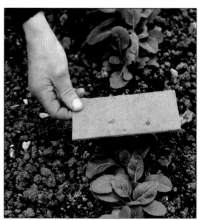

2 *Holding the board grease-side down, pass it along the row of seedlings about 1–2in (2.5–5cm) above them. The beetles jump up and stick to the grease.*

WHITEFLIES

These tiny insects suck the sap of many greenhouse and outdoor plants, and those which affect cabbages are especially persistent and resilient.

WHAT TO DO Whiteflies are strongly attracted to anything yellow, so the trick is to hang up a yellow card or square of plastic, coated with thin grease, in the greenhouse. The whiteflies are attracted to the card and stick to the grease, like flies on an old-fashioned fly paper.

The cabbage whitefly can survive outdoors in the winter, so you must ensure that there is no garden debris left around on which they can feed.

OTHER PESTS

Woodlice can do a lot of damage to seedlings and young plants, coming out at night to nibble on roots, stems, and leaves.

Millipedes are small black insects with short legs. They usually remain beneath the soil surface, feeding on roots and aggravating damage caused by other pests such as slugs.

Snails pose similar problems to those caused by slugs (*see opposite*), eating seedlings and all parts of mature plants.

WHAT TO DO In each of the above cases, the pests hide and breed under stones or garden debris during the day, only coming out at night to feed. The most sensible solution is therefore to keep the garden as neat as possible. Regular and thorough cultivation of the soil will expose millipedes and woodlice to birds, hedgehogs, and ground beetles. The snails can be detected by watching out for their slime trails. Pick them off the plants and drop them into a jar of paraffin, or use one of the other methods described for dealing with slugs (*see opposite*).

ENCOURAGING NATURAL PREDATORS

The organic garden is a far more conducive environment to all forms of wildlife than a chemically controlled one, and the natural balance ensures that there are predators that will feed on garden pests. A simple rule to follow in order to distinguish between "friend" and "foe" in the garden, is that pests are generally slow-moving and predators faster and more agile. By careful observation of this pattern, we can learn to let nature take its course and plan to attract helpful creatures into the garden, often eradicating or lessening the need for other forms of pest control.

BIRDS
Although they are usually regarded as somewhat of a garden pest in the productive garden, birds in fact do more good than harm. They eat numerous grubs, caterpillars, slugs, and aphids, and can be encouraged into the garden by incorporating food tables, bird baths, and nest boxes in your garden plan. Nesting requirements for different birds vary; you can obtain more information from the National Audubon Society (*see telephone directory for address*).

GROUND BEETLES
Black garden beetles feed on eelworms, cutworms, and leatherjackets, and other larvae and insect eggs. You can encourage them in your ornamental garden by keeping the ground covered, so that they have leaf cover or a mulch to hide under during the day. At night they will come out to feed on the pests. Use the closely planted deep bed system in the vegetable garden to keep the ground covered (*see p. 136*) and grow a green-manure plant between crops (*see p. 32*).

CENTIPEDES
Centipedes are fast-moving predators of many small insects and slugs. They are light brown with longer legs than millipedes. Like the black beetle, centipedes need ground cover to hide under during the day. At night they will emerge in search of prey, even climbing the plants to reach it.

FROGS AND TOADS
You should definitely try and encourage frogs and toads into the garden, because they are an excellent means of slug control. They also eat woodlice and other small insects. A garden pond is perhaps the ideal environment for them, but they really only need the water for breeding purposes.

HEDGEHOGS
A family of hedgehogs is a great boon to any garden, as the creatures devour slugs, cutworms, woodlice, millipedes, and wireworms. It is difficult to attract them into the garden but encourage them to stay if you have them. They will hide under piles of logs or hedges so leave a saucer of milk and water or bread soaked in milk near the suspected hiding place.

HOVERFLIES
It is the larvae of these creatures, which resemble "thin wasps," that are very useful in the natural control of aphids. The adult flies lay their eggs directly in the aphid colonies and the hatched young are voracious feeders. Hoverflies can be attracted into the garden by planting certain species of flowers such as marigolds (*Tagetes* and *Calendula*) and nasturtiums (*Tropaeolum* sp.), (*see* Companion planting, *p. 45*).

LACEWINGS
Again, it is the larvae who have an insatiable appetite for aphids. Adult lacewings lay their eggs on the undersides of leaves. Although they do not feed on flowers they can be encouraged into the garden by varied planting (*see* Companion planting, *p. 45*).

LADYBUGS
Both the easily identifiable adult ladybug and its less-familiar, slate-gray larvae eat vast quantities of aphids. They cannot be attracted by specific plants but will be encouraged into the garden by cultivating a varied selection of plants.

Ladybugs *These insects are very attractive and eat aphids.*

General garden diseases

Many diseases only affect specific types of plants and these are dealt with in the relevant sections of the book. Other problems are more general, occurring on the whole range of plants grown in the garden, and some of the most common of these are described below.

TREATING COMMON DISEASES

BOTRYTIS (Gray mold) This is probably the most common garden disease. It appears as brown spotting or blotching, followed by furry gray mold. Botrytis thrives in cold, damp conditions.

Treating botrytis *Careful handling of seedlings and the provision of good air circulation are essential if botrytis is to be avoided. Be sparing with fertilizers and avoid over watering, wet mulches, and planting in low, shady areas. Infected shoots should be cut off and burned.*

POWDERY AND DOWNY MILDEWS A mealy, pale gray coating forms on leaves, buds, flowers, and young shoots of a wide range of plants, resulting in yellowing and a general loss of vigor. Downy mildew gets right inside the plant and can eventually kill it, where powdery mildew stays on the surface. Powdery mildew is most common on herbaceous plants and roses and is at its worst when plant roots are dry.

Treating mildew *Both diseases thrive in cool, damp, and humid conditions. Downy mildew should be treated in the same way as botrytis. Mulching and hand watering will keep it at bay. Remove and burn leaves showing signs of powdery mildew. Spray with a copper fungicide (see opposite).*

SOOTY MOLD This is a superficial black fungus that grows on the sticky secretions of pests such as aphids (*see p. 50*). It is not a serious problem but it restricts plant yields.

Treating sooty mold *Control the aphids (see p. 50). Once they are eliminated, the mold will disappear.*

FUNGUS LEAF SPOT Leaf spotting can affect the foliage of most plants, especially in wet and high humidity. The black spot disease of roses is a common strain. Leaf spots may merge into large dead areas that drop out, and leaves may wither and die.

Treating fungus leaf spot *Proper crop rotation (see p. 134) and the provision of adequate air circulation are important factors in the prevention of this disease. Infected plants or parts of plants should be removed. Hard pruning of roses in the fall will kill off any overwintering spores; pick up all infected foliage and compost. Rose black spot can also be treated with a 50:50 solution of milk and water, which is surprisingly effective.*

RUST There are many different types of rust affecting a wide range of plants. Leaves and young stems develop yellow, red, brown, or black raised pustules. Leaves may then wither and fall and, in severe cases, whole plants can become stunted and even die.

Treating rust *Remove and burn leaves that have rust spots. Spray the rest of the plant with dispersible sulfur (see opposite). In the case of plants grown in the greenhouse, ensure that the humidity level is not too high and avoid wetting the foliage (see pp. 252–254).*

Biological control

Continued research into developing nature's own technique of using one organism to combat another is making significant advances in the area of pest and disease control. This involves using a parasitic insect or fungus, that is, one that lives off one particular living organism known as "the host." This "biological control" is now become a major way of controlling pests and diseases. It won't kill off all pests and diseases, but will help to keep them at acceptable levels.

The first discovery was the parasitic wasp *Encarsia formosa*, which has long been used by growers and large-scale gardeners to control whitefly in greenhouses. You simply hang a card containing several wasp pupae in the greenhouse and, when the adults emerge, they lay their eggs in the larvae of the whitefly. Control may not always be total but the whitefly are always reduced to acceptable levels.

Red spider mite in greenhouses can be very destructive and are difficult to kill. But by introducing another predatory mite, *Phytoseiulus persimilis*, very effective control can be achieved. You can buy this insect either on leaves or even in small shaker bottles. There are other very useful greenhouse controls, such

as *Aphidius* for controlling aphids, *Cryptolaemus montrouzieri* against mealy bugs, *Metaphycus helvolus* for scale insect, various nematodes for the control of vine weevils, ants, chafer grubs, and leatherjackets, *Amblyseius cucumeris* to control thrips, and *Hypoaspis miles* to control sciaris flies.

There are also parasites that can be used on crops outside. Perhaps one of the most beneficial of these is *Phasmarhabditis hermaphrodita*. This nematode is used as to control slugs and snails and is watered onto the ground from where the nematodes penetrate the slugs and snails, usually preventing them from feeding within three days and ultimately dying within a week. Another very useful nematode is *Steinernema carpcapse*. The adults penetrate the bodies of caterpillars and use them to breed in. You can spray a solution onto the foliage, making sure it comes into contact with caterpillars; for soil-borne cutworms apply the solution to the soil as a drench at the base of the plants. There are several other biological controls available to deter a variety of pests, but as with all control measures, use them according to the manufacturers instructions. Adding more or less is wasteful.

Research into the control of disease by using other diseases is still in its infancy but some progress has been achieved. Silver leaf disease commonly attacks plums but is sometimes found in other tree fruit. It causes leaves to adopt a silvery sheen and, if allowed to develop, will kill an entire branch. It is caused by the fungus *Stereum purpureum* and can largely be controlled by using a parasitic fungus, *Trichoderma viride*. This can be bought in the form of pellets that are pushed into holes drilled round the tree trunk at about 3in (7cm) intervals. If this is done before the silver leaf fungus establishes itself, a satisfactory level of control can be achieved. Some success has been reported using the same treatment against Dutch elm disease.

Organic chemicals

There may be situations when physical pest control does not work or is not suitable, and you have to resort to chemical control. If you are intent on completely blemish-free fruit and sanitized borders then this will be the case. If a plant has a fungus disease that is not cured by picking off the affected area in the early stages, a fungicide is the only answer.

There are several organic pesticides available that will not harm you or your "friends" in the garden, provided they are used with care. The principle of organic pesticides is that they are non-persistent.

Most remain active for no more than a day and nearly all are derived from plants.

Organic fungicides are a bit of a gray area. They could not really be said to be organically derived though they are certainly non-persistent. More research is needed in this area but, in the meantime, the fungicides recommended will not harm you or the beneficial wildlife in the garden. The organic chemicals recommended are safe if they come into contact with each other, can be used outside, provided there is no wind, and in the greenhouse.

PERMITTED PESTICIDES AND FUNGICIDES

INSECTICIDAL SOAP This is a potassium-salt soap and is more effective than soft soap in the control of aphids, whitefly, red spider mites, scale insects, and mealy bugs. Control can only be achieved by hitting the insect, and the soap persists for only one day.

SOFT SOAP A traditional control for all kinds of aphids and red spider mite. It can also be mixed with other sprays as a wetting agent, ensuring a better spread and more "stickability" of the insecticide. Soft soap will only kill insects it touches and is persistent for only one day.

FERRIC PHOSPHATE These organic slug pellets are effective against both slugs and snails, but totally harmless to other wildlife, pets, and children. They can be used around ornamental as well as edible plants and once eaten the slugs or snails are unable to feed, returning to the soil to die.

SKIM MILK AND WATER A simple but effective spray to prevent black spot from occurring on roses. Regular sprays of equal parts skim milk and water will cover the leaves. When the milk spoils, the lactic acid produced lowers the pH level on the leaf, producing an unsuitable environment for black spot to thrive. Depending on the season and therefore the likelihood of black spot occurring, apply every week or two.

PYRETHRUM Derived from the pyrethrum (*Chrysanthemum coccineum*) plant, it is effective against most insects, especially aphids. Unfortunately, beneficial insects will also succumb but since it is a non-persistent pesticide and acts quickly, it is possible, if you use it carefully, to spray only the pests.

RAPESEED OIL This is useful for controlling greenfly, blackfly, whitefly, thrips, and red spider mite. Do not spray on fuchsias, begonias, or seedlings as it can damage the foliage.

COPPER FUNGICIDE Several types of copper fungicide are used to control mildews and blights including Bordeaux mixture, a mixture of copper sulfate and slaked lime, and Burgundy mixture which contains copper sulfate and washing soda. All are based on copper sulfate and consist of liquids or powders that are mixed with water. They coat the leaves and stay active for several weeks, but new growth formed in that time is uncoated and therefore vulnerable.

DISPERSIBLE SULFUR Allowed as a fungicide, but only rarely. In my view it is not necessary in a well-run organic garden. It is an effective control for rust, against which copper fungicides rarely work satisfactorily, and most fungi.

POTASSIUM BICARBONATE This fungicide is a cure, not a preventative spray. Applied weekly, it can be effective against powdery mildew, black spot, and downy mildew on a range of plants such as roses, zucchinis, cucumbers and fruit.

USING PESTICIDES AND FUNGICIDES

When handling even these "safe" pesticides and fungicides, it is important to treat them as if they were dangerous.
• Put concentrates in a place where children or curious pets cannot reach them.
• Always leave chemicals in their own bottles.
• Dilute as specified on the bottle.
• Avoid spraying beneficial insects because these chemicals are not selective.

• Use a good sprayer to apply the chemicals and wash it out thoroughly after use between sprayings. Never keep the leftover solution, pour it down the drain.
• Spray only on a windless day and always in the cool of the late evening, when all the good, respectable insects have turned in for the night.
• Never spray any open flowers, especially of fruit, for fear of harming bees.

ORGANIC WEED CONTROL

THERE IS NO SUCH THING as an organic weedkiller, and whatever may be claimed about the safety of chemical weedkillers, there is always danger in their use. If there wasn't, there would be no need for the elaborate testing and strict controls enforced by governments. Chemical manufacturers have, however, tried to persuade us that we must follow the commercial grower in soaking our plants and our soil with poisons when there are very few advantages and many dangers in doing so. The commercial grower's problem is just not the same as ours, and there is no doubt that prolonged use of chemicals has a very damaging effect on soil organisms.

It may seem attractive to use a chemical to kill everything in a new garden so that you can start clean and stay on top of the weeds. It is certainly an easier way out, but it is done at the risk of killing the beneficial inhabitants of the soil and even harming yourself. At a horticultural research station in England a few years ago, during a quite unconnected experiment on soils, it was noticed that in the soil on land that had been regularly treated with a paraquat/diquat mixture there were no earthworms. Subsequent examination revealed that most other beneficial soil organisms were either reduced in numbers or not present.

Having tested chemical weedkillers under garden conditions for many years, I am also strongly of the opinion that there is no advantage in their use in order to save labor. It is so awkward and time consuming to apply them between cultivated plants, and the process often takes longer than the traditional organic methods. Of course there are some weeds that are very troublesome, such as couch grass (*Agropyron repens*) and ground elder (*Aegopodium podagraria*), but it is always possible to control them, and eventually to eradicate them, without resorting to chemicals, though in some cases it may take quite a long time. Weeds with tap roots, fleshy roots that go straight down into the soil, such as dandelions, can be a problem. As an experiment, I once nailed a big old dock root to the shed door and left it there for two years to suffer scorching sun, drying winds, and frost. When I planted it again two years later it flourished as if the rest had done it good! There is only one way with these perennials and that is to dig them out and put them in your regular garbage can, not your compost bin.

THE PRINCIPLES OF WEED CONTROL

Whether you are trying to clear a new garden of weeds or deal with their habitual menace in an established one, there are many physical methods of weed control outlined on the following pages. The basic principles to remember all the time are as follows:
- All green plants must have access to sunshine to survive. There are a variety of light-deprivation measures that can be used by the organic gardener to control weeds.
- Constant vigilance is very important: remove weeds as soon as you see them. Regular hoeing will deny persistent weeds a foothold.
- Never let weeds flower or seed. Cutting them down and digging out the roots takes a moment, while coping with the hundreds of seedlings they may disperse is a time-consuming job.

Clearing uncultivated ground

If you are starting a brand new garden, taking over a weed-infested one, or incorporating a new area, the first stage in weed control is to make the ground as clean as possible right from the start. First, clear the ground completely by digging it, removing weeds as you progress.

Then cover the ground; sow the lawn area; and plant a "cleaning crop" in the borders.

DIGGING THE ENTIRE PLOT
Begin by digging over the whole site and removing as much as you possibly can. If the ground is

▲ **Controlling weeds with gravel**
*Spreading a layer of coarse gravel, at least
2in (5cm) thick, around ornamental plants
provides an effective and attractive barrier
against weed growth.*

▲ **Covering soil with plastic** *Although
black plastic is not suitable for the ornamental
garden, it is a cheap, yet effective, way of
covering soil to inhibit weed growth in
the vegetable garden.*

◀ **Mulching with bark** *A covering of
pine bark chippings controls weeds by blocking
the light. It looks attractive and lasts for
several years.*

infested with one of the more pernicious weeds, like couch grass (*Agropyron repens*) or ground elder (*Aegopodium podagraria*), you should not expect to be totally succesful the first time because any tiny piece of root that is left in the soil may multiply to form a massive root again.

Annual weeds can then be put on to the compost heap provided they have not been allowed to seed (*see p. 21*). Roots of other perennial weeds, those that continue year after year, such as dandelions (*Taraxacum officinale*), and docks (*Rumex* sp.) should be thrown away or burned. Never put any perennial weeds on the compost heap because they will only be transplanted again when you spread the compost.

SOWING THE LAWN AREA

If you plan to seed a lawn, the area can be sown right away after digging (*see p. 79*). Even if the weeds do come through again, regular use of a mower will eventually eradicate all but the "rosetted" types like dandelions and daisies that grow close to the ground. They are easy to control afterward by simply dropping a pinch of table salt into the center of the rosette (*see p. 80*) or by digging them out of the lawn with a penknife. You may have to repeat the process a few times but they will disappear.

PLANTING A "CLEANING CROP"

Areas planned for ornamental borders or vegetable and fruit plots, in fact any bare soil, should be planted for the first year with a "cleaning crop." There is none better than potatoes, which will not only help clean the soil of weeds but will pay for themselves into the bargain. Potatoes have two great virtues as a cleaning crop. First of all their cultivation entails turning over the soil three times in the year—once when they are planted, a second time when they are earthed up, and finally at harvest time. Second, they grow a dense canopy of leaves that excludes the light from any weeds that may be bold enough to try to compete. Together, starvation of light and not being allowed a foothold encourage most weeds to give up the ghost.

Nonetheless, some weeds still survive. Plants that climb by twining round their competitors, such as bindweed (*Convolvulus arvensis*), will not be crowded out so easily. Their climbing habit enables them to reach the sunlight even through a dense canopy of leaves so they can always make enough food to store in their labyrinthine root system. So, in the second year, you will still have problems. But, on a small scale, they are not difficult to overcome.

PREVENTING WEEDS FROM SPREADING

There are two sources of nuisance—weed seeds flying over the fence and settling on your land, and weeds with creeping roots coming underneath the fence. The first problem is solved by asking your neighbors for permission to cut down any weeds before they seed. Accompany your request with a couple heads of your fresh lettuces and you may even shame them into doing it themselves. To cope with weeds that creep under the fence, you will have to install a barrier that runs deep into the soil to discourage encroaching roots. This provides effective protection for life.

1 *Close the hole between the bottom of the fence and the ground by digging out a little soil and nailing a 6 × 1in (15 × 2.5cm) board along the base of the fencing panels.*

2 *Dig a trench along the entire length of the fence. The trench must be deep enough to remove up to 6in (15cm) of subsoil.*

3 *Then put in a "wall" of heavy-gauge plastic. Nail one edge to the bottom of the wooden board so that the sheet hangs down to the bottom of the trench.*

Hoeing

The hoe is the most effective tool in your armory, and it should be used regularly, preferably during dry weather. By pulling it through the top layer of soil you can uproot any weeds that appear.

If you are waging war against persistent weeds like bindweed (*Convolvulus arvensis*), horsetail (*Equisetum arvense*) or couch grass (*Agropyron repens*), you should never allow them to reach that stage. The rule here is to hoe before you see any weeds at all on the surface. If you do that you will cut off the growing tips while they are still beneath the surface and before they have had a chance to benefit from the sun.

It is fairly easy to cope with weeds in the vegetable plot because they are easily seen, but in the borders they have a habit of hiding under foliage. So, when you take your evening walk around the garden in spring and summer, take a Dutch hoe with you and make a point of tickling between a few plants with it. Naturally, if you see so much as a glimpse of a weed, you must remove it immediately.

It must be stressed that hoeing will only kill persistent perennial weeds if you prevent them from getting above the soil surface. If you allow such weeds to do this, and you then turn them in or, even worse, chop them up with a rotavator, you will simply propagate them and make matters much worse.

DUTCH HOE

For weeding, a Dutch hoe is probably best (*see p. 259*). It should be used walking backward to avoid treading on the weeds once they are uprooted. If you walk forward, you will probably push them back into the soil and effectively transplant them, while walking backward leaves any weeds sitting on the soil surface, a prey to drying winds and the heat of the sun.

WHEEL HOE

I would never be without a wheel hoe, particularly in the vegetable garden. This is a hand-pushed tool with a single wheel at the front and a cutting blade behind it. It may seem that there would be very little advantage in this over the conventional Dutch hoe but it is, in fact, much quicker. Once you have hoed between the rows a couple of times to create a soft layer of soil on the top of the path, it is no trouble to push the hoe along at a slow walking pace.

If you do decide to invest in one, it is a good idea to adjust the distance between the rows when planting to suit the width of the hoe. If this makes the rows too close together so that plants are in danger of competing with one another or too far apart so that land is being wasted, simply adjust the planting width in the row. So, if you would normally plant, say, onions with 9in (23cm) between the rows and 6in (15cm) between each onion in the row, make the rows 12in (30cm) apart to suit the hoe width and allow 3in (7cm) between the plants in the row. This will save you a lot of time.

◀ **Using a Dutch hoe**
Most crops have shallow roots so keep the blade of the hoe no more than ½in (15mm) below the surface of the soil.

▶ **Using a wheel hoe**
Push the blade at the back of the hoe into the ground between two rows of vegetables, again keeping it shallow.

Mulching

An effective way to exclude light and prevent weeds from appearing is by mulching (covering the soil surface with a layer of one of several materials). Some mulching materials are not very attractive to look at, so you will want to use different materials in the vegetable and fruit garden from those used in the ornamental borders. Bear in mind, though, that the most effective and attractive method of keeping weeds out of the ornamental borders is to provide competition in the form of plants that create a canopy over the soil. Ground cover plants are useful in this respect (*see p. 90*).

BLACK PLASTIC SHEETING

One of the most effective mulches for eradicating perennial weeds is black plastic sheeting. When the plastic is laid over the soil, no light at all can reach the leaves and the weeds will die. They will try to work their way to the sides of the mulch and appear there, so keep a special lookout at the edges of the sheeting and be ready with the hoe. The sheeting must be anchored securely or high winds will get underneath and tear it or even blow it away (*see below*).

Black plastic sheeting is an ideal method in the vegetable garden or between rows of fruit. Before laying the sheeting, cultivate the soil between the rows and mound it slightly in the center so that the rain will run off the sheet towards the base of the plants.

Another method is to lay a wider sheet across the entire bed and plant through it by cutting small cross slits. This is ideal for strawberries and potatoes, and there is no reason why it should not be used for any other long-term crops like cabbages, cauliflower, and Brussels sprouts. This is particularly useful for potatoes because they will not need to be earthed up (*see p. 185*).

The advantage with a wide strip is that a much bigger area can be kept weed free with no chance of weeds sprouting out between the edges of the sheeting. The disadvantage is that it is very difficult to water. The best way is to lay a seep hose (*see p. 260*) underneath the sheeting and leave it there for the season. This will seep water along its whole length, so all you need to do is attach a hose to it at intervals to give the soil a good soaking. There will be little water loss through surface evaporation so less water will be required than normal.

Naturally, plastic sheeting is not attractive enough to be used on its own on the borders. It can, on the other hand, be covered with gravel or even a thin layer of soil to enhance the appearance.

PAPER AND BIODEGRADABLE PLASTIC

Of the biodegradable materials available, use tough brown paper rather than the biodegradable plastic. The latter is supposed to avoid the necessity of removing the mulch when the crop has been harvested but, in fact, the plastic deteriorates into strips which blow around all over the garden. The tough brown paper is used in exactly the same way as plastic—simply roll it out onto cultivated and

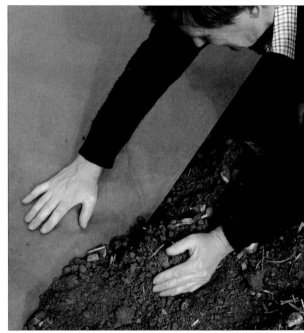

Weighting down plastic *It is essential to ensure that plastic sheeting is well held down with bricks. If it is not secure, wind will blow it away and this could damage plants.*

Digging in plastic or paper *The best way to secure plastic or paper is to bury the edges in shallow trenches around the edge of the bed.*

Spreading a bark mulch *Push the chippings right under the plants to cover all exposed soil in the border.*

USING A SHREDDER

Most electric shredders will efficiently get rid of all your woody prunings. The wood chips may look rather obtrusive in the borders, but they soon lose their stark white appearance.

Using an electric chipping machine *Put a bucket under the front of the machine to catch the chippings, then feed two or three lengths of tree prunings into the machine at a time.*

leveled soil, anchor the edges by burying them in a shallow trench, and then plant through pre-cut slits. After the crops have been harvested, it is either dug or cultivated into the soil, where it will rot down. This is ideal for use on deep beds. Paper can also be used in the ornamental garden without a covering of gravel since it is much less obtrusive than plastic (*see opposite*).

NEWSPAPER

A cheaper, but more time-consuming, alternative is to use newspaper. Lay about six sheets on top of one another, and again, anchor the edges by burying them. The paper tends to become quite hard and will certainly not rot for quite some time or until it is dug into the soil after harvesting.

COMPOST

A much more attractive mulch can be achieved using a 3in (7cm) layer of a loose material such as garden and green compost. This is a fairly inert material and therefore inhospitable to weed seedlings, but it needs to be at least 3in (7cm) or more deep. It won't prevent all weed seedlings from germinating but will reduce numbers and make them easier to pull out. Animal manure can also be used as a mulch, but again it should be well-rotted. Apply in a thick layer, like compost. Fresh manure can damage plants by scorching young shoots.

BARK MULCHES

The most effective material in the ornamental borders is either shredded or chipped bark. It is available in various grades of coarseness and it does not seem to make much difference which one is used. They should all go on at about 3in (7cm) thick and this should be sufficient to control all annual weeds and many perennials too. I have used it on a bed previously plagued with creeping thistle (*Cirsium arvense*) and not had to weed at all for two years.

The big disadvantage with bark of all types is the price. It is very expensive, although one application will last several years. A cheaper alternative is to invest in a wood chipper (*see above*) and make your own wood chips, even though it does take some time to make enough.

GRASS CUTTINGS

If they are applied thickly enough straight from the mower bag, grass cuttings are effective as a mulch for weed control. However, they must be at least 6in (15cm) deep, and this can lead to problems. If the layer is too thick, no air will reach the bottom, and if rotted down anaerobically (*see p. 21*), they become a smelly, slimy mass and are not only unpleasant but also quite useless as a soil conditioner. Grass cuttings do not look very attractive either, so I would rather put them on the compost heap and use them after they have rotted down.

Recognizing weeds

Of course, not all weeds are to be despised, and the organic gardener who gets rid of them all is wasting a valuable natural asset. Many weeds will attract insect predators, some also provide food for birds and butterflies and others, like the clovers (*Trifolium* sp.), can be used to fix nitrogen in the soil (*see p. 34*). So, before making an indiscriminate onslaught on native plants, pause for thought. Indeed, I recommend growing cultivated plants in the ornamental garden that are close to their original wild species because they will attract the same insect life.

However, I am not suggesting that you allow nature to take over, as your cultivated "foreigners" will be at the mercy of some pretty tough "locals," who will give scant regard to "world peace." Most weeds must be rigorously controlled, but there are a few that should be allowed to stay if you have room. I have grouped together those which have to be removed ("bad weeds") and those which can be beneficial ("good weeds").

BAD WEEDS

The underground creepers should never be allowed to flourish or they will take over in next to no time. Among these be particularly ruthless with ground elder (*Aegopodium podagraria*), bindweed (*Convolvulus arvensis*), couch grass (*Agropyron repens*), creeping thistle (*Cirsium arvense*), rosebay willow-herb (*Epilobium angustifolium*), and Japanese knotweed (*Polygonum cuspidatum*). The surface creepers like creeping buttercup (*Ranunculus repens*), ground ivy (*Glechoma hederacea*), and cinquefoil (*Potentilla* sp.) are slightly easier to control, but be diligent.

Weeds that spread by seed are not difficult to control, provided they are pulled out or cut down before they have a chance to seed. Keep an eye out for spear thistle (*Cirsium vulgare*) and broad-leaved willow-herb (*Epilobium montanum*).

Plants with tap roots (long, thick, fleshy roots that go straight down into the soil) like docks (*Rumex* sp.) and cow parsley (*Anthriscus sylvestris*) should be dug out.

Storage roots (tubers, corms, bulbs, or rhizomes) often break off in the soil when the plant is pulled up and this can be a means of propagation. The worst of the lot is oxalis, which must be dealt with as soon as it shows even an exploratory leaf! Constant hoeing is the only answer, unless you can leave a sheet of black plastic in place for at least a year.

GOOD WEEDS

Having made sure that the real villains are banished forever, try to give room to some of the less invasive plants. As gardeners, our interest lies in the cultivation of plants for beauty and interest and for the purpose of feeding our families. How far you allow nature to take over is a matter of judgment and will depend largely on the size of your garden, and the range of wild plants you can grow will depend upon the soil, site, and location. In my own garden the pretty yellow snapdragon flowers of toadflax (*Linaria vulgaris*) and the pure white clusters of white campion (*Lychnis alba*) or red campion (*Lychnis dioica*) are always allowed to remain. In the borders where these "weeds" have access to artificially fertile soil, they really thrive and produce flowers that rival any cultivated hybrid.

It has been said that if the dandelion (*Taraxacum officinale*) only grew in Tibet, we would be sending plant hunters to collect it and we would pay huge sums of money to nurseries to propagate it. It may be common, but it is an undeniably pretty flower. Do not let it seed, however, or it will outstay its welcome.

The stinging nettle (*Urtica dioica*) is an antisocial plant, but allow some to remain if you can because it is an extremely important food for butterflies.

The corn poppy (*Papaver rhoeas*) used to be a common sight before chemical weedkillers made it virtually extinct in cornfields. It is a favorite with finches when it seeds, so it is certainly worth growing.

Groundsel (*Senecio vulgaris*) and herb robert (*Geranium robertianum*) are valuable nectar plants for butterflies and bees, but can be a nuisance if allowed to seed.

If you have an old tree stump in the garden, you can make an attractive feature of it by covering it with ivy (*Hedera helix*). Many birds and insects use ivy as a home and a food plant.

Allow chickweed (*Stellaria media*) to grow in the winter to help prevent the ground from becoming waterlogged. It will rot down after digging in, supplementing compost and manure. Do not let it grow in the summer because, once it gets a hold, it can be particularly troublesome.

The teasel (*Dipsacus fullonum*) is a tall, stately plant with large seed heads that attract goldfinches, who will travel far for the seeds. The flowers attract butterflies and other insects.

Another insect attractor is fat hen (*Chenopodium album*), which was a favorite vegetable in the Middle Ages.

Finally, there are the leguminous plants that will fix nitrogen and release it into the soil once they are dug in. For example, the medicks (*Medicago* sp.) and clovers (*Trifolium* sp.) can be allowed to remain in winter.

WEEDS TO REMOVE FROM THE GARDEN

GROUND IVY ▲
Glechoma hederacea
A vigorous perennial that quickly becomes invasive. Its small, hairy leaves have serrated edges and a distinctive minty smell.

▲ **CINQUEFOIL**
Potentilla sp.
A persistent perennial weed with very long, creeping stems. Each leaf is made up of five leaflets.

CREEPING BUTTERCUP ▶
Ranunculus repens
Found on damp soils, this weed produces long creeping stems that spread across the soil. It also spreads by seeding.

◀ **BROAD-LEAVED WILLOW-HERB**
Epilobium montanum
This very common weed has pointed oval leaves and small purple flowers with yellow centers. Pull plants out as soon as you see them.

COW PARSLEY ▲
Anthriscus sylvestris
The fernlike leaves are pale green in color. The distinctive flower heads are made up of a mass of tiny white flowers.

▲ **SPEAR THISTLE**
Cirsium vulgare
The leaves are sharply pointed and spined. The purple flowers produce numerous seeds.

OXALIS ▲
Oxalis sp.
Control by hoeing, preferably before the leaves reach the surface, or by covering the ground with black plastic.

BROAD-LEAVED DOCK ▲
Rumex obtusifolius
Docks have a fleshy tap root and long, broad, dark-green leaves.

▼ **ROSEBAY WILLOW-HERB**
Epilobium angustifolium
The purple flowers produce many seeds making this a very invasive weed.

◀ **GROUND ELDER**
Aegopodium podagraria
The oval leaves have a strong smell if crushed. It spreads very quickly, soon taking over if allowed to remain.

▼ **BINDWEED**
Convolvulus arvensis
Although its flowers are attractive, this fast-growing weed quickly smothers any ornamental plants.

▼ **COUCH GRASS**
Agropyron repens
A very invasive grass. Its roots spread quickly to form a dense underground mat. A tiny piece broken from this can produce a new plant.

▼ **CREEPING THISTLE**
Cirsium arvense
The serrated leaves are very prickly and flowers are a pale lilac color. The flower stalks do not bear thorns as most other thistles do.

JAPANESE KNOTWEED ▼
Polygonum cuspidatum
This weed has oval leaves and small white flowers. Its roots are difficult to destroy.

Useful weeds

Not all weeds are to be despised, and the gardener who pulls them all out regardless is wasting a valuable natural asset. Of course, weeds should not be grown where they will compete with cultivated plants but, next time, think again before you dig up the useful weeds shown here.

▼ DANDELION
Taraxacum officinale
Rich in minerals, young dandelion leaves blend wonderfully into salads and the roots make a caffeine-free coffee substitute. Also attracts butterflies and bullfinches.

HERB ROBERT ▶
Geranium robertianum
An attractive annual that seeds and colonizes quickly. It will quickly cover even the poorest soil, thus providing cover for pest predators and organic matter for the soil when it dies down.

▲ BLACK MEDICK
Medicago lupulina
A nitrogen-fixing plant. It also attracts butterflies, bees, and hoverflies.

FAT HEN ▶
Chenopodium album
Attracts hoverflies, which eat aphids, and bees. High in iron, protein, calcium, and vitamin B, and an excellent spinach substitute.

RED CAMPION ▶
Lychnis dioica
Attracts bees which pollinate flowers. Also butterflies and moths—drawn by a perfume released by the plant at night—which attract birds. When cultivated, the size of the flowers increases.

▼ CHICKWEED
Stellaria media
Good source of green manure because it grows rapidly. Birds like to eat the seeds of this plant.

▲ TOADFLAX
Linaria vulgaris
Good source of nectar; a decorative plant with delicate, yellow flowers.

▲ CLOVER
Trifolium sp.
Nitrogen-fixing plant, taking nitrogen from the air and fixing it in the soil in a form which is later accessible to other plants.

POPPY ▶
Papaver rhoeas
Butterflies and bees are attracted by the red flowers and birds are drawn to the seeds.

◀ NETTLE
Urtica dioica
Important food plant for butterflies, the young leaves can be boiled and eaten as a spinach substitute.

▲ TEASEL
Dipsacus fullonum
An outstanding biennial, often cultivated in the ornamental garden for its striking seed heads. Birds are attracted to the seeds in the fall.

◀ GROUNDSEL
Senecio vulgaris
Good source of nectar for butterflies and bees, although not an attractive plant.

◀ IVY
Hedera helix
Provides nesting ground and vital cover for birds. Attracts butterflies and bees.

PLANNING YOUR GARDEN

A SUCCESSFUL ORGANIC GARDEN depends upon growing a wide diversity of plants, including as many native plants as possible, in order to attract wildlife and useful pest predators. The result will inevitably be informal. There is, however, no reason why an informal garden should look neglected or untidy and, indeed, there is every reason why it should not. Pests and diseases go hand-in-hand with a lazy approach to gardening; a neat and tidy garden, where regular cultivation keeps unwanted weeds at bay and where you remove trash before it has a chance to accumulate, is bound to be more efficient and productive.

My own belief is that a garden is essentially a personal place, and so its final design must be something that you have conceived and put into practice yourself. We all have the innate creative ability to transform that muddy patch of ground outside the back door into a beautiful, productive and, above all, enjoyable place in which to be. And bear in mind that, no matter how inexperienced you are, nature will give you a hand along the way.

WHERE DO YOU START?

First, take account of the physical characteristics of your garden—the soil type, the direction it faces, and so on. Second, draw up lists of the features that you need to include in your garden such as windbreaks or a garbage can—and the features you would like to include such as a vegetable garden, compost bins, a greenhouse, or a leveled terrace. Then, before you start any real gardening, draw up a plan of your garden and work out where you want to place things in relation to each other. These principles apply if you are starting a garden from scratch, taking over an established garden, or simply changing to organic gardening.

The physical characteristics of your garden

When contemplating the overall plan of your garden, consider its physical characteristics such as the direction it faces, your local climate, and the type of soil you have to work with—clay, peat, silt, sand, and chalk (*see pp. 14–15*).

The features that are within your power to change, or improve, include drainage and the quality of your soil and the contour of the land. The techniques for improving them, however, will vary according to the soil type of your situation (*see below and pp. 18–34*).

Aspect and climate

It is not possible to do anything about your garden's orientation, and you can rarely remove shade, which is generally caused by the house, walls, or fences. Likewise you can do nothing about the weather. Altitude, rainfall, and the wind will all dictate certain features of the

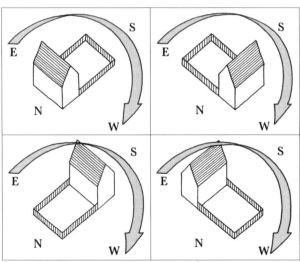

The garden's aspect *The direction your house and garden face will affect the amount of sun the garden receives. The diagrams above show the difference between north-, south-, east-, and west-facing gardens: north-facing gardens can be cold and sunless, while a south-facing garden receives full sun all day.*

Frost pockets *Cold air tends to flow downhill so hollows in the land may trap frost. If your garden is in a frost hollow, choose late-flowering or hardier plants that can withstand the cold.*

garden such as the amount of shade and protection you need to provide. If frosts are a regular occurrence, or you live in a frost-pocket (a low-lying area where frost accumulates), make sure that you use the correct type of hedging or fencing to minimize the problem (*see above*), and that you choose late-flowering or especially hardy plants that are not going to lose fruit and flowers every time the weather turns cold.

Soil types

There are five main soil types—clay, silt, sand, chalk, and peat—and each one is made up of a mixture of minerals, the proportions of which are highly variable even within a small area. An important consideration with soil types is the degree of acidity or alkalinity, or the lime content (*see p. 35*). Certain plants prefer certain types of soil and, while you can do much to improve the general fertility or drainage qualities of a poor soil (*see pp. 262–265*), and even make special provisions for "unsuitable plants," it is easier, in the ornamental areas, to grow plants that are happy in the existing soil conditions. You may, though, have to take measures to alter the soil pH for your vegetable and fruit areas (*see pp. 35–37*).

Steep slopes

Steep slopes are difficult to maintain. It is much better to terrace the garden to form a series of "plateaus" linked by paths or steps even though this involves a great deal of hard work initially.

It is not good enough simply to level the topsoil because that results in an extra deep layer of topsoil at the front and very little at the back. The only satisfactory way is to dig off all the topsoil from the area and level the subsoil before replacing it (*see right*).

FENCING

The easiest material to use for fencing on a slope is a wire fence, a length of plastic windbreak, or even posts and rails because they can be made to follow the general fall of the land. Don't, however, try to follow every little rise and fall or the top of the fence will go up and down like a

ELIMINATING A SLOPE

The only satisfactory method of removing a slope is to dig off the topsoil and then level the subsoil before re-spreading the topsoil. The new soil level should be held back by building either retaining walls or banks.

Link the different levels of the garden with ramps or a series of stone or paved steps. Alternatively, make steps out of strong wood (old railroad ties are ideal) held in position with stout stakes firmly secured in the ground. Fill in the area between the railroad ties with soil, gravel, or chipped bark. These informal steps blend in particularly well if you have planned the garden on the "cottage-garden" principle (*see p. 71*). It is also possible to connect different levels of a garden with ramps if this is more convenient for you.

Leveling slopes *If you want to form a series of "stepped" borders, remove all the topsoil from the area, level the subsoil, then replace the topsoil, spreading it evenly. Build a supporting wall at the front to hold the topsoil in the bed.*

▲ **Wooden steps** *A cheap way of linking parts of your garden is with wooden steps. The steps shown here were made with railroad ties. Hammer stakes into the ground behind them and nail them to the ties.*

▶ **Stone steps** *Slabs of stone can be used to make attractive steps. Use stone or brick to make the step "risers."*

switchback: try instead to even it out to form one overall slope.

Panel fencing is difficult to put up on a slope because the panels cannot be erected to follow the line of the slope; it would mean putting the posts in at an angle. On gently sloping ground, you can erect the panels vertically in a series of "steps." Make sure you take this into account when you buy your fencing material because you may need to order a few more panels and longer fence posts than normal. Panel fencing is unsuitable for steeply sloping ground because you will get gaps at one end of each panel.

FENCING FOR SLOPES

If your garden slopes, putting up fencing needs a little thought. Choose a type that can be made to follow the slope and make sure that the fence posts are exactly vertical.

Post-and-wire link fence

Post-and-rail fence

Fencing along a slope *These fences are ideal for slopes because they can be built to follow the line of the slope. You can plant a hedge in front of a post-and-rail fence or grow climbing plants up a wire fence.*

Fencing across a slope *If you have to build a fence across a slope, leave at least 1ft (30cm) of space between the bottom of the fence and the ground so that cold air can flow underneath and out of the garden.*

On sloping ground, fencing built across a slope can act as a barrier that prevents frost-laden air from moving downhill and out of the garden, creating a frost pocket. To avoid the problem, raise the bottom of the fence slightly to allow air to flow underneath.

Improving drainage

It is easy to recognize a badly drained site, since the garden, or large parts of it, will be wet underfoot and water may lie on the top, particularly in winter. Compacted topsoil or an impervious layer of compacted soil beneath the soil surface, particularly on a new garden, are common reasons for bad drainage. You can do a great deal to improve the drainage by good soil management (*see p. 262*). A heavy soil such as clay, for example, can be greatly improved by digging in organic matter and coarse sand.

In very badly drained gardens, however, you may have to install a drainage system, and you will have to do this before anything else.

DRAINAGE SYSTEMS

If your soil really drains badly, you need to install a drainage system. It is relatively easy to install the drain pipes, but not as simple to dispose of the water. If you have a ditch at the end of your garden, there is no problem. Otherwise, you should run your land drains into the storm drains that feed into the sewer system or the local authority's drainage system. Seek permission from the local authority before connecting up your garden drains in this way because it is illegal in some areas. Installing a drainage system is discussed in more detail in *Basic Techniques* (*see p. 262*).

Garden boundaries

You will almost certainly need some sort of fencing or hedge around your garden for privacy. There are many different types of man-made fencing available so choose one to suit your needs and to blend with your house and style of garden.

In addition, if you live in an exposed position, fencing or hedging can go a long way to protecting your plants from high winds. Winds can be particularly damaging to all plants, especially in the winter if they are not protected by a covering of snow. If protected, your fruit and vegetables will produce heavier crops and your ornamental plants will grow and flower better too.

BARRIERS FOR WIND PROTECTION

The most effective windbreaks are those that merely slow the wind down such as hedges, slatted wooden fences, or barriers made from

Enhancing a brick wall *You can soften the effect of a brick wall by removing individual bricks, filling the gaps with soil, and planting alpine plants, such as these pink lewisias.*

Disguising a barrier *A wooden trellis serves as a practical barrier but can also become a decorative feature when shrubs or climbers, such as scented roses, are trained against it.*

perforated plastic windbreak material. Solid barriers can be worse than useless as wind protection unless they are extremely high. When the wind comes up against a solid obstruction, it tends to whip over the top and swirl around on the other side, increasing in speed during the process. If you are using man-made barriers, make sure that the posts are sunk deep into the ground and, if you are using a plastic windbreak material, fix it to the fence posts with battens. Do this by laying the windbreak material against the posts then nailing battens over the top.

HEDGES
Hedges make very good garden boundaries as they are far less obtrusive than man-made barriers. They also make the best windbreaks. You can choose from either formal hedges or informal ones, those that are allowed to flower (*see p. 76*). Hedges do, however, take up a lot of growing room because they will compete with other plants for water and nutrients. Never, for example, choose privet (*Ligustrum ovalifolium*) unless you are prepared to sacrifice at least 1 yard/meter along either side of the length of the hedge. If your garden is small, choose a formal hedge that can be kept compact by clipping. Choose informal hedges only if your garden is large because they need at least 3–6ft (1–2m) of growing room on either side.

If your garden is on a slope, make sure your hedge does not act as a barrier, preventing frost-laden air from escaping (*see opposite*). Keep the area under the hedge cleaned out to allow air to pass through freely and to stop pests from using the debris as winter cover.

Features to include in your garden

While you are carrying out the necessary groundwork, you must think about the features you want to include in the garden and the eventual scheme you wish to achieve. Working out a plan isn't easy because there are so many possibilities. Take time over it and put your ideas onto paper first. Your budget may not allow you to complete your chosen garden design all at once but an overall plan will at least give cohesion to the finished product.

ALLOWING FOR THE ESSENTIALS
Start by making a list of the features that you simply must include in your garden—a clothesline, for example, a storage building or wood shed, a place to hide the garbage cans, or a gate to stop children from running out into the road. If you are simply changing over to organic methods, then you may already have these features; nonetheless, put them on the list in case you want to improve them, move them, or even do away with them completely.

DESIRABLE FEATURES
In my experience, the things you would like to include in your garden always exceed the space available, so draw up a list in order of priority. If you have a family, you may decide that a large vegetable and fruit plot is most important, but that you also need an area in which the

children can play, and a leisure area for yourself. After all, gardening is not all hard work!

In any organic garden, you will certainly need an ornamental area where you can grow some of the plants that attract birds and insect predators (*see pp. 45 and 51*). If you have space for a greenhouse or a cold frame, make sure you include this. And don't forget to allow room for the utility area— the compost containers, the manure heap (if you are lucky enough to be able to get any), and the storage shed.

Water

From a strictly practical point of view, a water supply is absolutely essential to allow you to maintain the garden. Ideally, you should have an outside tap and a hose long enough to allow you to water every part of the garden. With long gardens, you might want to install a standpipe at the far end. If this is your intention, then make sure you lay the necessary pipes at an early stage of garden preparation.

Hard surfaces

It is important to decide the position of the hard surfaces, such as terraces and paths, before you decide anything else because they determine the level and position of many other garden features. Bear in mind right at the planning stage that areas of concrete or gravel can look stark against the background of a plant-filled garden, so try to

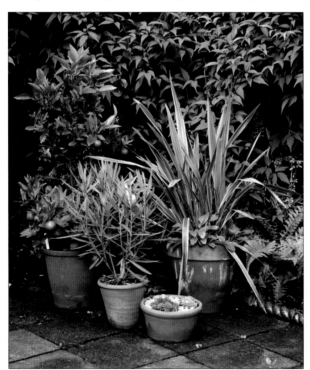

Positioning plants in containers *Large areas of paving are an integral part of many gardens, but they can look stark. Here, the problem is countered by a variety of potted plants.*

allow for softening by including raised beds or leaving space for plant-filled pots.

TERRACES

If you decide on an area of paving for sitting out in the garden, you do not necessarily have to build it against the house, though this is certainly the most convenient place. For example, if the back of your house faces north, it will be a bleak place to sit; on the other hand, if you live in a hot sunny climate, you may prefer to sit out in the shade.

Make the area a useful shape. A narrow strip of paving or concrete running along the back of the house is almost useless since there is simply not enough room for a table and chairs. A square or triangular area in one corner is more practical and requires no more paving.

If you decide to butt paving up against the side of the house, take a careful look at the level of the damp-proof course on your house or any airbricks. Paving slabs must finish no less than two rows of bricks below the level or you risk having water creep into the house.

Use paving material that blends in with your style of garden and the house itself. Soften stark and intrusive lines by leaving a few spaces between the slabs and then include some low-growing plants such as alpines (*see pp. 123–124*) that thrive in a well-drained soil and need sun.

Edging paved areas with raised flower beds allows you to bring color right up to the house; edging them with a hedge provides both privacy and a windbreak, if this is necessary. If you plan for it at the outset, it is relatively easy to build a barbecue into the paving.

PATHS

In my view, you should only use paths where they are absolutely essential because they tend to cut gardens into pieces. In a small garden, that is a disaster. If you must have a path, make it curved, so that it disappears from view here and there, giving the illusion of hidden nooks and crannies. In large gardens you can use paths extremely effectively to link one feature with another. I like to see them in either gravel or, better still, grass. Never make a dead straight path in a small, informal garden or allow a path to run either across the plot or straight down the middle.

There are some situations where a path is essential—however large or small your garden. If you have children, there is likely to be a lot of washing so you may need easy access, via a path, to a clothesline. In this case, it will probably also have to be straight, so try to place it at the edge of the garden where you can hide it with a border of flowers.

An extremely attractive way of making paths, particularly in small gardens, is to use stepping stones set in gravel. Space the stones out so that

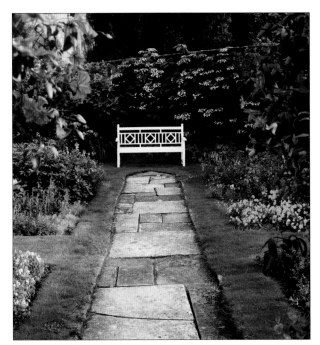

Using bold lines *Although a path is generally considered a necessity, it also adds another feature to a formal garden. Here, paving slabs of different sizes and shades have been put together to create a tessellated route to a bench.*

A subtle approach *This simple gravel path is designed to act as an inconspicuous foil to the shrubs and perennials, which vary in color through the seasons. Its soft curves serve to define the shape of the central ornamental bed without distracting attention from it.*

they deliberately slow you down, giving you the opportunity to enjoy the beauty of your garden, and plant alpines in the spaces (*see p. 124*).

The lawn area

An area of grass is a highly desirable garden feature. It makes an excellent feeding place for birds, a comfortable playing surface for children, and a superb "foil" to the plants in the borders.

When planning a lawn you will also, as a result, be shaping the flower borders. Bear in mind that, if you are going to adopt traditional "cottage garden" mixed borders—with swathes of tall and short annuals and perennials, including many native plants to attract suitable wildlife, then there is no place for formality. You should lay out the edges of the grass in

long, sweeping curves to produce borders of varying widths. Long, simplified sweeps of grass make the garden look bigger and are easier to cut.

If you have the room, allow a small patch of grass to grow tall and sow some wild flowers to help attract useful insect predators (*see p. 125*). The "miniature meadow" will soon become a very attractive feature. You can also include some bulbs with the wildflowers (*see p. 118*).

Ponds

An area of water is particularly useful in an organic garden if you want to increase the range of wildlife you attract. If you have a small pool, you will attract birds and insects, frogs, and many other pest predators. You can make a pool by digging a hole and lining it with a butyl-rubber liner (*see p. 122*) or simply bury plastic containers and fill them with water.

Remember, though, that any water is dangerous if you have young children. It may be worth including a bird bath until they are older.

Plan your pool with rounded edges, instead of harsh angles, to blend in with a more informal garden. And allow for very shallow water at the edges, or provide a ledge in the side of the pond, so that you can include marginal or bog-loving plants and a marshy area. If you are lucky, you will also attract frogs and that keeps your slug problem under control.

If you want moving water in the form of a waterfall or fountain, provide an underground electricity supply before laying paving or lawns.

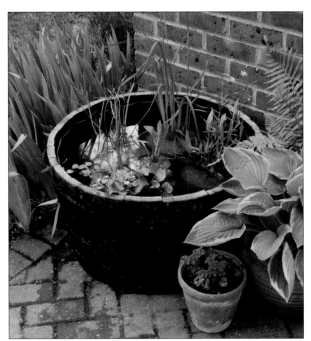

Miniature ponds *If you do not have room for a large pond in your garden, you can still benefit from the advantages water brings. Fill tubs with water, and you can then grow aquatic plants and attract pond wildlife.*

Growing vegetables

Fresh, homegrown vegetables are part of the organic gardener's way of life, so allow as much room as possible for the vegetable plot. The idea that vegetable plants are unsightly is nonsense; a well-ordered and productive vegetable plot is a truly heartening sight. (*See also* The Vegetable Garden, *pp. 132–201*).

Plan to position the plot in a sunny part of the garden and never plant a screening hedge between the vegetables and their source of sun.

If space is limited, grow your vegetables on the deep bed system, a method of cultivation where vegetables are grown in blocks rather than rows. The soil is deeply dug to form a very deep topsoil, or root zone. This encourages their roots to grow downward, enabling them to be planted very close together (*see p. 135*). It is important to note that the beds need to be about 4ft (1.2m) wide with a 12–18in (30–45cm) path between each one. If possible, leave extra room for crops such as Brussels sprouts and runner beans, which are not suited to this method of cultivation. There is no reason at all why you should not have an irregular-shaped vegetable plot if this helps it to blend in better with the rest of the garden.

If your garden is too small for even the most restricted vegetable plot, grow a few fresh greens and some of the more ornamental vegetables in among the flowers in the borders.

Growing fruit

Not so long ago, growing fruit trees in a tiny garden would have been impossible because of their size. However, you can now grow many types of fruit on special dwarfing rootstocks and, with modern pruning methods, these can be restricted so that they will grow happily in the smallest of spaces (*see* The Fruit Garden, *pp. 202–235*).

If you have a sunny wall or fence, reserve it for a peach tree grown as a fan and trained close to the wall or fence so that it takes up virtually no space at all. Use a north wall for a fan-trained Morello cherry, which will produce masses of delicious black fruits, and look extremely attractive into the bargain. You can also train apples and pears up walls or fences, as either fans or espaliers (*see p. 209*); east- or west-facing walls are best for these. Alternatively, you can grow them as cordons, planting the trees 2–3ft (60–90cm) apart and training them to grow parallel to each other at a 45-degree angle, to form a hedge wherever a barrier is needed. You can even train some soft fruits, such as gooseberries and currants, as cordons against a wall if space is limited. More compact still are single-tier espaliers, or stepovers, which form trees no more than 12in (30cm) high. These are ideal as a low hedge around the vegetable plot.

Decorative vegetable gardens *With an imaginative layout, the vegetable garden can be made an attractive feature—an important point in a small garden where everything can be seen.*

Birds are the biggest nuisance in the fruit garden. If you have enough space for a fruit cage, try to plan it into your scheme. In fact, if you can erect a cage to protect your vegetables as well, you will find it well worthwhile.

Growing under glass

A greenhouse is an asset to any garden, and is well worth finding space for. Obviously, it needs as sunny a place as possible. It is also best placed as near to the house as possible, since this makes the installation of electricity or gas for heating cheaper, and, above all, makes the trip to attend to it on chilly winter nights less daunting.

There is a lot of controversy surrounding the question of which way to situate a greenhouse, but in my view it does not really matter if it faces east-west or north-south. There are many different greenhouses to choose from. Rectangular ones are the most common, but bear in mind that, if your garden is small, a hexagonal greenhouse may be more suitable. Greenhouses are widely available with frames made of wood or aluminium (*see p. 247*).

COLD FRAME

If you plan to raise your own plants for setting out in the garden, try to find the space for a cold frame, a wood, metal, or brick frame with a glass top (*see p. 254*). This is essential for acclimatizing plants to outside temperatures before planting them out, a process known as "hardening off." Site it as close to the greenhouse as possible.

The utility area

Organic gardeners are usually do-it-yourselfers by nature, and they tend to accumulate plenty of material that other people would call trash. I find it difficult to throw away a piece of wood, I keep all my old styrofoam coffee cups for use as pots, and compost bags pile up by the hundreds to make growing bags (*see p. 253*) and tree ties, or for mulching between rows of vegetables for weed control. Throwing away a length of nylon string is anathema. So plenty of room is needed to store these valuable, money-saving materials.

If you have room for a garden shed, there is no problem. There is no need to hide it, since a few climbing plants will soon transform it into a thing of beauty. If you do not have room for a shed and you don't have any room in the garage, arrange some kind of cover for tools and equipment. It is possible to buy garden "chests" or "lockers" now; I have even seen an old wardrobe pressed into service as a "mini-shed."

You will also need room for the compost heaps— at least two and preferably three—perhaps a pile of manure, certainly a container for leaf mold, and an area for storing bales of peat or bags of fertilizer (if you don't have a shed, buy them in plastic sacks and keep them outside). Set aside a general-purpose utility area for all these things and arrange to screen it from the rest of the garden. You can tuck it behind tall-growing shrubs or conceal it by planting some hedging plants in front of it. But, if space is limited, the best method of screening is to erect a trellis (or posts and wires) and plant some fast-growing climbing plants in front of it.

Choosing ornamental plants

The aim of planting in an organic garden, apart from the obvious aesthetic one, is to attract and encourage as many predators of pests as possible. The right selection of ornamental plants helps to create a natural balance of wildlife in the garden and increases the interest and pleasure you'll derive from the garden, while also reducing attacks from pests.

COTTAGE-GARDEN PLANTING

For the average gardener with just a moderately sized garden, the "cottage-garden" design offers some distinct advantages over other styles of garden. This style was developed by the old "cottagers" in England as a way of combining a productive garden with ornamental plants and later developed and romanticized by the Victorians in the 19th century. It is also a style that is endlessly adaptable and suits modern architecture and building materials just as well as it did old stone cottages with roses around the door and windows.

Its advantages are that, first, it allows you to grow a mixture of ornamental and vegetable plants in the same beds, making maximum use of any available space; and that, second, the informality of the style encourages the use of native plants, which will attract useful insects and pest predators into your garden. A side effect of the close-planting technique adopted in this style of garden is the suppression of weeds and the saving of a lot of tedious labor.

There is no need to plan all the borders at the outset. It is much better to collect all your plants slowly, learning about them first from visits to nurseries, garden centers, and other gardens. Permanent plants such as trees and shrubs form the framework of the garden. Remember, though, that in ten years time, they will look very different from the small specimens that you plant, and they dislike being moved. So, before buying them, check their final spread and height to ensure that you plant them in the right place the first time. Other types of plants can be moved at will, and many benefit from being moved. This is discussed in *The Ornamental Garden* (*see pp. 81–125*).

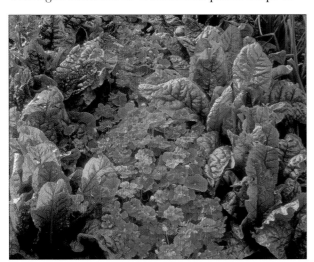

Varied planting *A perfect partnership of vibrant red nasturtiums with the textured leaves and bright stems of chard combine to make an ornamental feature of the vegetable patch.*

Dramatic colors *In this informal garden large areas of concentrated color are created by dividing the plants into bold clumps of purple, pink, and red.*

Drawing up a plan

Once you have made your lists and have a good idea of your priorities, you should make a detailed plan of how you will carry the work through to completion. First, measure the boundaries of the garden, draw the area onto a piece of paper, then transfer it onto some grid paper. If your house and garden are absolutely rectangular, it is easy to measure and transfer this to paper. If it is not, you will have to use a system of measurement known as "triangulation" (*see below*).

STARTING WORK ON THE GARDEN

Once you have finalized your plan, you can start work. Transferring your ideas from paper to the ground can be tricky, and it is a good idea to set a "datum line." This is simply a line down the middle of the garden from which you can take all your measurements. Then it is relatively easy to work out curves from the drawing and transfer them to the garden itself, marking out each step with stakes.

Be prepared to be flexible when you start to dig the garden or cut the lawn edges. If, for example, the curve on a border looks wrong when it comes to cutting it out of the lawn, don't stick slavishly to the plan. There is nothing to stop you making an alteration here and there in order to perfect the final garden layout. Remember, if it looks right, it *is* right.

MEASURING YOUR GARDEN

It is rare to find a perfectly rectangular plot; most gardens are not exactly at right angles to the house. So, in order to measure accurately, you will need to master the simple skill of triangulation.

For this you need two fixed points from which to measure everything. The corners of the house are ideal. Since walls are generally at right angles to each other, you can be pretty certain that the house itself will be more or less straight. Start by measuring the house, then measure the distance to each corner of the boundary, first from one corner of the house and then from the other, and make a note of these measurements on your rough plan. Use the same method to determine the position of any features, such as trees, that you don't intend to change.

When you come to draw up your master plan, decide on a scale to use. It is best to work in units of ten—1in:1ft, for example (or, alternatively, 1cm:1m). Start by transferring your house measurements to the paper. If you use grid paper you will find it easier to obtain accurate angles and lengths. Then, set a pair of compasses to the relevant scale distances for each feature and draw an arc from both points marking the corners of the house. The point where the arcs intersect gives the precise location of the feature in question. Draw all these details on the master plan in ink. Then fix a piece of tracing paper over the top of the grid paper. This gives you the opportunity to experiment with various designs (and make mistakes) without spoiling the master plan itself. There will inevitably be plenty of mistakes and mind changing before the process is completely to your satisfaction. There are two plans opposite to give you an idea of how you can allocate space. The large one is based on the measurements taken for these diagrams (*see right*).

▶ **Measuring the existing features** *On a rough piece of paper, mark down the distance between the corners of the house and the boundary, and the house and existing features such as trees.*

▼ **Drawing the plan** *Choose a scale to work to and draw the outline of the garden and existing features on to squared paper using compasses.*

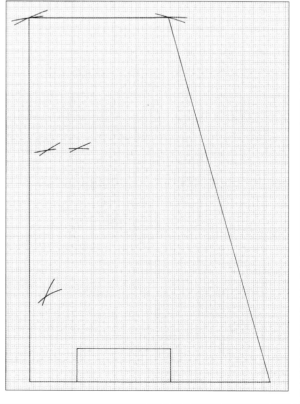

LAYING OUT A GARDEN

Below are ideas for two gardens: one for a large garden and one for a small one. Both demonstrate clearly how many different elements you can incorporate into any sized garden. The small garden is rectangular, the large garden is narrower at one end and slopes away from the house.

Compost bins

Greenhouse and cold frames

Mixed border

Herb garden

Pond

Mixed border

Deep beds

Fan fruit trees

Vegetable plot

N   Scale 1:2

Ornamental trees

Wildflower meadow

Rock garden

Wooden steps to productive garden

Stone steps to lawn with low retaining wall

Ornamental climbers growing against fence

Paved area with plants in cracks

Greenhouse and cold frames

Utility area with space for compost bins and manure heap

Shed

Fruit cage

Fruit trees

Raised bed for acid-loving plants

Pond and marsh garden

Herb garden

Mixed border

Wooden pergola covered with climbers

Trash Area

N   Scale 1:10

THE ORNAMENTAL GARDEN

You MAY THINK that it is not important to manage the ornamental part of your garden organically. After all, you are never going to eat anything from the flower borders. So what does it matter if the roses are cleared of greenfly with chemicals? Why shouldn't the slugs be kept at bay with toxic pellets? And what difference does it make if the weeds are killed with herbicides?

A BALANCED COMMUNITY

In fact, it matters very much. The ornamental garden is an integral part of the organic garden. One of its main functions, after the purely aesthetic one, is to attract insects, birds and, if you are lucky, small mammals, thus creating a completely balanced wild community. This balance is the one way you can ensure that no pest gets the upper hand and manages to build up a dominance that threatens not only the rest of the community but your cultivated plants too. The only way to make the system work properly is nature's way.

Creditable though they certainly are, our attempts at controlling one insect pest with a predatory insect (*see p. 46*) will always have their imperfections. The problem is that, once the pests have been killed, the introduced predators die out because they have nothing left to eat. So, we have to wait for another infestation of the pests and then introduce another supply of predators to kill them. And so it goes on. By a skillful juggling trick, however, nature's system somehow manages to arrange it so that the pests are never completely wiped out and there is, therefore, always enough food for just a few predators. In other words, each is in control of the other's destiny. The predators keep the pests down to numbers that are acceptable, not only to the plants but to you as well, while the pests control the build-up of the predators by the simple process of reducing their food supply. What you must do, instead of supplying the predators, is to supply the plants that will attract them and then let nature do the rest.

Insects and birds are particularly attracted to our gardens by the colors and perfumes of flowers, the fresh green of foliage, and the exotic reds and yellows of berries—all the features that make plants attractive to us too. Create a framework of trees and hedge plants and fill the ornamental borders with a glorious jumble of shrubs, herbaceous plants, wildflowers, and even vegetables. Plant as many native plants as you possibly can. The choice of plants is wide, but it is very important to include the right types. It is easy, for example, to attract a whole range of butterflies by planting the ice plant (*Sedum spectabile*). It will be covered with them throughout its late summer flowering period. In order to get butterflies to breed in your garden, however, you will also need to grow those plants that provide food for their caterpillars. Without them, the life cycle cannot be completed.

CHOOSING PLANTS FOR THE ORNAMENTAL GARDEN

The range of plants to choose from varies not only with the country in which you live, but also the area within that country. There is one rule to follow: when planting, try to vary the types as much as possible—the wider the variety, the wider the range of wildlife you are likely to attract.

If you are lucky enough to be moving into a completely new garden, you can manage it organically right from the outset, choosing the plants and deciding on the position of the features. Start by digging over the entire garden area and preparing the soil thoroughly. Next, organize the hedging, fencing, and trees to give the garden a framework and privacy, then prepare the lawn area—you could, in fact, grass over the whole garden and cut out the ornamental borders later, when time or money are more plentiful.

However, if you are moving to an established garden, it may be advisable to wait a year before putting any plans into action. This will enable you to discover exactly what the garden contains in its borders, and how much work will be necessary to create your ideal, organically managed garden. Obviously, during that time, you can start preparing certain areas, and begin the attack on any pernicious weeds.

Preparing the soil

The basic raw material of gardening is the soil and it is worthwhile taking time and trouble over its initial preparation. Your soil will be one of the five different types or, more probably, a mixture. Soil type varies according to where your garden is situated, and each has a slightly different management technique. This is discussed in greater detail in the second chapter, *The Soil* (*see pp. 12–17*).

TESTING YOUR SOIL

Always begin by identifying your soil type properly (*see p. 14*), as it will affect the way you prepare the soil. If you are taking over a completely new garden, you should test the nutrient content and establish the soil's acidity or alkalinity (*see p. 19*).

In an established garden, it is not absolutely essential to test for nutrient content, because organic management will not take long to correct any nutrient deficiencies, but testing for the degree of acidity or alkalinity certainly is (*see p. 36*). This is determined by the lime content in the soil and will indicate not only whether you should add lime during cultivation, but also determine the types of plants you can grow. While it is possible to make special provision for plants that need conditions other than those prevailing in your soil, it is unwise to spend time and money trying to grow plants that find your soil entirely alien. Since, for example, one acid-loving rhododendron costs a great deal more than a kit to test your soil, it would be unwise not to test the pH before buying the plants.

WHERE YOU SHOULD START

Prepare the soil carefully; remember, once you have planted the trees and shrubs and laid the lawn, there is no opportunity to dig organic matter into the lower levels. Since you can only do it once, you must do it well.

The first job is to get rid of all the perennial weeds (*see p. 55*). If the borders are infested with pernicious perennial weeds like couch grass (*Agropyron repens*) and ground elder (*Aegopodium podagraria*), it is a good idea to grow a "cleaning crop" like potatoes (*see p. 56*) and wait a year before converting the ground into ornamental borders.

Generally, such measures are not necessary. The horrifying stories of gardeners who spend their lifetimes fighting couch grass or ground elder are always due to poor soil preparation and subsequent lack of vigilance (*see p. 56*).

If you don't use a cleaning crop, begin weeding by double digging the entire garden (*see p. 264*), removing every bit of weed possible. It is hard work, but very satisfying. Take your time and do

it thoroughly. Obviously, no perennial weed roots should go on the compost heap or green recycling bin—they should be burned or put in plastic bags and thrown away. Everything else can be put on the compost heap (*see p. 21*).

As the digging and weeding progresses, you are aerating the topsoil and breaking up the subsoil. Double digging also gives you the opportunity to incorporate manure, compost, or one of the alternatives (*see p. 30*) at the rate of 20–30lb (10–15kg) per square yard/meter.

RAISING THE BORDERS

It is a good idea, particularly if you have heavy soil, to raise the borders above the level of the lawn. Double digging and the addition of organic matter will do this. It will not only improve the drainage in the upper levels, but it will also raise the temperature by opening up the soil.

If your soil drains poorly, putting one to two bucketfuls of gravel per square yard/meter onto the soil you are digging and working it in will help to improve drainage and raise the border even further.

Improving drainage *If your soil is heavy and badly drained, raise the borders above the level of the lawn by digging in organic matter and sand. The borders will drain more freely and excess water on the lawn will drain straight into the subsoil.*

Hedges

All gardens, and gardeners, need a certain amount of privacy and shelter from strong wind. There are several ways of achieving this: fencing, informal or formal hedging, or even a wire fence covered with climbing plants. What you use depends largely on the space available. If your garden is tiny, you will not have the space to devote to a hedge of any kind, so a fence or wall may be more suitable. A solid barrier, however, prevents the free flow of frost-laden air and can create a frost pocket (*see p. 65*).

Hedging provides the most effective windbreak because it filters the wind, slowing it down, and allows cold air to escape from the garden. If you need a windbreak and you do not have room for a hedge, a good alternative is to build a post-and-wire fence and train climbing plants up it (*see p. 119*).

CHOOSING HEDGING PLANTS

There are two main types of hedging plant: those that can be neatly clipped and not allowed to flower, creating a formal hedge, and those that are allowed to grow in their natural state and flower, forming an informal hedge.

Formal hedges can be clipped back to reduce the amount of space they take up. Though the essence of the small garden is informality, a well-clipped coniferous hedge, such as the Lawson cypress (*Chamaecyparis lawsoniana*) or yew (*Taxus baccata*), or the shiny foliage of laurel (*Prunus laurocerasus*), makes a fine background to the ornamental garden. As a windbreak, the close foliage of a formal hedge is unbeatable.

Informal hedges require a lot more room, as they are allowed to grow in their natural way. For most, you should allow for a spread of at least 3–6ft (1–2m) either side of the planting line. However, they do have the advantage of flowers, which are not cut off as they would be with a formally trimmed hedge. Almost any tall-growing flowering shrub can be used. Escallonia is particularly attractive; an evergreen, it is covered in pink, red, or white flowers in summer. If you are trying to keep animals out of the garden, choose a hedging plant with thorns, for example, the barberry (*Berberis* sp.).

BUYING HEDGING PLANTS

Hedging plants can be bought bare root, container-grown, or balled. Each type has advantages and disadvantages. Bare root plants are grown in the open ground and dug up for sale. They are cheaper than container-grown plants; the disadvantage is that they can only be planted in winter, when they are dormant. Generally, shrubs like beech, privet, and hawthorn are only available as bare root plants. Container-grown plants can be planted at any time of year provided the ground is not frozen. Ensure that they have actually been grown in the container; if they pull out easily, they have just been lifted from the nursery and run a high risk of failing when planted out. Conifers are often sold balled. They are grown on a nursery and dug out for sale. The soil is left around the roots and wrapped in burlap or plastic. They should be planted in spring or fall.

Whichever type of plant you decide to buy, ensure that the roots are well-developed and free from disease. Bare root deciduous plants should have closed leaf buds.

Formal hedging *This yew hedge (*Taxus *sp.) is kept tightly clipped to restrict its height and spread. It also provides a neat backdrop to the lavender.*

Informal hedging *A whole range of shrubs may be grown together to create informal screens or boundaries that present different features of interest through the year.*

PLANTING A HEDGE

The essence of a good hedge is to provide effective cover quickly. It is important to prepare the soil thoroughly, to give the hedge a good start in life.

The best time to plant hedging plants is in their dormant period. The plant used below is Lawson cypress (*Chamaecyparis lawsoniana*).

1 *Mark out the hedge line with string and dig a trench at least 2ft (60cm) deep and 3ft (90cm) wide along the line. Take out the topsoil to the depth of the spade and break up the subsoil thoroughly.*

2 *Put a 3in (7.5cm) layer of well-rotted compost or manure in the trench. Cover with a layer of soil, then more organic matter, and refill. Cover with two handfuls of blood, fish, and bone meal per yard/meter length. Allow the soil to settle for two weeks.*

3 *If the plants are container-grown, carefully disentangle any roots that may be running around the bottom of the pot. This is especially important when planting conifers.*

4 *Plant each shrub at the recommended planting distance (see below). Use a planting board (see p. 260) as a guide to ensure even planting. Water well after planting.*

RECOMMENDED PLANTING DISTANCES

When planting a hedge, there is little point in spacing the shrubs too closely. Planted at the distances recommended in the table below, they will quickly grow together, forming a close hedge at a much lower cost. The table also gives the maximum height of the shrubs.

Plant	Planting distance					Maximum height
	12in (30cm)	18in (45cm)	2ft (60cm)	2ft 6in (75cm)	3ft (90cm)	
Formal hedge shrubs						
Lawson cypress (*Chamaecyparis lawsoniana*)				🌲		40ft (12m)
Leyland cypress (*Cupressocyparis leylandii*)				🌲		45ft (14m)
Western red cedar (*Thuja plicata*)				🌲		50ft (16m)
Yew (*Taxus baccata*)		🌲				15ft (4.5m)
Hawthorn (*Crataegus monogyna*)	🌲					25–30ft (7.5–9m)
Common laurel (*Prunus laurocerasus*)				🌲		15–20ft (4.5–6m)
Holly (*Ilex aquifolium*)					🌲	18–22ft (5.5–6.5m)
Privet (*Ligustrum ovalifolium*)	🌲					12–15ft (3.5–4.5m)
Beech (*Fagus sylvatica*)		🌲				40ft (12m)
Informal hedge shrubs						
Barberry (*Berberis* sp.)			🌲			8–10ft (2.5–3m)
Escallonia (*Escallonia* sp.)			🌲			15ft (4.5m)
Griselinia (*Griselinia* sp.)			🌲			10–25ft (3–7.5m)
Pittosporum (*Pittosporum* sp.)			🌲			15ft (4.5m)

MAINTAINING A HEDGE

Feeding Hedges tend to get neglected, but they should be treated like any other shrub in the garden. Feed them in early spring with blood, fish, and bone meal. Mulch with well-rotted compost or manure immediately after feeding.

Pruning Some plants, such as quick thorn (*Crataegus* sp.) or privet (*Ligustrum ovalifolium*), need to be pruned back hard immediately after planting (*see below*). This may appear to be defeating the purpose, but it ensures that the hedge will be bushy and well established at ground level.

Trim conifer hedges only when they reach the required height. The top shoots can then be cut out to limit upward growth. Prune the sides of the hedge annually in late summer. This is a good time to prune other slow-growing evergreens, but faster-growing hedges, like privet, must be pruned with shears regularly throughout the growing season too.

Clearing the hedge bottom The bottom of the hedge tends to trap all kinds of trash. Leaves, grass, and bits of paper, for example, will blow there and remain. This will trap frost-laden air and is an ideal place for pests and diseases to winter. Make a habit of cleaning out the bottom of your hedge in the fall.

Pests and diseases Hedges can harbor pests and diseases on their leaves which may spread to other garden plants. Native species will attract more pests but this increase is offset by a greater

attraction to the pest predators. If your garden is planted with a wide variety of species, hedge-dwelling pests should not be a problem as their natural predators will keep numbers under control (*see p. 43*).

Lawns

An area of grass is not essential in the organic garden, but it makes a good foreground to the ornamental borders and provides an area for children to play and you to relax in.

New lawns can be made from seed or turf. Seed is cheaper, but turf is much quicker to establish. An alternative is to use chamomile (*Chamaemelum nobile*), which makes a thick, bright green lawn. It is more drought resistant than grass so will remain green even in fairly dry conditions.

If you are buying seed, make sure that you choose a mixture that will suit your management regime. Very fine mixtures will need regular maintenance if the lawn is to remain high quality. Coarse mixtures are hard wearing, which is worth bearing in mind if you have children.

PREPARING THE SITE

Preparation is the same whether you intend to start from seed or turf. To the organic gardener, this is the most important phase of the lawn's life, because the best way to beat weed or moss problems in the lawn is to get the grass growing so well that it chokes out the unwanted plants. This requires healthy, fertile soil (*see p. 18*), with an active animal community (*see p. 11*). I have never understood, for example, the chemical gardeners who kill earthworms with chlordane poison just to avoid wormcasts on their lawn. Then they have to spend hours aerating the soil with a fork, because there are no worms to do it for them. Yet it takes no more than a few minutes to sweep the wormcasts over the lawn before mowing. Remember, not only do worms aerate the soil, and therefore improve drainage, but their pellets help break nutrients down into a form that is more readily available to plants (*see p. 31*). Encourage earthworms and all your other allies in the soil by digging in organic matter in the form of manure, compost, or one of the alternatives (*see p. 30*) at the rate of at least 20lb (10kg) per square yard/meter. A layer of gravel under heavy soil will improve drainage (*see p. 16*). Do this job thoroughly because it is the last chance you will get to dig below the level of the grass.

Seed lawns

Sowing seed is the cheapest way to lay a new lawn, and allows you to control the different types of grasses making up the lawn. The only

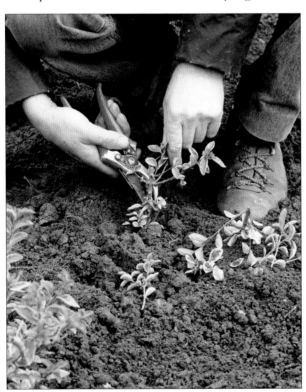

Cutting back after planting *It is recommended that some shrubs, such as privet* (Ligustrum ovalifolium), *are cut right back to within 1in (2.5cm) of the ground immediately after planting. This will encourage shoots to grow out from the base.*

disadvantage of a seed lawn is that it takes three months to establish if sown in the spring. If sown in the fall, it should not be used until the following spring.

MAINTAINING A NEW SEED LAWN

Watering With only a limited root system, a new lawn is very vulnerable in dry weather. Water using a lawn sprinkler to apply a fine spray at regular intervals (*see p. 266*).

Mowing When the grass is about 3in (7cm) high, it is ready for cutting. First, roll it with the mower with the blades right off the ground to push in any loose stones. This also bruises the grass stems, causing the buds at their base to grow out, greatly thickening up the lawn. Then, raise the mower blades as far as they will go and trim the tips of the new grass. The blades can be lowered progressively with each cut, until they are about ½in (1cm) above the soil surface.

Any weeds growing through the new grass will be sliced off regularly. The annuals will disappear quickly and, if you missed any of the perennials during preparation, most will soon succumb. Only rosetted weeds will survive regular mowing and these can be coped with later (*see next page*).

Turf lawns

A turf lawn is very much an "instant lawn." It looks good right away and is ready for use about six weeks after laying, if put down in the spring. Turf must be bought from a reliable source to ensure that the grass is good quality.

MAINTAINING A NEW TURF LAWN

Watering Make sure the sod isn never short of water. It takes only a little drying out to cause the pieces to shrink, leaving ugly gaps, so use the sprinkler little and often.

Mowing You will know when the grass has rooted because it starts to look greener and stands up. It can then be cut in the way recommended for a seed lawn (*see left*).

SOWING A SEED LAWN

Grass seed should be sown in early spring or early fall, when some wet weather can be expected. Avoid the driest months as this means constant watering. If sowing grass seed along the edge of paving, raise the level of the lawn above the paving to ensure easy mowing.

1 *Start with a stale seed bed (see p. 269). Rake the area roughly level with the back of a fork to take out any local undulations before consolidating the soil.*

2 *If your soil is light or lacks organic matter, apply a 2in (5cm) layer of compost and rake it in with the fork. If the soil is heavy, use coarse sand.*

3 *Rake in two handfuls of blood, fish, and bone meal every square yard/meter. To consolidate the soil, walk over the whole area with your weight on your heels; this will prevent the soil from sinking.*

4 *Rake the area level. It helps to see the local undulations if you take a step back from time to time, crouch down, and squint across the surface, although a completely level lawn is rarely necessary.*

5 *Sow the seed at 1–1½oz (25–35g) per square yard/meter. This is about two handfuls of seed. If you put your feet as wide apart as you can and lean forward as far as possible, you will cover about 1 square yard/meter.*

6 *Rake the seed in, aiming to cover about half with soil and, to speed up germination and protect the seed from birds, cover with perforated plastic. Remove the plastic when the first seed germinates.*

LAYING A TURF LAWN

Prepare the soil (*as shown on p. 78*) and rake it flat, then lay the sod as described below. Always work from boards, as you should never walk on the turf you have just laid or the leveled soil. Scaffolding boards are ideal and can be lifted very easily.

1 *Place a board along the longest straight edge of the lawn and lay the first row of turf. Lay rows of turf all the way around the edge of the proposed lawn. Tap down the strips with the back of a rake to put them into close contact with the soil.*

2 *Lay a board on the first row of turf. Standing on the board, lay a second row of turf parallel to the first and pull it into the first with the back of the rake. There's no need to bond the pieces together as is sometimes recommended.*

3 *When you get to the end of a row, butt the last turf up to the edging turf by laying it on top and cutting off the excess with a penknife. When the whole lawn is down, you can shape the edges with an edging knife.*

4 *When you have finished the lawn, put a sprinkler on the area. Keep the pieces well watered after laying to prevent shrinking. Once the grass has established its roots, water less frequently.*

Established lawns

If you already have a lawn in your garden, you can't dig in organic matter, but you can care for the grass to keep it in good condition.

Drainage To get the grass growing really well, proper drainage is necessary. You can improve it by adding sand or organic matter. If the drainage is poor, the soil will become waterlogged, preventing air from getting to the roots. If the lawn drains too quickly, the grass will soon become brown and unhealthy looking.

Feeding Lawns can be fed in two ways. You can use slow-release blood, fish, and bone meal once or, at most, twice a year in early spring, and again in early summer. Alternatively, if you want the instant greening results obtained by a chemical lawn fertilizer, use a liquid manure feed high in nitrogen (*see pp. 40–41*).

Weeding If you keep the grass growing well and cut it regularly, you will not be bothered by a lot of weeds. But, inevitably, some rosetted weeds, like dandelions or daisies, creep in. They can be kept under control by cutting them out regularly with a knife, or by dropping ordinary table salt on the growing point.

Repairing coarse patches of lawn Sometimes patches of coarse grass appear though, if you start with good seed or cultivated turf, this should be rare.

▲ **Improving drainage or water retention** *Work over the lawn with a hollow-tined fork, removing cores of soil. If your soil is heavy, put sand into the holes to fill them. For light soil, use garden compost.*

▶ **Killing rosetted weeds in lawns** *Pour table salt into the center of the weeds; this causes them to shrivel up and die overnight. Alternatively, cut them out with a penknife.*

If it does happen, it can be repaired by hatching and reseeding. Score the coarse patch in a criss-cross fashion with a penknife and reseed, using an equal-parts mixture of seed, moist peat, and good soil.

MOWING A LAWN

Mow your lawn only during the growing season. The grass stops growing in winter and does not need cutting then. Begin by raking any earthworm casts around the lawn, otherwise the mower flattens them, making perfect seedbeds for weeds.

The lawn should be cut in opposite directions on alternate cuts (*see below*). Never mow the lawn too close as this encourages bare patches which will be colonized by moss and weeds. Always leave the grass ½in (1cm) long and remove the cuttings to prevent a build-up of dead material and the possibility of attack by fungus diseases. Grass cuttings are also the best composting material possible, so never throw them away (*see p. 21*). Rake the lawn with a spring-tine rake at least once a year in spring to remove dead grass before you start mowing.

The correct way to mow *Cut once around the entire edge of the lawn. Then, starting in one corner, cut diagonally across the lawn. Mark your starting point so that you can work in the opposite direction the next time you cut the lawn.*

Trimming the edges *When you have finished mowing the lawn, tidy the edges by trimming the pieces the mower missed with long-handled shears, taking the clippers as close to the edge as possible.*

Trees

Ornamental trees serve many purposes. First, they provide shade, which extends the range of plants you can grow. Second, along with the hedges and lawns, they form the framework of the garden and can be planted to act as windbreaks, especially in the larger garden. And third, they attract wildlife to feed and breed.

Birds use them for perching and nesting and as a source of food, especially the berrying and fruiting trees such as cotoneaster (*Cotoneaster waterii*), mountain ash (*Sorbus* sp.), and flowering crab apple (*Malus* sp.). Trees with deeply furrowed or flaking bark, for example some of the birches (*Betula* sp.), provide homes for insects, which are themselves food for the birds.

Flowering trees attract pollinating insects, which are important if you are growing fruit. The flowering crab apple *Malus* "Golden Hornet," for example, pollinates most varieties of apple and, as it is bred for maximum flower, there is always ample pollen.

CHOOSING TREES

When choosing trees, the first consideration should be the ultimate height and spread. Trees will compete with plants growing near them for water and nutrients and, if you plant a large tree, it will throw your whole garden into deep shade. Many gardeners have lived to regret planting the lovely weeping willow (*Salix alba* "Tritis"), which can reach heights of up to 40ft (12m). There are many small trees which would be more suitable. For example, the Kilmarnock willow (*Salix caprea* "Kilmarnock") would be a better choice for a small garden. It makes an attractive weeping tree that will always remain small and manageable, with a maximum height of 10ft (3m). Remember, you can always ask your local nursery if you are unsure. A selection of deciduous and coniferous trees is shown on pp. 84–87.

Do not plant vigorous trees less than about 40ft (12m) from the house. Roots of trees like willows (*Salix* sp.) and poplars (*Populus* sp.) will seek out cracked drains, quickly blocking them. Worse still, they can cause soil shrinkage. When water is withdrawn from the soil by the tree, it shrinks away from underneath the foundations of the house, causing cracking and settling. This is particularly dangerous on clay soils.

BUYING TREES

Trees can be bought container-grown or bare root and should come from a reputable nursery. Container-grown trees are smaller and more expensive than bare root ones—their advantage is that they can be planted at any time of year. Bare root trees can only be planted in their dormant season.

PLANTING TREES

Never plant trees in holes dug in uncultivated soil. If you simply dig a hole in hard ground, it acts as a sump for all the surrounding water. If the hole fills up with water in the winter, the tree's roots will then be cold and deprived of air. So prepare the soil properly. Even if you are planting trees in an area of grass, you should prepare as big a hole as you can—at least 3ft (90cm) square. Break up the subsoil to improve drainage and work in plenty of organic matter—compost, manure, or one of the alternatives (*see pp. 29–30*). Do not use spent mushroom compost as it contains lime (*see p. 30*)

and most trees (and shrubs) prefer a slightly acid soil. It is essential not to use it on lime haters like the snowy mespilus (*Amelanchier lamarckii*). Spread two handfuls of blood, fish, and bone meal fertilizer over the soil too.

All young trees need staking when first planted. The type of stake is different for bare root and container-grown trees. If they are bare root, the stake should be a simple post, placed as near to the trunk as possible (*see opposite*). If they are container-grown, they should be supported with a crossbar stake (*see below*). It has been found that the movement of the trunk in the wind thickens the base and improves the root system, so the stake should anchor the base and the roots and come one-third of the way up the trunk, leaving the rest

PLANTING CONTAINER-GROWN TREES

These can be planted at any time of year. Watering is the most important aspect of planting this type of tree; lack of water is the main cause of failure. The roots will not spread out into the soil for several weeks, so the root ball must be hand watered, especially in dry weather.

1 Dig a hole large enough to accommodate the root ball. Water the tree while it is in the container. This will help the root ball slide out of the container more easily.

2 Put the tree in the hole, leaving the roots undisturbed, unless they have begun to run around the pot. Check that the hole is deep enough by laying a spade across the hole.

3 If your soil is short of organic matter, add compost to the pile of soil you have dug out and, as compost contains few nutrients, supplement it with two handfuls of blood, fish, and bone meal.

4 With a spade, mix up the soil and peat around the edge of the hole, and use this mixture to cover the root ball. Firm down gently with the ball of your foot.

5 Water retention around the root ball is vital. Use some of the dug-out soil to make a small retaining wall around the tree so that the soil can be really soaked later.

6 Hammer two 2 × 2in (5 × 5cm) stakes inside the soil walls. They should go 1ft 6in (45cm) into the ground and come one-third of the way up the trunk. Nail a crossbar between the stakes.

7 Tie the trunk to the crossbar using a special tree tie with a collar to prevent chafing. Water thoroughly and make sure you check the soil regularly for drying out.

8 A month to six weeks later—when the tree should have rooted properly—level out the soil wall and mulch thickly around the trunk with well-rotted manure or compost.

of the stem free to move. Secure the tree to the stake with a special tree tie or strip of plastic; never use wire or nylon twine; they cut through the trunk as the tree grows.

MAINTAINING TREES

Feeding Trees that are growing in borders will normally be fed every year when the rest of the plants receive fertilizer. In addition to two handfuls of blood, fish, and bone meal every spring, try to spread a layer of manure, compost, or one of the alternatives (*see p. 30*) around the roots every fall (avoiding spent mushroom compost, *see p. 30*).

If trees are growing in grass, they should be fed in the same way, but just a little earlier—say midwinter—so that the fertilizer is washed down into the soil before the grass starts growing and using up nutrients.

Pruning Ornamental trees need little pruning in the first years after planting; it is generally only a case of removing branches that are dead, diseased, crossing, or overcrowding during the dormant season. If you notice any branches growing toward the center of the tree, or that are beginning to grow across other branches, take them out right away. That way you will avoid having to remove large branches later, which spoils the shape of the tree.

Tree ties These should be checked at least every fall. You may find that they have become too loose to hold the tree in winter storms, or that the tie is now restricting further growth. Remove and replace them as necessary.

PLANTING BARE ROOT TREES

This can only be done in the tree's dormant season. Never plant in freezing or waterlogged conditions. If the trees arrive when the ground is frozen, leave them unpacked, in a frost-free building, until better weather, or "heel in" in a V-shaped slit trench (*see p.113*).

1 *Keep the roots covered with a burlap sack until the planting area has been prepared. This will prevent dehydration of the roots in sunny or windy weather.*

2 *Plant at the level of the old soil mark on the stem. Put the tree in the hole and lay a spade across the edge of the hole—the handle should line up with the soil mark if the tree is at the correct depth.*

3 *Take the tree out of the hole and drive a stake 18in (45cm) into the soil. It should be at least twice as thick as the stem and should come about one-third of the way up the tree.*

4 *Cover the soil you have dug out with a bucketful of organic matter. Compost can be used but, as it contains few nutrients, sprinkle on two handfuls of bone meal fertilizer.*

5 *Place the tree in the hole and put a little fine soil over the roots and then, holding the stem, jerk it up and down a few times to settle some of the soil around the roots.*

6 *Refill half the hole and pack down the soil with the ball of your foot. While the soil around the roots should be firm, it should not be over-compressed. Completely fill the hole and pack it down.*

7 *Tie the stem to the stake with either a tree tie or a length of thick plastic, tied in a figure eight to form a collar between the tree and the stake. Nail the tie or plastic to the stake.*

8 *Mulch around the stem with a layer of well-rotted compost or manure immediately after planting to conserve moisture and inhibit weed growth.*

Deciduous trees

These are trees that shed their leaves before the cold or dry season. Prior to this the leaves often turn orange, red, or yellow. New leaves appear in the spring. There are many different shapes and sizes and those shown here are just a tiny selection. When choosing a tree for your garden, check the eventual height and spread and remember that most trees will give shade, affecting the type of plants that will grow nearby. *For details of tree planting, see pp.82–83.*

WILLOW-LEAVED PEAR
Pyrus salicifolia "Pendula"
As the name suggests, this ornamental pear tree has willow-like leaves. They are gray-green in color and covered in fine, downy hairs. This variety is best suited to smaller gardens because it has a maximum height of 15ft (4.5m) and spread of 8 ft (2.4m).

WILD CHERRY
Prunus avium "Plena"
This variety is grown for its plentiful, double, white flowers which open at the same time as the leaves. They are followed in the fall by small, shiny plum-colored fruits. The leaves turn red in the fall. Height up to 40ft (12m), spread 30ft (10m).

MOUNTAIN ASH
Sorbus "Joseph Rock"
This is a small tree with leaves that turn from glossy green to deep, fiery red in the fall. In the spring, clusters of cream-colored flowers appear; these develop into amber-yellow fruits by early fall. Height up to 18ft (5.5m), spread 8ft (2.4m).

AUTUMN CHERRY
Prunus subhirtella "Autumnalis"
This ornamental cherry tree produces white, semi-double flowers intermittently from late fall to spring. It does not fruit. In most years the leaves turn an attractive red in the fall. Height up to 30ft (10m), spread 30ft (10m).

LABURNUM
Laburnum vossii
A small tree suitable for most soils and situations. The three-lobed leaves are deep green and the tree is covered with a profusion of bright-yellow flowers in late spring and early summer. All parts are poisonous. Height up to 18ft (5.5m), spread 12ft (4m).

GUM TREE
Eucalyptus gunnii
This tree is, in fact, an evergreen, constantly shedding and replacing a few leaves at a time. Like all eucalyptus, it should be planted in a sheltered position. When they are young the leaves are round. Height up to 50ft (15m), spread 20ft (6m).

SALLOW
Salix caprea
The leaves have dark-green upper surfaces with gray undersides. Yellow catkins appear on male plants in the spring, while female plants bear silver catkins. The Kilmarnock willow (*S. c.* "Pendula") is ideal for a small garden, reaching only 10ft (3m).

BIRCH
Betula platyphylla
Birches are grown for their beautiful bark that, on some species, constantly peels to reveal the new, lighter bark beneath. The leaves turn yellow in the fall and the trees bear catkins in spring. Height up to 30ft (10m), spread 15–20ft (4.5–6m).

HONEY LOCUST
Gleditsia triacanthos
The leaflets are bright yellow in spring, turning light green in summer, and back to yellow in fall. The branches bear spines. Green flowers are produced in spring and brown seed pods in fall. Height up to 30ft (10m), spread 15ft (4.5m).

NORWAY MAPLE
Acer platanoides
Large, handsome trees grown for their leaves, which turn yellow, and sometimes red, in the fall. There are several attractive forms with various foliage colors including white and green variegation. Height up to 30ft (10m), spread 20ft (6m).

PAPERBARK MAPLE
Acer griseum
Grow this tree for its beautiful fall coloring. The leaves turn orange-red in the fall and the peeling bark also contributes to its beauty. The brown outer bark peels away constantly to reveal the new, orange bark beneath. Height up to 20ft (6m), spread 8ft (2.4m).

THE ORNAMENTAL GARDEN

Coniferous trees

Shown here is a small selection of the many coniferous trees available. Their leaves are small and waxy, in the form of scales and needles that are usually retained all year.

There is a great variety of colors, shapes, and sizes—from dwarf forms for the rock garden or tubs, to large specimen and hedging varieties.

It is best to buy conifers in containers as they do not move well when bare root, unless lifted with a sizable root ball. *For details of tree planting, see pp. 82–83.*

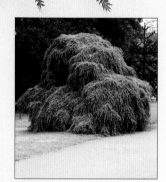

EASTERN HEMLOCK
Tsuga canadensis
The branches of this graceful conifer rest on the ground when they are long enough. The shoots are covered with small, dark-green needles and oval-shaped cones. It is best as a free-standing specimen tree. Height up to 30ft (10m), spread 20ft (6m).

MAIDENHAIR TREE
Ginkgo biloba
An unusual conifer as its leaves resemble those of the maidenhair fern. During the summer they are dark green, becoming a beautiful transparent yellow in fall. It is deciduous. Height up to 30ft (10m), spread 10ft (3m).

PENCIL CEDAR
Juniperus virgineana
"Skyrocket"
This species is one of the narrowest junipers. It is an ideal specimen for adding interest to a low planting. The foliage is made up of mid-green leaves loosely arranged on the shoots. Height up to 15ft (5m), spread 1ft (30cm).

MOUNTAIN PINE
Pinus mugo
The long narrow needles of this pine are arranged in pairs around the stems. The brown, oval cones are about 2in (5cm) long. Its prostrate habit and slow growth rate makes it an ideal subject for the rock garden. Height up to 15ft (4.5m), spread 15ft (4.5m).

DEODAR
Cedrus deodara
Deodars look best grown as specimen trees in a large lawn. When young, the needles are light green. They darken as they become older. The branches droop as the tree matures, giving it a weeping appearance. Height up to 40ft (12m), spread 10ft (3m).

LAWSON CYPRESS
Chamaecyparis lawsoniana
"Allumii"
As the tree gets older it widens at the base, making an attractive "candle-flame" shape suitable for formal planting. It can also be used for hedging. The leaves are blue-gray in color. Height up to 20ft (6m), spread 5ft (1.5m).

WESTERN RED CEDAR
Thuja plicata
This species is the fastest growing of the thujas and is a tall, conical tree when fully mature. The flattened sprays of scalelike leaves have a distinctive fruity scent. The cultivar "Atrovirens" makes an excellent hedge. Height up to 55ft (16.5m), spread 20ft (6m).

HINOKI CYPRESS
Chamaecyparis obtusa
"Nana Gracilis"
This conical bush is very slow growing, though it will eventually become a large shrub or small tree. A popular conifer for the rock garden, it will take many years to outgrow its space. Height up to 10ft (3m), spread 6ft (2m).

LEYLAND CYPRESS
Cupressocyparis leylandii
The Leyland cypress can grow very tall and is one of the fastest growing conifers available. It makes an excellent dense hedge growing, in good soil, 2–3ft (60–90cm) a year. Height up to 50ft (15m), spread 15ft (4.5m).

COMMON YEW
Taxus baccata
This hardy species is tolerant of most adverse conditions and makes a good hedge. The narrow, waxy leaves are dark green. The red, cup-shaped berries are the only part of the tree that is not poisonous. Height up to 15ft (4.5m), spread 15ft (4.5m).

COLORADO SPRUCE
Picea pungens "Koster"
A very popular blue spruce, used widely as a specimen tree. It makes an ideal lawn planting. The needles are arranged spirally so that each shoot looks like a small bottle brush. The brown cones are 4in (10cm) long. Height up to 25ft (7.5m), spread 10ft (3m).

Planting ornamental borders

The essence of planting an organic garden is to create as wide a diversity as possible so that you will attract a balanced community of wildlife that will include pests and predators, so that no one species will build up to an unacceptable level. The "cottage-garden" style is ideal. Here each border contains a mixture of permanent plants such as trees, shrubs, perennials (soft-stemmed plants that die back in the winter every year then reappear in spring), bulbs that flower in different seasons, bedding plants in the form of annuals and biennials to provide extra color during the growing season, and even vegetables. Annuals are plants that complete their life cycle in one year; biennials are plants that are sown one year and flower the next. It is important that a number of plants native to your area are included in this type of planting. If you are not sure which are the native plants, look

them up in a plant directory. Unless your garden is large, there is no place for "sophisticated" planting of, perhaps, single-color borders or areas that come to a peak at one particular time and provide nothing for the rest of the year. To create a real balance you need flowers and fruits for as long a period as possible to attract and feed insects, birds, and small mammals. A selection of suitable plants is shown on pp. 92–111.

Of course, you'll need to consider the type of soil in your garden, as this will govern the type of plants you can grow. If you have chalky or alkaline soil, for example, you should avoid acid-loving plants such as azaleas.

Consider the aspect of the garden too—that is, the direction it faces, and how much direct sun it gets. This will also have a bearing on the plants you can grow (*see p. 64*).

▲ **Mixed planting** *Some vegetables make attractive plants to mix into the ornamental borders. This is an ideal way of growing them in very small gardens and has the advantage that the flowers will attract or encourage insect predators like hoverflies and ladybugs to control aphids, while the dense ground cover provides ideal conditions for insects such as ground beetles that prey on caterpillars.*

◀ **The mature border** *This wide, mature border illustrates very well the principle of mixed, "cottage-garden" planting. All types of plants have been used together and some tall plants have been brought near the front of the border to create an attractive undulating profile.*

CREATING A COLORFUL INSTANT BORDER

Permanent plants like shrubs and herbaceous perennials take some time to fill their allotted space. However, it's not difficult to create instant borders full of summer color by interplanting the shrubs with blocks of annuals. You may occasionally need to trim back the annuals a little to ensure that they do not inhibit the growth of the more permanent plants.

1 *Prepare the soil in the normal way, digging out any perennial weeds and working in plenty of well-rotted manure or compost through the top as well as the lower levels.*

2 *Sprinkle a light dusting of blood, fish, and bone meal, at the rate of one handful per square yard/meter, over the surface of the soil before planting.*

3 *The annuals are planted in "drifts," using several plants together to create a more dramatic effect. Be sure to leave plenty of room for the permanent plants to grow. A tomato plant will not look out of place in this border.*

4 *Plants with open, flat flowers like French marigolds (Tagetes patula) are particularly useful for attracting hoverflies that feed on their pollen before laying their eggs among groups of aphids.*

The finished border

By using annuals, the border will be a blaze of color throughout the summer. By mixing the productive with the ornamental in this way, vegetable plants are camouflaged from insect pests attracted by sight and scent; the diversity of planting creates a natural balance of pest and predator.

Clematis
Cauliflower
Onion
Tomato
Gilia
Marigolds

Pepper
Fuchsia
Chives
Geranium
Sea kale
Antirrhinum

When you have a general idea of your plan, it is worth putting it down on paper to prevent any costly mistakes (*see p. 72*). You do not necessarily have to follow it religiously, but it will give you a starting point. If you have just taken over an established garden, and you are planning to change an existing border planting, leave it for one growing season to see what the border contains and start planning the new planting program in the winter or early spring of the following year.

WHAT TO PLANT FIRST

When you are planting a new border, it is best to start with the shrubs. Herbaceous plants can be put in later, they can easily be dug up and moved if you feel you have made a mistake—in fact they may actually benefit from being moved occasionally. Shrubs, on the other hand, need to establish themselves; they will suffer every time they are moved.

Shrubs such as roses can also be included as a part of the border framework. This way, there is an opportunity for companion planting to help keep pests away (*see p. 45*).

FILLING BETWEEN THE SHRUBS

Once the framework of shrubs has been planted, perennials can be intermingled with them to fill up the spaces. Bear in mind, however, that they grow very fast so do not allow them to overcrowd and inhibit the growth of the shrubs.

For instant color, particularly in the first few years of the border, annuals and biennials can be used (*see p. 89*). They are ideal for filling the spaces around young shrubs though a certain amount of care is needed. Don't plant them too close to growing shrubs or they will compete for light and inhibit the growth of the shrubs. If you find them encroaching, trim them back. Even when the borders are mature, you should leave some space for annuals and biennials to brighten the garden with color, and often perfume.

Also useful in the mixed borders are bulbs (and here I include tubers, corms, and rhizomes). Spring-flowering bulbs can be planted among shrubs and herbaceous plants to make a show when other plants are still dormant. Then, when the herbaceous plants or shrubs grow and are in full leaf, the messy, post-flowering bulb foliage is hidden from view. By choosing the species carefully it is possible to have bulbs in flower all year-round. If you are planting in a fairly young mixed border, put the bulbs very close to the shrubs. As you should never dig near the roots of shrubs for fear of damage, the bulbs will not be dug up accidentally when planting other herbaceous plants in the border.

GIVING A BORDER HEIGHT

Climbing plants can be included in informal borders to add height—especially those in front of a wall or hedge that a climber can be allowed to ramble over. Climbers can also be used to cover any ugly features in the garden, such as a garage or central air compressor. And some, like the less vigorous cultivars of the clematis, are invaluable, climbing over shrubs and in trees. If you choose a variety that is in flower when the tree or shrub is not, you can extend the flowering season of your border.

GENERAL MAINTENANCE OF ORNAMENTAL BORDERS

Feeding Maintain a regular supply of nutrients to the border by mulching annually with well-rotted manure or compost. Give the whole border a coating of blood, fish, and bone meal in early spring. Every three years apply a layer of kelp meal to ensure that the trace elements are in plentiful supply.

Watering Make sure the border plants get plenty of water in dry weather, and ensure they do not dry out immediately after planting. This is particularly important with container-grown shrubs. (*See* Watering plants, *p. 266*).

Pest and disease control Ornamental plants are susceptible to many of the general pests and diseases listed on pp. 46–52. Constant vigilance and companion planting will help to keep problems to a minimum.

Weed control Covering any exposed soil with bark chippings or ground-cover plants suppresses weed growth, greatly reducing the workload. Bark mulch looks good but can be rather expensive and needs to be replaced every few years. Ground-cover plants quickly cover the soil and give the borders a more complete look. There are plenty of low-growing plants available that are dense enough to suppress weeds, and the most attractive way of using them is to plant several different species to make a tapestry of colors and leaf textures under and around the taller plants. For colored leaves, plant bugle (*Ajuga reptans*) or euonymus, cinquefoil, heathers (*Erica* sp.), and periwinkles (*Vinca* sp.), all of which form flat, dense mats over the ground. Bear in mind that some plants, such as periwinkle (*Vinca minor*) and knotweed (*Polygonum* sp.), sold as ground cover, can become as invasive as the weeds if their growth is not restricted.

There are problems, however, with ground-cover plants. In the early stages, before dense cover is established, a great deal of weeding will be necessary and it can only be done by hand. Once they have spread, however, to cover the soil completely and form a dense carpet that excludes light, annual weeds will rarely be able to compete so weeding will consist only of pulling out the rare perennial weed. There are other forms of organic weed control that work on the principle of depriving any possible weeds of light (*see pp. 55–59*).

▲ Naturalizing bulbs
Spring-flowering bulbs such as daffodils
*(*Narcissus*) and crocuses can transform an*
area of rough grass into a joyful sea of color—
and the long grass provides a haven for insects.

▶ Attracting insects
A varied insect population is vital
in the organic garden. Butterflies and
hoverflies are attracted to the ice plant
*(*Sedum spectabile*) by its brightly*
colored, nectar-filled flowers.

▼ Covering a pergola
If your garden is small, grow fast-growing
climbing plants, such as clematis, over a
pergola to add height to your plantings. This
is C. orientalis, *which produces brilliant*
yellow flowers throughout summer.

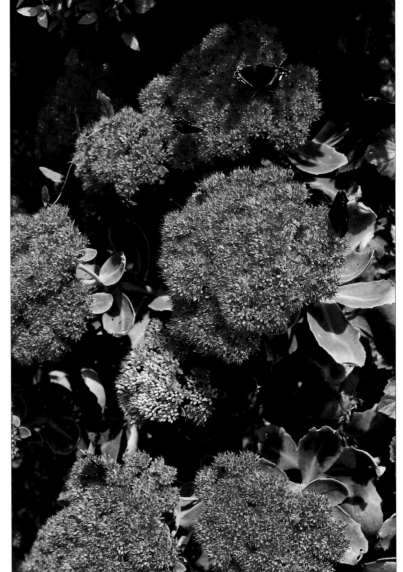

Choosing suitable plants

It is important to choose plants that suit the type of soil in your garden in order to achieve the best results. The charts below show a selection of plants for each soil type. The lists are divided according to the different plant types and further divided to indicate their tolerance of sun and shade. Bulbs, annuals, and biennials are not included in these lists because they are tolerant of most soil conditions and light levels.

On the following pages (pp. 94–111), you will find a photographic season-by-season guide to ornamental garden plants. Each plant illustrated on these pages has been given a set of symbols to explain its type and to indicate its sun and soil preferences—the symbols are explained in the panel opposite.

PLANTS FOR CLAY AND SILT SOILS

Many plants will grow very well in heavy clay and silt soils provided drainage is reasonable and organic matter is applied regularly to improve the heavy texture. The following are examples of those plants that grow particularly well on clay and silt soils.

SHRUBS
Sun
Rose (*Rosa* sp.) *see p. 105*
Flowering currant (*Ribes* sp.)
see p. 98
Snowberry (*Symphoricarpos* sp.)
Shade
Spotted laurel (*Aucuba japonica*)
Skimmia (*Skimmia* sp.)
Oregon grape (*Mahonia* sp.) *see p. 95*
Tolerant
Witch hazel (*Hamamelis* sp.) *see p. 94*
Honeysuckle (*Lonicera* sp.) *see p. 96*

Hazel (*Corylus* sp.) *see p. 95*
Aronia (*Aronia* sp.)

PERENNIALS
Sun
Bear's breeches (*Acanthus* sp.)
Marigold (*Tagetes* sp.)
Bugle (*Ajuga* sp.) *see p. 103*
Pearly everlasting (*Anaphalis* sp.)
see p. 109
Shade
Solomon's seal (*Polygonatum* sp.)
see p. 102
Comfrey (*Symphytum* sp.)
Brunnera (*Brunnera* sp.)
Barrenwort (*Epimedium* sp.)
Tolerant
Daylily (*Hemerocallis* sp.)
Primula (*Primula* sp.) *see p. 97*
Hellebore (*Helleborus* sp.) *see p. 95*
Hepatica (*Hepatica* sp.) *see p. 95*

CLIMBERS
Ivy (*Hedera* sp.)
Wisteria (*Wisteria* sp.)

Skimmia japonica "Rubella"

Primula (*Primula* sp.)

PLANTS FOR SANDY SOIL

A light, free-draining soil. Most plants will grow on sandy soil provided plenty of organic matter is incorporated regularly to improve water-holding capacity (*see pp. 17–19*). The following are examples of those plants that grow particularly well on sandy soil.

SHRUBS
Sun
Artemisia (*Artemisia* sp.)
Broom (*Cytisus* sp.) *see p. 103*
Cinquefoil (*Potentilla* sp.) *see p. 102*
Rock rose (*Cistus* sp.)
Shade
Shrubby germander (*Teucrium fruticans*)
Ornamental bramble (*Rubus* sp.)
Barberry (*Berberis* sp.) *see p. 98*
Tolerant
Eleagnus (*Eleagnus* sp.)
Rose of Sharon (*Hypericum* sp.)

Barberry (*Berberis* sp.) *see p. 98*
Cotoneaster (*Cotoneaster* sp.)
see p. 111

PERENNIALS
Sun
Bear's breeches (*Acanthus* sp.)
Yarrow (*Achillea* sp.)
Aubrieta (*Aubrieta* sp.) *see p. 96*
Campion (*Lychnis* sp.)
Shade
Bergenia (*Bergenia cordifolia*)
Liriope (*Liriope muscari*)
Piggyback plant (*Tolmeia menziesii*)
Cranesbill (*Geranium macrorhizum*)
Tolerant
Cranesbill (*Geranium* sp.)
Phlomis (*Phlomis* sp.)
Euphorbia (*Euphorbia* sp.)
see p. 101
Phygelius (*Phygelius* sp.) *see p. 108*

CLIMBERS
Honeysuckle (*Lonicera* sp.)
see p. 96
Rose (*Rosa* sp.) *see p. 105*

Artemisia "Powis Castle"

Campion (*Lychnis* sp.)

THE PLANT SYMBOLS

"Plant type" symbols indicate whether the plant is a tree, shrub, perennial, annual, biennial, bulb, or climbing plant.

"Sun preference" symbols indicate the amount of sun each plant prefers to receive. Many require full sun, full shade, or partial shade at all times. Others will grow in partial shade as long as they get some full sun and are given the "sun" and "partial shade" symbols. Those that grow in a range of positions are given a "tolerant" symbol.

"Soil preference" symbols indicate whether the plant prefers an acid soil or an alkaline soil. (*See also p. 35*). Some plants will tolerate a range of soil pHs and are given the "tolerant" symbol.

PLANTS FOR CHALKY SOIL

A chalky, or alkaline, soil tends to be dry because it drains quickly. It has a very high pH and many plants won't tolerate this as it leads to certain nutrient deficiencies. The following are examples of those plants that grow particularly well on chalky soil.

SHRUBS
Sun
Wintersweet (*Chimonanthus* sp.) *see p. 95*
Mock orange (*Philadelphus*) *see p. 106*
Lilac (*Syringa* sp.) *see p. 102*
Butterfly bush (*Buddleja davidii*) *see p. 108*
Shade
Periwinkle (*Vinca* sp.) *see p. 99*
Oregon grape (*Mahonia* sp.) *see p. 95*

Tolerant
Spirea (*Spiraea* sp.) *see p. 99*
Forsythia (*Forsythia* sp.) *see p. 99*
Yucca (*Yucca filamentosa*)

PERENNIALS
Sun
Peruvian lily (*Alstromeria* sp.)
Peony (*Paeonia* sp.) *see p. 102*
Dutch iris (*Iris* sp.) *see p. 106*
Anemone (*Anemone* sp.) *see p. 99*
Shade
Dicentra (*Dicentra* sp.)
Primula (*Primula* sp.) *see p. 97*
Primrose (*Primula vulgaris*)
Plantain lily (*Hosta* sp.) *see p. 110*
Tolerant
Hellebore (*Helleborus* sp.) *see p. 95*
Columbine (*Aquilegia* sp.) *see p. 100*
Cinquefoil (*Potentilla* sp.) *see p. 102*

CLIMBERS
Honeysuckle (*Lonicera* sp.) *see p. 96*
Clematis (*Clematis* sp.) *see p. 97*

Yucca (*Yucca gloriosa* "Variegata")

Cinquefoil (*Potentilla* sp.)

PLANTS FOR ACID SOILS

Most plants prefer a very slightly acid soil, although the ones listed below will not tolerate anything but an acid soil. Acid soils are often moisture-retentive, so incorporate plenty of organic matter to improve drainage. The following are examples of those plants that grow particularly well on acid soil.

SHRUBS
Sun
Broom (*Cytisus* sp.) *see p. 103*
Bearberry (*Arctostaphylos sp.*)
Rock rose (*Helianthemum* sp.)
Gorse (*Ulex* sp.)
Shade
Magnolia (*Magnolia* sp.) *see p. 101*
Rhododendron (*Rhododendron* sp.) *see p. 94*
Azalea (*Rhododendron* sp.)
Snowy mespilus (*Amelanchier* sp.)
Pieris (*Pieris* sp.) *see p. 98*

Tolerant
Witch hazel (*Hamamelis* sp.) *see p. 94*
Heather (*Erica* sp.) *see p. 95*
Dogwood (*Cornus* sp.)
Camellia (*Camellia* sp.) *see p. 97*

PERENNIALS
Sun
Carex (*Carex* sp.)
Lily (*Lilium* sp.) *see p. 107*
Lupin (*Lupinus* sp.) *see p. 106*
Allium (*Allium* sp.)
Shade
Solomon's seal (*Polygonatum* sp.) *see p. 102*
Gentian (*Gentiana* sp.) *see p. 101*
Japanese primrose (*Primula* sp.)
Tolerant
Woodrush (*Luzula maxima*)
Campion (*Lychnis* sp.)

CLIMBERS
Trumpet vine (*Campsis radicans*)
Wisteria (*Wisteria* sp.)

Heather (*Erica* sp.)

Lily (*Lilium* sp.)

Winter plants

Even in the winter the garden can be interesting.
Some bulbs and tubers flower at this time of
year and many shrubs have interesting leaves,
flowers, or catkins. Even when leafless, shrubs
with colored or twisted stems are attractive.

▼ GARDEN PANSY
Viola wittrockiana

Much valued for its long
flowering period. Some hybrids
flower all summer, others bloom
intermittently during the winter.
See Perennials, *p. 115.*

▼ CHINESE WITCH HAZEL
Hamamelis mollis
"Goldcrest"

This shrub bears
scented flowers.
Height 8–10ft
(2.5–3m). *See*
Shrubs, *p. 112.*

SKIMMIA ▶
Skimmia japonica
"Rubella"

A small shrub with
evergreen leaves and
red buds. Height
3–5ft (1.1–5m). *See*
Shrubs *p. 112.*

▼ RHODODENDRON
Rhododendron "Praecox"

One of the many hybrids
available in a wide range
of flower colors and sizes.
Height 3–5ft (1–1.5m).
See Shrubs, *p. 112.*

▼ IRIS
Iris reticulata

One of the best
known early
flowering irises.
Plant 2–3in
(5–7cm) deep
in well-drained
soil. *See* Bulbs,
p. 117.

▼ CYCLAMEN
Cyclamen coum

An attractive hardy
species. They dislike
exposed situations.
See Bulbs, *p. 117.*

◀ WILLOW
Salix sachalinensis
"Sekka"

One of the many attractive
willows with winter appeal.
The chestnut-brown shoots
are covered in furry buds
in winter. Height 15–20ft
(4.5–6m). *See* Shrubs, *p. 112.*

◀ **MAHONIA**
Mahonia "Charity"

This shrub has very fragrant yellow flowers. Height 6–10ft (1.8–3m). *See* Shrubs, *p. 112.*

Plant type
Tree · Shrub · Perennial · Annual · Biennial · Bulb · Climbing plants

Sun preference
Sun · Partial shade · Shade · Tolerant

Soil preference
Acid · Alkaline · Tolerant

HELLEBORE ▼
Helleborus corsicus

A sprawling plant that can look untidy unless staked. Like all hellebores they prefer deep, well-drained soil. *See* Perennials, *p. 115.*

◀ **MEZEREON**
Daphne mezereum

A small shrub with fragrant, pink, purple, or white flowers. Height 5ft (1.5m). *See* Shrubs, *p. 112.*

WINTERSWEET ▶
Chimonanthus praecox

The flowers have a superb perfume. The plant is best grown against a south- or west-facing wall. Height 8–10ft (2.5–3m). *See* Shrubs, *p. 112.*

▼ **SNOWDROP**
Galanthus nivalis

One of the earliest winter flowers. *See* Bulbs, *p. 117.*

▼ **CORKSCREW HAZEL**
Corylus avellana "Contorta"

A curiously contorted form of the common hazel. Height 8–10ft (2.5–3m). *See* Shrubs, *p. 112.*

▼ **HEPATICA**
Hepatica nobilis

There are several named varieties in shades of blue, white, red, or purple. *See* Perennials, *p. 115.*

▼ **CHRISTMAS ROSE**
Helleborus niger

These attractive perennials take some time to build up large clumps but are worth the wait. *See* Perennials, *p. 115.*

▼ **HEATHER**
Erica darleyensis

This is one of the many varieties of heathers, available in several colors from white through pink and red to deep purple. *See* Shrubs, *p. 112.*

Early spring plants

This is a selection of plants that are at their best in early spring. Some, such as the almond and the camellia, have been chosen because they have spectacular blooms at this time of year; others, for example, photinia, because they have particularly attractive new growth. Combined in the same border, these plants make a very impressive early spring display.

▼ CROWN IMPERIAL
Fritillaria imperialis

A majestic bulb that flowers freely on most soils. Available in red and yellow. *See* Bulbs, *p. 117.*

▶ FLOWERING ALMOND
Prunus triloba

A pink-blossomed shrub which reaches a height and spread of 10–14ft (3–4.5m). *See* Shrubs, *p. 112.*

◀ HONEYSUCKLE
Lonicera japonica "Aureoreticulata"

A rampant evergreen climber. The leaves are bright green with conspicuous golden veining. Height up to 30ft (10m). *See* Climbing plants, *p. 119.*

HYACINTH ▼
Hyacinthus hybrid

One of the many hybrids in a range of colors, with an intense fragrance. It grows in most soils but likes a sunny location. *See* Bulbs, *p. 117.*

▼ AUBRIETA
Aubrieta deltoidea

An easy-to-grow small plant for border edges, walls, or rock gardens. There are several varieties in shades of purple and pink. *See* Perennials, *p. 115.*

RED ROBIN
...otinia fraseri

...is evergreen shrub is
...own for its brilliant-red
...ung growth. Height up
...6–10ft (2–3m), spread
...6ft (1.5–2m). *See*
...rubs, *p. 112.*

◄ **CAMELLIA**
Camellia japonica

An exotic-looking but hardy
shrub, available in a range
of colors. Height up to 6ft
(1.8m), spread 11ft (3.5m)
See Shrubs, *p. 112.*

CLEMATIS ►
Clematis macropetala

This plant grows in full
sun or part shade and
will climb up a trellis
or over shrubs. Height
up to 11ft (3.5m). *See*
Climbing plants, *p. 119.*

◄ **DAFFODIL**
Narcissus sp.

These bulbs grow
in any type of
fertile soil. *See*
Bulbs, *p. 117.*

◄ **PRIMROSE**
Primula hybrid

A hybrid of the wild *Primula
vulgaris.* Primroses are
available in many colors. *See*
Perennials, *p. 115.*

Mid-spring plants

As the season begins to warm up, the variety of ornamental plants in flower in the garden begins to change. By mid-spring the tulips, in all their various colors and shapes, have flowered. Shrubs like forsythia will be covered in golden-yellow flowers and fresh green leaves will begin to appear. The colorful foliage of the barberry is welcome at this time of year too.

FLOWERING CURRANT ▶

Ribes sanguineum

This relative of the black currant bears bunches of tiny red or pink flowers. The berries produced are not edible. Height up to 8ft (2.4m), spread 5ft (1.5m). *See* Shrubs *p. 112.*

BARBERRY ▶

Berberis thunbergii "Atropurpurea Nana"

This shrub has deep-red foliage. Height up to 3ft (1m), spread 2ft (60cm). *See* Shrubs, *p. 112.*

▼ TULIP *Tulipa greigii* "Good Luck"

There are many species and hybrids of tulips that extend the flowering period for several weeks. A few have attractively marked foliage. *See* Bulbs, *p. 117.*

▼ ROCK CRESS

Arabis ferdinandi-coburgi

This plant forms mats of green leave They do best on well-drained soil. *S* Perennials, *p. 115.*

PIERIS ▶

Pieris formosa "Forest Flame"

The foliage of this evergreen is red when it is young, turning pink, through yellow to deep green as it matures. Height and spread up to 10ft (3m). *See* Shrubs, *p. 112.*

Plant type							Sun preference				Soil preference		
Tree	Shrub	Perennial	Annual	Biennial	Bulb	Climbing plants	Sun	Partial shade	Shade	Tolerant	Acid	Alkaline	Tolerant

▼ **FORSYTHIA**
Forsythia intermedia
"Lynwood"

One of the most popular spring-flowering shrubs, the forsythia bears bright yellow flowers that appear before the leaves. Height and spread up to 8ft (2.4m). *See* Shrubs, *p. 112.*

SPIREA ▶
Spiraea bumalda
"Goldflame"

A small shrub grown for its spring foliage. Red flowers appear in summer. Height up to 2ft 6in (75cm). *See* Shrubs, *p. 112.*

Spirea

WALLFLOWER ▶
Cheiranthus cheiri

Very popular bedding plants, wallflowers are easily grown from seed. *See* Biennials, *p. 117.*

▼ **PERIWINKLE**
Vinca minor

A rapidly spreading plant used extensively for ground cover but can become invasive. Height up to 12in (30cm), spread, unlimited. *See* Perennials, *p. 115.*

▼ **WINDFLOWER**
Anemone blanda

A colorful plant for the spring rock garden. *See* Bulbs, *p. 117.*

DRUMSTICK PRIMROSE ▶
Primula denticulata

The flowers may be blue, white, crimson, or lilac. *See* Perennials, *p. 115.*

THE ORNAMENTAL GARDEN

Late spring plants

As the season progresses, a whole new range of plants comes into flower. Trees have attractive late-spring foliage too—for example, the maple has pale orange leaves at this time of year. Combined together, this range of plants can make an interesting border.

BARBERRY ▶
Berberis stenophylla

This evergreen shrub becomes covered in small yellow flowers in spring. Plant it in well-drained soil. *See* Shrubs, *p. 112.*

▼ MAPLE
Acer pseudoplatanus "Brilliantissimum"

Avoid planting in a windy site since exposed conditions will damage the foliage. *See* Trees, *p. 81.*

CHERRY PLUM ▶
Prunus cerasifera "Nigra"

This small tree is a prolific flowerer. *See* Trees, *p. 81.*

▲ SPIREA
Spiraea sp.

A useful, informal hedging shrub. *See* Shrubs, *p. 112.*

SYMPHYANDRA ▼
Symphyandra wanneri

An uncommon plant closely related to the bellflowers (*Campanula* sp.). *See* Perennials, *p. 115.*

▼ FORGET-ME-NOT
Myosotis alpestris

A good plant for edging borders. *See* Biennials, *p. 117.*

COLUMBINE ▶
Aquilegia vulgaris

The flowers have distinctive spurred petals. *See* Perennials, *p. 115.*

▼ ALYSSUM
Lobularia "Maritima"

A popular plant for rock gardens or walls. *See* Annuals, *p. 116.*

MAGNOLIA ▶

Magnolia soulangiana

Plant spring-flowering magnolias in a sheltered spot as their blooms can be blemished by frost. Height up to 20ft (6m), spread 15ft (4.5m). *See* Shrubs, *p. 112.*

Plant type Tree Shrub Perennial Annual Biennial Bulb Climbing plants **Sun preference** Sun Partial shade Shade Tolerant **Soil preference** Acid Alkaline Tolerant

DWARF RUSSIAN ALMOND ▶

Prunus tenella "Fire Hill"

A small shrub that is covered with flowers every spring. *See* Shrubs, *p. 112.*

▼ COWSLIP

Primula veris

A native British wildflower, the cowslip can easily be grown in the garden. *See* Perennials, *p. 115.*

▲ FLOWERING CHERRY

Prunus "Kanzan"

Do not plant too deeply as they are shallow rooting. Height up to 30ft (10m), spread 15ft (4.5m). *See* Trees, *p. 81.*

◀ RHODODENDRON

Rhododendron "Elizabeth"

Grow in a raised bed if your soil is alkaline. *See* Shrubs, *p. 112.*

◀ GRAPE HYACINTH

Muscari armeniacum

An ideal edging for a border. They should be grown in well-drained soil. *See* Bulbs, *p. 117.*

◀ EUPHORBIA

Euphorbia polychroma

An attractive, dome-shaped bush. *See* Perennials, *p. 115.*

Early summer plants

Summer is the most abundant time of year in the ornamental garden. The range of colors, shapes, and fragrances of both flowers and foliage available in this season is immense. On the following pages, the summer plants are subdivided by flowering period, although actual flowering times may vary with your location and the position of the plant in the garden.

LILAC ▶
Syringa vulgaris

Once established, lilac bushes require very little care. *See* Shrubs, *p. 112.*

HEBE ▲
Hebe pinguifolia "Pagei"

Height up to 9in (20cm), spread 3ft (1m).*See* Shrubs, *p. 112.*

◀ **CINQUEFOIL**
Potentilla fruticosa

These compact shrubs have butter-yellow flowers. Height and spread up to 5ft (1.5m). *See* Shrubs, *p. 112.*

FUCHSIA ▶
Fuchsia "Peggy King"

The many hybrids of this plant produce a striking display of flowers all summer. Height and spread up to 18in (45cm). *See* Shrubs, *p. 112.*

◀ **SOLOMON'S SEAL**
Polygonatum hybridum

The roots of this plant should always be shaded. *See* Perennials, *p. 115.*

◀ **PEONY**
Paeonia officinalis "Alba Plena"

Prepare the soil well before planting peonies. They dislike root disturbance. *See* Perennials, *p. 115.*

CATMINT ▶
Nepeta faassenii

An excellent ground cover plant. *See* Perennials, *p. 115.*

▼ **WARMINSTER BROOM**
Cytisus praecox

The green stems become covered with a mass of creamy-yellow flowers in early summer. Height and spread up to 6ft (2m). *See* Shrubs, *p. 112.*

Plant type							Sun preference				Soil preference		
Tree	Shrub	Perennial	Annual	Biennial	Bulb	Climbing plants	Sun	Partial shade	Shade	Tolerant	Acid	Alkaline	Tolerant

◀ **ROSEMARY**
Rosemarinus officinalis

This attractive shrub is widely grown as an herb. They thrive in well-drained soil. Height and spread up to 6ft (2m). *See* Shrubs, *p. 112.*

KNOTWEED ▶
Polygonum
"Donald Lowndes"

A good ground-cover plant as it spreads rapidly. *See* Perennials, *p. 115.*

CLEMATIS ▶
Clematis montana "Rubens"

A popular climbing plant. They require full sun but roots should be shaded by a bush. Height up to 40ft (12m), spread 20ft (6m). *See* Climbing plants, *p. 119.*

◀ **MASTERWORT**
Astrantia major
"Rubra"

The flowers of astrantias have an interesting and attractive shape. They spread by underground runners. *See* Perennials, *p. 115.*

◀ **BUGLE**
Ajuga reptans
"Burgundy Glow"

A useful ground-cover plant. They require a moist soil. *See* Perennials, *p. 115.*

◀ **LILY-OF-THE-VALLEY**
Convallaria majalis

These plants have very fragrant flowers and should be grown in a cool, shady spot. *See* Perennials, *p. 115.*

Midsummer plants

The borders will be a blaze of color at this time of year. The following four pages show just a selection of the large variety of plants which will not only look attractive in the borders but will also encourage the diversity of wildlife necessary in the organic garden.

▼ **BITTERSWEET**
Solanum dulcamara
"Variegata"

Not for gardens where children play as the berries are poisonous. *See* Climbers, *p. 119.*

FOXGLOVE ▶
Digitalis purpurea

Normally grown as a biennial but can be left in year after year in peaty soil. *See* Biennials and Perennials, *pp. 115 and 117.*

▼ **POTENTILLA**
Potentilla fruticosa

A small, compact shrub that will flower throughout summer. Height and spread up to 5ft (1.5m). *See* Shrubs, *p. 112.*

◀ **YARROW**
Achillea filipendulina
"Cloth of Gold"

Grow yarrow in well-drained soils. It grows particularly well in chalky soil. *See* Perennials, *p. 115.*

▼ **FREESIA**
Freesia kewensis

The flowers are available in a wide range of colors. *See* Bulbs, *p. 117.*

▼ **BELLFLOWER**
Campanula glomerata
"Superba"

If grown in fertile, well-drained soil, these perennials will spread quickly. They can become invasive. *See* Perennials, *p. 115.*

▼ **DAHLIA**
Dahlia "Coltness"

Small bedding dahlias are raised annually from seed. The flowers attract hoverflies. *See* Annuals, *p. 116.*

Plant type Tree Shrub Perennial Annual Biennial Bulb Climbing plants **Sun preference** Sun Partial shade Shade Tolerant **Soil preference** Acid Alkaline Tolerant

◀ **DELPHINIUM**
Delphinium
"Dreaming Spires"

The tall flower spikes need to be staked for support. *See* Perennials, *p. 115.*

▼ **ROSE**
Rosa "King's Ransom"

The modern hybrid roses are easy to cultivate and very soil tolerant. *See* Roses *p. 114.*

ESCALLONIA ▶
Escallonia
"Slieve Donard"

Compact evergreen shrubs that make good informal hedges. Height up to 8ft (2.5m). *See* Shrubs, *p. 112.*

◀ **PLANTAIN LILY**
Hosta
"Thomas Hogg"

If grown on rich, damp soil, the foliage will form large, dense clumps. *See* Perennials, *p. 115.*

▼ **DIASCIA**
Diascia barberae

Remove dead flower heads regularly to encourage more flowers. *See* Annuals, *p. 116.*

▼ **TUBEROUS BEGONIA**
Begonia tuberosa

Store the tubers in peat over the winter. *See* Bulbs, *p. 117.*

LUPIN ▼

Lupinus "New Generation"

There are many varieties of lupin, some of which have two-color flowers. They all have deeply divided, dark green leaves and are easily raised from seed sown outside in spring. *See* Perennials, *p. 115.*

RUGOSA ROSE ▼

Rosa rugosa "Blanc Double de Coubert"

Rugosa roses can be grown as hedging plants, forming a dense, wind-resistant barrier, or as specimen shrubs. Height up to 6ft (2m). *See* Shrubs, *p. 112.*

MOCK ORANGE ▶

Philadelphus "Virginal"

Probably the best of the double-flowered *Philadelphus*, they have a strong fragrance resembling that of orange blossom. The soil must be well drained. Height and sprea up to 10ft (3m). *See* Shrubs, *p. 112*

PINK ▼

Dianthus allwoodii

The modern pinks have a long flowering period, but should be propagated at least every three years to maintain the number of flowers. *See* Perennials, *p. 115.*

ALPINE POPPY ▼

Papaver alpinum

Grow these poppies in rock gardens, between paving slabs, or wherever the drainage is good. *See* Perennials, *p. 115.*

▼ DUTCH IRIS

Iris "Xiphium" hybrids

These elegant-looking flowers are available in many different colors. *See* Bulbs, *p. 117.*

FRENCH MARIGOLD ▼

Tagetes patula "Royal Crested"

The brightly colored, open flowers attract hoverflies. *See* Annuals, *p. 116.*

Plant type
Tree | Shrub | Perennial | Annual | Biennial | Bulb | Climbing plants
Sun preference
Sun | Partial shade | Shade | Tolerant
Soil preference
Acid | Alkaline | Tolerant

SWEET ROCKET ▶

Hesperis matronalis

Although a perennial, it
is best to raise new plants
from seed every few years.
See Perennials, *p. 115.*

◀ BEAUTY BUSH

Kolkwitzia amabilis

Blooms beginning
in midspring. *See*
Shrubs, *p. 112.*

LILY ▼

Lilium "Pandora"

Lilies are easy to grow in
a sheltered, well-drained
site. *See* Bulbs, *p. 117.*

LADY'S MANTLE ▼

Alchemilla mollis

Remove the seedheads after
flowering or they will
become invasive. *See*
Perennials, *p. 115.*

CAMPION ▼

Lychnis flos-jovis

These are easy to raise
from seed and will grow
in almost any soil. *See*
Perennials, *p. 115.*

PETUNIA ▼

Petunia hybrida
"Peppermint Daddy"

Grow them in borders or hanging
baskets. *See* Annuals, *p. 116.*

THE ORNAMENTAL GARDEN

Late summer plants

As summer draws to a close, the "cottage garden" borders will continue to provide food for insects and birds. This is one of the best seasons for flowers and fruits, and the wildlife activity in your garden is likely to increase at this time of year.

PHLOX ▷

Phlox paniculata "Eva Cullum"

This tall perennial responds well to mulching with organic matter. *See* Perennials, *p. 115.*

PHYGELIUS ▽

Phygelius aequalis

This plant is not truly hardy and should be grown against a wall for protection. *See* Shrubs, *p. 112.*

BUTTERFLY BUSH ▷

Buddleja davidii "Royal Purple"

The flowers attract many butterflies. *See* Shrubs, *p. 112.*

GENTIAN ▽

Gentiana septemfida

One of the easiest gentians to cultivate. They can be raised from seed. *See* Perennials, *p. 115.*

◁ HAREBELL

Campanula rotundifolia

Naturalize this graceful perennial in large clumps. *See* Perennials, *p. 115.*

◁ TICKSEED

Coreopsis verticillata "Grandiflora"

Easy to raise from seed sown outside. *See* Perennials, *p. 115.*

Plant type — Tree, Shrub, Perennial, Annual, Biennial, Bulb, Climbing plants   **Sun preference** — Sun, Partial shade, Shade, Tolerant   **Soil preference** — Acid, Alkaline, Tolerant

◄ **PASSION FLOWER**

Passiflora caerulea

A very vigorous climber
that should be grown
on a warm south-facing
wall against a trellis or
wires. *See* Climbers, *p. 119.*

AFRICAN LILY ▼

Agapanthus "Bressingham Blue"

In temperate areas these plants should
be grown in a sheltered, sunny position.
See Perennials, *p. 115.*

PURPLE LOOSESTRIFE ▼

Lythrum salicaria "Robert"

An ideal plant for growing
in a damp area in the garden
as it requires moist soil
and partial shade. *See*
Perennials, *p. 115.*

◄ **GLADIOLUS**

Gladiolus "Peter Pears"

The flowers bloom
on tall spikes.
These arise from
underground corms.
See Bulbs, *p. 117.*

**PEARLY
EVERLASTING** ▼

Anaphalis triplinervis

Unlike other gray-leaved
plants, this perennial
will not tolerate drought.
See Perennials, *p. 115.*

Fall plants

At this time of year the borders are an interesting mixture of flower and foliage color. Fall-flowering bulbs are available and can add color to the rock garden and borders. Many of the plants, like the species roses and the cotoneasters, produce colorful hips and berries to brighten borders in the fall.

CARYOPTERIS ▶
Caryopteris clandonensis "Heavenly Blue"

This erect, compact shrub is native to the US and is one of the best deep blues available. *See* Shrubs, *p. 112.*

MEADOW RUE ▼
Thalictrum dipterocarpum

These plants should be staked if grown in an exposed site as they can grow as tall as 6ft (2m) high. *See* Perennials, *p. 11*

SMOKE TREE ▶
Cotinus coggygria "Flame"

The purple foliage of this shrub turns a bright orange-red in fall. *See* Shrubs, *p. 112.*

◀ PLANTAIN LILY
Hosta fortunei "Aureomarginata"

The large, ribbed leaves are edged in pale yellow. They are good ground cover plants and can be left undisturbed for many years. *See* Perennials, *p. 115.*

HYDRANGEA ▼
Hydrangea "Sybille"

Plant in a sheltered position to protect from frost. *See* Shrubs, *p. 112.*

▼ AUTUMN CROCUS
Colchicum byzantinum

They can be naturalized in grass or the borders. *See* Bulbs, *p. 117.*

CROCUS ▶
Crocus scharojanii

Plant them beneath trees or near shrubs where they are less likely to be disturbed by digging. *See* Bulbs, *p. 117.*

Plant type							Sun preference				Soil preference		
Tree	Shrub	Perennial	Annual	Biennial	Bulb	Climbing plants	Sun	Partial shade	Shade	Tolerant	Acid	Alkaline	Tolerant
⊛	⊛	⊛	⊛	⊛	⊛	⊛	○	◐	⦿	⦿	⊖	⊕	±

◀ **ROSE**
Rosa moyesii "Geranium"
These roses have geranium-red flowers in summer and bright orange hips in fall. *See* Shrubs, *p. 112.*

◀ **COTONEASTER**
Cotoneaster conspicuus "Decorus"
Cotoneasters are easy to grow and an excellent source of food for birds. This one is useful for covering banks and as ground cover. Spread up to 3ft (1m). *See* Shrubs, *p. 112.*

TIENTURIER GRAPE ▶
Vitis vinifera "Purpurea"
When they first appear, the leaves are claret-red, gradually deepening to a dark purple color. Height up to 20 ft (6m). *See* Climbers, *p. 119.*

ICE PLANT ▼
Sedum spectabile "Brilliant"
The flat heads of tiny pink flowers attract many butterflies. *See* Perennials, *p. 115.*

MICHAELMAS DAISY ▼
Aster sp.
Asters are easy to grow if the soil is kept moist during the flowering period. Some varieties are prone to mildew. *See* Perennials, *p. 115.*

GOOD-LUCK PLANT ▼
Oxalis deppei
Low-growing plants forming dense mats. The leaves and flowers close at night. *See* Bulbs, *p. 117.*

◀ **STERNBERGIA**
Sternbergia clusiana
The bulbs can be planted in drifts which can be left undisturbed for many years. *See* Bulbs, *p. 117.*

Cultivation of border plants

The following pages give the cultivation details of the many different groups of ornamental plants that can be included in the border. You will find advice on choosing and buying, and on the method of planting each type of plant. A section on maintenance gives general information on taking care of the plants once they have been planted.

Shrubs

These form the framework of any border as well as attracting birds, butterflies, and other insects. Some plants, like the beautiful butterfly bush (*Buddleja davidii*), prove irresistible to butterflies, which cluster round every nectar-filled bloom in the summer.

Birds make use of shrubs for cover and food too. They particularly appreciate the berried shrubs like the snowberry (*Symphoricarpos doorenbosii*)—a favorite because of its white berries and the dense cover it provides. Try to include a few native plants in the your plan because these are what will be most appreciated by the wildlife.

CHOOSING SHRUBS

When choosing shrubs, think into the future at least 10 years, to the time when the shrubs have grown to their maximum height and spread. After checking height and spread, think about a color scheme, not forgetting to take into account the flowering season of the shrub and any others near it. It is also important to check preferences for shade or sunshine, soil type, and acidity tolerance (*see pp. 92–93*) before making your final selection. Remember that you can fill the spaces between small, young shrubs with annuals or other plants that have a shorter life.

BUYING SHRUBS

Like hedges, shrubs for borders can be bought as bare root or container-grown plants. Container-grown plants tend to be smaller and more expensive—their advantage is that they can be planted at any time of the year instead of having to wait for the dormant season like you would with a bare root plant.

Check all shrubs for signs of pests or disease (*see p. 44*) and make sure they have a healthy root system.

PLANTING A SHRUB

Although shrubs can be planted at any time of the year from containers, there is, in my view, an advantage in buying field-grown, bare root plants from a traditional nursery and planting during the fall or early winter. A container-grown plant is more likely to suffer from the root ball drying out, so even if you do buy a plant in a container, it is still safer to wait until the fall when the plant will not be losing so much water and the soil is more likely to remain moist.

If you plant shrubs (or trees) in an exposed spot, they dehydrate very quickly—this is especially so with conifers and other evergreens. Strong winds evaporate water from the leaf surfaces faster than the unestablished roots can absorb it again, so cells dry out and die. In a windy spot, it is essential, therefore, to protect newly planted specimens with a windbreak until they are established and their roots have had a chance to spread out.

1 Dig a hole large enough for the roots or root ball. Mix the dug out soil with a bucketful of organic matter.

2 Water the plant well and remove the plastic container by cutting it off, being careful not to damage the roots with the knife.

3 Plant at the level of the old soil mark on the stem. Sprinkle a little fine soil over the roots. Refill the hole and press the soil down.

4 Mulch around the shrub with a layer of organic matter to conserve moisture and inhibit weed growth.

MAINTAINING SHRUBS

Feeding If you can provide shrubs with an annual mulch of well-rotted manure or compost, they will require little more. If not, give the whole border a dressing of blood, fish, and bone meal in early spring, and a dressing of kelp meal once every three years.

Watering Always pay particular attention to watering, especially in the first year while the shrubs are becoming established. This is particularly important with container-grown plants.

Pruning For many shrubs this should be carried out regularly. All shrubs can be shaped and, to some extent, kept smaller by regular cutting back, and many are pruned annually to produce flowering stems. Shrubs, such as the forsythia and the flowering currant (*Ribes* sp.), should be cut back hard immediately after flowering to encourage the bush to produce long shoots. The longer the shoots, the more flowers they are able to carry. Others like heathers (*Erica*) and lavender (*Lavandula*) are trimmed with shears after flowering in order to keep them compact and prevent them dying out in the center. Plants like broom (*Cytisus* hybrids) are pruned after flowering to prevent them from producing seed.

Some shrubs, like the butterfly bush (*Buddleja davidii*), flower on wood made during the same season. These make long growths from buds that have been resting over the winter, and they flower late in the summer. To increase the size of the blooms, all shoots made the previous year should be cut back hard in early spring.

Removing flower heads It is an advantage to remove the dead flower heads from many shrubs to increase the flower yield the following year. This is known as "deadheading." Plants like the heathers can be trimmed with shears immediately after flowering. Other shrubs like rhododendrons, have to be deadheaded by hand (*see below left*).

Winter care If you plant in the fall, winter frosts can lift the plants out of the ground again, so check them at regular intervals and, if they have been lifted, press them back in.

Pests and diseases Pests like greenfly and diseases such as leaf spot attack a wide variety of shrubs, so check plants regularly and treat as necessary (*see pp. 49–53*).

TEMPORARY PLANTING

If plants arrive when the weather is cold and the ground is frozen or if the soil is waterlogged, planting cannot go ahead. If you cannot plant immediately, it is wise to set the plants in a temporary trench, a technique known as "heeling in." Shrubs can be heeled in for several weeks and lifted and planted in the normal way when favorable conditions return.

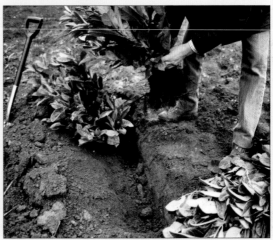

1 *Cut a shallow, V-shaped slit trench—building the soil up on the back wall. Lay the shrubs in a single row in the trench, at an angle of 45°, so that their roots are in the trench and their tops resting on the soil you have built up. This will ensure that they do not blow around, causing root damage.*

2 *Cover the roots and lower stem with soil or peat and firm down with your boot. Cover with soil dug out of a second trench if you have a lot of shrubs to heel in.*

Removing flower heads from rhododendrons *Remove the dead flowers very carefully as next year's buds are immediately beneath and could come off with the old bloom. Pinch off the flowers between finger and thumb. This tidies up the plant and promotes more flowers for the following year.*

Roses

There are many types of roses and their classification can be confusing. Species roses are the original ancestors of modern, hybrid roses and should be grown in the same way as other shrubs. The modern, hybrid roses can be grown as bushes or standards—standard roses are simply bush roses budded on to a long stem to make a short tree. Many varieties of climbing and rambling roses are also available.

CHOOSING ROSES

With the wide variety of shapes and colors available, choosing roses can be difficult. In my view, bush standards are too formal for mixed borders in very small gardens, though "weeping standards" fit into a mixed border quite well—these are rambler roses on a long stem, with their branches allowed to hang down instead of being trained upward.

BUYING ROSES

Roses can be bought bare root in the winter or container grown at any time of the year. Check all plants for signs of mildew and black spot (*see p. 52*) before buying them.

PLANTING ROSES

Unlike other shrubs, bush roses should be planted a little lower than they were grown at the nursery in order to encourage the growth of new shoots from below ground. About 1in (2.5cm) deeper is generally sufficient, but make sure that the point at which the variety is budded onto the rootstock is below ground. If you are planting roses in the fall, they should be pruned back hard immediately after planting (*see below*).

MAINTAINING ROSES

Feeding Feed like other shrubs, mulching annually with well-rotted manure or compost.

Watering Water well in the first year after planting. In subsequent years ensure the roots do not dry out in warm weather.

Pruning This is carried out every year on hybrid bush roses in early spring, just before the bushes start into their growth stage, as you will be able to assess the amount of frost damage and cut it out. The principle of pruning is that the harder you cut back, the stronger the branch will grow. So get into the habit of always cutting back weak branches further than the stronger-growing ones to balance the bush. Weak branches should be pruned to leave one or two buds while stronger ones can have three or four. Bush standards are pruned just like the ordinary bush hybrids, while weeping standards are pruned after flowering, merely removing very old, diseased, or overcrowded wood.

Suckers Rose varieties are usually grown by being grafted onto a rootstock. Occasionally the rootstock will send out a vigorous shoot, known as a sucker, which has no ornamental merit. These are easy to spot as they are light green and are usually covered with more thorns than the variety. If allowed to develop, suckers will sap the energy of the variety so they must be removed (*see below*).

Removing flower heads Removing the flowers of continuous-flowering varieties as they fade will ensure a supply of blooms all the way through summer and fall and often into early winter too.

Pests and diseases Check all roses regularly for signs of pest or disease attack, particularly of mildew, black spot, or greenfly (*see pp. 50 and 52 for treatment*).

Pruning rose bushes *Cut all the shoots back to an outward- or downward-facing bud to encourage them to grow outward, away from the center of the bush.*

Removing a rose sucker *Scrape away a little soil where the sucker arises from the root, and pull it off if you can. If not, cut it as near to the stem as possible.*

Deadheading a rose *Remove the fading flower by breaking the stem about ½in (1cm) below the seedhead with your thumb and forefinger.*

Perennials

These can be defined as plants with soft stems that generally die down every winter and produce new growth in the spring, lasting for many years. Since perennials number in the hundreds, there is a good selection for every soil type and sun preference (*see pp. 92–93*).

CHOOSING PERENNIALS

Confusingly sold as "herbaceous perennials," "herbaceous plants," "hardy plants," "hardy perennials," and "hardy herbaceous perennials," they are all the same thing. Half-hardy perennials are merely perennials that need to spend the winter indoors.

BUYING PERENNIALS

Most perennials can be raised from seed or propagated by division (*see p. 274*) of an existing clump. They can be bought all year-round as container-grown plants or bare root in the spring and the fall.

The plants you choose will be governed by the soil type and aspect of your border, but try to include as varied a selection as possible.

PLANTING PERENNIALS

Unlike shrubs, I prefer to plant perennials in the spring, just as new growth is starting. Planted in the fall, they may suffer from cold, frozen soil, or from waterlogging, which can rot the soft parts of the plant. In spring they will start to grow and make roots right away and, provided you water them regularly, they will flourish. If you have a large area to fill, you can plant in groups of three to five to create blocks of color.

MAINTAINING PERENNIALS

Feeding General border feeding should be sufficient to maintain perennials (*see p. 90*).
Watering Perennials should be well watered when they are planted—deep soaking is the best method (*see above right*). Afterward they need to be watered as necessary (*see p. 266*).
Supporting Many perennials require staking because their stems are often weak and floppy. Others grow tall and are likely to be bent and broken in high winds. Tall perennials, such as delphiniums, should be staked fairly early in the season, using a bamboo cane and tying the stems to the stake as they grow longer. Medium-sized perennials like hellebores can be held erect with a few twigs or sticks that also look less obtrusive than stakes. Some shorter perennials like oriental poppies (*Papaver orientale*) need staking to stop them from flopping, so use a special wire support or put a piece of wide-mesh wire netting over the young plants and allow them to grow up through it. The mesh will soon be hidden by a mass of new leaves.

PLANTING PERENNIALS

When planting container-grown perennials, it is important to ensure that the root ball does not dry out. Deep soaking ensures that the plants get enough water when first planted.

1 *Remove the plant from its pot and dig a hole large enough to accommodate the root ball. Sprinkle a handful of a general fertilizer, such as blood, fish, and bone meal, around the rim.*

2 *Once the plant is in the prepared hole, gently press the soil down. Give the plant enough water so a puddle forms on the soil surface.*

Propagation Most perennials should be divided and replanted every few years. Otherwise, they form large clumps that simply get tired. The young plants thrive on the outside of the clump, but the center often becomees bare or dies out altogether. To rejuvenate the clump, dig and divide the whole plant every three to five years (*see p. 274*).

Half-hardy perennials can be propagated by taking cuttings in late summer or early spring.
Pests and diseases Some perennials—for example, Michaelmas daisies (*Aster novi-belgii*),

Staking a delphinium *Stick an 8ft (2.5m) bamboo cane into the ground next to the plant and tie the stem with soft string. Add further ties as the plant grows.*

delphiniums, and poppies (*Papaver*), are susceptible to mildew in dry conditions. Pull out any affected plants and increase watering around the others, particularly if the weather is very dry (*see p. 266*). Always throw diseased plants away; never compost them.

Annuals

These are defined as plants that grow from seed, flower, and die in the same year. Though annuals need to be replaced each year, they provide a very bright display of color through the whole summer and can be very useful for covering soil and providing flowers in a new bed until you have planned your planting. They also attract many beneficial insects into the garden, including bees for pollination (*see p. 203*) and hoverflies for the natural control of greenfly and other aphids (*see p. 50*).

CHOOSING ANNUALS

There are so many different varieties of annuals that it is often difficult to choose which ones to grow. Annuals are divided into those that are able to stand a certain amount of frost and those that are not. They are known as "hardy" and "half-hardy" annuals respectively.

Annuals range from the sprawling sweet pea (*Lathyrus odorata*) and the carpeting alyssum (*Lobularia* "Maritima") to the taller cornflower (*Centaurea*) and love-in-a-mist (*Nigella*).

BUYING ANNUALS

Annuals can be raised from seed or bought in trays as bedding plants, ready to plant out in the garden. Avoid all plants with diseased or blemished leaves. Check that the annuals you choose are suitable for the soil type and amount of sun that your border receives (*see pp. 92–93*).

PLANTING ANNUALS

Preferably the soil for sowing or planting any kind of annual should not be too rich. In poor soil, they

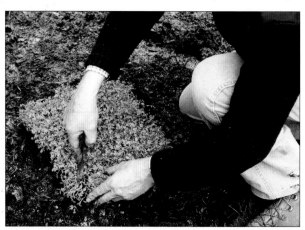

Planting hardy annuals *Sow the seeds fairly thickly in a seed tray in early spring. When the seedlings are 1in (2.5cm) or so tall, take the block out of the tray and cut into small squares with a penknife. Plant the clumps.*

will make more flower and less leaf growth. Of course, in the small garden border where all the plants are mixed together, it is best to fertilize for the shrubs and perennials and let the annuals take their chances.

Growing hardy annuals These are the easiest annuals to grow and can be raised from seed sown in open ground in the spring, as soon as the soil is dry and warm enough. There is little point in sowing until the soil temperature has reached 45°F (7°C).

Mark out the area you wish to sow and sow seeds into shallow seed rows 6in (15cm) apart. When the seedlings are large enough to handle, carefully thin out to about 6–9in (15–20cm) apart, depending on the variety. Alternatively, sow seeds in a seed tray. Allow them to grow without thinning out and plant them in clumps when they are tall enough (*see below*). This is also a much better method if your soil is heavy and stays wet in the early spring.

Growing half-hardy annuals These are much more difficult to grow than hardy annuals, but are generally worth the extra effort. They must be sown either in a heated greenhouse (*see p. 249*), or they can be germinated in a heated propagator in the greenhouse or on the kitchen windowsill. Most require a temperature of about 65°F (18°C).

As soon as they germinate, bring them into the light and grow them until they can be handled without danger of damaging the delicate stems. Transfer them to another seed tray with wider spacing and grow them until all danger of frost has passed for the year, then plant them out in the garden. Before planting, ensure that they are "hardened off," or acclimated to the lower temperatures outside, by putting them first into a closed cold frame (*see p. 254*), then increasing the ventilation gradually over a week or so.

When you are certain that frost will not recur, plant them out in soil that has been prepared with manure or compost. Don't add fertilizer or you will encourage too much leaf growth at the expense of flowers. If frost is threatened after planting, cover the plants with a plastic cloche until warmer weather arrives.

MAINTAINING ANNUALS

Feeding Do not fertilize annuals unless they have stopped growing completely since this encourages them to grow leaves at the expense of the flowers.

Watering Annuals need careful watering when first planted, and further watering if the weather is very dry (*see p. 266*).

Pests and diseases Some annuals are prone to fungus diseases such as botrytis in cold, damp weather. If you see signs of disease, remove the affected leaves immediately to prevent it from spreading (*see p. 52*).

Biennials

These are defined as plants that are sown one year and flower the next, after which they die. Some, such as pansies, are really perennials, but they are best grown as biennials because they flower better in the first year.

CHOOSING BIENNIALS

If carefully chosen, biennials will give you a fine display of flowers throughout spring and summer. They grow in most soils, and include some of the true cottage-garden plants like sweet Williams (*Dianthus barbatus*) and Canterbury bells (*Campanula medium*).

BUYING BIENNIALS

Biennials can be bought as seed or small bedding plants in trays. Check items for diseased or blemished leaves and make sure that you can supply the right soil and sun requirements in your garden.

PLANTING BIENNIALS

They require much the same conditions as annuals. Avoid fertilizer at planting time, but incorporate well-rotted manure or compost into the soil (*see pp. 18–34*).

You will need a small area set aside as a seed bed and a little more for growing. Biennials are very easy to raise from seed sown outside in early summer (*see p. 268*). When the seedlings are sturdy enough to handle without damaging them they are best transplanted about 4in (10cm) apart in rows in a corner of the garden and then transplanted again to their final positions in early fall, after the summer-flowering annuals have finished.

Spring-flowering biennials will flower until early summer, when they can be pulled up, put on the compost heap, and replaced with clumps of summer-flowering annuals.

Bulbs

I include corms, rhizomes, and tubers with bulbs as they are all types of food-storage organs. After flowering, the foliage dies down and food is stored in the bulb through the dormant season. New growth appears the following season.

Bulbs are ideal for filling spaces between shrubs in the border with color. Moreover, if spring-flowering types are planted at the base of deciduous shrubs, they will be in full flower when the shrubs are dormant and then later in the season their unattractive foliage will be masked by the new growth of the shrubs.

CHOOSING BULBS

Bulbs should not be considered as merely spring-flowering plants—with careful planning and planting it is possible to have a year-round display of color.

BUYING BULBS

When buying, inspect each bulb carefully. Check that the skin is intact and the bulb feels firm. If not, this will indicate that it is rotten or shriveled inside.

PLANTING BULBS

Most bulbs do well when grown in groups, which is a convenient way of creating blocks of color. Do not mix different varieties in blocks because they all flower at slightly different times.

Bulbs can be planted in any type of soil as long as it is well drained. Because they are soft and fleshy, bulbs cannot survive with bad drainage; it quickly leads to rotting. So, if your soil is heavy, make sure it is deeply dug and preferably raised above the level of the lawn or the surrounding soil, and plant the bulbs on a layer of gravel.

Depth of planting varies, of course, with the bulb, but, as a general rule, plant twice as deep

Spreading forget-me-nots *Do not buy forget-me-not* (Myosotis alpestris) *seeds; simply pull up a seeded plant and shake it over the border to disperse its seeds.*

Planting bulbs in heavy soil *Dig a hole about 2ft (60cm) diameter and 12in (30cm) deep. Put a bucketful of gravel in the bottom, sit the bulbs on the gravel, then cover with soil.*

as the depth of the bulb in light and normal soil, and the same depth as the bulb if your soil is very heavy, not forgetting to allow for the layer of gravel. This is important since some bulbs will not produce flowers if they are planted too near the surface. Make sure, too, that the bulbs are right side up—it can be difficult to tell sometimes—the "nose," or pointed end, is the top.

Some summer-flowering bulbs, such as lilies, do better with their heads in sunshine and their feet in the shade, so planting in the shade of a low-growing shrub is ideal. The bulb will grow through the shrub to expose its flower to the sun while the roots stay cool.

Spring-flowering bulbs should be planted in the late summer, and fall- and summer-flowering types in the spring or early summer.

TEMPORARY STORAGE OF BULBS

Sometimes you may want to dig up bulbs after flowering to make space for annual flowers. If so, dig them up with as much root as possible and make sure the foliage remains intact. Then, in a sheltered corner of the garden, replant them in a row in a slit trench. This is known as "heeling in." They can be close together as long as the foliage is exposed to the sun. Give them a couple of liquid feeds before the foliage dies down.

1 *Dig a V-shaped slit trench, building up the soil on the back wall. Lay the bulbs in a single row against the back wall of the trench. They can be kept close together if space is at a premium in your garden.*

2 *Cover the bulbs with soil, leaving the foliage exposed to the sun. Replant the following season. If you are planting several different types of bulb, it may be worth labeling them to avoid confusion when replanting.*

Bulbs can also be planted in grass—a technique known as "naturalizing." This is especially attractive in areas where the grass is cut only two or three times a year. If you want to plant bulbs on a lawn that is mown regularly, you should choose those that flower very early, otherwise cutting the grass will be delayed several weeks until the foliage has died down. Bulbs for naturalizing are best planted informally, so scatter them about haphazardly on the grass and then plant them with a bulb planter, a tool that removes a core of soil, enabling you to put the bulb in the bottom of the hole and then replace the soil and grass in one piece.

MAINTAINING BULBS

Feeding It is not enough to plant bulbs and then leave them to their own devices. Bear in mind that the flower you see in the first year after planting is the result of the efforts of the grower in the previous year. To achieve as good a result the following year, you have to do what he did. After flowering, it is important to ensure that there is a plentiful supply of potash (*see p. 38*); this encourages a good flower the following year. If the bulbs are in the borders, you will be applying sufficient manure or fertilizer when you feed the soil for the benefit of the shrubs and herbaceous plants. If they are planted on their own, in tubs or in beds under large trees, they will benefit from a couple of liquid feeds after flowering—kelp or liquid manure is ideal (*see pp. 40–42*). Once the foliage has died down, mulch the soil over the bulbs with well-rotted manure or compost.

Watering The soil should be moist at all times but ensure that drainage is good, otherwise the bulbs will rot (*see p. 117*).

Post-flowering care It is essential, after bulbs have flowered, that you allow the foliage to remain attached so that it can build up a flower for next year. Remove the leaves only after they have turned yellow; then cut them off and compost them. If you cut them off too early or, as some gardeners do, tie them in neat little knots, the plant cannot use sunlight to make food. Consequently, the bulb gets smaller and smaller and eventually disappears. Personally, I do not object to the foliage of bulbs in the borders, provided it is fairly quickly masked by other foliage. I make sure of this by planting those bulbs with a tendency to look scruffy next to foliage plants. Daffodils (*Narcissus*), for example, can be planted next to large-leaved plantain lilies (*Hosta* sp.). When the daffodils are flowering, the lilies are dormant. Then, almost as soon as the daffodils finish, the lilies produce large leaves to cover the daffodil foliage.

Lifting and storing Some of the more tender summer-flowering bulbs like gladioli and dahlias must be lifted to prevent frost damage. Dig them up just before heavy frosts threaten. Then dry them off, clean them, and store them over the winter in a cool, frost-free shed until planting time next season.

Climbing plants

Whether they cover the wall of the house, hide an ugly feature, scramble through trees or shrubs, or soften the artificial look of a wooden fence, climbers are invaluable. There is no quicker way of achieving height in the garden and no better way to disguise the inevitable "man-made" look of barriers and buildings.

True climbers are plants that have some means of clinging on to a support—either tendrils, curling leaf stalks, adventitious roots, or by twining. Many shrubs and some roses can, however, be trained to cover a wall or fence by regularly tying their branches onto supports.

CHOOSING CLIMBERS

The site and function of the climber will determine the type you can grow. Some climbers, especially clematis and roses (*Rosa* sp.), can be trained to grow through trees and other shrubs to give either a contrast in flower color or to extend the season by flowering when the tree has finished. But avoid the vigorous types like *Clematis montana* and the Russian vine (*Polygonum baldschuanicum*) for this purpose, because they will swamp the tree. Other climbers, such as ivy (*Hedera* sp.), make useful ground cover plants for weed suppression (*see p. 90*). Many, like the ornamental vines (*Vitis* sp.) and Virginia creeper (*Parthenocissus quinquefolia*), are grown for their dense, colorful foliage rather than their flowers.

BUYING CLIMBERS

Climbers are normally bought as container-grown plants, at any time of year. When choosing them, look at the growth at the base of the plant rather than that at the top. It is much better to have one with short, strong branches growing from the base than a long bare stem with branches at the top.

PLANTING CLIMBERS

Good preparation is essential, especially if the plants are to be grown against a wall of your house. In most cases this will put them in the driest spot in the garden because they are likely to be "protected" from rain by the overhanging eaves. Yet, because they are vigorous growers, they need all the moisture and food they can get. Make sure the planting area is generously enriched with well-rotted manure, compost, or one of the alternatives (*see p. 30*). For each climber, try to prepare a planting site at least 4ft (1.2m) square, double dig it, and work in at least a wheelbarrow of organic matter. Supplement this with two good handfuls of blood, fish, and bone meal.

Most climbers, like shrubs, should be planted at the level of the soil mark on the stem. The exception is clematis. It is subject to a fungus disease called "clematis wilt," which causes the plant to wilt from the top—branches suddenly collapse and die. But if

Supporting climbers *The neatest and least obtrusive way to train climbers that do not stick to the wall or fence is with horizontal wires. These can be fixed to the wall with vine eyes driven into the mortar joints (see p. 267). This beautiful clematis (Clematis montana 'Rubens') has tendrils which will twist around the wires and disguise them from view.*

you cut it back hard as soon as you see any signs of the disease, new shoots, free from the fungus, will appear from below ground. So plant clematis about 4–6in (10–15cm) deeper than it grew at the nursery to ensure plenty of new buds form underground.

After planting, cover the soil with a layer of coarse material such as pine bark to shade the roots (they like to be cool), prevent evaporation of water, help keep slugs at bay, and suppress the growth of weeds.

TRAINING CLIMBERS

Climbing plants can be divided into groups according to the way they are trained. Some can support themselves, while others need to be provided with wires or a trellis. Some shrubs can be used as climbers if they are trained properly—these are known as wall shrubs.

Self-clinging climbers These are the easiest climbers to train, and include ivy (*Hedera* sp.), Virginia creeper (*Parthenocissus quinquefolia*), and climbing hydrangea (*Hydrangea petiolaris*). Simply plant them at the bottom of the wall and point them in the right direction. They will find their own way after that. They will not grow very quickly until they attach but, once they do so, they will soon make up for the delay.

Twining climbers This group of climbers needs support. Some, like honeysuckle (*Lonicera*) or wisteria, will twist themselves around any kind of support, while others, like clematis, have either tendrils or leaf stalks that are designed to twist around a support to hold up the stem. Both types will be happy climbing up wires, trellis, or netting.

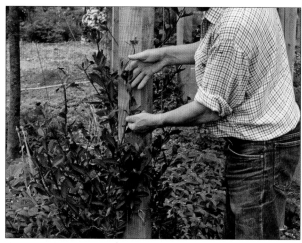

Supporting climbing stems *Climbers that are not self-supporting, such as honeysuckle, should have their new branches twisted around their supports.*

Making a rose-covered pillar *Carefully wind the rose stem around the pillar and tie it in with soft string. As you are doing so, try to pull the branches down to form a flat spiral, which will increase the number of flowers produced.*

Wall shrubs Some shrubs can be trained upward, to give the same effect as climbing plants; climbing roses are often used to decorate pergolas and arches. They are not really climbers at all, but very vigorous shrubs, sending out long shoots. These shoots need to be tied in to the support as they appear. As with climbing roses on a wall, try to pull the branches down almost horizontally as they grow to increase flowering. It takes a little longer to cover the support this way, but the restriction of the flow of sap will ensure that many more flowers will be produced.

Other wall shrubs include cotoneaster and firethorn (*Pyracantha* "Lalandei"). Both of these plants can be trained to cover a wall or fence.

MAINTAINING CLIMBERS

Watering If the soil has been well prepared, climbers will only need watering in very dry weather. Climbers on walls need extra watering if they are protected by overhanging eaves.

Feeding If the soil has been well prepared, general border feeding should be sufficient.

Cutting back Self-clingers only need to be prevented from straying where they are unwelcome. They should be cut away from windows or they will block out the daylight quickly. Do this with pruning shears whenever it is necessary. Spring is the best time.

Pruning Climbers should be pruned annually to improve flowering. They can be divided into two pruning groups—the early-flowering plants, which should be pruned and dead-headed immediately after flowering, and those that flower later in the season, which should be cut back the following spring (*see below*).

GROUPING CLIMBERS FOR PRUNING

Early-flowering climbers	Late-flowering climbers
Clematis montana	*Clematis jackmannii*
Clematis macropetala	*Clematis* "Ville de Lyon"
Clematis "The President"	*Clematis* "Hagley Hybrid"
Wisteria	Trumpet vine
Summer jasmine	Russian vine
Honeysuckle (Woodbine)	Winter jasmine
Chinese gooseberry	Chilean glory flower
Akebia quinata	*Lapageria rosea*

Preventing climbers from straying *Never let a climbing plant get a firm hold on a roof. The tendrils will get beneath the tiles and could dislodge them. Cut back stems with shears.*

Ponds and aquatic plants

The organic garden will be more attractive to wildlife if it contains a pond, because it provides drinking water for birds and small mammals, and a home for many aquatic animals. Some, like frogs and toads, should be encouraged because they eat large quantities of slugs and snails. A pond will also enable you to grow a much wider range of plants in your garden.

AQUATIC PLANTS

These can be divided into four groups—deep-water aquatics, floating plants, submerged oxygenating plants, and marginal plants. Try to include plants from each group in your pond.

Deep-water aquatics are plants that root at the bottom of the pond but whose leaves float on the surface. This group includes the water lilies (*Nymphaea* sp.), which are not only very decorative but also useful in reducing the growth of algae, which turn the water green and murky. Algae live on mineral salts and sunlight, so the more leaf cover there is on the surface of the water, the better. Attractive deep-water aquatics include the white water lily (*Nymphaea alba*) and water crowfoot (*Ranunculus aquatilis*).

Floating plants also reduce the amount of sunlight that reaches the surface of the water and include the water hyacinth (*Eichornia crassipes*) and the water chestnut (*Trapa natans*).

Submerged oxygenating plants are not decorative but they aerate the water, and are, therefore, essential to the health of the pond. Suitable plants include spiked water milfoil (*Myriophyllum spicatum*), Canadian pondweed (*Elodea canadensis*), and curly pondweed (*Potamogeton crispus*).

Marginal plants grow in the shallowest parts of the pond and the boggy soil around the edges. There is a great range of preferences for the amount of water above the roots. They range from those that must be planted in water an inch or so deep, like the sweet-scented rush (*Acorus calamus*), to the primulas, which should be planted in the marshy soil.

▲ **Floating plants**
The water chestnut (Trapa natans), *helps to exclude light and thus algae.*

▶ **Deep-water aquatics**
Plant the water crowfoot (Ranunculus aquatilis) *in a deep part of the pond.*

▲ **Submerged oxygenators**
The spiked milfoil (Myriophyllum spicatum) *will oxygenate the water.*

▶ **Marginal plants**
Grow moisture lovers like irises around the edge of the pond.

CONSTRUCTING AND PLANTING A POND

There are several ways of making a pond. The simplest is to buy a ready-made fiberglass shell and dig a hole for it. Alternatively, you can dig a hole to your own specifications and line it with plastic, although this will eventually disintegrate. Slightly more expensive but much more durable is a rubber pond liner. This also enables you to choose the shape of the pond.

Dig a hole to the required size with a slope on one side. A shelf can also be cut out at the edge for the marginal plants. Line the hole with a thick layer of soft material to protect the liner from damage by sharp rocks in the soil. To calculate the minimum size of liner, measure the maximum length and width of the pond. Add to these measurements twice the maximum depth.

Planting marginal plants
These should be planted on the pond shelf or in the special marsh garden.

The marsh garden
A gently sloping, shallow area that provides an ideal habitat for plants that like to grow in damp soil.

Planting in pots Use heavy garden soil or rotted turf. Do not use soil rich in organic matter; it will putrefy as it rots down. A thin layer of gravel on top of the soil prevents it from floating to the surface and stops curious fish from disturbing it.

The marginal shelf
This provides a planting area for plants that like to grow in shallow water. Make it very shallow in places as a refuge for fish.

Hibernation site
Put rocks in the marsh garden to provide a place for frogs to hibernate.

Planting floating plants
Put these into the pond in spring. You simply throw them in. Use one plant every sq yard/meter.

Edging the pond Paving stones make the planting and maintenance of the pond easy. They also help to secure the rubber liner.

Protecting the liner Cover the soil with a special blanket, sand, or newspaper before laying the rubber liner.

Planting submerged oxygenating plants
These are sold in bunches, with a small weight fixed to the stalks. To plant them, throw the bunch into the pond in spring, using one bunch per 2sq yard/meter of water.

Plastic containers
Put plants into the pond in plastic buckets of soil.

Planting deep-water aquatics These should be planted in containers during late spring and summer. Cut off all the old leaves and lower the container to the bottom of the pond. The new leaves will soon grow up to the surface.

The pond in cross-section

Shallow area

Marginal shelf

Deep-water area

The marsh garden should consist of damp soil. The shallow area should be 2in (5cm) deep for those plants that like their roots covered with shallow water. The marginal shelf should be wide enough to hold containers of plants and be 3–5in (7–12cm) deep. The deep water area should be at least 18in (45cm) deep. This will accommodate most water lilies.

PLANTING DEPTHS FOR AQUATIC PLANTS

Deep-water plants	
Water hawthorn (*Aponogeton distachyum*)	6–18in (15–45cm)
Water violet (*Hottonia palustris*)	12in (30cm)
Water lily varieties (*Nymphaea* sp.)	
N. 'Alba'	1–3ft (30–90cm)
N. 'Sunrise'	6–18in (15–45cm)
N. 'Firecrest'	6–18in (15–45cm)
N. pygmae 'Alba'	4–9in (10–20cm)
Marginal plants	
Sweet-scented rush (*Aconus calamus*)	3–5in (7–12cm)
Flowering rush (*Butomus umbellatus*)	3–5in (7–12cm)
Bog arum (*Calla palustris*)	2–4in (5–10cm)
Marsh marigold (*Caltha palustris*)	0–3in (0–7cm)
Arrowhead (*Saggitaria japonica*)	3–5in (7–12cm)
Water forget-me-not (*Myosotis palustris*)	0–3in (0–7cm)
Primula (*Primula* sp.)	0–3in (0–7cm)
Note: *Depths refer to water above the planting soil in the pool.*	

LOCATING THE POND

Ideally, the pond should form a feature in the garden, rather than being tucked away out of view. Choose a site that receives plenty of sunlight for at least part of the day. Most aquatic plants prefer sunny conditions and certainly fish prefer warmer water, although they don't like very sudden changes in temperature.

Site the pond as far from deciduous trees as possible. If leaves fall into the pond they will turn the water sour as they rot anaerobically. Trees will also shade the pond.

If you have small children, even a small pond can be very dangerous. Make sure you site it where it can easily be seen from the house and, if there is any risk, it is best not to build one at all until the children are older.

MAINTAINING THE POND

Algae growth Soon after filling the pond, the water may turn pea-green in color. This is due to rapid algae growth. Pond water contains minerals and receives plenty of sunlight right at the beginning, so the algae flourish. Do not empty out the water and replace it with fresh. If you do, you are giving the algae another supply of mineral salts, which will cause them to flourish again. Leave the water in the pond as the supply of minerals is soon depleted. And, as the water plants grow larger, the other source of food—sunlight—will be excluded. Deprived of food, the algae die, and the water in the pond begins to clear.

Thinning plants You may need to thin out the oxygenating plants occasionally; this is easy to do, just pull some out by hand. Return any animal life on the plants to the pond and throw the plants on the compost heap.

Blanket weed infestation You may be unlucky enough to get an infestation of blanket weed. This is a slimy, ugly-looking green weed that floats on top of the pond and chokes out other vegetation. Remove it as soon as you see it. Provided you do this regularly, you will prevent further infestation.

Leaves Keep leaves out of the pond, or they will turn the water sour as they rot. Try to avoid building the pond near deciduous trees; if this is impossible, cover the surface with a piece of netting in the fall.

Keeping ornamental fish If you decide to keep fish, you should make special provision for their offspring. Fish have a habit of eating the eggs they lay, plus the tiny "fry" when they hatch, and any frog spawn that you may be lucky enough to attract. To foil them, include a very shallow area in the pond, no more than 2in (5cm) deep, which is too shallow for the larger fish to swim in. Here, the smallest fish will gather, because it will be warmer, and you can make sure that you guide any frog spawn into the area yourself.

Alpines

Cultivated varieties of wildflowers from the high, mountainous areas of the world are among the most beautiful garden flowers we have. They are unique in the organic garden because most have little or no value in attracting wildlife and, therefore, pest predators. Nonetheless, once you have grown a few, you will want to make room for some more. In fact, they take up very little room because the best way to grow them is in a rock garden, a scree garden, or in holes in walls or between paving slabs.

CHOOSING ALPINES

The choice of plants is enormous, providing attractive flower colors and shapes, and interesting foliage. Many alpines need an alkaline soil; others, such as some of the gentians, are lime haters and need an acid soil.

PLANTING ALPINES

Plant alpines in spring or fall, and sow alpine seeds in the winter because they need a period of cold before they will germinate (*see p. 270*). The one really important factor for success is good drainage. In the wild, alpines grow in cracks in rocks or in the gravel, known as scree, that has broken off and rolled down the mountainside. This is the type of environment that you need to reproduce.

One way of growing alpines that really works is in a miniature scree garden (*see below*). Alpines can also be grown in drinking troughs or old stone sinks. If you grow them in containers, make sure they have drainage material in the bottom then fill them with a free-draining compost (*see p. 128*).

If you grow alpines in a rock garden, make special planting pockets by arranging the rocks

A scree garden *The very formal shape of this scree garden is softened by the informal planting and the stepping stones. A wide range of ground cover plants will thrive in this well-drained site. To construct the garden, dig a hole at least 2ft (60cm) deep and put in about 9in (23cm) of sawdust. Refill with equal parts of good soil, sphagnum peat, and coarse gravel.*

GROWING ALPINES

Alpines originate from rocky habitats, which provide them with a well-drained site. In the garden you can recreate this by growing them in a rock garden, in gaps between paving stones, or in a hole in the garden wall.

A rock garden can be as large or as small as you wish and is often used as a means of growing plants on an awkward, sloping site. Walls for growing alpines can be specially constructed; build a hollow wall and fill it with soil.

Growing alpines in a wall

1 *Cut a piece of turf large enough to cover the root ball of the plant. Leave it upside down until the grass dies completely, then soak it in water.*

2 *When the turf is thoroughly wet, roll it around the root ball of the plant.*

3 *Push the turf-wrapped root ball firmly into the hole.*

Making soil pockets in a rock garden

Arrange the rocks in small horseshoe-shaped pockets and fill the area between them with a mixture of equal parts soil, peat, and coarse gravel. Plant with a wide variety of alpines to ensure that the color and shape of the garden will change constantly. The two photographs, right, were taken two months apart; the first one was taken in late spring, the second in midsummer.

Late spring

Midsummer

into horseshoe shapes and filling the spaces with a special soil mixture. It is possible to grow plants that need different soil types in the same rock garden provided you fill the pockets with suitable soils.

Alpines can also be grown in cracks and crevices in walls. Particularly successful are plants that do not tolerate being wet. Plant them in the fall, by wrapping the roots in old turf and pushing them into the hole (*see above*).

You can also plant them between stone slabs when making a path. Leave gaps between some of the slabs, fill with a suitable soil, and plant with trailing alpines.

MAINTAINING ALPINES

Feeding Fertilizer is rarely required. Only feed alpines if they look as though they have completely stopped growing—which should not be more often than every five or six years. Give them a light dusting of blood, fish, and bone meal.

Watering Alpines need water only in very dry weather. Ensure they have good drainage.

Weeding This can be time consuming among alpines, especially when the plants are very small. Weeds can be kept to a minimum by covering any bare soil with coarse gravel.

Protection In their natural habitat, alpines are covered with snow that protects them in the winter, so many, especially those with gray, woolly foliage, are not happy in the wet climate of lower areas. It is a good idea, therefore, to cover any susceptible plants with a small piece of glass supported by wire to keep the foliage dry.

Cultivating wildflowers

Wildflowers can be grown in the borders or, in large gardens, as a wildflower meadow. In fact in many cases, what is a wildflower, or even a weed, in some countries, is a desirable border plant in others. Also, some native wildflowers looked upon with scorn by gardeners can, when grown in the fertile conditions of the border, become very attractive indeed. In my own garden, I leave seedlings of red campion (*Lychnis dioica*) and white campion (*Lychnis alba*) that blow in from the nearby fields. When they grow in my manured and fertilized borders they become much bigger plants, bearing many more flowers. And, even when cultivated in this way, they are just as attractive to native insects and birds, so helping to control pests by attracting their natural predators.

CHOOSING WILDFLOWERS

There are several specialists who sell wildflower seeds and most retail seed catalogs carry a selection. Special mixtures are available, aiming to attract butterflies, bees, or birds. Other seed mixtures may include old-fashioned cornfield flowers such as the corncockle (*Agrostemma githago*) and cornflower (*Centaurea cyanus*).

BUYING WILDFLOWERS

Some wildflower suppliers sell rooted plants that are ready for planting; never take plants from the wild— this is how they become rare or extinct. Check the soil and habitat preferences of each species before planting.

PLANTING WILDFLOWERS

Wildflowers can be raised from seed, either sown directly in the ground in the spring, or in seed trays in an unheated greenhouse. If sowing straight into the ground, ensure the site is well-drained. Ideally, choose a piece of soil that has not been cultivated in the recent past; in a new garden, subsoil dug up by builders is suitable. Wildflowers thrive on poor land, so do not add fertilizer or the coarser weeds will take over. Harden off seedlings raised in the greenhouse (*see p. 254*) before planting in the border.

▲ **Underplanting with wildflowers** *Bluebells bring color to a woodland border, and also suppress weeds.*

▶ **A summer meadow** *Scarlet poppies, blue cornflowers, and white ox-eye daisies attract butterflies and other insects. Later, the seedheads will attract a wide variety of birds.*

SOWING A WILDFLOWER MEADOW

A wildflower meadow is suitable for larger gardens, as one of the advantages of this method is the ease of maintenance; in a large garden this could be a boon. The flower population will change a little as conditions generally favor one species or another, but there always needs to be a varied selection to attract the insects and birds that help control pests.

If possible, choose a patch of land with low fertility. Prepare and sow it as you would for a lawn (*see p. 79*), using a mixture of grasses and flowers suitable for your soil type.

The meadow only needs cutting twice a year, once in early spring just as growth starts, and again after the wildflowers have set seed in late summer. Use the seed for next year's meadow.

THE CONTAINER GARDEN

Just as a houseplant on the windowsill immediately transforms a room into a "living room," so the harder man-made surfaces outside can be softened with plants in containers. By using plants in pots, tubs, or window boxes, you can integrate these otherwise barren areas with the rest of the garden.

Every gardener needs those hard areas of paving or concrete as paths or patios, steps, or driveways, but they always stand out a little in a plant-filled organic garden. A little softening makes all the difference. Try hanging a flowering basket on either side of the front door, for example, or position a stone trough filled with alpines over an unsightly drain cover.

You can fill containers with permanent plants or you can use them for seasonal displays or a combination. Fill tubs or window boxes, for example, with small shrubs surrounded by suitable annuals and biennials for winter and summer color.

Types of container

Good garden centers stock a wide range of containers made from different materials and they will also have a choice of styles—from simple wire baskets to plastic and "Greek" urns, wooden barrels, and concrete vases. Provided the containers have adequate drainage, or you can drill suitable holes through the bottom, plants will grow in all of them quite well.

PLASTIC

Containers made of plastic are certainly the cheapest and some can be quite attractive. Since most are made without drainage holes, make sure you drill holes in the bottom before planting; an ordinary wood drill will do for this. It is better to overdrain the pot, so make ½in (1cm) holes about 6in (15cm) apart.

Some plastic containers used for cooking oil or orange juice can make attractive containers when you cut the top off, and remember they will very soon be at least partially covered by plants. Again, you must drill drainage holes in the bottom.

If the container does not have a base to lift it off of the ground, raise it slightly on a few pieces of slate or brick so that the drainage holes are not in contact with the ground.

CLAY, STONEWARE, AND CONCRETE

Clay pots in terra-cotta color blend in particularly well in the organic cottage garden. They do have one disadvantage, however: most are not frost proof and will crack or flake in really cold weather. Again, drainage is vital.

Stoneware containers cost a little more but they stand up to even hard frosts so they are worth the extra investment. There is also a wide range of pots and tubs available made from reconstituted stone or concrete, but they, too, are generally expensive. This type of pot is very heavy when full of soil, so put it in its permanent position before filling and planting.

Old stone drinking troughs or wash basins look extremely attractive filled with plants and covered with moss and algae on the outside. However, they can be difficult to find.

WOOD

Wooden containers are available in various designs and a range of prices. Softwoods used to make containers, with the exception of cedar, must be pressure-treated with copper-based preservative at the manufacturing stage. Hard woods, such as iroko and teak, will last for many years without treatment.

Half barrels make excellent containers if you can find them, but they are becoming scarce and, therefore, expensive. Most are made of oak, so you do not have to treat them, but the metal hoops will need painting from time to time. Of course, avoid buying barrels that have contained any poisonous substances.

▲ Traditional urn
This urn is made from cheaper reconstituted stone and filled with bedding plants.

◄ Herbs in containers
A convenient and attractive way to grow herbs such as sage, thyme, and feverfew.

▼ Wooden tubs
Tubs filled with annuals and biennials brighten the terrace.

WINDOW BOXES

These are readily available in either wood or plastic, alternatively you can make one yourself from hardwood or softwood treated with a copper-based preservative. Whichever type you use, it is very important to secure the window box to the windowsill or wall properly.

Making a wooden window box
Make the box from 9 × 1½in (20 × 3.5cm) wood cut to a suitable length. Secure the corners with 1 × 1in (2.5 × 2.5cm) blocks of wood fixed in place with brass or galvanized screws. If your window box is more than 3ft (1m) long, include a cross support in the middle. Drill ½in (1cm) holes in the base—one hole every 6in (15cm).

Planting in containers

Though containers can be filled with permanent plants, there is no doubt that the most colorful and eye-catching display will come from seasonal plantings, using mainly annuals and tender perennials. In temperate regions, you normally plant in spring for a late spring and summer display and in fall for an early spring show. You can make up an extremely effective winter display using hardy plants such as winter-flowering heathers (*Erica cornea*), pansies (*Viola wittrockiana*), and euonymus (*Euonymus fortunei*) varieties.

You can use any of the plants suggested for seasonal plantings in containers on their own.

Tubs of daffodils, for example, followed by perhaps fuchsias or geraniums look fine. I am especially fond of the continental geranium called "Mini Cascade," which you can obtain in bright red or pink. See also *The Ornamental Garden* for a season-by-season collection of plants (*see pp. 94–111*).

Whatever type of container or planting program you use, it is very important that you use the correct compost (*see next page*).

LATE SPRING AND SUMMER COLOR
Do not consider starting the spring planting until all danger of frost has passed. Then, start

planting at the middle of the container, using a central plant to give height. This could be a geranium (*Pelargonium zonale*) or a hybrid fuchsia (*Fuchsia blumeii*), perhaps a flame nettle (*Coleus*), or a taller-growing begonia (*Begonia tuberosa*). Around this, position slightly shorter plants such as petunias (*Petunia hybrida*), salvias (*Salvia splendens*), nemesia (*Nemesia strumosa*), impatiens (*Impatiens walleriana*), or slipper flowers (*Calceolaria integrifolia*). At the edges of the container, plant low-growing, compact plants, such as ageratum (*Ageratum houstonianum*), lobelia (*Lobelia erinus*), or alyssum (*Lobuiaria* "Maritima"), interspersed with trailing plants. You could use trailing varieties of geraniums or fuchsias, trailing lobelia, thunbergia (*Thunbergia alata*), or ground ivy (*Nepeta hederacea*). While planting, sow a few seeds of the trailing nasturtium (*Tropaeolum majus*) to flower a little later and brighten up the container when it may be beginning to look a little tired.

REPLANTING FOR EARLY SPRING

In the early fall remove the summer display and freshen up the compost (*see below*) by taking out the top 9in (23cm) and mixing in some well-rotted garden compost or manure. Then refill and plant with your spring plants, again using a taller central plant surrounded by lower-growing and trailing ones. Here you could use pansies (*Viola wittrockiana*), polyanthus (*Primula polyantha*), primulas, forget-me-nots (*Myosotis alpestris*), dwarf daisies (*Bellis perennis*) and, of course, spring bulbs.

Spring bulbs

Nearly all the spring bulbs are suitable for containers but it is best to avoid tall varieties, especially if your container is in an exposed position. They will simply be broken down by heavy rain and wind. Of the shorter-growing daffodils, for example, perhaps the best for container planting are the *Narcissus cyclamineus*, *N. triandrus*, and wild jonquil (*N. jonquilla*) hybrids. Of the tulips, I would recommend *Tulipa tarda*, water-lily tulip (*T. kaufmanniana*), *T. greigii*, and *T. praestans*. All the hyacinths are short enough to survive and, of course, the early crocus and iris species and the anemones work especially well.

Permanent plants

Containers planted with shrubs or herbaceous perennials require less maintenance than those that are regularly replanted, but they don't give the same flamboyant display of color over such a long period. If, however, you cannot devote much time to maintaining your containers, then you should seriously consider some of the easy-to-care-for plants.

CONIFERS

Dwarf conifers make good tub plants but you must make sure that they really are dwarf. The taller-growing species will flourish for a year or two but they will soon begin to show their displeasure at being confined. You will then have to find room for them in the garden.

One of the best real dwarfs is the Noah's ark juniper (*Juniperus communis* "Compressa"), which forms a perfect upright spire of green. Alberta white spruce (*Picea glauca* "Albertiana Conica") will last for many years in a tub, but it is plagued by red spider mite, which can cause defoliation (*see p. 257*).

Lawson cypress (*Chamaecyparis lawsoniana* "Minima Glauca") is slow growing and forms a rounded bush of sea green, while its near relative, *C. l.* "Minima Aurea" is bright golden yellow. There are other cultivars of Lawson cypress that are suitable for a few years: *C. l.* "Ellwoodii" forms a dense blue-green spire, while *C. l.* "Ellwoods Gold" is slower growing and, of course, yellow in color.

COMPOST FOR CONTAINERS

In containers that are to remain outside, never use a peat-based compost because it dries out very quickly and is very difficult to rewet. You cannot rely on rainwater to water the containers because there is rarely enough. Instead, fill them with a soil-based compost using high-quality topsoil from a garden center or fibrous loam made from stacked turf. *See p. 252 for details of how to "grow" your own loam.*

Making soil-based compost

Mix 7 parts loam, 3 parts coir, and 2 parts coarse gravel. To each 2 gallon (9 liter) bucketful, add 1oz (30g) of garden lime and 5oz (150g) of blood, fish, and bone meal.

You can replace the coir with very well-rotted compost or manure or, even better, with worm-worked material or leaf mold.

Making acid compost

If you are including acid-loving plants in a container then use a commercial ericaceous compost, but if you cannot find one you like make your own using a mixture of equal parts coir, pine bark, and sharp sand with the fertilizer at the same rate as above.

Filling containers with compost

When you fill the containers, start by covering the holes with crocks—broken pots—laid concave-side down. Cover these with a little gravel and then either a piece of turf or some old sacking. This will prevent the compost from clogging the drainage holes. If the pot and/or the plant is tall it would be beneficial to put a layer of coarse sand at the bottom to act as ballast. When filling with compost always leave a 1in (2.5cm) between the top of the compost and top of the container to make watering easier.

There are several varieties of small and prostrate junipers like *Juniperus horizontalis* "Alpina" or *J. h.* "Plumosa,'" and a couple of thujas that you can use such as *Thuja occidentalis* "Rheingold" and *T. o.* "Midget."

SHRUBS

Certain shrubs last a long time in containers, and the root constraint tends to force them into regular and prolific flowering. One of my favorites is the evergreen pieris (*Pieris* "Forest Flame"). Its leaves pass from red in the early spring, through pink to creamy white and then green, and it has the bonus of creamy-white flowers resembling lily-of-the-valley. This plant needs to be planted in an acid compost (*see left*). Use the same compost to grow dwarf rhododendrons and azaleas (*Rhododendron* sp.), lithospermums (*Lithospermum diffusum*), pernettyas (*Pernettya mucronata*), heathers (*Erica* sp.), camellias (*Camellia japonica*), and other acid-loving shrubs. Bear in mind that you will have to water these containers with rainwater, since most tap water contains lime. The dwarf lilac (*Syringa velutina*), on the other hand, is excellent for limy compost, as are any of the variegated euonymus (*Euonymus fortunei*) species.

PERENNIALS

Planted in conjunction with shrubs, ivies (*Hedera* sp.) look excellent in containers. They will trail over the sides and break up any hard lines. Most low-growing perennials are suitable but many of them die down in winter.

FOLIAGE PLANTS

Ferns and grasses make an attractive change from the usual choices you see in containers, particularly when combined with other plants. A tub of plantain lilies (*Hosta*) mixed with ferns and one or two colored grasses makes a fine foliage tub for any shady area.

HERBS

Herbs are an obvious choice for containers when space in the garden is limited. They are all good looking plants and you will have the advantage of a source of fresh herbs conveniently close to the kitchen door. Stick to the shorter-growing types, such as thyme (*Thymus vulgaris*), sage (*Salvia officinalis*), chives (*Allium schoenoprasum*), rosemary (*Rosmarinus officinalis*), and parsley (*Petroselinum crispum*).

ALPINES

These low-growing plants make interesting and eye-catching troughs and they are especially useful for shallow containers. Almost any alpine plant will grow happily in a trough provided that there is good drainage. This means making sure there are plenty of drainage holes in the bottom of the container and using a free-draining compost made from equal parts of loam (made from stacked turf—*see p. 252*), peat, and coarse sand. There is no need to add fertilizer for alpines but include 1oz (30g) of lime per 2 gallon (9 liter) bucketful. When you have mixed it, you may think that the compost looks much too coarse and well drained, but remember that these plants live naturally in the most inhospitable conditions such as cracks in rocks or among the broken stones at the bottom of mountains. They should thrive in this type of compost without any feeding (*see* Maintaining alpines, *p. 124*).

TENDER PLANTS

In colder areas containers can be used to grow a whole range of exotic plants, such as agaves (*Agave* sp.), yuccas (*Yucca filamentosa*), manukas (*Leptospermum scoparium* varieties), and several ornamental flaxes (*Phormium* sp.) that would otherwise be impossible to grow. You can put them outside in the summer and bring them into a warm, light place in the winter.

Fruit and vegetables

If you only have limited space, there is no reason at all why you should not grow fruit and vegetables in containers. I have seen them successfully grown on balconies where no other form of gardening is possible.

Apples, pears, and plums do well grown this way but remember that they must be budded onto a dwarfing rootstock (*see pp. 203–204*). Standard gooseberries and red currant bushes make splendid tub plants, while strawberries do exceptionally well.

CONTAINER-GROWING STRAWBERRIES

The best way to grow strawberries is in shallow containers. You can also grow them in traditional strawberry pots, barrel-shaped containers with "cups" in the sides, but you may encounter mixed results. The top plants tend to do well but those growing out of the holes farther down will not thrive because

Growing in traditional strawberry barrels
It can be difficult to ensure water reaches the plants at the bottom of strawberry pots. So, put two stones into the bottom of the pot and rest a length of drainpipe on them. Surround the pipe with small stones, or similar drainage material as you fill the pot with compost.

they don't receive enough water. One method I have found reasonably successful is to put a short length of drainpipe into the barrel before filling it with soil. This way, by watering the top and filling the pipe, you will manage to get some water down to the lower plants.

MIXING VEGETABLES AND FLOWERS

Most shorter-growing vegetables do well in containers. Mix them with a few flowers, not just to improve their looks but to attract useful insects, too. A tub of lettuce, onions, carrots, and a few marigolds is a good combination and they will all grow well together, while bush tomatoes on their own look every bit as good as flowers.

Maintaining container plants

Feeding Plants in containers need regular feeding because nutrients will be continually washed through the compost. Feed weekly with liquid kelp or animal manure during the growing season. No feeding is necessary in the winter.

Watering Only very heavy rain will provide enough water for a container so regular watering is necessary. In summer you may need to water the containers daily. Water in winter only when the weather is very dry.

Removing flower heads Deadhead plants as the blooms die back to extend the flowering season.

Hanging baskets

You can brighten up walls considerably in summer and winter by adding a few flowering hanging baskets. They do, however, require a commitment to keep them well maintained. You will need to water them and feed them regularly, and remove the dead flowers to extend the flowering season.

The secret of success with hanging baskets is to plant them so that they create a complete ball of flowers. This means that you need deep baskets that can be planted on top and through the sides. The shallow plastic types sold widely will not hold enough plants and they cannot be planted through the sides. The best types to choose are those made of coated wire or plastic mesh, or you can make your own (*see opposite*). Hang the basket on a special bracket; choose one long enough for the basket to hang clear of the wall. As with window boxes, it is absolutely essential to fix brackets firmly, since a planted basket can be very heavy and therefore dangerous if it should fall.

Trailing hanging baskets *The basket on the left is in full summer glory. The basket on the right shows coir matting used as a basket liner.*

FILLING AND PLANTING WIRE HANGING BASKETS

You will need to line all wire or mesh baskets before filling them. Traditionally this was done with sphagnum moss, but this is no longer an option as it is becoming endangered. There are many alternatives available. You can buy mats made from coir, or liners made from a variety of other materials, such as wool waste. Whatever you choose to line your basket will eventually be covered by the plants.

1 *Support the basket on a flower pot and line with a coir or wool liner. Cover the base with plastic and extend it part way up the sides to retain moisture.*

2 *Half fill the basket with the peat-free compost. Position the central plant and some slightly smaller plants around it. Then fill the basket with some more compost.*

3 *Plant smaller plants in the compost nearer the edge. Allow a few trailing plants to hang over the edge.*

4 *Take a few trailing plants, squeeze their root balls together, and push them through the liner between the mesh of the sides of the basket and into the compost. Finally, top the basket off with compost, leaving space for watering.*

PLANTS FOR HANGING BASKETS

It is quite possible to have hanging baskets for spring, summer, or winter color. Use any of the plants recommended for tubs and other containers (*see pp. 128–129*). A selection of flowering plants for different seasons is also shown in *The Ornamental Garden* (*see pp. 94–111*).

For a summer basket, begin by planting a central "bushy" plant—geraniums or fuchsias are ideal. Surround this with several smaller potted plants such as petunias and include plants such as French marigolds (*Tagetes patula*), alyssum (*Lobularia* "Maritima"), and impatiens (*Impatiens*) near the edges of the basket. You can then add trailing varieties of lobelia (*Lobelia erinus* "Pendula"), geranium, bidens, and ground ivy (*Glechoma hederacea*) at the edge of the basket or in the sides of the mesh so that they grow and form a flower "ball."

I would not recommend vegetables in hanging baskets, but they are ideal, if fairly temporary, places for herbs. Again, as with other containers, choose the low-growing ones such as sage (*Salvia officinalis*), parsley (*Petroselinum crispum*), and thyme (*Thymus vulgaris*).

In the fall, when the baskets start to look tired, discard their contents onto the compost heap and throw the old soil and lining material away. Reline the basket, fill it with fresh soil, and replant for a winter show. In all but the warmest areas you will need to use frost-hardy plants. If there is any chance of a frost, use small shrubs such as the variegated pieris (*Pieris japonica* "Variegata") or the deep pink-flowered *P. j.* "Christmas Cheer." Surround this plant with winter-flowering or foliage heathers (*Erica carnea*) and, to trail over the sides, use ivies (*Hedera* sp.) or small plants of the evergreen honeysuckle (*Lonicera japonica* "Aureoreticulata'). Alternatively, use the variegated euonymus (*Euonymus fortunei* "Emerald 'n' Gold" or *E. f.* "Emerald Gaiety"). You can raise any of these plants from cuttings so, once you have bought your first basketful, you will not have to replace them even though the original plants will, after the first year, have outgrown their container (*see* Taking cuttings, *pp. 274–275*).

There is no reason why you should not put a few spring bulbs into a winter hanging basket, or even plant an early spring basket with bulbs such as crocus and species tulips (*Tulipa* sp.), early irises and anemones, with perhaps pansies (*Viola wittrockiana*) and forget-me-nots (*Myosotis alpestris*), or early polyanthus (*Primula polyantha*) and primroses (*Primula vulgaris*).

MAINTAINING HANGING BASKETS

Feeding Spring and summer hanging baskets will need feeding once a week with a liquid kelp or animal-manure fertilizer.

Plants in winter hanging baskets will hardly be growing at all so need no feeding.

Watering Spring and summer hanging baskets need to be watered regularly. In the summer they should be watered at least daily and, if they are in a particularly warm, sunny position, they may need watering twice a day.

In the winter the weather is much wetter so they may not need watering but, if the weather is unusually dry, keep an eye on the compost; water only when the top feels dry.

MAKING A WOODEN HANGING BASKET

You can make your own wooden baskets. In the past, I have made them from pieces of packing case obtained free from a local factory.

You need:
- *18 lengths of 1½ × 1in (3.5 × 2.5cm) wood 15in (40cm) long with two ¼in (5mm) holes in 16 of them, 1½in (3.5cm) from either end. Use more pieces of wood if you want a deeper basket.*
- *4 × 1yd (1m) lengths of nylon string. Tie a knot in one end of each piece of string. Heat the other end with a match and roll it between your fingers to make sure it does not fray.*
- *4 short nails.*

1 *Lay the first two struts on the work surface so that they are parallel to each other. Nail the two struts without holes across them at right angles to form the base. Thread a piece of string through each hole. Start threading more pieces of wood onto the string for the sides.*

2 *Continue working on alternate sides until all the sides are complete. Tie the strings together at the top, making sure that the basket hangs straight as you do so.*

3 *Line the basket with strips of plastic. You can cut up an old compost bag or anything similar.*

4 *Fill the basket with compost and plant in the usual way, leaving space for watering. Hang the basket on a well-secured wall bracket.*

THE VEGETABLE GARDEN

THE ORGANIC GARDEN must always be treated as a complete entity. While the fruit and vegetable gardens produce the edible crops, the ornamental section attracts the useful wildlife that helps ensure they are free from pests and diseases. In return, the vegetable and fruit gardens provide material for the compost heap. Herbs also play an important part in attracting predators, and insects to pollinate the fruit garden.

In the ornamental garden, it is smart to choose plants that are suited to your particular soil type. But, in the vegetable garden, you will want to grow a wide range of crops with differing soil requirements. It is therefore necessary to adjust the amount of organic matter and the soil pH to specific levels that will ensure optimum growth and quality (see pp. 18–37).

It is, however, the vegetable plot that really emphasizes the advantages of non-chemical gardening. For it is here that the transition to natural growing techniques will have a really positive effect on the health and general well-being of you and your family.

Cultivating your own vegetables is often cheaper than relying on store-bought produce, but of far greater consequence are the benefits in freshness, improved taste, and, above all, freedom from pollution.

If your garden is small, adopt the "cottage-garden" approach and combine vegetables and flowers in mixed borders (see pp. 71 and 88). You can also use the deep bed system, which encourages roots to grow downward rather than spreading outward, so crops can be planted closer together, giving far heavier yields.

There would be little point in growing your own food if you grew the same varieties, and used the same fertilizers and pesticides as the commercial grower. You may save a little money, but you would end up with comparatively tasteless vegetables that contain residues of often highly toxic chemicals. By combining the best of both traditional and modern gardening methods, you can have higher yields of better-tasting vegetables that you know are doing you nothing but good.

Crop rotation

All vegetables have specific soil and mineral requirements. By grouping together crops that have similar needs and planting them in a different place each year, you will be able to make much better use of your resources and allow the soil to replenish lost minerals. This practice is known as crop rotation. If you divide your vegetable plot into three, for example, you only need to manure a third of it each year and grow in that section those vegetables that will most appreciate it. The slightly less demanding crops can move to that plot the following year and those that are happy in poorer soil go there in the third year. You will also make the most efficient use of fertilizer and lime in this way. Because most vegetables are cultivated as annuals, there is no difficulty in growing them in a new plot each season. Those that dislike being moved must be kept in a permanent place.

Devising a viable rotation plan is not, however, as easy as it may at first seem. For example, following peas and beans with cabbages is fine in theory, but it's likely that the cabbages will need considerably more room than the peas and beans. Or you may find that putting the runner beans anywhere but at the same end of the plot each year would prevent the sunlight from reaching the rest of the crops. That might have a more damaging effect than an attack of greenfly or a mild case of mildew. So, do not be too rigid in your application of the system—serious problems are unlikely to occur if you have to deviate slightly from a strict rotation for some reason.

Though the rotation plan I have suggested provides for only one plot to be manured, it is a good idea to treat the whole vegetable patch if you can get enough manure. The idea that root vegetables will fork and split in manured soil is a

▲ **Growing vegetables in a mixed border** *If your garden is very small, and you wish it to be both decorative and productive, you can combine flowers, fruit, and vegetables in a mixed border. Here, crops such as sweet corn, tomatoes, and ruby chard are growing alongside a small apple tree and an assortment of flowers.*

◄ **Tending plants in a deep bed** *Plants can be spaced very close together if they are grown in deep beds of loose, organically enriched soil (see p. 135). To avoid treading on and compacting the soil, the crops are tended from paths that run beside the narrow beds.*

myth; provided you always use well-rotted manure, you will achieve far better results in soil that has been made water- and nutrient-retentive in this way. If you are using the deep bed system (*see opposite*), you should, in any case, manure all the plots every year. Dig the manure in during the fall and lime in the spring just prior to sowing or planting.

PEST AND DISEASE CONTROL

Crop rotation will help guard against attacks from pests and diseases by promoting generally healthier and more robust plants. However, while moving the crops each year allows the mineral balance of the vegetable plot to be maintained, it is not always an effective means of actually deterring pests and diseases altogether. For example, where growing cabbages in the same bed in consecutive years certainly encourages a build-up of clubroot spores in the soil (*see p. 45*), millions of these spores can be transported from one part of the garden to another in just the few bits of soil that cling to your boots or spade. Similarly, many pests are capable of flying considerable distances, so simply moving susceptible plants in no way guarantees freedom from attack. However, there is no doubt that annual crop rotation, as described below, does significantly delay the build-up of disease spores in the soil.

THE THREE-YEAR CROP ROTATION PLAN

This three-year rotation scheme is suitable for most gardens. Divide your vegetable garden into three plots and the crops you want to grow into three groups, as detailed below. Every year, prepare the plots as described and move each group to the next plot, so that two years elapse before any crop returns to its original site. This period allows the mineral balance of the soil to be maintained, reduces the risk of disease, and makes best use of organic matter.

PLOT A
Cultivation: Double digging (*see p. 264*), incorporating manure in upper and lower levels, plus two handfuls of blood, fish, and bone meal per square yard/meter. Some crops in this group may need extra feeding.
Suitable crops: Potatoes, carrots, beets, parsnips, onions, shallots, leeks, garlic, tomatoes, zucchini, squash, pumpkins, celery, Florence fennel, eggplants, peppers, cucumbers, melons, celeriac, Hamburg parsley, salsify, scorzonera.

PLOT B
Cultivation: Single digging (*see p. 264*) and application of blood, fish, and bone meal at the rate of two handfuls per square yard/meter, over the whole plot, two or three weeks before sowing the first crops of the season.
Suitable crops: Peas, green beans, runner beans, broad beans, Lima beans, soybeans, peanuts, sweet corn, okra, spinach, chard, Swiss chard, lettuce, chicory, endive, cresses, globe artichokes.

PLOT C
Cultivation: Single digging (*see p. 264*) and application of blood, fish, and bone meal (as on plot B), and lime to bring the pH level up to 6.5–7.0. Some crops may need extra feeding during the season— refer to specific entries in this chapter.
Suitable crops:
Cauliflower, cabbages, nappa cabbages, Brussels sprouts, broccoli rabe and broccoli, kale, rutabagas, turnips, radishes, kohlrabi.

PLOT D
Space must also be left for the permanent crops, which occupy a plot of their own and do not come within the rotation plan. These are: asparagus, globe artichokes, Jerusalem artichokes, rhubarb, sea kale, and herbs. (The globe artichokes are included in both plots because they can be grown as perennials or annuals—*see p. 150*).

In a small garden it is sensible to grow some permanent crops in the ornamental border (*see p. 71*).

Year 1

A   B   C   D

Year 2

B   C   A   D

Year 3

C   A   B   D

Ensuring a continuous supply of vegetables

Making sure that you always have fresh vegetables in the garden is not as simple as it may seem. Successional sowing plans are a good idea, but there is no accounting for the variations in weather conditions that can make crops late. Although having a strict timetable is out of the question it is a good idea to keep a diary that can act as a rough guide. In the first year, write down when you should be sowing or planting to provide a succession of cropping. Then record when you actually got around to doing the job and also the reason you were either delayed or early. Note too when you harvested each crop. Eventually, after two or three years, a fairly accurate pattern will emerge.

Many modern vegetable varieties are bred to remain in the ground, without deteriorating, for some time after maturing, so there is a fair amount of leeway. Others, such as main crop onions, can be stored throughout the winter and will last almost until the next crop is ready to harvest. Ensuring continuity is easy, therefore, and you can fill in with a very early-maturing set-grown variety or shallots. I have indicated in the individual vegetable entries where it is possible to achieve a continuous supply by successional sowing and planting.

Stick to your original rotation plan and, when it's time to sow a particular vegetable, use whatever space is available in the correct plot. If you find that there will be an area of vacant soil for more than about a month in the main season, sow a quick-maturing green-manure cover crop like mustard (*see p. 34*). It is also worth growing a green-manure crop in the winter, particularly if your soil is light (*see p. 32*). If you have sufficient space, plan a four-year rotation and separate out the vegetable groups to give more growing space and a longer rotation period.

Preparing vegetable beds

The best way to ensure good-quality vegetables is to grow them in the best soil possible. Soil types vary widely (*see pp. 13–14*) but, even if you start off with a poor-quality soil, it is not difficult to make substantial improvements by working in plenty of organic matter (*see p. 20*). The techniques involved in preparing and maintaining a vegetable plot are explained fully in *Soil Improvement* and *Fertilizers* (*pp. 18–42*). Refer to the individual vegetable entries for specific soil preferences and preparations. If you choose not to use the crop-rotation plan, you should still prepare the soil in the way recommended for the vegetables in each group.

The deep bed system

The deep bed method of growing vegetables has been practiced around the world for centuries. The system is basically very simple: instead of the vegetables being grown in long rows, with an access path between each row, the crops are grown in beds 4ft (1.25m) wide, with all the work being done from narrow paths at the sides.

By cutting out the unproductive paths, it's possible to double the amount of land available for crops. This is an important consideration, especially if you have a small garden.

HOW THE SYSTEM WORKS

By digging deeply, breaking up the subsoil, and incorporating plenty of bulky organic matter, a deep root zone is produced that allows plants to draw nutrients from a much greater depth. Because their roots are encouraged to grow downward, crops can be planted closer together than would otherwise be possible. Deep beds dug in heavy soils drain more easily if they are raised and the water retention of light soils is improved by working extra bulky organic matter into the top couple inches.

Most crops can be grown successfully using the deep bed system. The exceptions are runner beans, which are not manageable in such short rows (*see p. 159*), and Brussels sprouts—because they still need to be spaced about 18in (45cm) apart if you are to get good-sized sprouts.

CULTIVATION

Before sowing, rake into the top inch of soil about two handfuls of blood, fish, and bone meal per square yard/meter, and cover the soil with about 2in (5cm) of well-rotted garden compost. If the bed was dug and manured in the winter, the manure will have probably worked down a little way, leaving the top layer of soil liable to dry out quickly. The additional compost will help retain the necessary moisture.

Crops that have been overwintering, such as spring cabbages, will need an extra boost in the spring. A little dried blood sprinkled around the base of each plant should be sufficient. Vegetables that use a lot of nutrients—known as gross feeders—include tomatoes, zucchini, squashes, and peppers, and these benefit from an application of liquid kelp every two weeks during the growing season.

Weeding deep beds is comparatively easy once the plants have matured. The close spacing means that they cover the surface of the soil and effectively smother any weeds. In the early stages, though, weeding can be time-consuming, as it often has to be done by hand. Always start with a stale seedbed (*see p. 269*) and cover the soil with a thick layer of well-rotted manure or compost (*see p. 20*). It is also possible to plant through sheets of paper or plastic sheeting; this is very effective as it completely eliminates weeds and the need for weeding (*see p. 58*).

SOWING AND PLANTING IN DEEP BEDS

Most vegetables can be sown so that they just touch their neighbor when the plants reach maturity. I have indicated the relevant planting distances under each separate entry.

Crops should be planted in blocks, rather than rows, with the plants set out in a series of staggered lines. Some seeds, such as those of the radish and early turnip, can be sown in a wide band. Make the row with a draw hoe, using the whole width of the hoe, and scatter the seeds thinly within it (*see p. 269*). You need not thin the seedlings, but harvest them selectively, starting when the roots are very small and allowing the rest to develop fully.

The increased drainage can make the top inch of the soil drier than usual, so water the row before sowing in dry weather, and then cover the seeds with dry soil.

Sometimes, vegetables that are sown with wide spacing can be "intercropped" with a fast-maturing crop. If you sow three or four rows of broad beans, for example, a crop of radishes can be sown in between them. You will be able to harvest them long before the beans are big enough to rob them of sunlight.

Deep beds are ideal for growing crops under cloches (*see p. 140*). You may not be able to buy a cloche wide enough to fit the whole bed, but it is not difficult to make your own.

Spacing out plants *In order to make the best possible use of the available space, sow seeds or seedlings in blocks, or staggered rows, forming a triangular pattern where each plant is the same distance from those surrounding it.*

DIGGING A DEEP BED

To achieve optimum results with a deep bed, it is important that the soil is loose and dug deeply, so that the roots can penetrate to the required depth, and that it is enriched with plenty of organic matter. You should never walk on the bed once it has been dug because this compacts the soil. If you find it too awkward to work from the access paths, use a wooden board to spread your weight evenly over as large an area as possible.

A conventional bed
The comparatively shallow and compacted layer of topsoil means that roots cannot penetrate deeply and have to be planted further apart. Root crops may be distorted and smaller than those grown in deep beds of loose soil.

A deep bed *A deep layer of loose, organically enriched soil encourages roots to penetrate downward, rather than spreading sideways. This means that crops can be planted much closer together, resulting in dramatically increased yields.*

Deep bed dimensions *The usual width of a deep bed is about 4ft (1.25m). The beds can be as long as is convenient. A 10 × 4ft (3 × 1.5m) bed gives a 40sq ft (4.5sq meter) planting area that should produce up to four times the yield of a conventional bed of the same size.*

Leave a narrow access path between beds.

Divide the beds into 2ft (60cm) sections to prepare the soil.

The most convenient width of the beds is 4ft (1.25m).

1 *Mark one edge of the bed with a planting line. Measure 4ft (1.25m) across using the planting board and set up another planting line parallel to the first.*

2 *Using stakes, mark a trench 2ft (60cm) wide. Dig out the trench one spade deep, put the soil in a wheelbarrow and take it to the other end of the bed; it is used to fill the last trench.*

3 *Break up the exposed subsoil in the bottom of the trench with a fork. This enables the vegetable roots to penetrate more deeply.*

4 *Put a 2–3in (5–8cm) layer of well-rotted manure into the bottom of the trench. This enriches the soil and improves its texture.*

5 *Leaving a stake in the corner of the first trench, measure the second 2ft (60cm) section with the other stake. Making all the trenches the same size ensures that they contain the same amount of soil.*

6 *Start digging the soil from the second trench and transfer it into the first trench, spreading it out to cover the layer of manure.*

7 *Put another 2–3in (5–8cm) layer of manure into the first trench. Because of the bulk of the added manure, the bed will be raised as you work.*

8 *Continue to dig out the soil from the second trench and cover the new layer of manure. This leaves a deep bed of loose, organically enriched soil in the first trench.*

9 *Scrape all the soil from the bottom of the second trench and break up the exposed soil. Repeat steps 4–8 and use the soil taken to the end of the plot to cover the manure in the final trench.*

Sowing

The vegetable-growing season begins with seed sowing, either directly into the ground outside or in pots or trays from which the developed seedlings are transplanted after a period of "hardening off" (*see p. 254*). You can save seeds from existing plants or buy them from the seed catalog or the garden center, but remember to avoid the "dressed" seeds, those that have been treated with fungicide. Seeds must be watched and tended carefully, and the seedlings spaced and thinned as required. Some crops can be multiple sown to make the best possible use of available space (*see below*). Plants that may be slow or difficult to germinate can sometimes be pre-germinated to encourage swift growth when they are planted, and others may benefit from some form of protection from the cold. The techniques suitable for each crop are described in the individual entries. A good harvest of vegetables at the end of the season largely depends on how well the seeds are sown initially.

Multiple sowing

In order to make the best use of the available land, aim to get the maximum yield per square yard/meter and to extend the harvesting period as much as possible. Deep beds will increase the yields, and planting under cloches means you can start earlier and continue later at the other end of the growing season (*see p. 140*).

The very earliest crops, however, are best started inside, either in a heated greenhouse or on a windowsill. They will be well-established plants before they go out under the cloches, so they can be harvested earlier still. In the interests of economy, you will want to keep heating costs down, so the less space these early vegetables take up, the better. The best way of achieving this economy of space is by multiple sowing. This involves sowing up to six or eight seeds together in cells, rather than individually. Leave them to grow as a clump and do not thin them out. When the seedlings are planted outside, the vegetables simply push and jostle for space. Onions, for example, actually push each other so far over that some of the bulbs grow horizontally instead of vertically (*see opposite*). Multiple sowing therefore enables you to save space in the ground as well as on the propagating bench or windowsill.

Commercial growers have been using this method successfully for many years, using individual blocks made from a special type of peat compost. The seedlings are sown in the blocks and planted out before the roots outgrow them. However, none of the composts used in

this way are organic, as far as I know, and it is difficult to make your own from peat and organic fertilizer, because the special type of peat is needed if the blocks are not to fall to pieces. Also, the blocks tend to become hard and airless.

A better method is to buy trays consisting of individual cells, called module trays. These can be made from either plastic, styrofoam, or compressed coir. Fill them with a good open compost like peat and worm casts, or one of the commercial animal-manure composts. The plants are easily removed at planting time (*see opposite*). If you cannot find anything like them, you can either divide a seed tray with cardboard strips to make squares about 1½in (4cm) across or use very small pots.

Pre-germinating seeds

Sometimes it is beneficial to pre-germinate seeds before sowing. Really slow germinators, like parsnips for example, will just sit in the ground doing nothing or may even rot if they are sown in cold and wet soil conditions. But, if they are pre-germinated in optimum conditions, and sown when the soil is slightly warmer, they'll grow right away and easily catch up during a normal season.

Other seeds can be inhibited, or fail to germinate, because the soil temperature is too high. For example, if lettuces are sown in a soil warmer than 65°F (19°C), they will not germinate. This is nature's way of preventing them from starting into growth during the dry season. But if they are pre-germinated in slightly cooler conditions, they can be sown and will grow normally, provided they have sufficient water.

The seeds are germinated by spreading them out on a piece of damp paper. It is possible to buy a special kit which includes a germinating dish and absorbent filter paper, but a cheaper alternative is to put a few paper towels into the bottom of a small plastic container. Cover them with water and drain off the excess.

Germinate the seeds in the pantry or in a kitchen cupboard, depending on the temperature required, and check on them daily. In ideal conditions, they will sprout a small root much quicker than they would in the soil outside. As soon as a few roots are about ⅛in (3mm) long, they are ready to sow.

If it is impossible to sow them right away, put the seeds in the refrigerator (but not in the freezer);

HOW TO MULTIPLE SOW

Multiple sowing is the most effective way of producing some of your early crops. Sow groups of seeds in trays of styrofoam or plastic cells, and put them in a warm greenhouse. When they germinate, move the trays to a cooler place until the seedlings are big enough to plant out under cloches (*see p. 140*). Deep beds are ideal for multiple-sown vegetables.

Styrofoam cells for multiple sowing *You can buy blocks of styrofoam or plastic cells and separate trays with a corresponding number of pegs. The compost blocks are released by pushing them down on the pegs.*

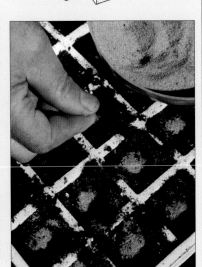

Vegetables suitable for multiple sowing

Not all vegetables are suitable for multiple sowing and there is no advantage with others. The crops listed below are some of those I have tried successfully.

LEEKS (*see p. 170*)
Sow and plant out exactly as for onions. There is no need to plant them in a trench since they will blanch each other by growing so closely together. Recommended varieties are *King Richard* and *Zermatt*.

CARROTS (*see p. 181*)
It's important to use the round varieties of carrots like *Atlas* or *Parmex*. The longer varieties will tend to wind around each other underground, making them useless for the kitchen. Sow six or seven seeds per cell in late winter and plant out 9in (23cm) apart in mid-spring.

BEETS (*see p. 184*)
Use a round variety like *Boltardy* or *Detroit 2*. Sow two beet seed clusters per cell. Harden off and transplant exactly as described for onions (*see below*).

TURNIPS (*see p. 183*)
Use an early variety like *Early Purple Top Milan* and sow six per block in late winter. Plant out after hardening off, 12in (30cm) apart in early spring.

SALAD ONIONS (*see p. 171*)
The best varieties are *White Lisbon* or *Shimonita*. Sow six seeds per cell in late winter and plant out 6in (15cm) apart, after hardening off in early spring.

ONIONS (*see p. 171*)
Sow six or seven seeds per cell in late winter, at a temperature of 60°F (15°C). After germination, the temperature can be lowered to 50°F (10°C). Harden off in a cold frame (*see p. 254*) in early spring and plant out 12in (30cm) square in mid-spring.
   Most varieties will do, but the best for me have been *Hystar* and *Sturon*.

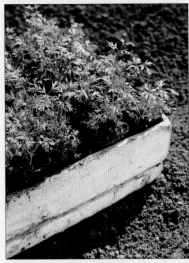

1 *Fill the cells with moist peat-free compost and make a small depression in each. Place your seeds—in this case carrots—on a piece of card and, with the back edge of a penknife blade, carefully scrape six or seven seeds into each cell.*

2 *Cover the seeds with a layer of silver sand. Water thoroughly, cover with opaque plastic, and place near a heat source. Once the seeds have germinated, remove the plastic and move plants to a cooler place to grow. Do not thin.*

3 *When the plants are about 1in (2.5cm) high, they are ready for planting outside. Take them outside, and water the plants thoroughly with a watering can. Then press the block of cells down onto the peg tray to push the compost and plants out of the cells.*

4 *Plant the clumps in staggered rows to save space. Using a planting board to measure accurately, plant a row of carrots so that the clumps are 9in (23cm) apart. Plant a second row 9in (23cm) from the first, staggering the clumps by 9in (23cm), and water them.*

Multiple-sown onions *The bulbs are forced to grow outward as they compete for space.*

they will keep in the refrigerator for three or four days without harm.

Of course, the difficulty lies in transferring the germinated seeds to the soil without breaking the tiny roots. They are at their most delicate stage and will not survive damage of any kind. Large seeds, like peas and beans, present no problem as they can be handled with ease. Even the medium-sized ones, like parsnips, can be carefully picked up with tweezers if you have infinite patience. But the smaller seeds, like lettuce, are impossible to sow in this way.

The answer is "fluid sowing," where the seeds are suspended in a "jelly." Special kits are available that include an alginate gel that is mixed with water, heated up, and allowed to cool before use. Equally effective is ordinary wallpaper paste, mixed to a stiff consistency. This does not need to be heated. Make sure you buy a paste that doesn't contain a fungicide.

FLUID SOWING WITH WALLPAPER PASTE

This method of sowing fragile pre-germinated seeds can be used for a number of vegetables, including parsnips, as shown here. If you are fluid sowing in the summer, water the newly sown seeds right away or you may find that the wallpaper paste hardens and traps the seeds inside. Gentle stirring enables the seeds to be distributed evenly through the paste. They can then be sown evenly, so only minimal thinning is needed when the seeds germinate.

1 Pre-germinate the seeds in a warm place, using moist paper towel (see p. 138). As soon as they are ready to sow, carefully wash the seeds off the paper into a strainer with cold running water.

2 Make up the wallpaper paste mixture in a jar and put the seeds into the paste, making sure you do not damage the shoots. Stir the seeds around gently and then pour the mixture into a plastic bag and tie a knot in it.

3 Before sowing, rake the soil to a fine tillage. Then draw the seed rows using the edge of a draw hoe (see p. 259) and water them with a liquid kelp or animal manure fertilizer (see p. 41).

4 Cut off the corner of the bag and squeeze the gel and the seeds down the row. Cover normally and gently consolidate the soil by tapping with the back of a rake. Water regularly and ensure that the seeds never dry out.

Protecting crops against cold

In temperate climates, the earliest crops have to be grown in a heated greenhouse (see pp. 246–257), but the sowing and harvesting dates of many vegetables can be brought forward by at least a month by using cloches— simple plastic or glass covers—outside, with no heating.

After raising an early crop, cloches can be used to cover tender vegetables like zucchinis, beans, and tomatoes. Since you will harvest these well before outside-sown crops are ready, you'll be eating them while market prices are still high. Then, at the end of the season, the cloches can be used again to grow late vegetables when those in the outside garden are finished. Once you have used cloches, you will not want to be without them—they will certainly pay for themselves easily in the first season.

Using cloches

Cloches are most useful for early planting out of multiple-sown seedlings or early sowings. I have included sowing times for each vegetable under the separate entry (starting on p. 146).

If your soil is heavy, start by incorporating well-rotted compost or peat into the top few inches (see pp. 15–16). This will help to aerate the soil and warm it up. Later, it helps retain moisture. If you are using peat, rake in blood, fish, and bone meal at about two handfuls per square yard/meter.

Position the cloche over the ground to be used about a month before sowing and planting, which should start in late winter. Be sure to

TYPES OF CLOCHE

Cloches can be made from glass or plastic, but glass is now so expensive that it is no longer feasible to use it for commercial cloche making. However, if you have some old glass panes, you can make a simple cloche using special cloche clips.

Fortunately, as the cost of glass has risen, the price of plastic sheeting has fallen. This is ideal cloche material but, for best results, it should be replaced each year. There are three main types of cloche: tunnel cloches, traditional rigid tent or barn cloches, and floating cloches.

Tunnel cloches

You can buy tunnel cloche kits that simply consist of a series of wire hoops over which plastic sheeting is draped. Make sure there is an adequate way of tying the sheeting down and tightening it up over the top, otherwise the plastic may flap around, damaging the plants as well as itself. The sides of a tunnel cloche can be pulled up to allow easy access for watering and harvesting. They are often very long—

up to 100ft (30m)—but you can always divide them up into smaller sections. It is also very simple to make your own (see next page).

Tunnel cloches for deep beds are harder to find and naturally more expensive. They need to be 5ft (1.5m) wide to allow a margin for growth at each side. There are a few available and these too are good value but, again, it's cheaper and very easy to make your own. Plastic greenhouses are made in much the same way.

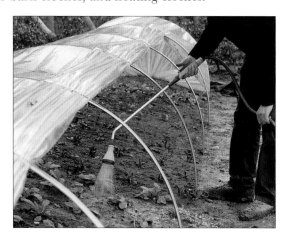

Rigid cloches

Many different designs of rigid glass or plastic cloches are available. Ensure that the ones you buy are tall enough and wide enough for the crops you intend to grow, and that there is a satisfactory means of anchoring them to the ground. Plastic cloches are light and can easily blow away if not properly anchored.

Plastic barn cloche

Glass tent cloche

Floating cloches

Cheapest of all are "floating cloches"—sheets of plastic, or as shown (right), garden fabric, which cover a crop from when it is sown or planted until a short time before harvesting. Perforated sheet plastic is available, but does not protect against frost. Much more efficient is garden fabric, which will protect plants from a few degrees

of frost. It can be used on all types of beds and is easy to fit and remove. Simply cover the area with a large sheet and weigh the edges down with bricks or cover them with soil, making sure the fit is loose over the crops. As the crops grow the fabric "floats" up. When the crops are ready to harvest, roll back the sheeting. For deep beds buy sheets at least 6ft (2m) wide.

measure the soil temperature—which should be 45°F (7°C) before sowing or planting anything.

The soil under the cloche will dry out faster than the open ground because the structure keeps the rain out, so make sure you water by hand when necessary. If you can, install a length of seep, or perforated, hose (see p. 260) along the length of cloche so that you only have to fit the end to the garden hose and leave it to "water itself." Remember too that a plastic

covering will exclude any pollinating insects so, if you grow a vegetable fruit or seed like eggplants or peas, which are pollinated by insects, open the cloche during the flowering period, at least during the day.

You will only need small amounts of very early pickings, so either grow several different vegetables in the same row—if you have room for a full-length cloche—or split the cloche into several lengths for adjacent rows.

MAKING YOUR OWN TUNNEL CLOCHE

A tunnel cloche is perhaps the best way of protecting crops planted outside, especially if you have a fairly large area to cover. It is quick and easy to make your own, using inexpensive and readily available materials. The technique described here can be adapted to make a cloche of any size; the measurements below will give you a cloche 18in (45cm) wide. Although they are fixed securely into the ground, tunnel cloches allow easy access to the crops they protect.

1 Fix bolts 6in (15cm) from one end of a 54in (1.35m) long piece of wood, and 12in (30cm) from the other. Cut a piece of stout wire the same length as the wood.

2 Starting at the shorter end, hold the wire at the end of the wood and wind it around the nearest bolt to leave a loop and a 6in (15cm) "leg" at one end.

3 Pull the wire taut and wrap it around the other bolt, making a second loop and another 6in (15cm) leg. Cut more pieces of wire and repeat the process.

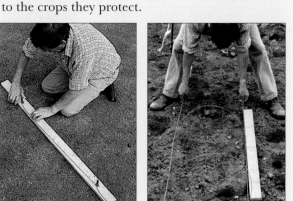

4 Peg two parallel planting lines 18in (45cm) apart. Bend the lengths of wire into hoops and push them into the soil at 2ft (60cm) intervals, using the lines as a guide.

5 Remove the planting lines and cover the hoops with a sheet of plastic. Dig a small hole and bury one end under the soil.

6 Pull the plastic tight over all the hoops and bury the other end in the same way. This prevents the wind from lifting the plastic.

7 Tie a length of nylon twine through one of the wire loops. Pull it tightly over the cloche and secure it to the opposite loop.

8 Repeat this process with the other loops to hold the whole cloche down securely. Slide the plastic up when the crops need watering.

Start by raising plants on the windowsill or in the heated greenhouse, sowing in late winter (*see p. 270*). Sow lettuce, early cabbage, and cauliflower in seed trays. Carrots, spring onions, spinach, early turnips, and beets should be multiple sown in blocks or cells (*see pp. 138–139*), and early peas sown in guttering (*see p. 157*). All these can be planted out under the cloches in early spring.

In warm climates, you can sow directly into the soil in late winter, depending on the soil temperature. Sow lettuces, which will mature later than the inside-sown ones, radishes, spinach, carrots, turnips, peas, broad beans, spring onions, and potatoes. Hopefully (it's never possible to be absolutely precise), these crops can be harvested by late spring, in time to use the same beds for

zucchini, eggplants, peppers, squash, tomatoes, green beans, and cucumbers.

In mid to late summer, another sowing can be made of the early varieties of the crops you sowed in early spring. These are sown uncovered and the cloches are put on in early fall to hasten maturity. The cloches can also be used to ripen vegetable fruits, like tomatoes, which may still be green at the end of summer.

Organic methods of increasing soil fertility are even more important under cloches. Every time you change crops, dig over the soil and work in as much well-rotted manure or compost as you can spare to increase the water-holding capacity of the soil.

The hoops are also useful as supports for netting, which provides protection against birds.

Choosing what to grow

On the following pages are listed over 50 different vegetables—obviously too many for the normal-sized garden to accommodate at the same time. You will have to resign yourself to the fact that you cannot grow everything, so you have to make choices—and that can be difficult.

The first step is to resolve to grow only what is needed by you and your family. If you grow more of a particular crop than you can use reasonably quickly, there is also the danger of plants "running to seed." This is where they are left in the ground too long before harvesting, so that they "bolt" and flower, then produce seed.

Sow short rows of fast-maturing varieties at frequent intervals for successional harvesting of peak-condition vegetables. And try to fit some of them in between wider spaced, long-term crops like Brussels sprouts and cauliflower.

You should also eliminate those vegetables that are easy to obtain organically grown and will cost no more to buy. Main crop potatoes, for example, take up a lot of room, and an organic farmer can grow them more cheaply than you. On the other hand, I plant a few early potatoes each year because they taste so much better when they're freshly dug.

If you choose vegetables that deteriorate rapidly after harvesting, you will get the full benefit of improved flavor. Sweet corn, for example, starts to turn its sugar into starch the very instant it is picked so, the sooner it is eaten, the better. Corn that has been in the grocery a day or two will not be worth buying. Leaf crops are not nearly as crisp and fresh, and tomatoes, which need sun to increase their sugar content, are often picked nearly green to ensure they have not become overripe by the time they reach the supermarket. There is no time for them to develop the characteristic sweetness associated with homegrown vegetables.

Finally, make your choice on cost and availability. The so-called "gourmet" vegetables—like asparagus, celeriac, sea kale, globe artichokes, and scorzonera—are ludicrously expensive, especially slightly out of season, so it is well worth growing them. I doubt too whether you will find most of those grown organically, so you may well *have* to grow your own.

BUYING SEEDS

In most countries, the quality of vegetable seeds is governmentally regulated, so it is unlikely that you will find one grower's products better or worse than those of another. However, seeds are expensive, so it is worth shopping around.

Some seeds, like peas and beans, are easy to save yourself—nearly all those you buy will be just as good sown the second year after buying as they were the first, provided they are properly stored. Start by buying seeds that have been foil-packed. Then open the packet in as dry an atmosphere as possible and take out what you need, then reseal the packet immediately and put it into an airtight container. I find the small plastic containers used for 35mm camera film are ideal. Label the container and store it in a cool, but frost-free, dry place.

There are several F1 vegetable hybrids available now (*see p. 45*) and all are much more expensive than the open-pollinated types. Before you consider buying these, remember that most have been bred with commercial growers in mind and that their requirements are often the reverse of yours. They need the entire crop to mature at the same time and to be of uniform size. You are looking for continuity of maturity and a range of sizes so you can choose a bigger cabbage when you have guests, for example.

The advantage of the F1 varieties is that they are often more vigorous, nearly always heavier cropping, and are sometimes bred for resistance to disease and pest attack, too. If they have these specific attributes and have not, as a result, had all their flavor bred out of them, they are an excellent choice. Otherwise, stick with the older, open-pollinated varieties.

In the pages that follow, I have recommended the varieties of each vegetable that I have found superior, but you may want to try others. Make a point also of growing at least one new variety, or even one entirely new vegetable, each year. If you simply keep planting the varieties you have used in the past, you may miss out on something much better.

PREPARING THE SOIL

Even if you decide not to use the three-year rotation plan, it pays to try and keep plants with the same requirements close together. You must also prepare the soil for each vegetable in much the same way, so refer to the rotation plan that will give a general idea of how to condition the soil before sowing or planting each crop. If any extra conditioning is needed, I have included recommendations in the relevant entry.

THE VEGETABLES

The vegetables are divided into groups according to basic characteristics, so each section deals with salad, leaf, or root vegetables, for example. Information regarding greenhouse cultivation is given where applicable and treatment for the pests and diseases that affect each group is discussed at the end of the chapter.

Salad vegetables

Growing your own salad vegetables is particularly beneficial, because their quality and flavor depends on freshness. They take up comparatively little space and most can be grown all year-round if some protection against frost is provided. Salad crops are fast-growing and are not usually troubled by many pests and diseases. They all require a moisture-retentive soil.

CHICORY ▶
Cichorium intybus
The example shown here is a "chicon" dug up and blanched in deep, moist peat. These and the unforced green leaves are used in winter salads. *For cultivation details, see p. 147.*

▲ MUSTARD AND CRESS
Brassica hirta and *Lepidium sativum*
Mustard and cress seedlings are quick and easy to grow, and can be eaten fresh all year. The seeds can be germinated on moist kitchen paper indoors. *For cultivation details, see p. 146.*

▲ WATERCRESS
Nasturtium officinale
Because it grows wild in fast-flowing streams, watercress needs shade, a moisture-retentive soil, and plenty of water. *For cultivation details, see p. 146.*

ROMAINE LETTUCE ▼
Lactuca sativa
A particularly crisp and refreshing salad vegetable, Romaine lettuce has erect bright-green leaves with a prominent central vein. *For cultivation details, see p. 147.*

◀ RED LEAF LETTUCE
Lactuca sativa
This distinctive form of lettuce has crinkle-edged leaves that are tinged with red. Like the other lettuces, it is a suitable crop for growing in the greenhouse. *For cultivation details, see p. 147.*

▲ CUT-AND-COME–AGAIN
LETTUCE
Lactuca sativa
This type of lettuce is so called
because new leaves grow to replace
those that have been harvested.
For cultivation details see p. 147.

▲ BUTTER LETTUCE
Lactuca sativa
Perhaps the most popular form of the
ubiquitous lettuce, which is often interplanted
between slower-maturing crops. The leaves
of the loose head varieties are especially soft.
For cultivation details, see p. 147.

▼ ENDIVE
Cichorium endivia
One salad vegetable that is often cooked, as well
as eaten raw, endive is harvested throughout fall
and winter. *For cultivation details, see p. 148.*

Cultivating salad vegetables

Mustard and cress

This combination is very easy to grow—either indoors during the winter or outside at other times. Mustard and cress are actually eaten at the seedling stage and are a popular salad ingredient, garnish, and sandwich filler.

VARIETIES There are no individual varieties.
SOIL AND SITE Mustard and cress are very fast-growing, taking most of their nourishment from the seed itself, so they will grow on very poor soil or, inside, on moist tissue or cotton balls.
• If you are using the three-year rotation plan (*see p. 134*), grow them in Plot B.
SOWING In the winter, put a little moist soil or a damp tissue into a plastic box and scatter the seed fairly thickly on it. Cover with a sheet of newspaper and put it in a warm spot. Sow the mustard, which germinates and grows faster, four days after sowing the cress. When the seed germinates, remove the paper and place the box in full sunlight.

Sowing mustard and cress indoors
Dampen the paper towel thoroughly but ensure any excess water is drained away. If the paper towel is too wet, the seedlings rot; if it is too dry, the crop won't mature.

In the summer, sow in the same way in a corner of the plot outside, or in a pot or tub. Sow every two weeks for a succession.
MAINTENANCE No further attention is needed during growth.
HARVESTING The shoots will be ready for harvesting in 15 to 20 days. Cut them with scissors.
PESTS AND DISEASES Mustard and cress are generally trouble free. See pp. 46–53 for general pests and diseases.

PLANTING AND HARVESTING TIMES

	Sow inside	Plant out	Sow outside	Harvest
Early spring	•			•
Mid-spring			•	•
Late spring			•	•
Early summer			•	•
Midsummer			•	•
Late summer			•	•
Early autumn			•	•
Mid-autumn	•			•
Late autumn	•			•
Early winter	•			•
Midwinter	•			•
Late winter	•			•

Watercress

This highly nutritious vegetable is an ingredient of salads, sauces, and soups. It grows wild in fast-flowing streams, but can be cultivated in soil without the aid of running water. It may be the ideal crop to fill a persistently damp corner of the garden.

VARIETIES There are no individual varieties.
SOIL AND SITE A moisture-retentive soil is essential. Choose a shady part of the garden, dig a trench 12in (30cm) deep, and half fill it with well-rotted manure or compost. Mix some more organic matter with the soil you have dug out and refill the trench.

SOWING AND PLANTING Sow indoors in seed trays in mid-spring at a temperature of about 55°F (12°C), or outside in shallow rows. Transfer the seedlings to wider spacing in another seed tray when they are big enough to handle (*see p. 272*). Plant outside in late spring or early summer, setting the plants 4in (10cm) apart. An easier way is to buy a bunch of watercress, select those shoots that have a few embryo roots showing and plant in the same way.
MAINTENANCE The moist conditions of the watercress bed are likely to encourage annual weeds, so hoe regularly to keep them at bay, and water frequently. No feeding will be necessary. As they grow, pinch out the leading shoots and remove flowers as soon as they are seen.

HARVESTING Cut shoots as required. This will encourage the production of more shoots, so harvesting can continue throughout the summer and fall.
PESTS AND DISEASES Watercress is generally trouble free. See pp. 46–53 for general pests and diseases.

PLANTING AND HARVESTING TIMES

	Sow inside	Plant out	Sow outside	Harvest
Early spring				
Mid-spring	•		•	
Late spring		•		
Early summer		•		
Midsummer				•
Late summer				•
Early autumn				•
Mid-autumn				•
Late autumn				•
Early winter				
Midwinter				
Late winter				

Chicory

There are two basic types of chicory. One is a white-blanched shoot—or "chicon"—grown for eating in the winter. In my view it is the finest winter salad vegetable. The other type needs no blanching; it can be harvested in the fall and eaten like lettuce. Chicory has a refreshing, slightly bitter flavor.

VARIETIES

The best varieties to grow for producing blanched chicons are *Witloof* and *Lightning*. For growing unblanched, use *Pain de Sucre* or *Rossa di Treviso*.

SOIL AND SITE Chicory likes a sunny location and does best in soil that is rich and moisture retentive, with a pH of 6.5. Apply two handfuls of blood, fish, and bone meal per square yard/meter, preferably two to three weeks before you start sowing.

• If you are using the three-year rotation plan (*see p. 134*), grow it in Plot B.

SOWING Do not sow until early summer or the plants may run to seed. Sow in shallow rows 12in (30cm) apart and thin the seedlings to 9in (23cm).

Deep beds Sow the blanching varieties in rows 8in (20cm) apart and thin to 8in (20cm) apart in the rows. Sow non-blanching varieties in rows 10in (25cm) apart and thin to 10in (25cm). (*See p. 135*.)

MAINTENANCE Weed and water non-blanching varieties when necessary. Dig up the chicon varieties in fall for blanching (*see right*).

HARVESTING If the chicon varieties are kept in a frost-free shed, they can be forced as required to ensure a supply of chicory throughout the winter (*see right*). The unblanched varieties are simply cut as soon as the hearts have filled out. They will last well into the early winter.

PESTS AND DISEASES Chicory is generally trouble-free. See pp. 46–53 for general pests and diseases.

BLANCHING CHICORY

Dig chicon varieties in the fall, trim the leaves to within ½in (1cm) of the root and lay them in a box of moist peat. Every three to four weeks, plunge some roots into a container full of peat. Use a deep box, such as an orange crate, so you can pack the peat tightly around the roots. This restricts the spread of the leaves and results in firm chicons.

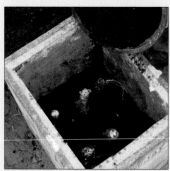

1 *Bury the roots upright in a box one-third full of peat and cover them with another 9in (23cm) layer. Make sure the peat is packed down. Put the box in a warm place.*

2 *After 4–5 weeks, the chicons will have grown to 6–8in (15–20cm) long. Remove them from the box and cut them away from the roots.*

PLANTING AND HARVESTING TIMES

	Sow inside	Plant out	Sow outside	Harvest
Early spring			•	
Mid-spring				
Late spring				
Early summer			•	
Midsummer				
Late summer				
Early autumn				
Mid-autumn				•
Late autumn				•
Early winter				•
Midwinter				•
Late winter				•

Lettuce

As the prime summer salad vegetable, lettuce is considered a "must" for the vegetable garden. In most climates it can be grown almost all year-round outside and, by using cloches (*see p. 140*) or cultivating in a heated greenhouse, you can harvest throughout the year.

VARIETIES For the earliest sowings choose a quick-maturing variety like *Tom Thumb* or *Buttercrunch*. For successional sowing outside, *Great Lakes* or *Avoncrisp* are recommended, or the Romaine varieties *Paris White* or *Lobjoits Green Cos*. If you prefer a loose-head lettuce, try *Salad Bowl* or the red-leaved *Lollo Rossa*. There are many cut-and-come-again mixtures available to suit all tastes, although I have found *Saladisi* to be a good variety.

SOIL AND SITE Lettuce prefers a water-retentive soil with a pH of about 6.5. Grow it in the soil that was manured for a previous crop as freshly manured soil is too rich and likely to cause rotting at the base. All varieties require a relatively cool spot so, if your garden is likely to become very hot in summer, sow them in semi-shade. They need no extra feeding.

Of course, lettuce is often interplanted between other, slower-maturing crops, such as Brussels sprouts or cabbages, in which case the soil preparation should always be for the main crop and you should leave the lettuce to take its chances.

• If you are using the three-year rotation plan (*see p. 134*), grow them in Plot B.

SOWING AND PLANTING Make the first sowing in seed trays in the heated greenhouse in late winter. Start the seeds off in a tray of organic compost (*see p. 252*) at a temperature of between 60–65°F (15–18°C). Transfer them to a larger tray, about 2in (5cm) apart, as soon as they are large enough to handle and grow them on at about 50°F (20°C). When the seedlings are about 2in (5cm) tall, plant them out under cloches, normally in early spring, 6in (15cm) apart in rows 6in (15cm) apart.

At the same time, sow a row of seed under the cloche to follow them, using one of the larger, later varieties. Leave some to grow under the cloche and transplant the others into the open ground 9in (23cm) apart, with 12in (30cm) between rows, as soon as they are large enough to handle. Continue sowing outside about every two weeks until midsummer, thinning the sown row so that the lettuces are about 9in (23cm) apart, and use the thinnings to plant another row or two.

Make the final sowing in midsummer. Plant out as before and cover with cloches in early fall to mature them.

Plant cut-and-come-again lettuce in a wide band, scattering the seed thinly. Make the first sowing outside in early spring.

Deep beds Sow as described above, but set the plants out in a block rather than rows (see p. 136). Space the seeds 6in (15cm) apart for the earliest sowings and 9in (23cm) apart for later, successional sowings.

MAINTENANCE Weed regularly between plants and water if necessary.

HARVESTING When the heart of the lettuce feels full and hard, pull out the whole plant, cut off the root, and put it on the compost heap. Leave cut-and-come-again lettuces in the ground. Cut the leaves near the base of the plant and more leaves will grow.

PESTS AND DISEASES
Millipedes, cutworms, slugs, aphids, botrytis, and downy mildew fungus can affect lettuce (see pp. 46–53). See p. 257 for greenhouse pests and diseases.

PLANTING AND HARVESTING TIMES

	Sow inside	Plant out	Sow outside	Harvest
Early spring		•	•	•
Mid-spring		•	•	
Late spring		•	•	
Early summer		•	•	
Midsummer		•	•	
Late summer	•		•	
Early autumn	•			•
Mid-autumn	•			•
Late autumn	•			•
Early winter				•
Midwinter	•			•
Late winter		•	•	•

CULTIVATING LETTUCE IN THE GREENHOUSE

Early lettuce can be raised as described for growing under cloches (see p. 140), or sown directly in greenhouse borders. Raise the beds to improve drainage (see p. 75) and dig in plenty of well-rotted compost. Rake in a handful of blood, fish, and bone meal per square yard/meter, and sow seeds in groups of three, 9in (23cm) apart each way. When they germinate, thin each group to one plant. Alternatively, sow in boxes and transplant (see p. 272) 9in (23cm) apart when the seedlings are 1½in (4cm) high. Plant at the same depth as the seedlings are growing in the box to prevent rotting at the base. This is especially important with overwintered crops.

Using the varieties *Magnet, Dandie, or Kellys,* start sowing in the heated greenhouse in late summer and continue through to midwinter. In the cold greenhouse, sow in late summer for cutting in late fall and again in late winter for harvesting from mid-spring onward.

Endive

Endive is a good salad vegetable for late summer, fall, and winter, although it tends to be slightly tough if not properly cultivated. Like chicory, it has a slightly bitter flavor.

VARIETIES *Moss Curled* or *Fine de Louvier* are varieties with heavily fringed leaves for late summer and fall cropping. For winter harvesting, *Batavian Broad Leaved* or *Bubikopf 2* are best.

SOIL AND SITE Endives need semi-shade because they may become bitter and run to seed in hot sunshine. They prefer a soil that is rich and moisture retentive, with a pH of about 6.5. Apply two handfuls of blood, fish, and bone meal per square yard/meter, preferably two to three weeks before sowing.

• If you use the three-year rotation plan (see p. 134), grow in Plot B.

SOWING Sow the earlier crops in early summer and winter types in late summer, in shallow rows 12in (30cm) apart, in a place where they can be cloched. Avoid transplanting endives as they may run to seed, so thin the rows to 12in (30cm) apart.

Deep beds Sow in shallow rows 9in (23cm) apart and thin to 9in (23cm). (See p. 135.)

MAINTENANCE Weed and water if necessary. Cover the latest-sown rows with cloches in late fall. About three months after sowing, blanch the plants by covering them with a flowerpot with the hole blocked with a lump of clay, or, provided the leaves are dry when you do it, cover the row with black plastic. Alternatively, lift the plants, tie the leaves together to exclude light from the hearts, and replant them in a box of moist soil in a cool but frost-free place.

HARVESTING About three weeks after blanching (see left), the hearts become creamy in color and lose their bitter taste. They are then ready to harvest.

PESTS AND DISEASES Endive is usually trouble free. See pp. 46–53 for general pests and diseases.

PLANTING AND HARVESTING TIMES

	Sow inside	Plant out	Sow outside	Harvest
Early spring				
Mid-spring				
Late spring				
Early summer			•	
Midsummer				
Late summer			•	
Early autumn				
Mid-autumn				•
Late autumn				•
Early winter				•
Midwinter				•
Late winter				•

Shoot vegetables

This diverse group of vegetables, grown for their succulent stems, provides an assortment of flavors and forms. Several are highly prized as "gourmet" delicacies and they certainly demand more careful attention during cultivation than most other crops. All the shoot vegetables require plenty of water.

Cynara scolymus
Grown as annuals
or perennials,
globe artichokes
need a sunny,
sheltered position.
*For cultivation
details, see p. 150.*

▲ FLORENCE FENNEL
Foeniculum vulgare dulce
Grown for its aniseed flavor,
Florence fennel needs moist
conditions to prevent it from
running to seed. *For cultivation
details, see p .151.*

▲ ASPARAGUS
Asparagus officinalis
A well-drained bed, sunshine,
and a lot of water are needed
to grow asparagus. *For
cultivation details, see p. 151.*

CELERY ▶
Apium graveolens
There are two
types of celery:
self-blanching
and blanched,
which is more
demanding. Both
need a moisture-
retentive soil. *For
cultivation details,
see p. 152.*

▲ RHUBARB
Rheum rhaponticum
Although eaten as a dessert, this hardy perennial
is technically a vegetable, as we eat the stem,
not the fruit. Rhubarb tolerates a wide range
of conditions. *For cultivation details, see p. 153.*

Cultivating shoot vegetables

Globe artichokes

Globe artichokes are a real "gourmet" vegetable, but they are faster-cropping and less demanding than many others. They can be grown as annuals or perennials and are decorative enough to grow in your flower borders if you have no room in the vegetable plot.

VARIETIES New varieties appear and disappear again from time to time, but, in my opinion, *Green Globe* has yet to be topped.

SOIL AND SITE Choose a sunny but sheltered part of the garden. Work in plenty of organic matter to improve the drainage quality of heavy soils (*see pp. 15–17*). Growing in deep beds will assist drainage too (*see p. 136*). If necessary, add lime to the soil to achieve a pH of 6.5.
• If you are growing artichokes as annuals, put them with the cabbages on plot C in the three-year crop rotation plan (*see p. 134*), but manure the area they will occupy. Otherwise, grow them in a plot of their own with the other perennials.

SOWING AND PLANTING
The traditional way is to buy "suckers"—shoots that arise from the roots of mature plants—and to plant them 3ft (1m) square in mid-spring. Alternatively, you can grow globe artichokes from seed. Sow in late winter in 3in (7.5cm) pots in a temperature of about 65°F (18°C). When the seedlings appear, put them in full sun in a temperature of 55°F (13°C). To grow them as perennials, plant them out 3ft (lm) square in mid-spring, or at the back of the ornamental border.

Deep beds The best way, in my opinion, is to grow globe artichokes as annuals in deep beds, planting them 18in (45cm) apart in mid-spring. That way, you will get the

▲ **Planting in a mixed border**
Globe artichokes are decorative enough to mix with plants in the ornamental border.

▶ **Harvesting selectively** *Each plant will produce 2–4 heads. Cut the biggest to encourage the others to grow.*

same number of heads per plant, quadrupling the yield per square yard/meter. (*See p. 136.*)

MAINTENANCE Artichokes need plenty of water, so mulch with well-rotted, compost or manure (*see p. 20*), and water them in dry weather.

HARVESTING Cut the heads while they are still fairly tightly closed. Once they start to open they become tough. Removing the sideshoots makes the individual heads bigger but reduces the yield.

After harvesting, cut the stems to within 12in (30cm) of the ground. New shoots will appear and, when they are about 2ft (60cm) long, tie them together and earth them up like celery (*see p. 152*) to blanch them. After a few weeks, the stems can be cooked and eaten.

PESTS AND DISEASES These plants are affected by slugs (*see p. 50*). See also p. 198 for pests and diseases that affect shoot vegetables.

PLANTING AND HARVESTING TIMES

	Sow inside	Plant out	Sow outside	Harvest
Early spring				
Mid-spring		•	•	
Late spring				
Early summer				
Midsummer				•
Late summer				•
Early autumn				•
Mid-autumn				
Late autumn				
Early winter				
Midwinter	•			
Late winter				

Asparagus

Asparagus is a perennial crop, much improved by organic husbandry. It takes up a lot of space for the amount harvested, and will not produce a full harvest of spears for three years, but the unique flavor of asparagus is well worth the time and space it demands.

VARIETIES The American variety *Mary Washington* is strong-growing and reliable, producing thick shoots. It is also resistant to rust disease. New European varieties like *Jersey Knight Improved* have the distinction of producing only male plants, so there is no reduction in yield brought about by producing seed.

SOIL AND SITE Good drainage and lots of sunshine are essential. If your soil is light, work in plenty of well-rotted manure or compost or one of the alternatives (*see pp. 21–28*) and grow the plants in flat beds rather than in raised beds. If you have heavy soil, raise the beds by working plenty of organic matter into the soil in the same way you would make a deep bed (*see p. 136*). Before planting, spread two handfuls of blood, fish, and bone meal per square yard/meter, and lime if needed to raise the soil pH above 6.5 (*see p. 36*).

SOWING AND PLANTING You can raise asparagus from seed but the range of available varieties is limited. Sow 1in (2.5cm) deep in a seedbed (*see p. 269*) in mid-spring and thin to 3in (7.5cm) apart when the seeds germinate. Transplant to the permanent position, 12in (30cm) apart, the following spring. Alternatively, buy one-year-old roots ("crowns"). Dig a trench 6in (15cm) deep and 12in (30cm) wide, with the bottom slightly raised in the center. As soon as you get the crowns, soak them in water for an hour and then plant them 12in (30cm) apart, spreading out their roots before covering them.

Cutting down asparagus ferns *In fall, cut back the yellowing stems and mulch around the plants.*

MAINTENANCE Make sure the plants never go short of water, especially in the first year. In early spring each year, repeat the application of fertilizer and, in the fall, spread well-rotted compost or manure around the plants. After about seven or eight years, start another bed and, when that is in full production, discontinue the first one.

HARVESTING Start light cutting in the second year, when the plants have begun to get established. You can take nearly a full crop in the third and subsequent years. Cut the shoots when there is about 4in (10cm) above ground and the tip is still tightly closed. Cut below ground down to the tough base. Always leave some shoots and continue cutting for no more than four weeks in the third year and six weeks in following years.

PESTS AND DISEASES Asparagus is affected by slugs, asparagus rust, and asparagus beetles (*see pp. 46–53 and 198*).

PLANTING AND HARVESTING TIMES

	Sow inside	Plant out	Sow outside	Harvest
Early spring				
Mid-spring		•	•	
Late spring				•
Early summer				•
Midsummer				
Late summer				
Early autumn				
Mid-autumn				
Late autumn				
Early winter				
Midwinter				
Late winter				

Florence fennel

Florence fennel is not an easy plant to grow, but worth persevering with for its unique aniseed flavor. The swollen stems can be eaten either raw or cooked.

VARIETIES For an early variety try either *Pronto* or *Amigo*, but for a main crop I recommend *Romanesco* and *Zeta Fino*.

SOIL AND SITE Florence fennel requires plenty of sunshine and a moisture-retentive soil rich in organic matter, with a pH of above 6.5.
• If you are using the three-year crop rotation plan (*see p. 134*), grow Florence fennel in Plot A.

SOWING Sow in shallow rows 18in (45cm) apart from mid-spring to late summer. Later, thin to 8in (20cm) apart. Sow little and often to avoid cropping all at once.

MAINTENANCE Ensure the plants do not dry out or they will run to seed (*see p. 143*). When the bases begin to swell to form bulbs about the size of golf balls, earth up around them (*see p. 186*) to keep them sweet and tender.

HARVESTING Cut the heads two or three weeks after earthing up.

PESTS AND DISEASES Fennel can be attacked by slugs (*see p. 50*) and the pests and diseases that affect shoot vegetables (*see p. 198*).

PLANTING AND HARVESTING TIMES

	Sow inside	Plant out	Sow outside	Harvest
Early spring				
Mid-spring			•	
Late spring			•	
Early summer			•	
Midsummer			•	•
Late summer			•	•
Early autumn				•
Mid-autumn				•
Late autumn				
Early winter				
Midwinter				
Late winter				

Celery

If you opt for the self-blanching varieties, celery is not difficult to grow. What may be difficult for the organic gardener is finding seed that has not been "dressed," or treated with a fungicide.

VARIETIES The blanched types are grown in trenches. Varieties include *Giant Red*, the color referring to the tinge at the base of the otherwise white sticks and *Giant Pascal*.

Self-blanching types are grown in flat ground and are much easier. They produce very light green shoots. Recommended varieties include *Lathom Self-Blanching* and *Golden Self-Blanching*.

SOIL AND SITE A moisture-retentive soil is imperative, so dig in plenty of organic matter (*see pp. 21–28*). Celery likes a soil pH of 6.5, so add lime if necessary. Trenches for blanched types must be dug out as described below.

To grow self-blanching celery, simply dig in plenty of well-rotted organic matter, and lime to a pH of 6.5.

• If you are using the three-year crop rotation plan (*see p. 134*), grow celery in Plot A.

SOWING AND PLANTING Sow both types in late winter at a temperature of 65°F (18°C). Sow on the surface of the potting compost in a seed tray and do not cover the seeds, as they need light to germinate. When they germinate, transfer them to a wider spacing in a seed tray and grow them at about 55°F (13°C) until late spring. Harden them off in a cold frame (*see p. 254*) and plant out in early summer.

Plant rows of blanched celery in trenches (*see below*) with 12in (30cm) between plants.

Plant out self-blanching varieties in blocks with 9in (23cm) between plants. This will help the plants to shade each other, which keeps the stems whiter.

MAINTENANCE The self-blanching types require only weeding and watering in dry weather. The blanched varieties need more attention.

They are prodigious feeders so give them a feed of animal-manure liquid fertilizer in midsummer and again a month later. Blanch the stems as described below and cover the rows with tunnel cloches in late fall (*see p. 141*).

Deep beds Self-blanching celery can be grown in deep beds at the same distances (*see p. 136*). Blanched celery is too awkward to manage from the edge of the bed, so is best grown separately.

HARVESTING Dig self-blanching celery before the first frost at the end of fall. Blanched types can be used from then onward, digging out a plant at a time and recovering the rest.

PESTS AND DISEASES These plants are affected by slugs, celery fly, and celery leaf spot (*see pp. 50 and 198*).

PLANTING AND HARVESTING TIMES

	Sow inside	Plant out	Sow outside	Harvest
Early spring				
Mid-spring				
Late spring		•		
Early summer		•		
Midsummer				
Late summer				•
Early autumn				•
Mid-autumn				•
Late autumn				•
Early winter				•
Midwinter				•
Late winter	•			•

BLANCHING CELERY

Certain varieties of celery must be blanched by keeping them out of direct sunlight. This is done by covering the stems with soil, but careful preparation is needed to prevent rotting.

1 Dig a trench one spade deep and 18in (45cm) wide, heaping the soil either side. Put 2in (5cm) of well-rotted compost or manure in the bottom, and cover this with 1in (2.5cm) of soil. Plant out the seedlings 12in (30cm) apart.

2 In midsummer, remove any suckers from near the base and wrap the bunches of stalks with corrugated cardboard, brown paper, or several layers of newspaper. This prevents soil from getting between the stalks.

3 Fill the trench with soil to the bottom of the leaves. As the celery grows, repeat this process twice more at three-week intervals, sloping the soil to drain off rain and prevent rotting.

Rhubarb

I have included rhubarb among the vegetables because we eat its stems rather than its fruit. It is easy to grow and can be harvested from late winter through to midsummer.

VARIETIES Recommended varieties are *Cawood Delight*, *Victoria*, *Timperley Early*, *Red Champagne*, and *Stockbridge Arrow*.

SOIL AND SITE Rhubarb likes a soil pH of 7.0, so add lime if necessary to attain this level. It also prefers a well-drained soil with plenty of well-rotted compost or manure dug in (*see pp. 21–28*). Apart from this, rhubarb is fairly tolerant and is frost hardy. Plant it in a bed reserved for perennials.

PLANTING Mature roots ("crowns") are generally planted in the winter, although you can also buy plants in pots for year-round planting. Most people will not require more than two or three plants but, if you wish to grow more, set the plants 2ft 6in (75cm) apart with 3ft (90cm) between rows. Cover the crowns with 1in (2.5cm) of soil.

MAINTENANCE Weed and water as necessary. Mulch with well-

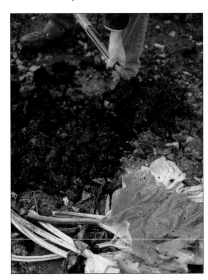

Mulching rhubarb *It is not practical to dig in organic matter around the plants, so mulch each fall instead.*

rotted compost or manure every year after the leaves have died down.

HARVESTING Leave the plants to grow during the first year. In subsequent years, pull the thickest sticks when they are long enough, but never strip the plant. Remove any flower spikes and put the leaves on the compost heap.

PESTS AND DISEASES Rhubarb is susceptible to aphid attack (*see p. 50*), and viruses (*see p. 199*).

PLANTING AND HARVESTING TIMES

	Sow inside	Plant out	Sow outside	Harvest
Early spring				•
Mid-spring				•
Late spring				•
Early summer				•
Midsummer				•
Late summer				
Early autumn				
Mid-autumn				
Late autumn			•	
Early winter			•	
Midwinter			•	
Late winter			•	•

Sea kale

Sea kale is a permanent plant, not at all difficult to grow. You can grow it outside for eating in the spring or bring it inside and force it for a superb winter delicacy.

VARIETIES *Lily White* is a little whiter than the common type and has a slightly better flavor.

SOIL AND SITE Sea kale requires plenty of sun and a soil rich in organic matter, so dig in lots of well-rotted compost or manure (*see pp. 21–28*). If necessary add lime to the soil to achieve a pH of above 6.5 (*see p. 36*).

SOWING AND PLANTING I recommend starting from root cuttings (called "thongs") or young plants bought from a specialty grower. Order them early for spring delivery and plant them 12in (30cm) square. Lay the thongs flat in the soil about 2in (5cm) deep. It is possible to obtain seed but, in my experience, it is rarely successful.

MAINTENANCE Hoe to keep beds weed free (*see p. 57*) and water as required.

HARVESTING Leave the plants to grow for the first and ideally the second year. If you cannot wait, you can actually begin forcing a few plants in the second year (*see below*). Allow the plants to regrow, and repeat the process for three more years. Then dig up the roots, take some root cuttings, and start again. Alternatively, you can then force a crop in the greenhouse or even on a windowsill. Lift the plants after the first frost and pot them into large pots of moist peat. Cover with another pot, excluding all light, and keep the temperature between 50–60°F (10–15°C). After forcing, the plants should be discarded.

PESTS AND DISEASES Sea kale is susceptible to attack by slugs and the pests and diseases that affect shoot vegetables (*see pp. 50 and 198*).

Forcing sea kale *In late winter, place black plastic pots over a few plants, covering any drainage holes with black plastic. Harvest the shoots in spring.*

PLANTING AND HARVESTING TIMES

	Sow inside	Plant out	Sow outside	Harvest
Early spring		•		•
Mid-spring				•
Late spring				•
Early summer				
Midsummer				
Late summer				
Early autumn				
Mid-autumn				
Late autumn				
Early winter				
Midwinter				
Late winter				

Pod and seed vegetables

The vegetables in this group, with the exception of okra and sweet corn, are all members of the *Leguminosae* family, and are an excellent source of protein and fiber. The nitrogen-fixing qualities of the peas and beans are another good reason why you should devote as much space as possible to growing them. When you have picked the vegetables, save some seeds for sowing the next year; the rest of the plants can be dug into the soil or removed to release their nitrogen on the compost heap (*see pp. 32–34*). Pod and seed vegetables are therefore doubly valuable.

▲ **OKRA** *Abelmoschus (syn. Hibiscus) esculenta*
In areas where the average temperature is at least 70°F (21°C), two crops of this fast-maturing vegetable can be harvested in a single year. It is also known as "gumbo" or "lady's fingers." *For cultivation details, see p. 156.*

▶ **SWEET CORN** *Zea mays*
Homegrown sweet corn has an especially sweet flavor as it can be eaten as soon as it is picked, before most of the sugar has turned into starch. The crop needs lots of sun and is wind-pollinated—so grow it in blocks, rather than rows, to aid pollination. *For cultivation details, see p. 156.*

▲ **SNOW PEAS** *Pisum sativum*
These vegetables, also known as "snap peas," are becoming increasingly popular. The whole pod is cooked and eaten with the tiny peas inside. *For cultivation details, see p. 157.*

▶ **PEAS** *Pisum sativum*
Like sweet corn, peas taste better when eaten soon after picking, before the sugar changes into starch. Sow early and main crop varieties for successional harvesting. *For cultivation details, see p. 157.*

◀ **BROAD BEANS** *Vicia faba*
A very rewarding vegetable to grow, broad beans are high in protein and a good source of green manure. They should be picked young and can be dried and stored for winter use. *For cultivation details, see p. 158.*

▶ **RUNNER BEANS** *Phaseolus coccineus*
This popular and very prolific summer vegetable has attractive flowers and foliage and is suitable for growing in the ornamental border or training up wigwams of poles. Runner beans need careful soil preparation and a water-retentive soil. *For cultivation details, see p. 159.*

◀ **GREEN BEANS**
Phaseolus vulgaris
These flat or rounded beans are a suitable crop for the greenhouse. Green beans are available in bush and climbing varieties and require warm soil conditions. *For cultivation details, see p. 160.*

▲ **LIMA BEANS** *Phaseolus lunatue*
Also commonly known as "butter beans," these highly nutritious seeds need particularly warm soil conditions to germinate, and can only be grown successfully in warm climates. They can be dried for winter use. *For cultivation details, see p. 161.*

▲ **SOYBEANS** *Glycine max*
Rich in protein and calcium, these highly versatile beans are considered the most important crop in many countries. However, they are only successful in warm climates and are comparatively low-yielding. *For cultivation details, see p. 161.*

▲ **PEANUTS** *Arachis hypogaea*
Suitable only for warm areas, peanuts need to be protected against frosts and require a light, sandy soil. This is because the plants sow their seeds into the soil where the nuts develop inside protective shells. *For cultivation details, see p. 161.*

Cultivating pod and seed vegetables

Okra

Sometimes known as "lady's fingers" or "gumbo," this crop is only suitable for warm climates. The yield decreases dramatically when average temperatures are below 70°F (21°C). The pods are eaten whole or shelled and eaten like peas.

VARIETIES *Cajun Delight* has been bred to cope with outdoor temperatures. *Clemson Spineless* is fast and very heavy yielding with pointed, spineless pods.
SOIL AND SITE A sunny position and a well-drained, fertile soil are essential. Dig in plenty of organic matter and, if the soil is badly drained, grow the plants on a raised deep bed (*see p. 136*).
• If you are using the three-year crop rotation plan (*see p. 134*), grow okra in Plot B.
SOWING AND PLANTING It is quite possible to produce two crops of this vegetable in a

single growing season, sowing the first when all danger of frost has passed in the spring and the second, for fall harvesting, in early or midsummer. Sow in shallow rows 3ft (90cm) apart and, when the plants are large enough to handle, thin them to 18in (45cm) apart. They can also be raised in the greenhouse or on a windowsill but, since they resent root disturbance, this should be done in 3in (8cm) pots. Plant out the seedlings at the same distances in late spring or early summer, when all danger of frost has passed.
MAINTENANCE Keep the plants weed free and slightly on the dry side to prevent rotting. Apply two handfuls of blood, fish, and bone meal per square yard/meter about a month after sowing, then mulch between the plants with well-rotted compost (*see p. 20*).
Some people suffer an allergic reaction when working with okra,

so avoid handling it when the crop is wet and, if you do have problems, wear gloves.
HARVESTING Pick every two or three days when the pods are small. If you want to keep the pods for more than two days, put them in a cool place and cover them with a damp cloth.
PESTS AND DISEASES Okra is susceptible to aphids and the pests and diseases that affect pod and seed vegetables (*see pp. 50 and 198*).

PLANTING AND HARVESTING TIMES

	Sow inside	Plant out	Sow outside	Harvest
Early spring	•			
Mid-spring	•		•	
Late spring		•	•	
Early summer		•	•	
Midsummer			•	•
Late summer				•
Early autumn				•
Mid-autumn				•
Late autumn				
Early winter				
Midwinter				
Late winter				

Sweet corn

As soon as a pod of sweet corn is picked from the plant, the sugar in it starts to turn to starch. Growing your own enables you to eat it freshly picked, when the cobs taste sweetest and are at their most nutritious.

VARIETIES Modern, fast-maturing varieties are easy to grow in most climates. The sweetest are the new hybrids like *Earlybird*, but they must be grown away from other varieties since cross-pollination will reduce the sugar content.
SOIL AND SITE Sweet corn likes plenty of sun and a soil pH of about 6.5.
• If you are using the three-year crop rotation plan (*see p. 134*), grow sweet corn in Plot B.

SOWING AND PLANTING
Normally, plants are raised in a heated greenhouse or on a windowsill. Sow pairs of seeds in mid-spring in 3in (8cm) pots at a temperature of 65°F (18°C), and thin to leave the strongest seedling if both germinate. Harden off in a cold frame in late spring (*see p. 254*) and plant outside in early summer in blocks, with 2ft (60cm) between plants.
Alternatively, sow them outside in mid-spring, in furrows 2ft (60cm) apart and about 6–9in (15–22cm) deep. Sow groups of two or three seeds every 2ft (60cm) in the bottom of the furrows and cover with 1in (2.5cm) of soil. Then cover with a sheet of plastic to protect against frost. The ridges of soil will support the sheeting and prevent the seedlings

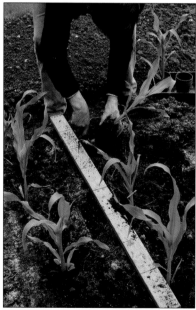

Planting in blocks to encourage pollination *Plant seedlings in a series of short, staggered rows to give the plants the best chance of wind pollination.*

Harvesting sweet corn *Break off ripe sweet corn by pulling the cob downward with one hand while bracing the rest of the plant with the other.*

from touching it. When the seedlings reach the sheeting in late spring, cut slits and help them through. When the plants come into flower, cut the sheeting away. The plants will be as far advanced as those raised in a greenhouse.

MAINTENANCE Keep the rows weed free and mulch with compost, manure, or paper (*see p. 58*). When the plants flower, they will benefit from extra watering.

HARVESTING When the tassels at the top of the cobs turn brown and then black, the cobs are ready for harvesting.

PESTS AND DISEASES Sweet corn is generally trouble free. See pp. 46–53 for general pests and diseases and p. 198 for pests and diseases that affect pod and seed vegetables.

PLANTING AND HARVESTING TIMES

	Sow inside	Plant out	Sow outside	Harvest
Early spring				
Mid-spring		•	•	
Late spring		•		
Early summer		•		
Midsummer				
Late summer				•
Early autumn				•
Mid-autumn				•
Late autumn				
Early winter				
Midwinter				
Late winter				

Peas

Despite what the processors of frozen peas may tell you about their freshness, there is no doubt that peas taste much better when they are grown organically and eaten minutes after picking.

VARIETIES Two varieties are necessary—an early one and a main crop type. Recommended for an early sowing are *Douce Provence* and *Meteor*, while *Hurst Green Shaft* and *Onward* are fine main crop varieties.

I also suggest that you try one of the snow pea or snap pea varieties—where the pods are eaten as well as the seeds. These have improved greatly over the past 10 years, and are now very succulent, with no stringiness. Try *Oregon Sugar Pod* and *Sugar Bon*.

SOIL AND SITE Peas, like all the other legumes, make their own nitrogen and require little extra feeding. Too rich a soil leads to a great deal of foliage but a small crop of vegetables. Peas like a soil pH of 6.5, so add lime to attain this level if necessary (*see p. 36*).

• If you are using the three-year crop rotation plan (*see p. 134*), grow peas in Plot B.

SOWING The earliest peas can be sown in the fall and overwintered. However, this is somewhat risky and, in a hard winter, the crop will be small. Alternatively, an early sowing can be made in plastic guttering (*see below*).

Next, plant in the open ground in early spring but cover with cloches (*see p. 140*). Peas are best sown in a wide trench dug with a spade. Make the row about 2in (5cm) deep and scatter the seeds in it so that they are roughly 2in (5cm) apart, cover, and firm down with the back of a rake.

Unprotected sowing starts in mid-spring, depending on the soil conditions, and is done in the same way, using maincrop varieties. Sow at two-week intervals until early summer.

Deep beds Most peas are difficult to support in deep beds so here I would recommend a semi-leafless variety like *Bikini*. This is a relatively new breeding breakthrough, producing plants with

SOWING PEAS IN GUTTERING

A useful way of raising an early pea crop without risking frost damage is to sow seeds in a length of plastic guttering in the greenhouse in late winter. Plant out the seedlings under cloches until they become established (*see p. 140*).

1 *Fill a length of plastic guttering with soil and sow peas at 2in (5cm) intervals. Make two staggered rows 1in (2.5cm) apart and cover with soil. Leave the seedlings in the greenhouse until they are about 3in (8cm) tall.*

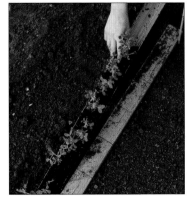

2 *Using a planting board as a guide, make a straight seed row with a draw hoe. Slide the entire contents of the guttering into the prepared furrow, firm in well, and water.*

few leaves but masses of tendrils. Sow the peas in a block with the rows 6in (15cm) apart and the seeds about 2in (5cm) apart in the rows (see p. 136), and they will grow into each other and form a completely self-supporting block of plants.

MAINTENANCE Apart from leafless varieties grown in the way described above, all types need to be supported with pea and bean netting or with sticks (see below). Hoe regularly to remove weeds and mulch with well-rotted compost or manure (see p. 58).

Supporting peas with sticks If you can find several twiggy sticks, cut them to a length of 4ft (1.2m) and push one into the ground beside each plant.

HARVESTING It is generally better to pick the pods just a little on the young side, because they are at their sweetest, but try to pick just before they are cooked to retain the sugar. When all the peas have been harvested, cut the foliage off and leave the roots in the ground to release their nitrogen.

PESTS AND DISEASES Peas may be affected by birds, mice, mildew, pea moths, and pea and bean weevils (see pp. 46–53 and p. 198).

PLANTING AND HARVESTING TIMES

	Sow inside	Plant out	Sow outside	Harvest
Early spring		•	•	
Mid-spring			•	
Late spring			•	•
Early summer			•	•
Midsummer				•
Late summer				•
Early autumn				•
Mid-autumn			•	•
Late autumn			•	
Early winter				
Midwinter				
Late winter		•		

Broad beans

Wonderful value in the vegetable plot, broad beans produce an early vegetable of unique flavor and just about the best green manure possible (see p. 32).

VARIETIES Aquadulce Claudia is the primary variety for early sowing. It is sown in late fall to give the first crop of the season. Express is a heavy-yielding maincrop variety, and Imperial Green Longpod has an excellent flavor.

SOIL AND SITE Broad beans, like all the other legumes, make their own nitrogen and require little extra feeding. They like a soil pH of 6.5, so add lime to attain this level if necessary (see p. 36).
• If you are using the three-year crop rotation plan (see p. 134), grow broad beans in Plot B.

SOWING AND PLANTING Sow Aquadulce Claudia in late fall or late winter, in double rows 12in (30cm) apart and 2in (5cm) deep, with about 4in (10cm) between seeds. If you grow more than one double row, allow 3ft (1m) between them. Follow with the main crop sowing at the same distances in early spring. Alternatively, sow the early crop under cloches in midwinter (see p. 140).

Deep beds Sow in staggered rows with 6in (15cm) between each seed (see p. 136).

MAINTENANCE Provide support in exposed gardens and for all winter-sown crops. A single string tied to posts either side of the

Supporting broad beans Tie nylon twine between wooden posts either side of the plants, at the end of each row.

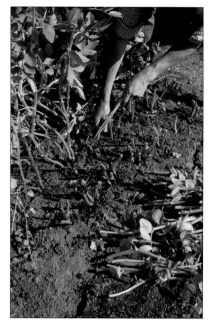

Cutting down broad beans If you garden in a warm climate, cut plants down to 2in (5cm) after harvesting. They will regrow to provide a second crop.

plants should suffice (see opposite). If plants are cloched, remove the cloches when the plants touch the tops. Water if necessary and mulch between rows with compost.

HARVESTING Pull the beans before the pods become tough and leathery. They are much more tasty when small and the plants will be encouraged to produce more. In warm climates, cut the plants back and allow them to regrow to give a second crop (see below). Dry beans in the sun and store in airtight bottles for winter use in soups and stews.

PESTS AND DISEASES Broad beans may be affected by blackfly, pea and bean weevils, and chocolate spot (see p. 198 and p. 233).

PLANTING AND HARVESTING TIMES

	Sow inside	Plant out	Sow outside	Harvest
Early spring			•	
Mid-spring			•	
Late spring				
Early summer				•
Midsummer				•
Late summer				•
Early autumn				•
Mid-autumn				
Late autumn			•	
Early winter				
Midwinter			•	
Late winter			•	

Runner beans

Runner beans are one of the most prolific of all summer vegetables. The flowers and foliage are attractive, so they make good subjects for growing in the borders (*see p. 71*), up a wigwam of canes, or on the fence.

VARIETIES *Painted Lady* is the one for the borders, since the flowers are an attractive red and white. *Mergoles* has white flowers followed by stringless green pods that freeze well, while *Polestar* is one of the very best for both yield and quality. *Pickwick* is a new dwarf variety that needs no support and is much earlier than anything else I have seen. Grow it like green beans (*see next page*).

SOIL AND SITE Thorough soil preparation is needed to prevent runner beans from drying out at the roots, since this discourages growth and could be responsible for failure of the flowers to set (*see p. 198*). Dig a trench one spade deep and at least 2ft (60cm) wide and break up the bottom. Half fill it with compost, manure, or even old newspapers twisted up and soaked in water, or better still, liquid manure. Then replace the soil and allow it to settle before planting. The soil pH should be about 6.5.

• If you are using the three-year crop rotation plan (*see p. 134*), grow runner beans in Plot B.

SOWING AND PLANTING Start the plants off in your greenhouse or on a windowsill in mid-spring, sowing one seed per 3in (8cm) pot. Plant out in late spring after hardening off (*see p. 254*). Alternatively, sow against poles set at 12in (30cm) intervals in a double row with 2ft (60cm) between the rows. The best time for this is about two weeks before you expect the last frost. Another way is to make a wigwam of between four and six poles spaced at about 18in–2ft (45–60cm) and tied at the top (*see below*). This is a more attractive method for the borders but is not as productive, because the plants lack light and air when they reach the top of the poles. Encourage the plants to twist around the poles.

Deep beds Runner beans are not a suitable crop for deep beds.

MAINTENANCE Protect the young plants from slugs right away by mulching with coarse pine bark (*see p. 50*). This also helps retain water and suppresses weeds. Pinch off the growing tips when the plants reach the top of their support.

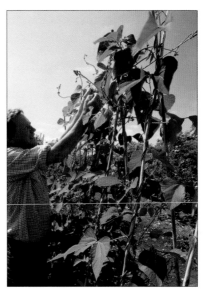

Pinching off *When the plants reach the top of their poles, pinch off the tips to encourage sideshoots to grow.*

TRAINING CLIMBING VEGETABLES

Climbing varieties of crops such as tomatoes, cucumbers, peas, and beans need to be supported as they grow. Peas are usually trained up plastic netting or twiggy sticks (*see facing page*), but other vegetables require different forms of support.

Making wigwams of poles *A wigwam of poles provides an attractive support for beans and cucumbers (see also p. 175). Sow four or five seeds in a circle and train the plants up poles that are tied together at the top.*

Using rows of stakes *Runner beans can be trained to grow up tall stakes. If you grow two rows, cross each pair of poles, tie them together, then run nylon twine through all the supports and peg it into the ground at either end.*

Training plants up strings *Bean and tomato plants will grow up lengths of nylon twine. Tie these to a pole or a nail fixed to a wall, and plant seedlings so that the root ball anchors the string in place.*

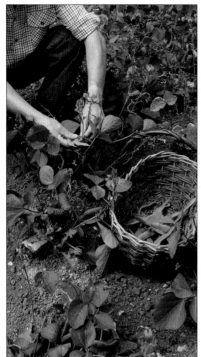

Harvesting dwarf runner beans
Dwarf varieties need no support and some can be harvested very early. Pick the beans when they are young and tender.

It is a popular misconception that spraying the open flowers with water will assist pollination, but there seems to be no evidence that this is true. However, supplying plenty of water to the plant's roots at flowering time does seem to help pollination.

HARVESTING Pick the pods when they are young and have not developed stringiness. This also encourages further production.

PESTS AND DISEASES Runner beans are liable to be affected by slugs, blackfly, halo blight, and failure to set (*see pp. 50, 198, and 233*).

PLANTING AND HARVESTING TIMES

	Sow inside	Plant out	Sow outside	Harvest
Early spring				
Mid-spring	•			
Late spring		•	•	
Early summer			•	
Midsummer				•
Late summer				•
Early autumn				•
Mid-autumn				•
Late autumn				
Early winter				
Midwinter				
Late winter				

Green beans

Dwarf green beans make a small bush, generally very heavy yielding. Climbing green beans need support (*see p. 159*) and will continue to produce over a long period. They are grown like runner beans.

VARIETIES There are two types of dwarf green beans—those that produce flat pods and the round, pencil-podded types. *Masterpiece* is one of the earliest and best flat types and, of the round varieties, *Tendergreen* is recommended. The best climbing varieties are *Hunter*, *Cobra*, and *Purple Podded*.

SOIL AND SITE Green beans, like all the other legumes, make their own nitrogen and require little extra feeding. They like a soil pH of 6.5, so add lime to attain this level if necessary (*see p. 36*).
• If you are using the three-year crop rotation plan (*see p. 134*), grow green beans in Plot B.

SOWING Because green beans need a warm soil, start the first ones off in a greenhouse in early spring. Plant out under cloches in mid-spring (*see p. 140*), setting the plants in rows 12in (30cm) apart with 8in (20cm) between plants. The next crop can be sown under the cloches in early spring putting two seeds every 8in (20cm), again in rows about 12in (30cm) apart and about 2in (5cm) deep. Outside sowings can start in mid-spring at the same distances.

Deep beds Grow bush varieties in staggered rows, 6in (15cm) apart. (*See p. 136*).

MAINTENANCE Hoe to keep beds weed free (*see p. 57*) and mulch between plants with compost, bark, plastic, or paper. Water if necessary in dry weather.

HARVESTING Pick the pods regularly when they are young, before they become stringy. If some pods are left on the plants to dry, they can be podded and stored in airtight jars for winter use. After harvesting, cut the plants off but leave the roots in the ground to release nitrogen into the soil.

PESTS AND DISEASES Slugs, aphids, and halo blight may attack Green beans (*see pp. 50 and 198*). See p. 257 for pests and diseases of greenhouse plants.

PLANTING AND HARVESTING TIMES

	Sow inside	Plant out	Sow outside	Harvest
Early spring	•		•	
Mid-spring		•	•	
Late spring			•	
Early summer			•	•
Midsummer				•
Late summer				•
Early autumn				•
Mid-autumn				•
Late autumn				
Early winter				
Midwinter				
Late winter				

CULTIVATING GREEN BEANS IN THE GREENHOUSE

Climbing varieties are preferable as they make the best use of the available space. *Romano* is fleshy and stringless, while *Purple Podded* is slightly earlier and very tasty.

Sow two seeds in 3in (8cm) pots of potting compost in early spring, at a temperature of 65–70°F (18–21°C). If both seeds germinate, thin to leave the strongest when they reach the first true leaf stage.

Plant in the borders in late spring, setting the plants 12in (30cm) apart and supporting them with a string (*see p. 159*).

The plants will twist around the strings of their own accord. Feed with liquid kelp at weekly intervals throughout the growing season and pinch off the tips when they reach the tops of the string supports.

Once the first crop has been stripped, remove all the lower leaves and drop the plants to the ground carefully, coiling the stems on the ground and allowing the new growth at the top to climb up the string again. This will encourage further growth and another full crop.

Lima beans

Lima, or butter, beans are nutritious and delicious, but they can only be grown in warm climates.

VARIETIES *Burpee Improved Bush* and *Burpee Fordhook* are both recommended. Climbing varieties like *Prizetaker* and *King of the Garden* crop later and are more difficult to grow.
SOIL AND SITE The beans need sunshine and a deep rich soil with plenty of organic matter (*see pp. 21–28*).
• If you are using the three-year crop rotation plan (*see p. 134*), grow them in Plot B.
SOWING Sow in late spring, or when the soil temperature reaches 65°F (18°C). Alternatively, start them off in pots inside at 70°F (21°C), to ensure rapid germination.
  Sow outside 1in (2.5cm) deep in rows 2ft (60cm) apart, with 4in (10cm) between seeds. Sow climbing varieties against 8ft (2.5m) poles set in a tripod, with 3ft (90cm) between the base of each pole. Sow four to six seeds per pole and thin to three.
MAINTENANCE Mulch around plants with well-rotted compost or manure (*see p. 20*) to help retain moisture.
HARVESTING Pick young pods regularly to encourage further production.
PESTS AND DISEASES Lima beans may be attacked by aphids and pea and bean weevils (*see pp. 50 and 198*).

PLANTING AND HARVESTING TIMES

	Sow inside	Plant out	Sow outside	Harvest
Early spring				
Mid-spring				
Late spring			•	
Early summer				
Midsummer				
Late summer				•
Early autumn				•
Mid-autumn				•
Late autumn				
Early winter				
Midwinter				
Late winter				

Soybeans

Extremely high in protein and calcium, soybeans are only suitable for warmer climates.

VARIETIES The best variety available is *Elena*, which has been purposely bred to be better suited to growing and producing in our climate.
SOIL AND SITE Soybeans prefer a well-drained soil, so dig in plenty of organic matter if your soil is heavy (*see pp. 21–28*). If necessary, add lime to raise the soil pH above 6.5.
• If you are using the three-year crop rotation plan (*see p. 134*), grow soybeans in Plot B.
SOWING During early or midsummer, sow seeds 1in (2.5cm) deep in rows 2ft 6in (75cm) apart, with 2in (5cm) between each seed.
MAINTENANCE Use a thick mulch of compost or manure to inhibit weeds and prevent water loss (*see p. 58*). Do not hoe because this would damage the shallow root system.
HARVESTING Harvest when all the leaves have fallen off and the beans can easily be removed and stored for winter. The yields are generally low in relation to the space taken up by the plants.
PESTS AND DISEASES Soybeans are generally trouble free. See pp. 46–53 for general pests and diseases and p. 198 for pests and diseases that affect pod and seed vegetables.

PLANTING AND HARVESTING TIMES

	Sow inside	Plant out	Sow outside	Harvest
Early spring				
Mid-spring				
Late spring				
Early summer			•	
Midsummer			•	
Late summer				•
Early autumn				•
Mid-autumn				•
Late autumn				
Early winter				
Midwinter				
Late winter				

Peanuts

Although capable of withstanding a slight frost, peanuts are only really suitable for cultivation in warm climates.

VARIETIES *Jumbo Virginia* produces high yields of rich-flavored nuts. *Early Spanish* is dwarf and early.
SOIL AND SITE Peanuts need a light soil, preferably well-enriched with organic matter (*see pp. 21–28*).
• If you are using the three-year crop rotation plan (*see p. 134*), grow peanuts in Plot B.
SOWING In cold areas, start the plants off in pots inside, one month before the last frost is due. Alternatively, wait until after the last frost and sow outside—2in (5cm) deep in rows 3ft (90cm) apart—setting the seeds 6in (15cm) apart. Thin the plants to 12in (30cm) apart.
MAINTENANCE Earth up the plants when they are 6in (15cm) tall (*see p. 186*). Then mulch with a deep layer of compost, manure, or grass cuttings (*see p. 58*). Stop watering when the plants begin to flower.
HARVESTING Five months after sowing, dig up the whole plant, dry the roots in the sun, and remove the peanuts.
PESTS AND DISEASES Peanuts are generally trouble free. See pp. 46–53 for general pests and diseases and p. 198 for pests and diseases that affect pod and seed vegetables.

PLANTING AND HARVESTING TIMES

	Sow inside	Plant out	Sow outside	Harvest
Early spring	•			
Mid-spring		•	•	
Late spring				
Early summer				
Midsummer				
Late summer				•
Early autumn				•
Mid-autumn				
Late autumn				
Early winter				
Midwinter				
Late winter				

Fruiting vegetables

Although these crops are technically fruits—the seeds of the plant encased by a fleshy pulp—they are usually classified as vegetables because we eat them as such. They are not frost hardy, and must therefore be started off under glass or grown to maturity in the greenhouse—where their brightly colored forms are extremely decorative. Although perennial in their native tropics, they are grown as annuals in temperate climates and need a rich, moist soil, and plenty of sunshine. The fruiting vegetables are all rich in Vitamin C.

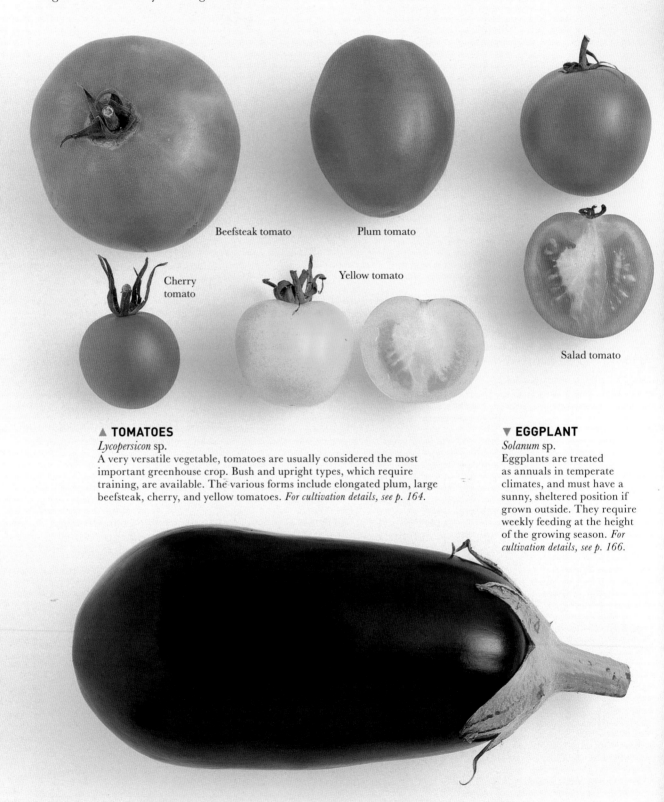

Beefsteak tomato

Plum tomato

Cherry tomato

Yellow tomato

Salad tomato

▲ TOMATOES
Lycopersicon sp.
A very versatile vegetable, tomatoes are usually considered the most important greenhouse crop. Bush and upright types, which require training, are available. The various forms include elongated plum, large beefsteak, cherry, and yellow tomatoes. *For cultivation details, see p. 164.*

▼ EGGPLANT
Solanum sp.
Eggplants are treated as annuals in temperate climates, and must have a sunny, sheltered position if grown outside. They require weekly feeding at the height of the growing season. *For cultivation details, see p. 166.*

Yellow pepper

Green pepper

Red pepper

▲ SWEET PEPPERS
Capsicum sp.
These attractive vegetables are available in an assortment of bright colors. The red peppers are merely green peppers left to ripen on the plant for longer. This gives them a slightly more spicy taste although, as a rule, color is not a reliable guide to flavor. *For cultivation details, see p. 167.*

Hot peppers

◄ HOT PEPPERS
Capsicum sp.
Hot or "chili" peppers are smaller and considerably hotter than sweet peppers. They are heavy-yielding plants, so only a small number is needed to provide an adequate crop. Peppers are raised in the greenhouse and then planted outside, but they need cloche protection in all but the warmest areas. *For cultivation details, see p. 167.*

Cultivating fruiting vegetables

Tomatoes

Tomatoes are a popular greenhouse crop (*see opposite*) but can also be grown outside in most climates. If you live in a cold area, choose early varieties, as the fruit on late-maturing plants will fail to ripen.

VARIETIES Tomatoes are obtainable as bush or upright types. The fruit of the bush types tends to be smaller. *Red Alert* is one of the best bush varieties, giving very early crops of small tasty fruits. *Incas* is an excellent disease-resistant bush variety that bears plum tomatoes.

Of the upright varieties, *Stupice* is tried and tested in cooler climates, while *Golden Sunrise*, a yellow variety, is recommended for flavor in warmer climates.

SOIL AND SITE Like all the vegetable fruits, tomatoes need sun and a well-manured soil that will retain moisture and plant nutrients. They like a pH of about 6.0.

• If you are using the three-year crop rotation plan (*see p. 134*), grow tomatoes in Plot A.

SOWING AND PLANTING Seeds for outdoor varieties must be raised inside a greenhouse or on a windowsill. Sow the seeds in trays (*see p. 271*), spacing them out about 1in (2.5cm) apart, in mid-spring. Transfer them into 3in (9cm) pots at the seed-leaf

Covering bush tomatoes *Protecting plants with a cloche at the end of the growing season extends the harvesting period by helping to ripen the green fruit.*

stage. Put them in the cold frame to harden off in late spring (*see p. 254*) and plant at the beginning of the summer. Set the plants 2ft (60cm) square and plant the climbing varieties against poles.

Deep beds Tomatoes are ideal subjects for the deep beds; plant them 20in (50cm) apart. (*See p. 136.*)

MAINTENANCE Tie the upright types to their poles regularly. Pinch off the tops when they have made three clusters of fruit—or four in warm climates. Remove the sideshoots arising from each leaf joint when they are still small. Bush varieties need no staking or side-shooting, but cover the soil underneath them with straw or bark to raise the fruit off the ground. Feed with a liquid kelp or animal-manure fertilizer at two-week intervals from midsummer to early fall.

HARVESTING Pick as soon as the fruits are ripe to get the

sweetest flavor and encourage the production of more fruits at the end of the season. Lay upright varieties flat on straw and cover with cloches (*see p. 140*).

PESTS AND DISEASES Tomatoes may be affected by whitefly, aphids, leaf mold, red spider mites, potato blight, and virus (*see pp. 46–53 and 199*). See p. 257 for the pests and diseases that affect plants grown in the greenhouse.

Supporting upright tomatoes *Use soft string to tie upright plants to 4ft (1.2m) poles as soon as they are planted.*

PLANTING AND HARVESTING TIMES

	Sow inside	Plant out	Sow outside	Harvest
Early spring	●			
Mid-spring	●			
Late spring			●	
Early summer		●		●
Midsummer				●
Late summer				●
Early autumn				●
Mid-autumn				●
Late autumn				
Early winter				
Midwinter				
Late winter				

CULTIVATING TOMATOES IN THE GREENHOUSE

Suitable varieties for the greenhouse are *Herald* and *Shirley*, which are both early and have good flavor, while the cherry-fruited *Gardener's Delight* and *Sweet Million*, though they crop later and are not resistant to disease, have a superb flavor.

Sow from midwinter onward, depending on the amount of heat you can give the plants. For cold greenhouse planting, sow in late winter at a temperature of 70°F (21°C). Transplant to individual 3in (8cm) pots as soon as the seedlings are big enough to handle. Grow them on at a temperature of 50–55°F (10–12°C), spacing them progressively so that they are not crowded, to produce short, bushy plants. Plant in the border soil or in growing bags 12 in (30cm) apart in mid-spring in the cold greenhouse. If planting in the border, use a variety resistant to root-rot, such as *Piranto* and flood the border with water about two weeks before planting to flush out excess mineral salts from the soil. Then dig in compost or manure and apply one handful of blood, fish, and bone meal per plant before planting.

Water the plants in initially and then leave them to search for water, thereby encouraging extensive root growth. Water again after about a week and from then on give each plant an average of about 2pts (1 liter) per day. The smaller cherry tomatoes *Gardener's Delight* and *Sweet Million*, however, only need about 3pts (1.5 liters) per week if they are to retain their sweetness. When the plants flower, spray them with water once a day to provide the humid conditions that favor good pollination.

After about eight weeks, start feeding with a liquid kelp or animal-manure fertilizer every time you water.

Remove the sideshoots from each leaf joint as they grow, and take off the bottom leaves when they turn yellow. Do not remove leaves above the fruit cluster that is ripening. Hose down daily (*see p. 255*) and shake the supporting wires to move the pollen around. When the plants reach the top of the greenhouse, pinch off the growing points.

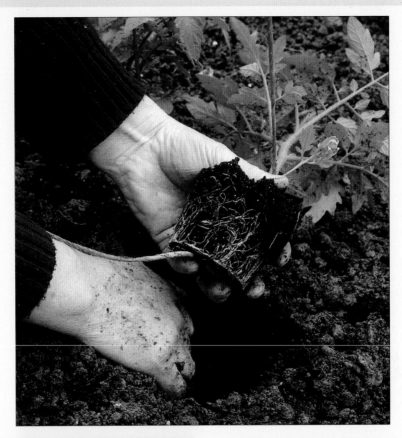

▲ **Training tomatoes** *Attach one end of a long piece of string to the top of the greenhouse, above where each seedling will be planted. Dig out a hole and flood it with water, then remove the young plant from its pot and loop the string around the root ball.*

◀ **Holding the strings in place** *Plant the young tomato plant in the prepared hole and firm it in well. The root ball anchors the string as the plant grows.*

▲ **Side-shooting** *Remove the sideshoots that develop from the angle between the leaf stems and the main stem of the plant.*

Eggplants

This is a good crop to grow outside in warm climates, where it can be cultivated as a perennial. In colder conditions it must be treated as a tender annual; it will certainly need cloche protection, and preferably a greenhouse or plastic tunnel (*see p. 247*).

VARIETIES The early varieties are preferable because they produce for a longer period of time. *Black Enorma* is very early and heavy yielding. *Black Beauty* is another early variety producing an excellent yield of large, pear-shaped fruit.

SOIL AND SITE Eggplants need plenty of sun and a sheltered location, and like soil that has been well manured. They prefer a pH of about 6.5, so add lime if necessary (*see p. 36*). In cold conditions, warm the soil by covering with cloches well before planting time (*see p. 140*). If you are using the three-year crop rotation plan (*see p. 134*), grow eggplants in Plot A.

SOWING AND PLANTING Raise the plants in a greenhouse or on a windowsill (*see below*). Pot them if necessary and move to the cold frame in mid-spring for hardening off (*see p. 254*). Plant out under cloches in late spring (*see p. 140*), setting the plants 2ft (60cm) apart. Stake them firmly and tie in the main stem. In warm climates, the cloches will not be necessary, so plant out in the open ground.

MAINTENANCE Plants should branch naturally but, if they don't, pinch off the growing point when they are 9in (23cm)

high. Allow no more than five fruits per plant; remove extra flowers when five have set and are swelling. Feed with a liquid animal-manure fertilizer at weekly intervals from midsummer until harvesting.

CARING FOR EGGPLANTS

Like the other fruiting vegetables, eggplants benefit from constant attention to their needs, whether you grow them outside or in the greenhouse.

Supporting and training
Grow eggplants up canes and tie in sideshoots as they develop.

Feeding *Bury a pot in the soil between plants, and pour liquid fertilizer into it. This enables the roots to get the maximum benefit from the feed.*

Harvesting eggplants *To ensure the sweetest possible flavor, cut the fruits when the flesh is most shiny.*

Deep beds Plant out 18in (45cm) apart in staggered rows, and protect with cloches in cold climates. (*See p. 136.*)

HARVESTING Start harvesting eggplants in late summer. Cut the fruits off before they lose their shine, or they will taste bitter.

PESTS AND DISEASES Whitefly and aphids may affect eggplants (*see pp. 46–53*). See p. 199 for pests and diseases that affect fruiting vegetables and p. 257 for those that affect greenhouse plants.

PLANTING AND HARVESTING TIMES

	Sow inside	Plant out	Sow outside	Harvest
Early spring	•			
Mid-spring	•	•		
Late spring			•	
Early summer				
Midsummer				
Late summer				•
Early autumn				•
Mid-autumn				•
Late autumn				
Early winter				
Midwinter				
Late winter	•			

CULTIVATING EGGPLANTS IN THE GREENHOUSE

I have tried many varieties and never found one better than *Black Beauty*. Sow in early spring in styrofoam cells or a seed tray (*see p. 271*), at a temperature of 65–70°F (18–21°C). Transfer to 3in (8cm) pots as soon as the seed leaves are large enough to handle comfortably.

In the cold greenhouse, plant outside in mid-spring, setting the plants 2ft–2ft 6in (60–75cm) apart in the borders. Or grow them three to a growing bag, or put them into 8in (20cm) pots of worm-worked potting compost (*see p. 81*). Support the plants with short stakes and feed at

every watering as shown above. Pinch off the top of the plant when it is about 12in (30cm) tall, and the tips of the sideshoots when the fruits have formed on them. Allow no more than about six fruits to develop on each plant. Harvest them when their flesh is shiny.

Peppers

Peppers are slightly easier to grow than eggplants in cold climates, though it is still worthwhile providing cloche protection (*see p. 140*). Red peppers are the same varieties as green, but are left to ripen longer. Hot peppers, or "chili peppers" are smaller and considerably hotter than the sweet varieties. They are very prolific so you will not need to grow many plants.

VARIETIES Of the sweet varieties, *Gypsy* produces very high yields. The fruits are a little yellow for some tastes but this does not affect their flavor. *Atris* is a good outdoor variety in a warm and sheltered position. It also does well in an unheated greenhouse

or under plastic cloches in temperate climates.

Chili Serrano is a very hot pepper suitable for cultivation in warm climates. *Numex Big Jim* is milder and can be grown under cloches in cooler climates.

SOIL AND SITE Peppers need plenty of sunshine and a sheltered location and like soil that has been well manured. They prefer a pH of about 6.0 or 6.5. In cold conditions, warm the soil by covering it with cloches well before planting time (*see p. 140*).
• If you are using the three-year crop rotation plan (*see p. 134*), grow peppers in Plot A.

SOWING AND PLANTING Sow in the greenhouse or on a windowsill (*see below*). Harden them off in a cold frame (*see p. 254*) from mid-spring and plant out under cloches or, in warm climates,

outside in late spring with 2ft (60cm) between plants.

Deep beds Plant out seedlings in staggered rows with 18in (45cm) between plants, during late spring. (*See p. 136*.)

MAINTENANCE Pinch off the growing point when the plants are 6in (15cm) high and tie them to a pole. Tie in the sideshoots as they grow. Water regularly and feed with a liquid kelp or animal-manure fertilizer every week (*see opposite*).

HARVESTING Harvest once the fruits have swollen (*see left*). Hot peppers can be dried in the sun and stored for use in the winter (*see left*).

PESTS AND DISEASES Slugs, whitefly, aphids, and red spider mites may affect peppers (*see pp. 46–53 and 199*). See p. 257 for pests and diseases that affect greenhouse plants.

Harvesting peppers *Pick the fruits when they are green or wait until they have turned red, when the flavor will be slightly more spicy.*

Drying chili peppers *Hot varieties can be dried outside on a raised wire frame then stored in airtight jars.*

PLANTING AND HARVESTING TIMES

	Sow inside	Plant out	Sow outside	Harvest
Early spring				
Mid-spring	•			
Late spring	•			
Early summer				
Midsummer				
Late summer				•
Early autumn				•
Mid-autumn				•
Late autumn				
Early winter				
Midwinter	•			
Late winter	•			

CULTIVATING PEPPERS IN THE GREENHOUSE

Both sweet and hot peppers are suitable for greenhouse cultivation. *Bell-Boy* is one of the most reliable sweet varieties. *De Cayenne* is a prolific hot pepper, while *Habanero Chocolate* are wrinkled, brown, and extremely hot!

Peppers need a temperature of 65–70°F (18–21°C). Sow in midwinter, if you can supply heat, but in early spring if you are growing them in a cold house. Peppers have a small root system, so prefer not to have too much cold compost around their roots. As soon as the seed leaves are big enough to handle comfortably, transplant to 3in (8cm) pots and

repot progressively into the next size up as the roots fill the pot. Again, space the plants early to give them plenty of light and air.

Plant out in mid-spring, either in the borders about 15in (35cm) apart or in growing bags. I have had my best results from peppers transplanted to 8in (20cm) pots of worm-worked potting compost. They seem to fruit better when the roots are restricted.

Peppers do not require any stopping and there is no need to remove sideshoots. Simply stake them and tie the plants in as they grow. Water the plants regularly and feed with liquid fertilizer at every watering.

Harvest when the peppers are green or wait until they turn red, for a spicier flavor.

Using a growing bag *Greenhouse peppers can be planted in growing bags which you can make yourself* (see p. 253).

Bulb vegetables

The edible bulbs of the onion family are in fact compacted layers of swollen leaf bases in which the plant stores food. They prefer a rich soil so are particularly suited to organic cultivation. The bulbs are among the easiest of all vegetables to grow and most of them store well, so it is not difficult to maintain a year-round supply.

ONIONS ▶
Allium cepa
One of the most useful vegetables in the kitchen, onions store well and can be used all year-round if a combination of main crop and other varieties are planted. *For cultivation details, see p. 171.*

▼ GARLIC
Allium sativum
Sometimes classified as an herb, garlic is one of the easiest vegetables to grow, needing only a warm, sunny location. It is sown from cloves—the individual segments of the bulb—and can be dried and stored for year-round use. *For cultivation details, see p. 170.*

LEEK ▶
Allium porrum
Hardy, easy to grow, and requiring little maintenance, this valuable winter vegetable can be left in the ground until needed in all but the very coldest conditions. It may run to seed if planted too early. *For cultivation details, see p. 170.*

GREEN ONIONS ▶
Allium cepa
Green onions are picked before the mature bulb forms. They have a milder flavor than the larger types. *For cultivation details, see p. 171.*

SHALLOTS ▼
Allium ascalonicum
Earlier to mature and with a milder flavor
than main crop onions, shallots require similar
growing conditions. They are easy to grow from
"sets," rarely troubled by diseases, and store well
for winter use. *For cultivation details, see p. 171.*

Cultivating bulb vegetables

Garlic

Garlic is one of the easiest of all vegetables to grow, provided you have a suitably sunny site.

VARIETIES Garlic is grown from cloves—the individual segments of the bulb. *California White* grow well in our climate, while *Silver Rose* stores very well. For something big and beautiful you might try *Elephant Garlic*.

SOIL AND SITE *See* Soil preparation for bulb vegetables, *right*.

PLANTING Separate the cloves and plant them, pointed end up, in holes 1in (2.5cm) deep and 6in (15cm) apart. Do this in late winter.

Deep beds Plant the cloves 6in (15cm) apart in staggered rows. (*See p. 136.*)

MAINTENANCE Keep the rows weed free and, if the site is exposed, support the stems to keep them from breaking off in the wind.

HARVESTING Dig up the bulbs in summer, clean them and dry them in the sun before stringing or storing in nets in a frost-free place.

PESTS AND DISEASES Garlic is generally trouble free. See pp. 46–53 for general pests and diseases and p. 199 for specific pests and diseases that affect bulbs.

SOIL PREPARATION FOR BULB VEGETABLES

All the bulb vegetables prefer sunshine and a soil rich in organic matter, so dig in plenty of well-rotted compost or manure. If necessary, add lime to raise the soil pH above 6.5 (*see p. 36*).
• If you are using the three-year crop rotation plan (*see p. 134*), grow the bulb vegetables in Plot A.

PLANTING AND HARVESTING TIMES

	Sow inside	Plant out	Sow outside	Harvest
Early spring		•		
Mid-spring				
Late spring				
Early summer				
Midsummer				•
Late summer				•
Early autumn				
Mid-autumn				
Late autumn				
Early winter				
Midwinter				
Late winter			•	

Leeks

A superb winter vegetable that is hardy in all but the very coldest climates, leeks are easy to grow, undemanding, and a valuable source of fresh greens in the winter.

VARIETIES *Musselburgh* is a popular variety, very hardy and with thick stems. *Titan* has a very long stem and a good blanched base. *The Lyon Prizetaker* has an excellent flavor and is also very hardy.

SOIL AND SITE *See* Soil preparation for bulb vegetables, *above*.

SOWING AND PLANTING Leeks can be multiple sown (*see p. 139*) or grown in seed boxes started in the greenhouse in mid-spring, at a temperature of about 60°F (15°C). Alternatively, sow them in a seedbed outside, in a shallow row, 6in (15cm) apart. Plant the young leeks in a deep furrow so they can be blanched as described at right.

Starting in early summer, make holes with a dibber (*see p. 260*), about 6–8in (15–20cm) deep and 6in (15cm) apart, with 12in (30cm) between rows. Trim the roots of the leeks by about two-thirds and the tops by about half, and drop a plant into each hole. Do not refill the holes, but pour a little water into each to wash some soil over the roots.

Deep beds Plant in the same way, setting the plants in a block of staggered rows with 6in (15cm) between plants each way. Alternatively, multiple sow them as described on p. 139 and plant them 12in (30cm) apart each way. (*See p. 136.*)

MAINTENANCE Hoe to keep the rows weed free (*see p. 57*) and, as the leeks grow, pull a little soil around the base of each stem to blanch them, taking care to prevent soil from getting between the leaves.

HARVESTING Leeks are quite hardy, and can usually be left in the ground until required. But, if there is a danger of very cold weather making the soil too hard to dig, remove a few plants and put them in a box of moist peat until required.

PESTS AND DISEASES Leeks are generally trouble free. See pp. 46–53 for general pests and diseases and p. 199 for specific pests and diseases that affect bulb vegetables.

PLANTING AND HARVESTING TIMES

	Sow inside	Plant out	Sow outside	Harvest
Early spring	•			•
Mid-spring	•	•		
Late spring				
Early summer		•		
Midsummer				
Late summer				
Early autumn				
Mid-autumn				•
Late autumn				•
Early winter				•
Midwinter				•
Late winter				

Onions

Onions store well so you can eat them all year-round.

VARIETIES Choose main crop varieties that store well, like *Walla Walla* and *Spanish*.

SOIL AND SITE All the bulb vegetables prefer sunshine an a soil rich in organic matter, so dig in plenty of well-rotted compost or manure. If necessary, use lime to raise the soil pH above 6.5 (*see p. 36*).

SOWING AND PLANTING Onions can be multiple sown (*see p. 139*) in midwinter in a heated greenhouse or sown outside in shallow rows 12in (30cm) apart in early spring. Use a stale seedbed (*see p. 269*) so the tiny seedlings are not swamped by weeds, and thin to 2in (5cm) apart. Sow other varieties in late summer and spread a handful of dried blood per square yard/ meter in the spring.

If your soil is heavy and wet, buy onion sets—tiny onion bulbs that have been specially treated to produce good-sized bulbs. Cut off any long growths of old foliage at the tips, to prevent birds pulling the sets out of the ground, and plant bulbs at the same distances, so the tips are just below soil level. Do not push the sets into the ground because they may push themselves out again when they grow roots.

Deep beds Sow or plant 2in (5cm) apart in staggered rows.

MAINTENANCE Keep onions weed free and water in dry weather.

HARVESTING In late summer, the onion foliage turns brown and withers. Dig the roots and leave the bulbs to dry in the sun. Then remove the tops and store the onions in nets in a frost-free spot. Alternatively, leave the leaves on, tie bunches of onions together with string.

PESTS AND DISEASES Onions may be affected by many of the general garden pests and diseases as well as onion fly, onion eelworm, neck rot, white rot, and storage rot (*see pp. 46–53 and 199*).

PLANTING AND HARVESTING TIMES

	Sow inside	Plant out	Sow outside	Harvest
Early spring		•	•	
Mid-spring		•	•	•
Late spring				•
Early summer				•
Midsummer				•
Late summer			•	•
Early autumn				•
Mid-autumn				•
Late autumn				
Early winter				
Midwinter	•			
Late winter	•	•	•	

GREEN ONIONS

The small green or salad onions have a milder flavor than other types and do not store well. *White Lisbon* and *Ishikuro* are recommended varieties. Sow them under cloches (*see p. 140*) in late winter, and in the open at three-week intervals begining in early spring. They will not need to be thinned. If you are using deep beds, scatter seeds in a wide row (*see p. 136*).

Shallots

These mild-flavored bulbs are much smaller than main crop onions and can be harvested earlier, in the summer. They are easy to grow from sets (*see above*).

VARIETIES *Golden Gourmet* (*Dutch Yellow*) and *Pikant* (*Dutch Red*) are two varieties having flavorful, large bulbs with excellent storage potential. The exhibition variety *Hative de Niort* produces bigger bulbs which do not keep as well.

SOIL AND SITE *See* Soil preparation for bulb vegetables, *opposite*.

SOWING AND PLANTING Remove any dead foliage and plant the sets in rows in early spring, putting them 6in (15cm) apart in rows 12in (30cm) apart. Ensure that the tip of the bulb is just below soil level and do not press the sets into the ground or they will push themselves out again when they grow roots.

Deep beds Plant in staggered rows with 6in (15cm) between sets. (See p. 136.)

MAINTENANCE Weed and water as required. In early summer, draw the soil away from the bulbs to assist ripening.

HARVESTING Dig when the foliage dies down in summer, clean the bulbs and store in nets in a frost-free place.

PESTS AND DISEASES Shallots are generally trouble free. See pp. 46–53 for general pests and diseases and p. 199 for specific pests and diseases that affect bulb vegetables.

Drying shallots *Put harvested bulbs on a piece of chicken wire raised off the ground so air can circulate around them.*

PLANTING AND HARVESTING TIMES

	Sow inside	Plant out	Sow outside	Harvest
Early spring		•		
Mid-spring				
Late spring				
Early summer				•
Midsummer				•
Late summer				•
Early autumn				
Mid-autumn				
Late autumn				
Early winter				
Midwinter				
Late winter			•	

THE VEGETABLE GARDEN

Squash vegetables

These crops are members of the *Cucurbitae* family, half-hardy annuals that can be grown outside in warm conditions. They require well-manured, slightly acid soil and plenty of water. Squashes and zucchinis form small, bushy plants, while cucumbers and melons trail across the garden. These need more room, but can be trained to grow up poles.

▼ **SQUASHES**
Cucurbita pepo
These large, fast-maturing vegetables require a soil enriched with as much organic matter as possible. Like pumpkins, squashes can be stored for a short time in nets and kept in a frost-free place. Pick the fruits before they get too large. *For cultivation details, see p. 174.*

▼ **ZUCCHINIS**
Cucurbita pepo
These are simply miniature squashes that are harvested early to give a superior flavor. They may be green, striped, or bright yellow. Pick the fruits regularly to encourage continued production. These bush plants take up relatively little space. *For cultivation details, see p. 174.*

CUCUMBERS ▶
Cucumis sativus
Cucumbers require a well-manured soil and can be trained to grow up wigwams of poles to save space. They can be grown in the greenhouse or outside. The newer "all-female" cucumber varieties are best for growing under glass. *For cultivation details, see p. 175.*

Honeydew

Cantaloupe

MELONS ▶
Cucumis melo
New fast-maturing
varieties are grown under
cloches or in the open in
warm areas. The heavy
fruits, which are juicy
and sweet-flavored, can be
supported by nets as they
mature. They require
plenty of water and must
be eaten fresh, as they do
not store. *For cultivation
details, see p. 176.*

PUMPKINS ▲
Cucurbita maxima and *C. moschata*
Because they take a long time to mature, true
pumpkins are best grown in warm areas, but
there are many related squashes that will do well
in cooler climates. They are used in both sweet
and savory dishes. All types can be stored in
nets for winter use. *For cultivation details, see p. 177.*

Cultivating squash vegetables

Squashes and zucchinis

Zucchinis are really only immature squashes, and both are grown in exactly the same way. If you are short of space, grow a zucchini variety and, toward the end of the season, allow a few fruits to grow into squashes.

VARIETIES *Zucchini* and the yellow *Orelia* are excellent zucchinis; while *One Ball* produces round, yellow fruit. *Long Green* is a fine trailing variety.

SOIL AND SITE Dig in plenty of compost or manure (*see pp. 21–28*). All squashes prefer a pH of about 6.0.

• If you are using the three-year crop rotation plan (*see p. 134*), grow your plants in Plot A.

SOWING AND PLANTING Sow squashes and zucchinis inside at a temperature of about 65°F (18°C) in mid-spring, putting two seeds in each 3in (8cm) pot. When they germinate, thin to one if necessary. Plant out 2ft (60cm) apart each way, in normal or deep beds (*see p. 136*). Alternatively, sow pairs of seeds outside two weeks before the last frost and protect them with cut-off plastic bottles or cloches.

MAINTENANCE If space is restricted, you can grow zucchinis up a tripod of poles (*see* Cucumbers *opposite*).

Mulching young zucchinis *Surrounding plants with a layer of ornamental pine bark (see p. 59) helps control weeds and deter slugs.*

Harvesting summer squash *Cut through the stem with a sharp knife.*

Keeping the plants in check *If you grow trailing varieties of squash flat on the ground, trim them regularly with a spade.*

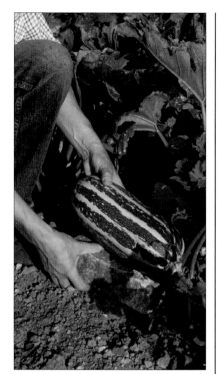

Ripening squashes *Put bricks under mature squashes to raise them off the ground and prevent rotting.*

Pinch off the tops when the plants reach the top of the poles. Feed at two-week intervals with a liquid kelp or animal-manure fertilizer from midsummer until harvesting.

HARVESTING AND STORING

Cut zucchinis when they are no more than 6in (15cm) long, to encourage further production. Cut squashes when they are large—up to 15in (35cm) long. You can ripen them at the end of the season and keep them for a short time in a frost-free place.

PESTS AND DISEASES See

pp. 46–53 for slugs, aphids, and mildew, and p. 199 for cucumber mosaic virus.

PLANTING AND HARVESTING TIMES

	Sow inside	Plant out	Sow outside	Harvest
Early spring				
Mid-spring	●			
Late spring	●	●	●	
Early summer		●	●	
Midsummer				●
Late summer				●
Early autumn				●
Mid-autumn				●
Late autumn				
Early winter				
Midwinter				
Late winter				

Cucumbers

New varieties of cucumbers make them well worth growing outside. These are now so good that I only use the greenhouse to grow the very earliest varieties.

VARIETIES *Marketmore* produces long, dark green fruits, while *Burpless Tasty Green* is said to be easier to digest than most varieties.

SOIL AND SITE All squashes prefer a pH of about 6.0 and a well-manured soil, so dig in plenty of compost or manure (*see pp. 21–28*).

• If you are using the three-year crop rotation plan (*see p. 134*), grow cucumbers in Plot A.

SOWING AND PLANTING Sow inside at a temperature of about 65°F (18°C) in mid-spring, putting two seeds in each 3in (8cm) pot. When they germinate, thin to leave the strongest seedling if necessary. Plant outside in late spring, setting the plants 2ft (60cm) apart. Alternatively, sow pairs of seeds outside in late spring, at the same spacings. Cover the sowing site with a cut-off plastic bottle or a cloche (*see p. 140*) to protect them from cold wind and slugs.

The most space-saving way to grow cucumbers is up a wigwam of poles (*see below*). This also keeps the fruits off the ground and out of reach of slugs, and looks attractive enough for the flower borders. If you decide to grow them flat on the ground, space them 3ft (90cm) apart.

Deep beds Cucumbers are suitable for deep beds. They should be grown up poles at 2ft (60cm) spacings. (*See p. 136.*)

MAINTENANCE If you grow plants up poles, tie them in often and trim the sideshoots back to two leaves regularly to encourage compact, bushy growth. Pinch off tops when the plants reach the top of the canes. Feed with liquid

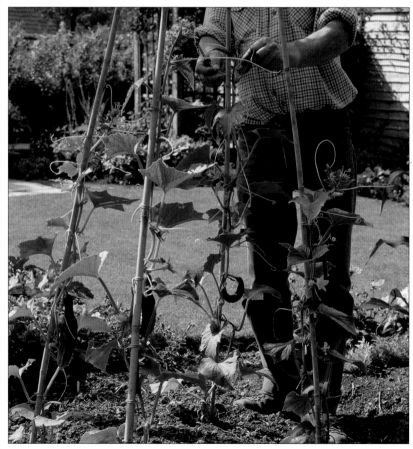

Training cucumbers up a wigwam of canes *Space four 8ft (2.5cm) poles 2ft (60cm) apart and tie them together at the top. Plant young plants at the base of each pole and tie them in with soft string as they grow.*

animal-manure fertilizer at two-week intervals from midsummer until harvesting. Do not remove the male flowers.

HARVESTING Cut the fruits when they are still young and have a bloom on them. Regular cutting encourages the plants to produce more fruit.

PESTS AND DISEASES See pp. 46–53 for slugs, aphids, and mildew, p. 199 for cucumber mosaic virus, and p. 257 for pests and diseases that affect greenhouse plants.

PLANTING AND HARVESTING TIMES

	Sow inside	Plant out	Sow outside	Harvest
Early spring	•			
Mid-spring	•			
Late spring	•	•	•	
Early summer		•		
Midsummer				•
Late summer				•
Early autumn				•
Mid-autumn				•
Late autumn				
Early winter				
Midwinter	•			
Late winter	•			

CULTIVATING CUCUMBERS IN THE GREENHOUSE

New varieties are sweet-tasting, vigorous, resistant to disease, and all female. *Hana* produces an abundant crop of short fruits, while *Carmen* is very heavy cropping. *Cumlaude RZ* will grow in an unheated greenhouse. *Athene* is ideal for slightly cooler conditions. All these grow perfectly well in the same temperature and humidity regime as tomatoes (*see p. 165*), so they can share the house.

Sow from midwinter if the greenhouse can be heated to about 50°F (10°C) during the early part of the growing year, and in mid-spring for growing in a cold house. Sow individually in 3in (8cm) pots of potting compost, and put them in a propagator at a temperature of 75–80°F (24–27°C). When they germinate, move them to a light, airy position at 60–65°F (15–18°C).

Prepare the border soil and plant in the borders or growing bags as for tomatoes (*see p. 165*). Support the plants in the same way as tomatoes (*see right and p. 165*), but handle the plants carefully when twisting them around the strings because they are delicate and can easily break.

Cucumbers like plenty of water and should never be allowed to dry out. They like a humid atmosphere, so wet down the paths and plants at least twice a day in the morning and early afternoon (*see p. 255*). Ventilate to keep the temperature around 65–75°F (18–24°C) during the day and keep the vents shut at night at least until the early summer. After about eight weeks, start feeding with liquid kelp or animal-manure fertilizer at every watering.

Trim the sideshoots regularly to leave two leaves. The newer varieties recommended here fruit mainly from the main stem. Other, older varieties may produce fruit mainly on the sideshoots, in which case remove any on the main stem.

Training greenhouse cucumbers
Guide the main stem so it winds around a string (see also p. 165).

Melons

New, quick-maturing varieties are ideal for cloche culture in cool climates (*see p. 140*) or growing outside in warmer areas.

VARIETIES The small-fruited varieties like *Ogen* and *Sweetheart* ripen quickly and are ideal for all areas.

SOIL AND SITE Melons need a well-manured soil, so dig in plenty of compost or manure (*see pp. 21–28*). They prefer a pH of about 6.0.

• If you are using the three-year crop rotation plan (*see p. 134*), grow melons in Plot A.

SOWING AND PLANTING Sow inside at 65°F (18°C) in mid-spring, putting two seeds in each 3in (8cm) pot and thinning to one if necessary. Plant outside under cloches in late spring with 3ft (90cm) between plants.

MAINTENANCE It is important to water regularly. When the plants have three leaves, pinch off the growing point. It will then make sideshoots that should again be stopped after three leaves, When the fruits form, pinch back to two leaves beyond the fruit.

HARVESTING Cut the fruits as soon as they feel soft when you press the ends.

PESTS AND DISEASES See pp. 46–53 for slugs, aphids, and mildew, p. 199 for cucumber mosaic virus, and p. 257 for pests and diseases that affect greenhouse plants.

PLANTING AND HARVESTING TIMES

	Sow inside	Plant out	Sow outside	Harvest
Early spring	•			
Mid-spring	•			
Late spring	•	•		
Early summer				
Midsummer				
Late summer				•
Early autumn				•
Mid-autumn				•
Late autumn				
Early winter				
Midwinter				
Late winter	•			

CULTIVATING MELONS IN THE GREENHOUSE

Because they can be grown without heat during the summer, needing only a little at the propagation stage, the modern Cantaloupe and F1 hybrid varieties have replaced the old-fashioned musk or sweet melons. In warm climates, these newer varieties are at home outside (*see left*). As well as those mentioned above, I recommend *Lunabel* for the greenhouse.

Sow individually in 3in (8cm) pots in early spring at a temperature of 70–75°F (21–24°C). Plant about 12–18in (30–45cm) apart in a well-manured border or, ideally, a hot bed (*see p. 253*). Alternatively, grow them in growing bags or even in pots, but they will need more careful watering. In the cold house, plant out in mid-spring.

Pinch off the growing point to keep only two true leaves, a

Supporting melons *Place nets around the maturing fruits to prevent the stems from snapping while they ripen. Melons may bruise or split if they fall to the ground.*

week after planting. Two sideshoots will grow from this point and they are allowed to grow on the ground or can be trained up wires. Stop these shoots after they have between seven and ten leaves. Secondary shoots and flowers will then appear. When the embryo fruits appear, stop two leaves past the fruit. Only allow about five fruits to develop on each plant. Allow insects access to the greenhouse in order to pollinate the plants. Spray over the leaves and wet down the paths and borders each morning (*see p. 255*), except when the fruit is ripening—then leave the atmosphere dry and ventilate freely. Feed the plants with liquid fertilizer at each watering.

Pumpkins

True pumpkins are best suited to warm climates, as they take four months to reach maturity. However, there are plenty of related squashes that can be grown for winter use, even in cooler climates, so some of these are included here. The method of cultivation is exactly the same.

VARIETIES The largest pumpkins are impractical for eating unless your family is very large or you want to use them to make jam, in which case *Big Max, Atlantic Giant,* or *Mammoth* are suitable varieties. The smaller *Uchiki Kuri* has a wonderful sweet, nutty flavor and stores very well. However, most seed catalogs now stock a wide range of different shapes, sizes, and tastes to suit everyone's needs. *Vegetable Spaghetti* is ideal and improves with keeping until midwinter.
SOIL AND SITE All squashes need a well-manured soil, so dig in plenty of compost or manure

(*see p. 21–28*). They prefer a pH of about 6.0.
• If you are using the three-year crop rotation plan (*see p. 134*), grow pumpkins in Plot A.
SOWING AND PLANTING Sow inside at a temperature of about 65°F (18°C) in mid-spring, putting two seeds in each 3in (8cm) pot and thinning to leave the strongest seedling if necessary. Most winter squashes are trailing varieties and require a lot of room, so plant them out at least 3ft (90cm) apart when all danger of frost has passed in the late spring. If sowing outside, do so about two weeks earlier than that.
MAINTENANCE Feed with a liquid animal-manure fertilizer at two-week intervals from midsummer to early fall. There is no need to remove the male flowers. Pinch back the trailing stems regularly to keep the plants in check.
HARVESTING AND STORING Leave winter squashes on the plant as long as possible, while there is

plenty of sunshine. At the end of the season, raise the fruits off the ground by putting them on a piece of wood or brick to avoid rotting. When they start to fade, cut off the fruit but leave them in the sun to continue ripening if possible. The harder the skins at the end of the season, the better the fruits will keep. Store them in a frost-free place and eat them in midwinter.
PESTS AND DISEASES See p. 46–53 for slugs, aphids, and mildew, and p. 199 for cucumber mosaic virus.

PLANTING AND HARVESTING TIMES

	Sow inside	Plant out	Sow outside	Harvest
Early spring				
Mid-spring	•			
Late spring	•	•	•	
Early summer		•	•	
Midsummer				
Late summer				•
Early autumn				•
Mid-autumn				•
Late autumn				
Early winter				
Midwinter				
Late winter				

Root vegetables

Most of the root vegetables are biennials; they store food in the swollen roots for use in the second year of the growth cycle, when the plants would normally flower and produce seed. By harvesting at the end of the first year, we benefit from this reserve of nourishment.

CARROTS ▶
Daucus carota sativus
Carrots are rich in vitamins and dietary fiber. *For cultivation details, see p. 181.*

▼ SALSIFY AND SCORZONERA
Tragopogon porrifolius and *Scorzonera hispanica*
These two vegetables both produce long, tapering roots. They are a good source of iron and are not difficult to grow. *For cultivation details, see p. 181.*

RADISHES ▶
Raphanus sativus
These roots are fast-maturing and very easy. *For cultivation details, see p. 180.*

KOHLRABI ▶
Brassica oleracea gongylodes
The swollen stem of this unusual vegetable is the part that is eaten. *For cultivation details, see p. 180.*

CELERIAC ▶
Apium graveolens
This is actually a swollen stem that grows just above the ground. *For cultivation details, see p. 182.*

JERUSALEM ARTICHOKES ▶
Helianthus tuberosus
An excellent winter alternative to potatoes, these large plants are easy to grow and can become invasive if not carefully controlled. *For cultivation details, see p. 182.*

Salsify

Scorzonera

TURNIPS ▼

Brassica rapa rapa
Turnips can be harvested
from spring to fall and
stored in a frost-free
place for winter use.
They need plenty of
water. *For cultivation
details, see p. 183.*

▼ BEETS

Beta vulgaris esculenta
This summer vegetable can also
be stored for winter use. Its delicate
roots will "bleed" if damaged. *For
cultivation details, see p. 184.*

RUTABAGA ▲

Brassica napus napobrassica
This member of the *Brassica* family is easy
to grow and can be stored for the whole
winter in moist peat or vermiculite. *For
cultivation details, see p.183.*

POTATOES ▲

Solanum tuberosum
Always grow a few early
potato varieties for their
delicious flavor. *For
cultivation details, see p. 185.*

▲ SWEET POTATOES

Ipomoea batatas
Sweet potatoes are only
suitable for cultivation
in warm climates. *For
cultivation details, see p. 187.*

▼ PARSNIPS AND
HAMBURG PARSLEY

Pastinaca sativa and
Petroselinum crispum
"Tuberosum"
These vegetables require
similar growing conditions.
For cultivation details, see p. 187.

Parsnip

Hamburg
parsley

Cultivating root vegetables

Radishes

Grow radishes as a catch-crop between rows of slower-maturing vegetables (*see p. 136*). They will put up with a wide range of soils and conditions, so they can be grown almost anywhere you have room to spare. Try to give them shade and moisture during the summer but full sun in early spring and fall.

VARIETIES *French Breakfast* is the best variety, with long, mildly-flavored, crisp roots. *Cherry Belle* is round and red and a good fast developer.

SOIL AND SITE Radishes will produce a reasonable crop in any soil, but they grow faster in land that is enriched with well-rotted compost or manure (*see pp. 21–28*).

• If you are using the three-year crop rotation plan (*see p. 134*), grow radishes in Plot C.

SOWING Sow the first crop under cloches in late winter (*see p. 140*), scattering seeds thinly in rows 6in (15cm) apart. Thinning

Harvesting multiple-sown radishes *To improve yields, multiple sow early crops indoors and plant outside under cloches* (see p. 139).

is not normally necessary. After that, sow small amounts outside every week until mid-fall.

Deep beds Sow in wide, shallow bands, scattering the seeds thinly across the band. (*See p. 136*).

MAINTENANCE Water if the soil is dry and keep the beds weed free by hoeing (*see p. 57*).

HARVESTING Pull regularly to avoid the roots becoming hot and woody.

PESTS AND DISEASES Radishes are susceptible to flea beetles and the pests and diseases that affect root vegetables (*see pp. 50 and 200*).

PLANTING AND HARVESTING TIMES

	Sow inside	Plant out	Sow outside	Harvest
Early spring			•	
Mid-spring			•	•
Late spring			•	•
Early summer			•	•
Midsummer			•	•
Late summer			•	•
Early autumn			•	•
Mid-autumn			•	•
Late autumn				•
Early winter				•
Midwinter				
Late winter	•			

Kohlrabi

This strange-looking vegetable is a member of the cabbage family. The swollen stem is the part that is eaten, rather than the leaves. New varieties are a great improvement on the old for flavor, and can even be eaten raw.

VARIETIES *Lanro* and *Purple Danube* are both excellent, with a sweet flavor. But keep a look out for *Blusta* that has intense purple roots and a nutty flavor.

SOIL AND SITE If your soil is heavy, use beds raised by digging in plenty of well-rotted compost or manure to improve the drainage (*see pp. 21–28*). Add lime to the soil to achieve a pH over 6.5.

• If you are using the three-year crop rotation plan (*see p. 134*), grow kohlrabi in Plot C.

SOWING AND PLANTING Sow in a seedbed, making successional sowings from mid-spring to midsummer. Transplant to rows 12in (30cm) apart with 9in (23cm) between plants.

Deep beds Transplant in staggered rows with 9in (23cm) between plants (*see p. 136*).

MAINTENANCE Hoe to keep the beds weed free (*see p. 57*).

HARVESTING Pull the roots during the summer before they get too big—about 2in (5cm) in diameter is ideal. Later, the whole crop can be lifted and stored for a short

time in boxes of moist peat in a frost-free place.

PESTS AND DISEASES Kohlrabi is generally trouble free. See pp. 46–53 for general pests and diseases and p. 200 for specific pests and diseases that affect root vegetables.

PLANTING AND HARVESTING TIMES

	Sow inside	Plant out	Sow outside	Harvest
Early spring				
Mid-spring			•	
Late spring			•	
Early summer			•	•
Midsummer			•	•
Late summer				•
Early autumn				•
Mid-autumn				•
Late autumn				•
Early winter				
Midwinter				
Late winter				

Carrots

Carrots are not hard to grow on good soil and it is possible to get a succession throughout the year. They are an excellent source of vitamins and dietary fiber.

VARIETIES For multiple sowing (*see p. 139*), use round types like *Parmex* and *Atlas*. Early outdoor sowings should be the fast-maturing varieties like *Adelaide* or one of the *Nantes* strains, but choose a larger variety, like *Autumn King* or *Chantenay Red Cored*, for main crop sowing.
SOIL AND SITE Carrots do best on light soil with plenty of well-rotted organic matter. They will not fork provided the compost or manure is well-rotted. If your soil is heavy, grow them in raised deep beds (*see p. 136*). Add lime to the soil to bring the pH over 6.5.

• If you are using the three-year crop rotation plan (*see p. 134*), grow carrots in Plot A.
SOWING Earliest crops are multiple sowings planted outside under cloches in mid- to late winter. Sow outside under cloches in late winter: sow around varieties in wide bands and long ones in rows 9in (23cm) apart. Thin long varieties when they are just big enough to eat. Sow every three weeks in rows 12in (30cm) apart, thinning to 3in (8cm) apart.
Deep beds Plant out multiple-sown carrots in staggered rows 6in (15cm) apart. Alternatively, make sowings of round varieties as above and successional sowings of long varieties in rows 6in (15cm) apart and thin to 3in (8cm) apart.
MAINTENANCE Hoe to keep the rows weed free and, as the carrots swell, pull a little soil up to them to prevent the "shoulders" from going green and to deter carrot fly (*see p. 200*).

HARVESTING Pull early and successional sowings when they are still young and crisp. In mid- or late fall pull the final sowing and store in moist peat or vermiculite. Do not leave them in the ground for a long time or some may split, attracting slugs.
PESTS AND DISEASES Carrots are affected by carrot fly and storage rot (*see p. 200*). See pp. 46–53 for general pests and diseases.

PLANTING AND HARVESTING TIMES

	Sow inside	Plant out	Sow outside	Harvest
Early spring		•	•	
Mid-spring			•	•
Late spring			•	•
Early summer			•	•
Midsummer			•	•
Late summer				•
Early autumn				•
Mid-autumn				•
Late autumn				•
Early winter				
Midwinter	•		•	
Late winter	•	•	•	

Salsify and scorzonera

These two gourmet vegetables are much alike in flavor and can be grown in the same way. Salsify has a white root while scorzonera is black skinned but pure white beneath. I prefer the taste of scorzonera, but you may disagree, so try both. Both are an excellent source of iron and are not difficult to grow. As well as the roots, you can eat the stems and leaves of both crops.

VARIETIES I find *Mammoth* and *Sandwich Island Mammoth* to be indistinguishable, and both are good varieties of salsify, while *Russian Giant* is the best scorzonera.
SOIL AND SITE Both scorzonera and salsify like a very deep, well-manured soil but ensure that the manure is well-rotted or the roots will fork. Scorzonera is a particularly deep-rooting vegetable.

• If you are using the three-year crop rotation plan (*see p. 134*), grow your plants in Plot A.
SOWING Sow outside in mid-spring in drills about 1in (2.5cm) deep and 12in (30cm) apart. Thin the seedlings to 6in (15cm) apart.
MAINTENANCE Hoe to keep the beds weed free (*see p. 57*) or, better still, mulch with well-rotted compost in the fall to safeguard against damage to the roots.
HARVESTING AND STORING In late fall, dig and store in moist peat in a frost-free shed.

Blanching salsify or scorzonera
After harvesting the roots you need, cover a few plants with soil to provide blanched leaves which can be used in salads.

Alternatively, the leaves and stems can be used. Leave some roots in the ground and cover them with soil to blanch them (*see below*). Then harvest them in the spring and use raw in salads or leave them unblanched and cook them like spinach.
PESTS AND DISEASES Salsify and scorzonera are both generally trouble free. See pp. 46–53 for treatment of general pests and diseases and p. 200 for specific pests and diseases that affect root vegetables.

PLANTING AND HARVESTING TIMES

	Sow inside	Plant out	Sow outside	Harvest
Early spring				
Mid-spring			•	
Late spring				
Early summer				
Midsummer				
Late summer				
Early autumn				
Mid-autumn				•
Late autumn				•
Early winter				
Midwinter				
Late winter				

Jerusalem artichokes

This superb winter vegetable has all the flavor of globe artichokes, but is much easier to grow. The plants can even become very invasive if not kept in check. They can attain a height of 9ft (3m), so they make a useful windbreak.

VARIETIES The best and least bumpy is *Fuseau*, although *Stampede* is a high yielding, smooth variety. If shorter top growth is required then *Dwarf Sunray* should fit the bill.

SOIL AND SITE Although they will grow practically anywhere, you can ensure bigger, smoother tubers by reserving a permanent, well-prepared site for them. Dig a trench about 2ft (60cm) wide and one spade deep. Break up the bottom and refill, working in as much well-rotted compost, manure, or one of the alternatives, as you can spare (*see pp. 21–28*). Jerusalem artichokes like an acid soil, so keep the pH down below 6.5.

PLANTING Plant as early in the year as the soil conditions will allow, usually late winter or early spring. Set the tubers 6in (15cm) deep and 12in (30cm) apart. You will generally only need one row but, if you want more, make the rows at least 5ft (1.5m) apart.

MAINTENANCE Weed and water as required. Mulch annually in

Using Jerusalem artichokes as a windbreak *You can position these tall vegetables to protect other plants from wind.*

Planting tubers *Make a deep trench for the tubers or some may force their way to the surface and turn green. Plant to avoid casting shade over other crops.*

early spring with well-rotted compost or manure (*see pp. 21–28*), and spread a handful of blood, fish, and bone meal per yard/meter of row. In exposed areas you may need to support plants with a length of nylon string tied between two posts (*see p. 159*).

HARVESTING AND STORING Cut down the stems in mid-fall to leave 12in (30cm), and dig up the tubers as required. Leave some in the ground to replace the crop for next season.

PESTS AND DISEASES Jerusalem artichokes are generally trouble-free. See pp. 46–53 for general pests and diseases and p. 200 for those that affect root vegetables.

PLANTING AND HARVESTING TIMES

	Sow inside	Plant out	Sow outside	Harvest
Early spring		•		
Mid-spring				
Late spring				
Early summer				
Midsummer				
Late summer				
Early autumn				
Mid-autumn				•
Late autumn				•
Early winter				•
Midwinter				•
Late winter	•			•

Celeriac

This superb vegetable is really a swollen stem that grows just above the ground. It has all the flavor of celery hearts.

VARIETIES There is little to distinguish between *Alabaster, Monarch,* and *Giant Prague*.

SOIL AND SITE Celeriac prefers plenty of sun and a water-retentive soil rich in organic matter (*see pp. 21–28*), with a pH of about 6.0.
• If you are using the three-year crop rotation plan (*see p. 134*), grow celeriac in Plot A.

SOWING AND PLANTING Sow in your greenhouse or on a windowsill at a temperature of about 65°F (18°C) in mid-spring. Do not be tempted to sow earlier or the crop will certainly run to seed. As soon as the first true leaf develops, transplant to a spot with wider spacing (*see p. 272*). Plant in late spring, after hardening off in the cold frame (*see p. 254*), so that the swelling at the base of the plant is at soil level. Plant 12in (30cm) apart with 15in (35cm) between rows.

Deep beds Plant in blocks, with 12in (30cm) between plants (*see p. 136*).

MAINTENANCE Mulch with well-rotted manure (*see p. 20*) and keep the plants well watered in dry weather. In early fall, draw soil around the stems to blanch them.

HARVESTING Dig regularly between mid- and late fall and store in boxes of moist peat in a frost-free shed.

PESTS AND DISEASES Celeriac is generally trouble-free. See pp. 46–53 for general pests and diseases and p. 200 for specific pests and diseases that affect root vegetables.

PLANTING AND HARVESTING TIMES

	Sow inside	Plant out	Sow outside	Harvest
Early spring				
Mid-spring	•			
Late spring		•		
Early summer				
Midsummer				
Late summer				
Early autumn				
Mid-autumn				•
Late autumn				•
Early winter				
Midwinter				
Late winter				

Turnips

One of the easiest root vegetables to grow, turnips can be harvested in succession from spring to fall, when they can be dug up and stored for winter use.

VARIETIES *Early Purple Top Milan* has tender white flesh and is undoubtedly best for the first crops and for successional sowings. *Tokyo Cross* is a flavorful variety that stores well, as does *Golden Ball*, which is quite hardy, with yellow flesh and an excellent flavor.

SOIL AND SITE Grow the earliest varieties in well-manured soil for fast growth. The main crop varieties and those for storage can be grown on the cabbage plot. You may need to add lime to the soil to bring the pH above 6.5.
• If you are using the three-year crop rotation plan (*see p. 134*), grow main crop turnips in Plot C.

Harvesting multiple-sown turnips
To improve yields, multiple sow early crops indoors and plant out under cloches.

SOWING AND PLANTING The earliest crop should be multiple sown (*see p. 138*) in late winter at a greenhouse temperature of 65°F (18°C) and planted out under cloches in early spring. Sow outside from mid-spring to midsummer, in shallow rows 12in (30cm) apart. Thin to leave the plants 6in (15cm) apart in the rows.
MAINTENANCE Keep the rows clean and weed free by hoeing (*see p. 57*) or handpulling, and water if necessary. Mulch between plants with well-rotted compost or manure (*see p. 20*), to help retain moisture and prevent the roots from becoming tough and stringy.
HARVESTING AND STORING Pull the first roots at golf ball size and the biggest at tennis ball size. In mid-fall, dig up the main crop varieties, twist off the tops, and store in moist peat.
PESTS AND DISEASES Turnips are affected by flea beetles and soft rot (*see pp. 50 and 200*).

PLANTING AND HARVESTING TIMES

	Sow inside	Plant out	Sow outside	Harvest
Early spring		•		
Mid-spring			•	
Late spring			•	•
Early summer			•	•
Midsummer			•	•
Late summer				•
Early autumn				•
Mid-autumn				•
Late autumn				
Early winter				
Midwinter				
Late winter	•			

Rutabagas

New varieties are a great improvement on the old ones that were grown mainly for cattle feed. A member of the *Brassica* family, rutabagas are one of the most straightforward vegetables to grow, although sometimes prone to clubroot (*see p. 201*).

VARIETIES *Brora* has a beautiful flavor with yellow flesh when dug up before Christmas, where *Ruby* can be harvested until February. For clubroot resistance and a long harvesting period few can beat *Willemsburger*.
SOIL AND SITE Provide a well-drained soil with a pH of over 6.5, to help combat clubroot (*see p. 201*).
• If you are using the three-year crop rotation plan (*see p. 134*), grow rutabagas in Plot C.

Sowing rutabagas *Sow seeds very thinly, as about 90 percent will germinate. Hold a few between your thumb and finger and sprinkle them down the row.*

SOWING Sow rutabagas late in the season—late spring or early summer—as a safeguard against mildew (*see p. 52*). Sow seeds in shallow rows 18in (45cm) apart and thin to 12in (30cm) in the rows.
MAINTENANCE Keep the plants free from weeds by hoeing (*see p. 57*), and water if necessary. Mulch with well-rotted manure or compost (*see p. 20*).
HARVESTING AND STORING Roots can be left in the soil in milder areas, but this may encourage disease so dig them after a frost in mid-fall, twist off the tops, and store in boxes of moist peat or vermiculite.
PESTS AND DISEASES Rutabagas are affected by flea beetles, mildew, soft rot, and clubroot (*see pp. 50, 52, and 200–201*).

PLANTING AND HARVESTING TIMES

	Sow inside	Plant out	Sow outside	Harvest
Early spring				
Mid-spring				
Late spring			•	
Early summer			•	
Midsummer				
Late summer				
Early autumn				
Mid-autumn				•
Late autumn				•
Early winter				
Midwinter				
Late winter				

Beets

A superb summer vegetable that can be eaten cold, hot, or pickled. Fall crops can also be stored to last well into the winter.

VARIETIES The earliest sowings should be of quick-maturing *Boltardy* or *Early Wonder*, which produce quite large round roots and store well. *Moneta* is a monogerm type, so no cluster of seeds, which eliminates the need for thinning seedlings. For successional sowings, you could also use *Cylindra* or *Burpees Golden*.

SOIL AND SITE Beets like a deep, rich soil, with a pH of about 6.5. Dig in plenty of well-rotted manure or compost to improve drainage.
• If you are using the three-year crop rotation plan (*see p. 134*), grow beetroot in Plot A.

SOWING Start by multiple sowing (*see p. 139*) in mid or late winter and plant out under cloches (*see p. 140*). Make the first sowings outside under cloches in early spring. The seeds come in "clusters," so put one or two clusters every 3in (8cm) in 1in (2.5cm) deep rows 12in (30cm) apart. Before sowing, put the seeds into a strainer and wash them vigorously under the tap. This removes chemicals that inhibit germination, encouraging the seedlings to germinate faster. Thin by pulling roots selectively when they are no bigger than a golf ball.

Continue sowing every three weeks until midsummer. The main crop sowing is done then and the roots are thinned to leave one every 3in (8cm).

Deep beds Sow the earliest crop in wide bands and pull selectively. Successional sowings are made in staggered rows 3in (8cm) apart, thinning to 3in (8cm) between plants.

MAINTENANCE Hoe regularly to remove weeds (*see p. 57*), taking great care not to damage the roots; they will "bleed" if the skin is broken. Mulch between plants with rotted compost, manure, or wet newspaper (*see p. 58*).

HARVESTING AND STORING Never let the roots get too big or they will become woody. Pull early sowings as "baby beets" at about golf ball size, and maincrops at about tennis ball size. Lift main crop roots in mid- or late fall and store for winter use (*see below*).

PESTS AND DISEASES Beets are susceptible to mildew (*see p. 52*). See also p. 200 for specific pest and diseases that affect root vegetables.

PLANTING AND HARVESTING TIMES

	Sow inside	Plant out	Sow outside	Harvest
Early spring			•	
Mid-spring			•	
Late spring			•	•
Early summer			•	•
Midsummer			•	•
Late summer				•
Early autumn				•
Mid-autumn				•
Late autumn				•
Early winter				
Midwinter	•			
Late winter	•	•	•	

LIFTING BEETS FOR WINTER STORAGE

Many of the root crops, such as rutabagas, turnips, and beets, can be harvested and stored in a similar way, ensuring a ready supply of fresh vegetables throughout the winter months. Beets will bleed if the skin is broken, so be careful when harvesting and handling. Store in a cool, frost-free location.

Preparing beet seeds *To encourage rapid germination, put the clusters of seeds into a strainer and wash them in cold running water.*

1 *Dig up the last of the plants in late fall. Trim the roots by twisting off the tops or cutting them with a knife, but leave 1in (2.5cm) of leaf stem.*

2 *Put some moist peat or vermiculite into a wooden box. Place trimmed roots on top and cover with more peat. Repeat until the box is full.*

Potatoes

The potato really does justify organic gardening methods, but it may not be worth growing main crop varieties in small gardens if you can find a supply of organically grown ones from a farmer or a local market. Potatoes take up a lot of room and are relatively cheap to buy. Early varieties, however, are desirable, because the flavor is so much better when they are eaten fresh from the garden. Maincrops make a wonderful cleaning crop in new gardens (*see p. 56*).

VARIETIES Always buy seed potatoes that have been certified free from disease and, if possible, select small tubers with few sprouts (*see right*). This avoids undue competition producing a larger number of inferior tubers.

Seed companies in the US supply potato eyes rather than the whole tuber. These are sold packed in moist vermiculite and can be potted and put in the greenhouse or on a windowsill until planting time.

Early varieties are dug and eaten right away. Recommended varieties are *Yukon Gold*, which produces an early, great-tasting crop of yellow-fleshed spuds; *Irish Cobbler*, an early and versatile potato with an excellent flavor, and *Adirondack Red*—a very early and flavorful variety. There are numerous varieties, and they perform differently in different areas, so try a few tubers of a different type each year. Main crop varieties are dug in the fall and stored for winter use. In the US, one of the best varieties is *Red Pontiac*.

SOIL AND SITE Potatoes need a water-retentive soil with plenty of organic matter for the best results. If you do not have enough well-rotted compost or manure for the whole potato plot, dig the planting furrows deep and put a layer in the bottom. The tubers can be set directly on it. Do not lime the potato plot at all, as potatoes prefer an acid soil.

• If you are using the three-year crop rotation plan (*see p. 134*), grow potatoes in Plot A.

PLANTING Buy seed potatoes as early in the year as possible and put them in boxes or—if you only have a few—in egg cartons, in a light place at a temperature of about 50°F (10°C). They will then form good, short, bushy green sprouts. Never put them in the a warm, dark place as this makes long, pale sprouts (*see right*).

The earliest crops come from tubers planted through black plastic sheeting under cloches in late winter (*see next page*). This is an ideal deep bed method (*see below*). Alternatively, plant in rows 2ft (60cm) apart, setting the tubers 12in (30cm) apart and about 6in (15cm) deep at the same time. The rows must then be covered with a sheet of woven polypropylene for protection against frost.

Plant the first unprotected crop using the early varieties at the

Good sprouts

Bad sprouts

Good and bad potato sprouts *To encourage healthy green sprouts, keep seed potatoes in cool, light conditions. If they are kept in a warm, dark place, they will produce pale and weak sprouts.*

GROWING POTATOES UNDER BLACK PLASTIC

Early varieties can be planted through holes made in black plastic sheeting. This restricts weeds and protects the young plants from frost by warming the soil. Lay the sheeting over the area to be sown and bury the edges or secure them with bricks.

1 *Cut slits in the plastic every 12in (30cm), in staggered rows 12in (30cm) apart. Plant the potatoes 6in (15cm) with the sprouts uppermost.*

2 *The plastic can be lifted or cut away and the tubers harvested as normal. Lift early varieties for immediate use, leaving the rest of the crop to continue.*

same distances in early or mid-spring. Main crop varieties are planted at the same time, but here the rows are spaced 2ft 6in (75cm) apart and the tubers spaced about 15in (35cm) apart (*see below*).

Planting tubers *Main crop potatoes can be planted directly onto a layer of well-rotted organic matter. Mound up the row slightly after planting.*

If plants are raised from eyes, plant them at the same distances after the last frost in late spring.

MAINTENANCE If shoots emerge before the danger of frost has passed, draw a little soil over them for protection.

When the shoots are 6–8in (15–20cm) tall, spread a handful of blood, fish, and bone meal dressing down each yard/meter of row. Then earth up by pulling soil from between the rows up to the shoots, leaving about an inch still showing. A second earthing up can be done later if the plants have not met in the rows in about three weeks. This is an excellent means of controlling weeds, as well as ensuring that the tubers do not push up into the light.

HARVESTING AND STORING Dig early potatoes when they begin to flower. Take only what is needed immediately, leaving the rest to continue growing.

Main crop types are dug in mid-fall. Cut down foliage and put it on the compost heap but, if there is any sign at all of

disease on the leaves, they must be burned. Dig from the sides of the ridges to avoid damaging the tubers, lift the potatoes and throw them into a pile, leaving them for a few hours to dry out. Then store them in paper or burlap bags in a frost-free place. Store only perfect tubers; those that are blemished must be used immediately.

PESTS AND DISEASES Potatoes are affected by slugs, wireworms, potato cyst eelworm, potato blight, scab, potato blackleg, spraing, and wart disease (*see pp. 49, 50 and 200*).

PLANTING AND HARVESTING TIMES

	Sow inside	Plant out	Sow outside	Harvest
Early spring	•			
Mid-spring	•			
Late spring	•			
Early summer				•
Midsummer				•
Late summer				•
Early autumn				•
Mid-autumn				•
Late autumn				•
Early winter				
Midwinter				
Late winter	•			

HARVESTING AND STORING POTATOES

Main crop potatoes are stored in a different way from many of the other root crops (*see p. 184 and opposite*). As with beets, care is needed when harvesting them, as damaged roots may rot.

1 *Cut off the potato foliage and inspect it carefully for signs of disease. If there are none, put it on the compost heap; otherwise burn it.*

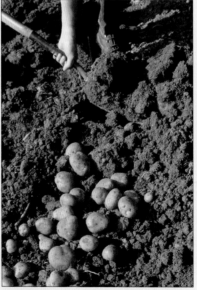

2 *Using a garden fork, dig from the side of the ridge and lift the plants. Shake off excess soil and leave the tubers to dry for a few hours. They are liable to rot if stored while damp.*

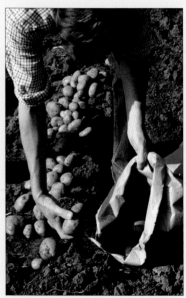

3 *Store blemish-free tubers in bags, reserving any damaged ones for immediate use. Inspect the stored crops regularly for signs of storage rot and remove any potatoes that are affected.*

Sweet potatoes

Sweet potatoes are very nutritious and tasty, but can only be grown in warm climates.

VARIETIES *Beauregard Improved* is the most reliable type of sweet potato in our climate, and has a sweet flesh.

SOIL AND SITE Sweet potatoes prefer a sandy soil but can be grown on heavier land with plenty of organic matter worked in. Make deep furrows and put a layer of compost or manure in the bottom. Then ridge up the soil to make mounds about 10in (25cm) high.

• If you are using the three-year crop rotation plan (*see p. 134*), grow sweet potatoes in Plot A.

PLANTING Buy plants from a nursery or seed company. Set them 12in (30cm) apart in the rows about a month after the last frost.

MAINTENANCE Keep the rows weeded until the plants meet in the rows to smother weeds. Sweet potatoes thrive in hot, dry weather so there is usually no need to water.

HARVESTING Dig and store in the same way as ordinary potatoes (*see opposite*) before the first frost of fall.

PESTS AND DISEASES Sweet potatoes are susceptible to slugs, wireworms, cutworms, aphids (*see pp. 46–53*). See p. 200 for pests and diseases that affect root vegetables.

PLANTING AND HARVESTING TIMES

	Sow inside	Plant out	Sow outside	Harvest
Early spring				
Mid-spring				
Late spring				
Early summer		•		
Midsummer				
Late summer				
Early autumn				•
Mid-autumn				•
Late autumn				
Early winter				
Midwinter				
Late winter				

Parsnips and Hamburg parsley

The distinctive sweet taste of parsnips makes them popular winter roots. In cool climates, they must be dug up and stored for the winter but, in warm areas, sow later and leave them in the ground. Hamburg parsley looks very much like parsnips and is grown in exactly the same way.

VARIETIES *Hollow Crown* and *Countess* form long, tapering roots of white flesh. *Avonresister* is smaller but has a marked resistance to canker disease (*see p. 200*) and forms longer roots. Hamburg parsley is simply sold as such.

SOIL AND SITE Parsnips and Hamburg parsley are tolerant of fairly poor conditions but will do best when plenty of well-rotted compost or manure is incorporated into the soil (*see pp. 21–28*). They prefer a soil pH of about 6.5, so add lime to the soil if necessary. If you want to grow long roots in stony soil, make holes at 6in (15cm) intervals with a crowbar, about 18in (45cm) deep and 3in (8cm) in diameter. Fill these with good soil or organic matter, then sow two or three seeds in each hole and later thin to leave one.

• If you are using the three-year crop rotation plan (*see p. 134*), grow these plants in Plot A.

SOWING The seeds germinate very slowly when the soil temperature is below 55°F (12°C), so there is little point in sowing too early. In cold climates, sow in mid-spring and in warmer climates in early fall. Sow two or three seeds at 6in (15cm) intervals in shallow rows 12in (30cm) apart. Always sow in a stale seedbed (*see p. 269*) and sow a few radishes in the drill to mark the rows for hoeing. Alternatively, pre-germinate the seeds and fluid sow them (*see p. 140*).

Deep beds Sow in blocks 6in (15cm) apart in each direction. (*See also p. 136.*)

Although they can be left in the ground, digging and storing these vegetables avoids the risk of pests and diseases.

1 *Lift the roots after the first frost. This will improve the flavor and kill off the top growth, so there is no need to remove the leaves by hand.*

2 *Loosely pack harvested parsnips and Hamburg parsley in boxes, between layers of moist peat or vermiculite. Store in a cool, frost-free place.*

MAINTENANCE Keep the rows weed free and the water supply fairly constant to prevent the roots from cracking.

PESTS AND DISEASES Both are affected by carrot root fly and parsnip canker (*see p. 200*). See pp. 46–53 for general pests and diseases.

PLANTING AND HARVESTING TIMES

	Sow inside	Plant out	Sow outside	Harvest
Early spring			•	
Mid-spring				
Late spring				
Early summer				
Midsummer				
Late summer				
Early autumn			•	
Mid-autumn				
Late autumn				•
Early winter				
Midwinter				
Late winter				

Leaf vegetables

Many of these vegetables are members of the *Brassica* family and are able to store large amounts of water in their leaves, making them fleshy and succulent. Because they are biennials, they also store nutrients during the first year of growth and these are available to us if the crops are harvested before they flower and seed. Many leaf vegetables are especially rich in iron and vitamins. The brassicas are prone to a wide range of pests and diseases, but correct cultivation techniques and strict crop rotation will prevent many of these problems.

◀ KALE
Brassica oleracea acephala
New varieties are a great improvement on the old, making kale a valuable winter vegetable, rich in vitamins. Smooth- and curly-leaved varieties are available. *For cultivation details, see p. 190.*

BRUSSELS SPROUTS ▲
Brassica oleracea gemmifera
These vegetables are often interplanted between other crops. New varieties can stay on the plant for a long time. *For cultivation details, see p. 190.*

CHARD ▶
Beta vulgaris cycla
This is even easier to grow than spinach and, as it is a biennial, there is no danger of it running to seed. Just two sowings will ensure a succession. *For cultivation details, see p. 192.*

◀ SWISS CHARD
Beta vulgaris cycla
The stems of this broad-leaved vegetable, also known as "sea kale beet," can be eaten as well as the leaves. *For cultivation details, see p. 192.*

SPINACH ▶
Spinacea oleracea
Very nutritious and easy to grow, spinach can be harvested throughout the year. It must be grown in shade to prevent it from running to seed. *For cultivation details, see p. 193.*

▲ CALABRESE AND BROCCOLI
Brassica oleracea italica
This easy-to-grow vegetable produces green or purple florets. Calabrese is simply broccoli that matures in summer. *For cultivation details, see p. 193.*

CAULIFLOWER ▲
Brassica oleracea botrytis
It is the central florets of the cauliflower that are actually eaten, not its leaves. There are three main seasonal types, so they can be harvested all year round. Cauliflowers are the most difficult of the brassicas to cultivate successfully. *For cultivation details, see p. 194.*

NAPPA CABBAGE ▶
Brassica pekinensis
Also known as "Chinese cabbage," this fairly demanding cabbage needs plenty of water and a moisture-retentive soil. *For cultivation details, see p. 196.*

Spring cabbage

Savoy cabbage

Red cabbage

White cabbage

CABBAGES ▲
Brassica oleracea capitata alba
It is possible to harvest cabbages throughout the entire year if the right spring, summer, and winter varieties are sown and transplanted at the correct time. Cabbages produce a large weight of edible material for the amount of space they occupy. As well as conical and round-hearted varieties, there are savoy and red cabbages. *For cultivation details, see p. 196.*

Cultivating leaf vegetables

Kale

Perhaps not the most flavorful of cabbage family (brassicas) but hardy and useful in hard winters, kale is also known as "Borecole"—which comes from the Dutch "Boerenkool," meaning "peasants' cabbage." It is a highly nutritious plant, especially rich in vitamins. The newer varieties are a great improvement on the older ones and are well worth a try.

VARIETIES There are curly- and smooth-leaved types. *Dwarf Green Curled* is the best flavored type, with *Redbor* having curly crimson leaves. *Nero Di Toscana* has long, narrow, smooth leaves.

SOIL AND SITE *See* Soil preparation for brassicas, *opposite*.

SOWING AND PLANTING Sow in a seedbed in mid- or late spring, in shallow rows 6in (15cm) apart. Plant out with 18in (45cm) between plants each way.

Deep beds Plant 15in (35cm) apart each way. (*See p. 136*.)

MAINTENANCE Water regularly, hoe and, if possible, mulch to keep the beds weed free (*see pp. 58-59*).

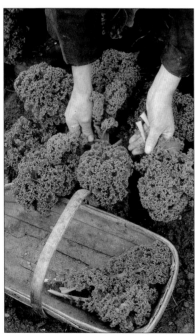

Harvesting kale *Pull young leaves from the center of each plant. Do not completely strip the plants.*

The plants may need support if the site is exposed.

HARVESTING Pull a few leaves from the center of each plant, while they are still young and tender.

Guarding against disease *After harvesting the young leaves, pull up the rest of the plant to deter the build-up of clubroot.*

PESTS AND DISEASES Kale can be affected by many of the general garden pests and diseases as well as cabbage butterflies, cabbage moth, cabbage root fly, and clubroot (*see pp. 46–53 and 201*).

PLANTING AND HARVESTING TIMES

	Sow inside	Plant out	Sow outside	Harvest
Early spring				•
Mid-spring		•		
Late spring		•		
Early summer				
Midsummer				
Late summer				
Early autumn				
Mid-autumn				
Late autumn				•
Early winter				•
Mid winter				•
Late winter				•

Brussels sprouts

Brussels sprouts are an invaluable winter vegetable, improved greatly by a touch of frost. Although they take up a fairly large area, fast-maturing vegetables like lettuce and radishes can be interplanted between rows in the early stages of development.

VARIETIES To ensure a long harvesting period and make the most of your space, grow those types that will stand for a long period without deteriorating. The more expensive F1 varieties are far superior in this respect. You will only need to grow two seasonal crops. *Romulus* is an early variety ready in early fall and continuing until midwinter. *Trafalgar* will then take over and go into early spring without losing quality or flavor.

SOIL AND SITE *See* Soil preparation for brassicas, *opposite*.

SOWING AND PLANTING Brussels sprouts need a longer growing period than most other brassicas, so start them in the seedbed in early or mid-spring. Sow seeds thinly in shallow rows 6in (15cm) apart, and use netting to protect the seedlings against birds (*see p. 47*).

Plant out when the seedlings are no more than 2–3in (5–8cm) tall. Space them 3ft (1m) square if you want them for eating fresh but, if you want smaller sprouts for freezing, plant them out 20in (50cm) square. Use a dibber (*see p. 260*) and press in well. Water afterward and then leave the plants for at least a week, before watering again.

Deep beds If your garden is committed to the system, Brussels sprouts can be grown perfectly well, planting out at the same distances, and you can plant other crops between rows. There is no need to firm the soil in the beds, but you may need to support the plants during the winter. However, because they

SOIL PREPARATION FOR BRASSICAS

Lime the soil if necessary to raise the pH to between 6.5 and 7.0, and dig in well-rotted compost or manure if you have it to spare. Add two handfuls of blood, fish, and bone meal per square yard/meter.

The soil for brassicas should be firm, so there is no need to dig after the last crop was lifted, except in the case of summer cabbages, which are planted in spring.

• If you are using the three-year crop rotation plan (*see p. 134*), grow all brassicas in Plot C. Since brassicas generally follow legumes in the rotation scheme, there will be a reserve of nitrogen in the soil from the bacteria in the root nodules of the peas and beans.

Never grow brassicas in the same plot in consecutive years. Strict crop rotation helps deter the build-up of clubroot disease (*see p. 45 and 201*).

require such wide spacing, the yield per square yard/meter is not increased by deep bed planting (*see p. 136*).

MAINTENANCE There is not much to do during the summer except keep the plants watered and the beds weed free. If you are not growing "catch-crops" between the plants (*see p. 143*), cover the soil between the rows with compost, paper, or black plastic to control weeds and reduce the need for watering. If you do grow lettuces, onions, radishes, or any other fast-maturing crop, be careful not to add too much extra fertilizer or the sprouts may become "soft." This is particularly important later in the season as winter approaches. On fertile organic soil, catch-crops grown between the rows should thrive without added fertilizer.

Pick off and remove yellowing leaves in the fall and compost them. Protect the plants against birds by covering them with netting (*see p. 47*).

Tall varieties may need staking in exposed areas; this can be done with a post at each end of the row and a length of nylon twine stretched either side of the plants (*see p. 158*).

HARVESTING Start in early fall, or when the bottom sprouts are firm, and go on until early spring. Always pick from the bottom upward, removing and composting yellowed leaves as you go to prevent fungus diseases. Once the plants have been stripped, remove them entirely and either shred them mechanically or pulverize them with a hammer

(*see below*). They can then be put on the compost heap, where they will rot down.

PESTS AND DISEASES Brussels sprouts can be affected by many of the general garden pests and diseases, as well as cabbage butterflies, cabbage moth, cabbage root fly, and clubroot (*see pp. 46–53 and 201*).

PLANTING AND HARVESTING TIMES

	Sow inside	Plant out	Sow outside	Harvest
Early spring			•	•
Mid-spring		•		
Late spring				
Early summer				
Midsummer				
Late summer				
Early autumn				•
Mid-autumn				•
Late autumn				•
Early winter				•
Mid winter				•
Late winter				•

Picking off leaves *It is important to pick off the large lower leaves as they turn yellow in the fall. They can easily be infected with fungus diseases that may spread to infect the whole crop.*

Harvesting Brussels sprouts *Pick from the bottom of the stem and work upward, as this is the order in which the sprouts mature. Snap them off at the base.*

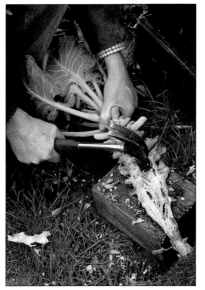

Pulverizing the stems *After harvesting, dig up the whole plant so the build-up of disease spores is deterred. Break up the stem with a hammer so it will rot down more quickly on the compost heap.*

Swiss chard

Sometimes also called "sea kale beet," this is an excellent, easy-to-grow vegetable. It is often regarded as a "spinach substitute," but has a quite different flavor and is considered a delicacy in some parts of the world.

VARIETIES It is generally just offered as *Swiss Chard. Rhubarb Chard* is also available, and this has distinctive blood-red stems. *Bright Lights* and *Rainbow Chard* are also very colorful and, although they have no advantage in flavor, their attractiveness means they can be grown in flower borders.
SOIL AND SITE A rich, moisture-retentive soil is best so, if you have some organic matter to spare, use it. Lime is generally required, so check that the soil pH is above 6.5.
• If you are using the three-year crop rotation plan (*see p. 134*), grow Swiss chard in Plot B.
SOWING Sow in shallow rows in mid-spring, setting the seeds 12in (30cm) apart in groups of two or three. The rows should be 15in (35cm) apart. Later, thin the clusters to leave the strongest seedlings. Make another sowing in midsummer for winter use. In very cold areas, sow where the crop can be cloched (*see p. 140*).
Deep beds Sow at the same time, so that the thinned plants are 9in (23cm) apart each way in staggered rows. (*See p. 136.*)
MAINTENANCE There is little to do except water and weed when necessary. In very cold winters, protect the plants by covering with cloches (*see p. 140*).
HARVESTING Start harvesting the leaves in midsummer. Pull them off the plant as you would rhubarb, as cutting them would cause bleeding. Take just a few leaves from the outside of the plant, leaving the remainder to continue growing. The fleshy mid-ribs are considered a delicacy and are sometimes cooked separately. Because it can withstand several degrees of frost, Swiss chard can be harvested throughout the winter.
PESTS AND DISEASES See p. 50 for slugs and p. 201 for specific pests and diseases that affect leaf vegetables.

Planting chard in the ornamental border *The dramatic bright-red* Ruby chard *is often grown for its decorative qualities as well as its flavor.*

PLANTING AND HARVESTING TIMES

	Sow inside	Plant out	Sow outside	Harvest
Early spring				
Mid-spring			•	
Late spring				
Early summer				
Midsummer			•	•
Late summer				•
Early autumn				•
Mid-autumn				•
Late autumn				•
Early winter				•
Midwinter				•
Late winter				•

Chard

This is an easier vegetable to grow than spinach (*see opposite*). Being a biennial, it will not run to seed (*see p. 143*) and will withstand very cold conditions, so it can generally be grown throughout the winter.

VARIETIES The seeds will usually be sold only as *Perpetual Spinach.*
SOIL AND SITE A rich, moisture-retentive soil is best so, if you have some organic matter to spare, use it. Lime is generally required, so check that the pH is above 6.5. Provide some shade if possible.
• If you are using the three-year crop rotation plan (*see p. 134*), grow your plants in Plot B.
SOWING Sow in rows about 1in (2.5cm) deep in spring for summer picking and again in summer for winter crops. Sow two seeds every 12in (30cm), with 12in (30cm) between rows. Thin to single seedlings.
Deep beds Sow in staggered rows with 9in (23cm) between seeds. (*See p. 136.*)
MAINTENANCE Water plenty in dry weather and keep the beds weed free by hoeing (*see p. 57*).
HARVESTING Pick a few outer leaves from each plant while they are still young and crisp. Never completely strip a plant, as the leaves will regrow and you can continue picking for most of the year.
PESTS AND DISEASES Chard may be attacked by slugs and birds (*see pp. 46 and 50*). See also p. 201 for pests and diseases that affect leaf vegetables.

PLANTING AND HARVESTING TIMES

	Sow inside	Plant out	Sow outside	Harvest
Early spring			•	•
Mid-spring			•	•
Late spring				•
Early summer				•
Midsummer			•	•
Late summer			•	•
Early autumn				•
Mid-autumn				•
Late autumn				•
Early winter				•
Midwinter				•
Late winter				•

Spinach

No garden should be without spinach. It is highly nutritious, easy to grow, and can be harvested in succession right through the year. Amaranth spinach, also known as "Timpala" or "Hinn Choy", has a spinach flavor with a hint of horseradish. It is worth growing, particularly in hot areas, as it will withstand high temperatures.

VARIETIES Spinach has a much better flavor than the spinach substitutes. *Scenic* produces an abundance of green leaves, while *Galaxy* is a baby-leaf type and both are resistant to mildew. *Bordeaux* has attractive green leaves and contrasting red stems and leaf veins.

SOIL AND SITE A rich, moisture-retentive soil is best so, if you have some organic matter to spare, use it. Lime is generally required, so check that the soil pH is above 6.5. Provide some shade, as spinach has a tendency to run to seed very quickly if it gets too much sun (*see p. 143*).

• If you are using the three-year crop rotation plan (*see p. 134*), grow spinach in Plot B.

SOWING AND PLANTING The first crop comes from a sowing in the greenhouse or on the windowsill in late winter at a temperature of about 65°F (18°C) (*see p. 256*). Sow pairs of seeds in styrofoam cells or small pots (*see p. 139*). Later, thin to leave the strongest seedling. These are planted outside under cloches in early spring, setting them 6in (15cm) apart in rows 12in (30cm) apart. From then on, make sowings at monthly intervals in shallow trenches 12in (30cm) apart and thin to 6in (15cm) apart in the rows. Continue until midsummer.

Sow amaranth spinach in late spring, when all danger of frost has passed, in shallow rows 8in (20cm) apart. Thin to 6in (15cm) apart.

Deep beds Plant out or sow in blocks with 8in (20cm) between plants each way. (*See p. 136.*)

MAINTENANCE There is little to do except water and weed as necessary.

HARVESTING Take a few leaves from each plant, which will enable the plants to keep growing. Pick amaranth spinach leaves regularly and use them like spinach in salads.

PESTS AND DISEASES See pp. 46–53 for aphids and downy mildew and p. 201 for mosaic virus.

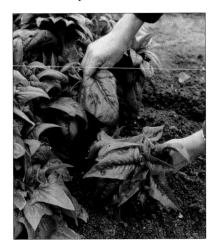

Harvesting spinach *Start picking the outer leaves 6–10 weeks after sowing.*

PLANTING AND HARVESTING TIMES

	Sow inside	Plant out	Sow outside	Harvest
Early spring		•	•	
Mid-spring			•	
Late spring			•	•
Early summer			•	•
Midsummer			•	•
Late summer				•
Early autumn				•
Mid-autumn				•
Late autumn				•
Early winter				•
Midwinter	•			
Late winter				

NEW ZEALAND SPINACH

This is a useful spinach substitute because it withstands the hottest weather without running to seed (*see p. 143*). It requires the same soil and conditions as spinach (*see above*). Sow the first crop indoors in small pots in late winter, then plant out 2ft (60cm) apart each way under cloches in mid-spring (*see p. 140*). Hoe to keep the beds weed free and pick 2–3in (5–8cm) shoots regularly from midsummer to the first frosts.

Calabrese and Broccoli

These brassicas are easy to grow and produce spears like the individual florets of cauliflower. Calabrese is simply broccoli that matures in summer.

VARIETIES For summer harvest use *Hydra*, which produces an abundance of sideshoots once the main head has been cut, or *Romanesco*, which makes creamy yellow heads of superb flavor in late summer and fall. For winter harvest, *Early Purple Sprouting* and *White Sprouting* will provide spears from midwinter to late spring.

SOIL AND SITE *See* Soil preparation for brassicas, *p. 191.*

SOWING AND PLANTING Sow calabrese in mid-spring and broccoli in late spring, both in shallow rows 6in (15cm) apart in the seedbed. Plant calabrese 6in (15cm) apart and broccoli at least 2ft (60cm) apart, with 2in (30cm) between rows.

MAINTENANCE Water regularly and keep the soil weed free by mulching with

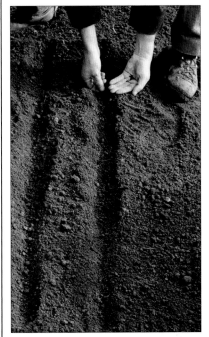

Sowing calabrese and broccoli *Always sow in a seedbed so that they can be transplanted easily. Sow in short rows with 6in (15cm) between plants.*

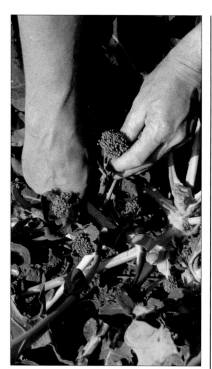

Harvesting broccoli *To maximize yields, cut the central stem first. Smaller sideshoots will then be encouraged.*

organic matter or, failing this, black plastic (*see p. 58–59*).

HARVESTING Cut the central shoot first, while it is still green, to encourage the production of sideshoots. If you can, try to prevent flowering, which will reduce yields. Broccoli will continue to produce sideshoots over a considerable period provided they are removed at regular intervals.

PESTS AND DISEASES These plants can be affected by many of the general garden pests and diseases, as well as cabbage butterflies, cabbage moth, cabbage root fly, and clubroot (*see pp. 46–53 and 201*).

PLANTING AND HARVESTING TIMES

	Sow inside	Plant out	Sow outside	Harvest
Early spring				•
Mid-spring		•	•	
Late spring		•	•	
Early summer			•	
Midsummer				•
Late summer				•
Early autumn				•
Mid-autumn				•
Late autumn				
Early winter				
Midwinter				
Late winter			•	

Cauliflower

Although cauliflower is the most difficult of the brassicas to cultivate, it is well worth growing if your land is free of clubroot disease (*see p. 201*). If you closely follow the cultivation methods outlined here, the plants will keep growing steadily and you should also avoid the problem of premature curding, where the plant flowers before it is big enough to support a decent-sized head, resulting in a small "button," which is useless. Like cabbages, there are three types: those that mature in summer, fall, and winter/spring.

VARIETIES

Summer cauliflower *Igloo* is ideal for growing on beds, *Purple Graffiti* has purple heads, while *Gypsy* is ideal for less fertile soils.

Autumn cauliflower *All the Year Round* lives up to its name but is best from late summer to early fall. *Dok Elgon* is a superb variety, which matures 16 weeks after planting and will go on to late fall. *Autumn Giant 3* matures in late fall and will stand until midwinter. It has firm white heads, well protected by leaves. To give a succession of curds, try the early fall *Violet Queen*, followed by *Sydney*, with bright white heads, and *Astral* for late fall harvest.

Winter/spring cauliflower For early winter, *Optimist* withstands both cold and wet conditions, but for real midwinter hardiness, *Deakin*, with its dense and firm white heads, is hard to beat. I rely on *White Dove* to give me the natural succession from midwinter until the spring varieties are ready. *Purple Cape* produces rich purple curds while the creamy-white heads of *Galleon* take me through to summer.

SOIL AND SITE *See* Soil preparation for brassicas, *p. 191*. Few plants in the garden will show such a marked reaction to nutrient deficiencies (*see opposite and pp. 38–39*). In a well-managed organic garden, none should occur but, if you are in the process of changing to organic techniques, be on

the lookout and take immediate steps to correct any deficiency. If the lime levels are correct and the symptoms still occur, hoe in about two handfuls of kelp meal per square yard/meter. This will ensure the necessary trace elements are replaced.

SOWING AND PLANTING

Summer cauliflower Make your earliest sowing in a heated greenhouse or on a windowsill in midwinter. Transfer the seedlings to wider spacings in a larger seed tray when plants are large enough to handle. Plant out under cloches 20in (50cm) square in late winter (*see p. 140*). Before transplanting, check each plant to make sure it has a growing point. Cauliflower sometimes goes "blind" and these plants are useless. Make sure too that the plants never stay too long in the trays. This will starve them and cause excessive root damage on planting, and may result in premature curding. Plant out when the seedlings are no more than 2in (5cm) high.

Sow the second crop in the same way in late winter and plant in the open in early spring. Continue sowing outside in a seedbed in

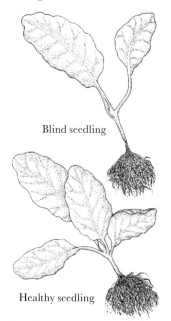

Blind seedling

Healthy seedling

Examining young cauliflower plants *When you take seedlings from the seed tray to be planted, inspect them carefully. They should have developed a tiny central bud. Any "blind" plants, without this bud, need to be discarded because they will not develop heads.*

MAINTAINING CAULIFLOWER

Cauliflower is generally considered to be among the most difficult vegetables to grow. However, while they certainly demand a lot of attention, proper soil preparation and maintenance should enable you to produce perfectly acceptable crops.

Supporting the plants *Draw a little soil around the roots of each cauliflower and press it down firmly with your heel to prevent the wind from rocking the plants.*

Protecting the heads *Cauliflower heads must be kept out of direct sunlight. A simple way of doing this is to bend one of the large leaves over to cover them.*

Storing summer cauliflower *Tie string around the stems and hang plants upside down in a cool shed. Spray regularly with water to keep them fresh.*

harvest time, and there will be no risk of them running to seed.

PESTS AND DISEASES

Cauliflower can be affected by many of the general garden pests and diseases, as well as cabbage butterflies, cabbage moth, cabbage root fly, and clubroot (*see pp. 46–53 and 201*).

Prompt action is especially important as an attack from any pest or disease could destroy the crop by causing premature curding (*see opposite*).

A shortage of molybdenum may result in a strange condition known as "whiptail," which makes the leaves thin and deformed. Boron deficiency causes small, bitter curds and makes the stems and leaves turn brown, while a shortage of magnesium may turn the leaves yellow, reddish, or purple. Prevent these deficiencies by correct soil management.

shallow rows 6in (15cm) apart at three-week intervals, from early to late spring, for a succession. Transplant at the same distances before the seedlings exceed 8cm (3in) and water before lifting and after transplanting.

Autumn cauliflower Sow in a seedbed in mid-spring in shallow rows 6in (15cm) apart. Plant out in early or midsummer, setting the plants no deeper than they were in the seedbed. Space the plants 2ft (60cm) square.

Winter spring/cauliflower Sow in a seedbed in mid- or late spring. Transplant 2ft 6in (75cm) square before the seedlings reach more than 3in (8cm) high.

Deep beds Plant out summer cauliflowers in staggered rows, 18in (45cm) apart each way, and other types 2ft (60cm) apart each way, at the same time as for ordinary beds. (*See p. 136.*)

MAINTENANCE Keep all plants weed free (*see p. 57*) and ensure they never go short of water. As a single day of dryness can result in the loss of an entire crop, cover the soil with a layer of organic matter

or with plastic or paper to retain moisture, and water by hand if the weather is dry.

Autumn cauliflower Provide support for the plants by firming them in the ground in late summer (*see above*).

Winter/spring cauliflower Bend plants over to face north in late fall to ensure that the sun doesn't strike the head first thing in the morning. This action prevents rapid thawing of frozen curds, which would cause discoloration and may also spoil the flavor.

HARVESTING AND STORING

Summer cauliflower Cut heads as they develop. Remove the stumps completely and put them on the compost heap. If too many are ready at the same time, summer cauliflower can be lifted and stored for a few weeks in a cool spot (*see right*).

Autumn and winter/spring cauliflower Break a few leaves over the curds when they mature and cut them as required, then remove the rest of the plant. You will not need to hang them, since they will have stopped growing by

PLANTING AND HARVESTING TIMES

	Sow inside	Plant out	Sow outside	Harvest
Early spring		•	•	•
Mid-spring		•	•	
Late spring			•	•
Early summer				•
Midsummer				•
Late summer				•
Early autumn				•
Mid-autumn				•
Late autumn				•
Early winter				•
Mid winter	•			•
Late winter	•	•		•

Nappa cabbage

Sometimes known as "Chinese cabbage," this vegetable is more difficult to grow than other types of cabbage. However, if you can provide favorable conditions, it is well worth growing.

VARIETIES The essence of a good variety is its resistance to bolting (*see p. 143*). *Blues* is very resistant, while *Wa Wa Sai* is a baby variety.

SOIL AND SITE *See* Soil preparation for brassicas, *p. 191*. Grow Chinese cabbages in shade, alongside the other brassicas, but dig a special bed for it with plenty of well-rotted compost or manure.

SOWING Sow in shallow rows about 12in (30cm) apart, from late spring to midsummer, putting in two seeds every 9in (23cm). Thin later to leave the strongest of each pair of seedlings.

Deep beds Sow in blocks, 9in (23cm) apart, and thin to 9in (23cm). (*See p. 136.*)

MAINTENANCE Always keep the soil moist and hoe regularly between plants (*see p. 57*) to eliminate weeds.

HARVESTING Harvest eight to ten weeks after sowing. As they do not store, sow at two-week intervals in short rows to ensure a succession.

PESTS AND DISEASES Flea beetles, slugs, millipedes, and clubroot may affect these plants (*see pp. 46–53 and 201*).

PLANTING AND HARVESTING TIMES

	Sow inside	Plant out	Sow outside	Harvest
Early spring				
Mid-spring				
Late spring			•	
Early summer			•	
Midsummer			•	•
Late summer				•
Early autumn				•
Mid-autumn				•
Late autumn				
Early winter				
Midwinter				
Late winter				

Cabbages

It is possible to harvest cabbages all year-round but, if you wish to be able to do this, you will need three different types: spring, summer, and autumn/winter cabbages.

VARIETIES

Spring cabbages *April* is a fine, pointed cabbage with a marked resistance to running to seed. *Durham Early* is an older variety producing good-quality, medium-sized heads that can stay in the ground for a long time.

Summer cabbages *Hispi* is probably the most popular variety and deservedly so. The pointed hearts are hard and crisp and the leaves make fine collards. *Greyhound* is similar and suited to raised beds. *Primo* is an improved strain of the old favorite *Golden Acre*, producing very heavy, solid heads.

Autumn/winter cabbages In order to maintain a succession you will need two varieties. For early fall harvesting, use *Minicole* or *Celtic*—which will go on through the winter too. Other good winter varieties are the savoys like *January King* or *Tarvoy*. Of the red cabbages, *Ruby Ball* is outstanding for quality and flavor.

SOIL AND SITE *See* Soil preparation for brassicas, *p. 191*.

SOWING AND PLANTING

Spring cabbages Sow in a seedbed (*see p. 269*) in mid- or late summer in shallow rows 6in (15cm) apart. Bear in mind that you'll only need a very short row—no more than 18in (45cm) long—to produce between 50 and 100 plants. Plant the seedlings as described below in early or mid-fall.

Summer cabbages Sow the earliest crop in seed trays in late winter. Put them on the windowsill or in the greenhouse and transplant them, when they are big enough to handle, to a wider spacing in the seed tray. Then harden them off (*see p. 254*) and plant out under cloches (*see p. 140*) in early spring, setting them 18in (45cm) apart each way. At the same time, plant hardened-off plants to be harvested later.

Using brown paper *A good way of controlling weeds is to plant cabbage seedlings through slits made in biodegradable brown paper.*

Sow seeds outside in mid-spring in a seedbed and transplant 18in (45cm) apart when they are large enough, in late spring or early summer.

Autumn/winter cabbages Sow autumn/winter and red cabbages in a seedbed in mid- or late spring in shallow rows about 6in (15cm) apart. Transplant the seedlings 18in (45cm) square in midsummer.

Deep beds Cabbages grown in a deep bed produce perfectly good results in the uncompacted soil. Plant out spring cabbages in blocks with the plants staggered and 6in (15cm) apart each way (*see p. 136*). For summer and autumn/winter cabbages the timings are the same as for a normal bed, but they can be planted out 15in (35cm) apart. Closer planting produces smaller heads, which you may prefer if you have a small family.

MAINTENANCE

Spring cabbages Weed around the plants and provide plenty of water in the early stages.

Deterring birds *Cover seedlings with netting to protect against birds.*

PLANTING OUT AND HARVESTING CABBAGES

All types of cabbage are normally transplanted. It is important that the development of the seedlings is not interrupted excessively. By following a few simple rules, you can encourage the plants to become re-established as quickly as possible.

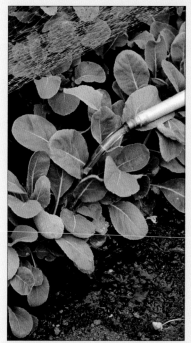

1 *The seedlings are ready to be planted out when they have grown to about 2–3in (5–8cm) high. Water the seedbed the night before you intend to dig them up. Lift clusters of seedlings with a small hand fork.*

2 *Fill a shallow trench with water and soak the roots of the young plants in it for about a minute until the roots are coated in muddy water. This ensures they do not dry out when they are planted.*

3 *Make holes with a dibber (see p. 260) 6in (15cm) deep every 18in (45cm), in rows 18in (45cm) apart. Plant the seedlings and firm in with your heel before watering.*

4 *When the hearts feel firm, harvest the cabbages by cutting through the base of the stems with a sharp knife. You can store certain varieties by hanging them upside down in a cool place.*

In late winter, they will benefit from a boost to get them growing again so apply one handful of dried blood per four plants.

Summer and autumn/winter cabbages Keep the beds weed free and the plants watered.

HARVESTING AND STORING

Spring cabbages Harvest the first pickings as "spring greens" or collards. Do this selectively to leave the final spacings at 12in (30cm) each way. Leave the remaining plants to heart up for later so you can harvest spring cabbages from early spring until early summer.

Summer cabbages Cut the plants when the hearts feel firm. If you cut a cross in the top of the remaining stem, a couple of new small cabbages will grow. Alternatively, dig up the root to avoid the possibility of attracting pests and diseases.

Autumn/winter cabbages Begin harvesting when the heads are firm and solid. Pull *Minicole* in late fall and hang it upside down with stalk attached, in a cold shed, where it will keep for about two months. Savoys stand any amount of frost, so can be left in the ground until needed.

Start cutting red cabbages as soon as the heads are firm and solid. Continue until late fall and then pull any that remain and hang them in a cool shed for use in the winter months.

PESTS AND DISEASES Cabbages can be affected by many of the general garden pests and diseases (*see pp. 46–53*), as well as cabbage butterflies, cabbage moth, cabbage root fly, and clubroot (*see p. 201*).

PLANTING AND HARVESTING TIMES

	Sow inside	Plant out	Sow outside	Harvest
Early spring		•	•	•
Mid-spring			•	•
Late spring			•	•
Early summer				•
Midsummer		•		•
Late summer		•		•
Early autumn				•
Mid-autumn				•
Late autumn				•
Early winter				•
Midwinter	•			•
Late winter	•	•		•

Vegetable pests and diseases

Most vegetables are susceptible to a range of specific pests and diseases in addition to those that may attack all garden plants (*see pp. 46–53*). Correct soil management techniques and crop rotation should prevent mineral deficiencies (*see pp. 38–39*), but it is important that the more serious problems are identified quickly and treated correctly.

Shoot vegetables

Mineral deficiencies can cause black or brown heart in celery (*see pp. 38–39*).

ASPARAGUS BEETLE

Adult beetles and their grubs feed on asparagus shoots and foliage. Severe attacks can strip foliage completely or girdle stems, killing the plant.
WHAT TO DO Spraying with Pyrethrum may have an effect. Pick off the larvae and adults and burn the fronds in late summer.

CELERY FLY

Damage is likely to be seen first in late spring, when leaves turn pale green, then brown and shriveled.
WHAT TO DO Remove affected leaves and burn them.

ASPARAGUS RUST

Rust appears as reddish pustules on stems and foliage in summer.
WHAT TO DO As soon as the first signs are seen, remove affected shoots and spray every two weeks with a copper fungicide until early fall.

CELERY LEAF SPOT

Brown spots on leaves and stems that develop into black pustules. Most celery seed is treated before selling, but their fungicide is not organic.
WHAT TO DO Remove affected leaves and spray with Bordeaux mixture every two weeks until two weeks before harvest.

Pod and seed vegetables

Birds (*see p. 47*) can be a major pest with pea crops, and broad beans are sometimes attacked by black bean aphid (*see p. 50*).

PEA MOTH

This moth is responsible for the small maggots that can make peas inedible. It lays its eggs on plants in flower throughout the summer. Pea moth is a difficult pest to control since a spray will also kill insects that are beneficial to the garden.
WHAT TO DO When peas begin to flower, cover the crop with enviromesh to prevent the moth from being able to lay its eggs. Phermone traps have been used by commercial growers for years and are now available to the amateur gardener. These consist of a sticky pad on which is placed pheromone—a chemical naturally secreted by the female pea moth to attract the male. The males stick to the pad, preventing them from mating with the female. The method is already available to catch codling moth adults which attack apples (*see p. 234*) and it works very well.

PEA AND BEAN WEEVIL

A grayish-brown beetle that attacks mainly peas and broad beans. It makes characteristic U-shaped notches in the margins of the leaves.
WHAT TO DO This is not a great problem unless young seedlings are being attacked, in which case pick them off by hand during early evening.

HALO BLIGHT

Angular spots on the leaves are surrounded by a lighter-colored halo. Later they turn reddish brown and can ooze white.
WHAT TO DO The disease is seed-borne, so buy only from a reputable company and, if you have been using home-saved seed, buy a fresh stock.

CHOCOLATE SPOT

This affects broad beans and shows as brown spots or streaks on leaves and stems. These marks may join up and stems can become completely blackened, leading to the death of the plant.
WHAT TO DO Avoid it by good cultivation methods (*see p. 158*), especially adequate feeding and manuring, and pull up and burn affected plants. As soon as you see signs of the problem, spray the whole crop with a copper fungicide (*see p. 53*).

FAILURE TO SET
The flowers of green and runner beans may drop off having failed to set, usually because the roots are dry or the plants have not been pollinated by insects.
WHAT TO DO Protect the plants from cold winds to encourage pollinating insects. In very dry weather, water the plants to prevent the flowers from wilting and closing, which makes it impossible for bees to reach the pollen without destroying the flower.

Fruiting vegetables

See also p. 257 for greenhouse pests and diseases.

RED SPIDER MITE

This will only be a problem in very dry years. The tiny mites cannot be seen with the naked eye, but they form visible webs and the leaves take on a characteristic mottled and yellowed appearance.
WHAT TO DO The mites like dry conditions, so avoid attack by spraying with water regularly.

POTATO BLIGHT

This shows as black or brown spots or patches on the leaves.
WHAT TO DO Spray with Bordeaux mixture at two-week intervals when the symptoms appear.

LEAF MOLD

Yellow patches on the upper surface of leaves and brown patches beneath are typical symptoms.
WHAT TO DO Most modern varieties are resistant. Spray once with copper fungicide to control any outbreak that does occur.

VIRUS

This shows as a stunting of the plant, and a yellowing and mottling of the leaves.
WHAT TO DO There is no cure. The disease is carried by aphids (*see p. 50*) so try to control them as a preventive measure.

Bulb vegetables

Although prone to a range of disorders, onions are most likely to suffer from those described here. Other bulbs are less susceptible.

ONION FLY

Damage is generally seen in early mid-summer, when the plants begin to yellow and die. If the soil is scraped from around the roots, white maggots can be found.
WHAT TO DO Hoe around the plants regularly to expose grubs to birds. The female fly is attracted by the scent of the onions, and this is strongest when the seedlings are thinned. Grow from sets or multi-sown blocks and you will not need to thin plants.

ONION EELWORM

These microscopic, soil-borne creatures get inside the bulbs, causing swelling and distortion.
WHAT TO DO Dig up affected plants and use the area to grow brassicas and lettuce for two, or preferably four, years to avoid providing a host for the eelworms to feed on.

WHITE ROT

This shows as a moldy growth near the neck of stored onions that then become soft and rotten.
WHAT TO DO Remove affected bulbs as soon as you see them. Do not overfeed and only store fully ripe bulbs. Never bend the tops over to induce ripening as this may encourage the disease.

NECK ROT

This shows as a white, fluffy fungal growth on the roots. Diseased plants turn yellow and eventually die.
WHAT TO DO Treat affected plants with Bordeaux mixture immediately and do not resow onions in the same area for at least two years to deter the build up of the disease.

STORAGE ROT

There are several different fungi that can attack bulbs in storage, causing them to go soft and slimy.
WHAT TO DO Try to ensure that the bulbs are completely ripe and that stored bulbs have plenty of air circulating around them. Inspect stored bulbs regularly and remove any that are affected right away.

Squash vegetables

Only one major disease affects crops grown outdoors. Greenhouse plants can also suffer from the diseases described on p. 257.

CUCUMBER MOSAIC VIRUS

This disease attacks all the squash vegetables, not just cucumbers. Affected plants develop puckered leaves which turn mottled and yellow, and growth is stunted.
WHAT TO DO Guard against aphids, which carry the disease (*see p. 50*). Destroy affected plants—there is no cure.

Root vegetables

The root crops include several members of the *Brassica* family, which are prone to the same disorders as cabbages (*see opposite*). Boron deficiency may cause corkiness in some roots (*see pp. 38–39*).

CARROT FLY

The female fly lays her eggs at the base of carrots, parsnips, parsley, and celery. The grubs burrow into the root, causing characteristic brown marks and tunnels.

WHAT TO DO There is a very simple solution to this problem: surround the row of plants with an enviromesh barrier supported by short posts. The pests fly an inch or so above the ground and, when they meet the barrier, they will fly upward and miss the crop. Erect the barrier as soon as the carrots are planted outside.

POTATO CYST EELWORM

A microscopic pest that causes premature death of the plants and results in undersized tubers.
WHAT TO DO Grow resistant varieties only and rotate crops annually (*see p. 134*).

POTATO BLIGHT

This fungus causes brown patches on leaves, especially in warm, wet weather. The patches spread and become black and the foliage dies. If left untreated, the spores can affect the tubers too, causing them to turn black inside and rot.
WHAT TO DO Spray with Bordeaux mixture in midsummer and at two-week intervals thereafter until harvesting.

SCAB

A disease that causes ugly corky marks on the outside of tubers.
WHAT TO DO Avoid trouble by incorporating plenty of organic matter into the soil and watering during dry spells. Use resistant varieties.

GANGRENE

A fungus disease attacking potatoes in storage, gangrene causes the inside of the tuber to rot. Only damaged or wet potatoes are likely to be affected.
WHAT TO DO Dig up and store potatoes as described on p. 186. Burn infected tubers.

POTATO BLACK LEG

A bacterial disease that causes the base of the stems to blacken and die. If tubers have formed, they too can be affected. It is transmitted through diseased seed tubers, so only buy seed that has been certified disease free from a reputable seed company.
WHAT TO DO Remove and burn affected plants as soon as the symptoms are seen.

SPRAING

The symptoms of spraing are red-brown lesions on the tubers. If you cut one in half you'll find wavy, semi-circular marks.
WHAT TO DO There is no cure, so grow resistant varieties only.

SOFT ROT

This bacterial disease affects rutabagas and turnips as a white or gray mushy rot. It is worse when soil is badly drained and not rotated.
WHAT TO DO Avoid by growing rutabagas and turnips on raised beds if your soil is heavy (*see p. 135*).

PARSNIP CANKER

This disease causes reddish brown marks on the shoulder of the root and these often spread further into the root, causing it to rot.
WHAT TO DO Concentrate on good cultivation methods (*see p. 187*) to produce healthy, fast growth, and use resistant varieties.

Leaf vegetables

The brassicas are especially prone to problems, but correct soil management and cultivation can avoid a lot of trouble. Boron deficiency causes brown heart in leaf crops (*see pp. 38–39*).

CATERPILLARS

Several butterflies lay their eggs on leaf crops and the caterpillars make characteristic round holes in the leaves. The attacks start in midsummer and continue through until fall. The worst offender is the cabbage white butterfly.

WHAT TO DO Simply pick off the caterpillars regularly and drop them into a jar of paraffin. The eggs can often be rubbed off by hand too. As a last resort, spray with the bacterium *Bacillus thuringiensis* or with nematodes.

MEALY CABBAGE APHID

Dense colonies of this aphid sometimes gather on the undersides of leaves, where they suck sap. It is rare in organic gardens.
WHAT TO DO Hoverflies and ladybugs generally set the balance straight. See p. 51 for ways of encouraging these natural predators into your garden. If the pests do build up, a spray with insecticidal soap will control them (*see p. 53*).

CABBAGE ROOT FLY

Perhaps the worst of all brassica pests, causing complete collapse of young plants. The adult fly lays her eggs in the soil right next to the stem. When the larvae hatch, they immediately burrow into the root and begin to feed. Symptoms are wilting and collapse of the plant, by which time it is too late to save it, so precautions must be taken at planting time.
WHAT TO DO The organic answer—and the only one, incidentally, that is completely successful—is to surround the stem at soil level with foam-rubber carpet pad or cardboard.

1 *Cut a piece of the pad into 6in (15cm) squares, make a slit in the center and a small cross slit at the end.*

2 *Slip the piece of carpet pad around the base of the plant, ensuring that it fits tightly.*

CLUBROOT

Undoubtedly the most debilitating disease of the cabbage family, clubroot is caused by a soil-borne fungus that distorts and thickens the root and causes stunting. Affected plants fail to develop at all. It is worse on badly drained soil and especially where acid conditions prevail, so make sure the soil drains well and add plenty of lime when you grow brassicas (*see p. 36*). Rutabagas can also be affected by clubroot.
WHAT TO DO There is no cure for clubroot and it will live in the soil indefinitely—certainly longer than the seven years often quoted. A method of overcoming it is to give plants a healthy start by raising them in pots in the greenhouse before planting them outside (*see p. 45*). Although the seedlings will still be partially affected by the disease, you will be able to produce decent crops—except for cauliflower, which must be discontinued. Rotate crops regularly.

MOSAIC VIRUS

Sometimes known as "spinach blight," this shows as a yellowing of the younger leaves and later of the older ones too.
WHAT TO DO There is no cure, but you can prevent the disease by controlling the aphids that spread it.

THE FRUIT GARDEN

As with vegetables, the advantages of growing fruit organically are mostly obvious. As you crunch that juicy apple, you will know that it hasn't been drenched with insecticide or coated with arsenic to improve shelf life; your strawberry jam will taste like real strawberries, without a hint of monosodium glutamate. You may have to put up with the odd blemish from the birds that were ridding your garden of aphids, but the organically grown crop is usually large enough to withstand a few bird attacks.

The plants in the fruit garden will be productive over a longer period than those in the vegetable garden. Most vegetables are annuals, cropping in the same year as they are planted, the plant then being discarded. Many fruit plants, however, take a few years to come into production, but will then continue to produce fruit for several seasons. The olive tree is an extreme example of longevity—it can bear fruit for 1,500 years!

Growing your own fruit frees you from having to rely on the small variety of relatively inferior fruit available in supermarkets. Commercial growers put flavor fairly low on their list of priorities, preferring to choose varieties that produce fruit that looks good, travels well, and has a long shelf life. Gardeners have a much wider choice and the fruits you grow in your own garden will often be far superior to any of the commercial ones.

GROWING FRUIT IN A SMALL GARDEN
Few people have room to set aside for a large fruit plot but, even if your garden is small, there is no reason why fruit should not be grown in the ornamental part. Most fruit trees are very decorative, giving a show of blossoms in the spring, followed by attractive fruit in the summer and fall. Certainly, walls should be utilized for growing fan-trained fruit (see p. 206). Even in temperate regions you can grow peaches, nectarines, and figs on warm, south-facing walls. Pears and apples can be grown on east- and west-facing walls and morello cherries and quinces on walls facing north. Vines also look good climbing up walls and will give a good crop of wine berries (see p. 231). Red currants and gooseberries can be grown as decorative double or triple cordons (see p. 208) against walls or fences.

Grow strawberries, gooseberries, red currants, and black currants in the ornamental borders and you should consider using a cherry, mulberry, orange, lemon, peach, plum, apple, or pear tree as a lawn feature. If you need a hedge to divide one part of the garden from another, think about using cordon apples and pears (see p. 206). You could even use single-tier espaliers, or stepovers (see p. 206), only 12in (30cm) high as a decorative and productive edging to the fruit plot.

THE EFFECT OF SITE
Many local features, such as slopes, which may cause frost pockets, altitude, and wind protection, will affect the fruit in your garden. There are, however, several simple measures you can take to prevent any adverse effects.

Frost is one of the main problems. If your garden is in a frost pocket (see p. 65), you may be limited to growing only varieties that flower late and so escape spring frosts. Recommendations are given in the appropriate cultivation sections (see pp. 215–231).

Strong winds can also be a problem since they destroy foliage, damage flowers, and discourage the vital pollinating insects (see opposite). If your site is exposed, it is worth protecting fruit; initially by erecting a temporary plastic windbreak and planting a hedge nearby to take over from the man-made windbreak when it has grown high enough. To avoid creating an artificial frost pocket in your garden by cutting off the escape route of cold air (see p. 65), raise the foot of the windbreak 12in (30cm) off the ground and keep the bottom of the hedge free of vegetation and rubbish (see p. 78). The best site for each type of fruit is given in the cultivation details (see pp. 215–231).

Soil preferences and optimum pH are also given for each plant in the cultivation details (see also pp. 215 and 225). Before planting fruit, it is essential to prepare the soil well. There are some plants that have specific requirements and these are dealt with in the relevant sections but, for most, the normal organic methods of soil care will ensure healthy trees and bushes and so produce bigger yields. Details of preparing and improving the soil are given in The Soil (see pp. 12–17) and Basic Techniques (see pp. 258–267).

Selecting plants

First, always buy your plants from a specialty grower to ensure a wider choice and better quality. If you can visit the nursery, you will have the opportunity of choosing the best-shaped trees and bushes—look for a uniform shape and a good root system.

Second, buy young plants; the old wives' tale that trees take seven years to begin fruiting, so the older the tree you buy the better, is untrue. In fact, the reverse is the case. Young trees establish very quickly and will crop earlier than those that have been languishing in a pot or a field for four or five years.

Third, I recommend buying fruit trees and bushes as bare root plants and planting in the late fall when they are dormant. Bare root plants tend to be better quality and cheaper than container-grown plants too.

There are several important points to remember when choosing varieties. Pollination is the first essential. Some varieties are self-fertile, while others need to be fertilized with pollen from a plant of a different variety—if this is so you will need to grow at least two varieties in your garden (*see below for details*).

The ultimate size of the tree is an important consideration too. If you have a large garden, a standard or bush tree can be very attractive. However, if your garden is small, many of the larger trees can be grown on "dwarfing rootstocks" (*see below for details*) to keep them small.

Take into account the storage qualities of the fruit too. Early apples, for example, though wonderful picked and eaten straight from the tree, will not keep as well as late-maturing varieties, so aim for a succession of harvesting.

Finally, bear in mind that, in most countries, fruit is covered by government regulation. If the nursery can't guarantee that their stock has been certified free from disease, go elsewhere.

POLLINATION

Many fruit trees will not produce a full crop unless they are pollinated by a different variety of the same species. If you choose to grow varieties that are not self-pollinating, you will have to grow at least two different ones, but make sure you choose two that will pollinate one another. These are generally varieties that flower at the same time.

Some varieties, known as "triploids," are incapable of pollinating others, but need pollinating by another variety so, if you want to grow a triploid variety, you will have to have at least three different varieties. If you only have the space for one tree, you could grow a "family tree," which has three or four compatible varieties budded onto the same tree. Apples and pears can both be grown in this way.

Pollen is usually transferred from flower to flower, and from tree to tree, by insects, who visit the flowers in search of nectar. The pollen sticks to the visiting insects and some of it is rubbed off in the next flower the insect goes to. Plants that flower very early in the year, before the pollinating insects are around, will have to be pollinated by hand. Pollen is transferred from flower to flower using a soft camel hair brush—simply dab the center of each flower. Plants in the greenhouse need hand-pollinating.

ROOTSTOCKS

Research into new "rootstocks," dwarf varieties of trees and pruning methods, means that fruit trees no longer have to be large, so you can grow trees in the smallest of spaces, even pots on a terrace.

A rootstock is a specially selected root system onto which is grafted the particular variety you wish to grow. The rootstock will control the growth rate and eventual size of the tree, while the grafted variety will decide the type of fruit produced. Rootstocks are labeled with special numbers or, in some cases, given a name, such as *Gisela, Pixy, Colt,* or *St. Julien A.*

When planting, make sure the grafting point is at least 4in (10cm) above the soil to prevent the variety from rooting into the soil—if this happens the vigor of the rootstock will be lost. Rootstocks can also confer resistance to certain diseases on the variety.

There are many rootstocks available and recommended types are listed in the appropriate cultivation details (*see pp. 215–231*).

You can buy trees already grafted or you can prepare your own (*see p. 276*).

The rootstock grafting point
The bump near the base of the stem is the graft between rootstock and variety.

Planting and training fruit trees and bushes

Fruit trees and bushes are generally planted in the same way as the ornamentals (*see pp. 82–83 and p. 112*). Most fruit plants are best planted in early winter, although container-grown ones can be planted at any time of year. However, if the plants arrive when the soil is frozen, do not plant them in their permanent position but heel them in, in the same way as the ornamentals (*see p. 113*). The one exception to the winter-planting rule is strawberries, which are planted in late summer and fall.

If you are growing fruit against a wall, plant so that the base of the plant is at least 12in (30cm) away from the wall. This is likely to be the driest spot in the garden and may even be protected by overhanging eaves, so ensure the plant has plenty of water immediately after planting. Later, the roots will spread away from the wall and find their own water.

If you buy one-year-old trees, it is often not necessary to stake them unless they are container-grown, or on a very dwarfing rootstock, when they should be staked with a short stake as recommended for ornamental trees (*see p. 82*). If you decide to grow trained fruit that requires a post-and-wire support, make sure you erect it first to avoid root disturbance later. (*See p. 266 for the different types of support.*)

PLANTING A CORDON APPLE TREE

All fruit trees should be planted in well-prepared soil. When planting a cordon, erect the post-and-wire support first. This can be free-standing as shown opposite or the wires can be put up against an existing fence, as shown below. (*For pruning details see p. 209.*)

1 *Attach three wires to the fence, one 2ft (60cm) from the bottom, one at the top, and one in the middle, and tie poles to them at an angle of 45°. The canes should be 2ft 6in (75cm) apart.*

2 *Prepare a strip of land along the fence. It should be at least 4ft (1.2m) wide. Dig deeply, breaking up the subsoil to the depth of the fork.*

3 *Incorporate plenty of well-rotted manure or compost throughout all levels of the trench.*

4 *Dig a hole at the base of each pole. Put the tree in the hole, planting it at the same angle as the pole. Cover the roots with soil.*

5 *Tie the stem of the tree to the pole at intervals, using soft string. The pole prevents the stem from chafing against the wires.*

6 *Mulch around the stem of each tree with well-rotted manure or compost to conserve moisture and suppress weed growth.*

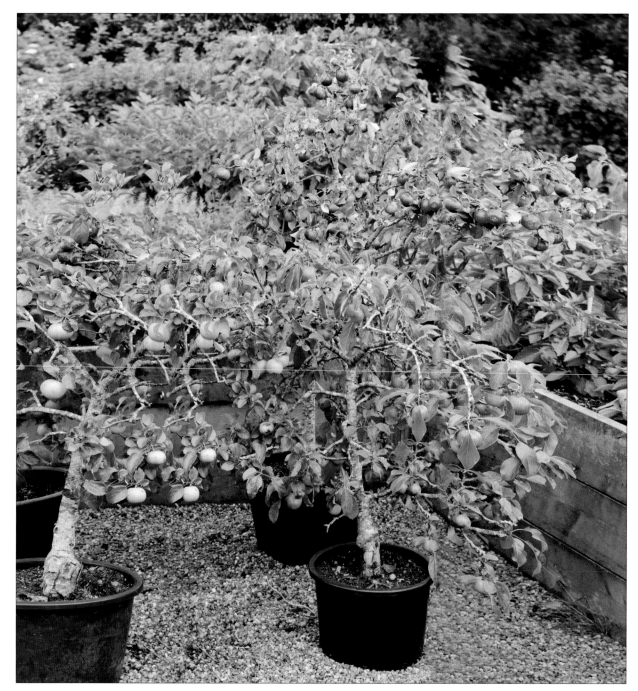

▲ **The effect of growing on a rootstock** *If a very dwarfing rootstock is used, a good crop can be produced from tiny trees grown in pots. The tree in the foreground shows clearly the grafting point between the rootstock and the variety.*

▶ **A screen of apple blossom** *This row of cordon-grown apple trees will produce an attractive display of blossoms in spring. As the trees mature they will form a dense, productive screen against the wall.*

TREE SHAPES

If you have a very large garden, you can grow tall, spreading fruit trees. These standard trees, and the slightly shorter bush trees, are attractive garden features. But if you have a small garden, your fruit trees are better trained into one of the space-saving shapes shown below. Training details are given on the following three pages. Fan-training involves complex pruning and is recommended mainly for cherries, plums, peaches, and nectarines (*see pp. 217–218*).

STANDARD TREE

This type of tree is grown on a tall stem. It makes a fine specimen tree but is difficult to pick and prune without working from a ladder. It needs no special pruning other than the removal of dead, diseased, or crossing branches. Height varies but ranges from 20–30ft (6–9m).

BUSH TREE

This is exactly the same as a standard tree, except that it is grown on a stem that is about 4ft (1.2m) shorter. However, it can still grow too large to pick and prune from the ground. Height varies according to the variety and rootstock but can be anything from 15–25ft (5–8m).

DWARF PYRAMID

This makes an attractive free-standing tree that is grown to a pyramidal shape, with the lower branches being longer than the upper ones. It is very easy to prune and pick. Apples, pears, and plums are suitable. Grow to a height of 8ft (2.5m), and a spread of 5ft (1.5m).

FAN

A fan is normally pruned so that two opposite shoots grow from the main stem. Shoots from these form the fan shape. Peaches, nectarines, plums, and cherries can be grown as fans. Grow them to a maximum height of 8ft (2.5m) and spread of 12ft (3.5m).

CORDON

Usually a single stem, grown at an angle of about 45° to the ground and supported on a post-and-wire support to make a hedge. Soft fruits such as gooseberries and red currants can be grown as single, double, or triple cordons. Grow cordons to a maximum height of 6ft (1.8m) and a spread of 2ft 6in (75cm).

FESTOONED TREE

A relatively new idea, where branches are bent down and tied either to the main stem or the branch below in a series of hoops, making an attractive small tree that can carry heavy crops. Apples and pears, and plums on *Pixy* rootstocks, can be grown as festooned trees. Grow them to about 6ft (1.8m) high with a spread of 3ft (90cm).

ESPALIER

This is trained so that its branches come horizontally from the stem at 12in (30cm) intervals. An espalier is normally trained against a wall or fence. Suitable fruits include apples and pears. Grow espaliers to a maximum height of 8ft (2.5m) and a spread of 15ft (4.5m).

STEPOVER

A shortened version of an espalier with only one branch on either side, so consisting of only one tier. Stepovers can be used as a productive edging around the vegetable garden or along paths. Apples and pears can be grown as stepovers and plums are possible on a *Pixy* rootstock. Grow to a maximum height of 12in (30cm).

TIPS FOR PLANTING AND TRAINING

There are several general guidelines that should be followed if you are buying and planting trees or bushes for training.
• Use one- or two-year-old trees or bushes.
• Buy and plant in the winter.
• Prepare as large an area as possible. Dig deeply and incorporate plenty of well-rotted manure or compost throughout all levels.
• Once the tree is planted, mulch around the stem with well-rotted manure or compost.
By judicious pruning and thinning at the start of growth, and throughout their life, you can train trees and bushes into a variety of shapes.

Each shape has its specific growth patterns, but there are some general pruning points to note.
• Always use a sharp pair of pruning shears that will make a clean cut.
• Always prune to a point just above a bud—if a stub of shoot is left it will die back and may introduce disease.
• If you cut out a branch altogether, cut back to ½in (1cm) beyond where it meets the main stem.
• A bud will grow out in the direction it is facing so always cut back to an outward-facing bud to prevent branches from growing into the middle of the tree or bush where they will cause congestion.

PRUNING TERMS AND TECHNIQUES

Pruning is the deliberate cutting back of plants, usually applied to trees and shrubs. It is a method of controlling size, training to shape, and encouraging flower or fruit buds to form. Commonly used pruning terms are listed below.

Sideshoot A shoot arising from the main stem of the plant.

Secondary shoot A shoot arising from a sideshoot.

Fruiting spur A collection of shoots on which the fruit is produced. Made by cutting sideshoots and secondary shoots back hard.

Secondary shoot

Sideshoot

Leading shoot The main stem (or stems) that extends the branch system.

Downward-facing bud Refers to the angle of the bud on the shoot. Buds can also be outward-, inward-, and upward-facing. They are used to advantage when training to shape. Remember that a bud grows in the direction it faces.

Making a cut A pruning cut should be angled away from the bud, and be made slightly above it. Do not leave too much stem above the bud as this "snag" will rot. Do not cut too close to the bud.

Too close   Too far away   Wrong angle   Correct

TRAINING A DWARF PYRAMID

If you want to grow a free-standing tree but don't have the room for a standard or bush tree, a dwarf pyramid is an ideal alternative. Its final shape resembles that of a Christmas tree and the initial pruning establishes the conical shape. After that, all pruning is done in summer to restrict growth. If you are growing more than one, they should be planted 5ft (1.5m) apart.

1 Immediately after planting, *cut the stem back to a bud within 2ft (60cm) of ground level.*

2 In the second winter, *select five or six evenly spaced lower branches that have a wide angle to the stem. Cut them back to a downward- or outward-facing bud to leave them 10in (25cm) long; if they are less than 10in (25cm) long, simply remove 1in (2.5cm) from the tip.*

3 At the same time, *any other branches at this level should be removed completely. Any branches above this level should be cut back to 6in (15m) to form a second tier. The tip of the main stem is cut back to leave it 12in (30cm) above the top branch.*

4 Every summer, *cut back the tip of each branch to leave 6in (15cm) of the current year's growth. Prune sideshoots to 4in (10cm) long and any secondary shoots to 2in (5cm).*

5 Every winter, *prune the leading shoot to leave 8in (20cm) of the last season's growth.*

6 Once the tree has reached the required height and width, *prune back twice as hard, so that new growth is cut back to 3in (7cm) long, sideshoots 2in (5cm) long, and secondary shoots 1in (2.5cm) long.*

TRAINING A CORDON

Cordon-grown fruit takes up very little room and becomes a decorative feature. The cordons should be grown against a post-and-wire support or wires strung at 2ft (60cm) intervals on an existing fence. Before planting, tie canes onto the wires to prevent the stems from chafing against them. Plant the trees 2ft 6in (75cm) apart. Plant bushes so that each will be 12in (30cm) from the next.

Double cordon   **Triple cordon**

Multiple bush cordons
Grow fruit bushes as cordons with one, two, or three arms. As they grow less vigorously than tree fruit, there is no need to restrict growth by training plants at an angle.

1 Immediately after planting, *cut the leading shoot back to remove a third of the growth it made that year. Cut back any sideshoots to a downward-facing bud, leaving each shoot 3in (7cm) long.*

2 In the first summer, *prune back sideshoots coming directly from the main stem to 3in (7cm). Prune any secondary shoots to 1in (2.5cm).*

3 In the second winter, *prune the leading shoot, cutting off one-third of that year's growth.*

4 Every summer, *prune in this way until the end of the cane is reached. Make more room by lowering the cane. When the tree is as long as you want it, prune the main shoot in summer, to 3in (7cm) and sideshoots to 1in (2.5cm).*

TRAINING A FESTOONED TREE

The aim of summer pruning fruit trees is to restrict growth and encourage the trees to produce fruiting buds instead. This can also be done by restricting the flow of sap by bending the branches into severe curves; this is known as festooning. Great care is needed in bending the branches and it must be done in the summer when they are young and supple. Plant trees 5ft (1.5m) apart.

1 At the end of the first summer, *pull the main shoot downward, bending it into a hoop. Secure it by tying the end to the base of the tree with soft string.*

2 In the second summer, *plenty of shoots will grow on top of the curve. Prune these back in the summer like cordons (see above).*

3 Also in the second summer, *select more shoots and bend them down into hoops. Secure to the main stem with soft string. Prune any unwanted branches.*

4 In subsequent summers, *prune all the fruiting spurs like cordons. The tree will be permanently bent in a festooned form.*

TRAINING AN ESPALIER

As they take up very little room, espaliers are suitable for small gardens and make a decorative feature of a bare wall. Plant the trees at least 12ft (3.6m), and preferably 15ft (4.5m), apart, against a wall or fence strung with wires at 2ft (60cm) intervals. Fix wires to a wall with vine eyes.

1 Immediately after planting, *prune to 2in (5cm) above the first wire. (This is 2ft (60cm) above the ground.) Make sure there are three good buds below the pruning position.*

2 In the spring, *train the resulting shoots onto canes fixed to the wires. Train the sideshoots at an angle of 45° from the main stem.*

3 In the first summer, *cut back any side branches that may have formed on the main stem to 3in (7cm).*

4 In the second winter, *tie the two branches that will form the first tier to the lower wire. Prune them back to remove a third of the previous season's growth. Prune the main stem to 2in (5cm) above the second wire to encourage three new buds to form the second tier.*

5 In the following summer, *prune the sideshoots on the lower two branches to 3in (7cm) and secondary shoots to 1in (2.5cm). Treat the second tier as you did the first in the previous summer.*

6 Every summer, *repeat the process for as many tiers as you wish. At the required height, select only two buds and train these horizontally as the final tier. After that, prune each arm as for cordon training, pruning in the summer (see step 4 opposite).*

TRAINING A STEPOVER

A modern variation of the espalier, stepovers are simply single-tier espaliers, developed to take advantage of every inch of space in a small garden. They should be grown on wires strung on short posts 2in (30cm) above the ground. Plant trees between 12–15ft (3.5–4.5m) apart.

1 Immediately after planting, *prune the main stem to 2in (5cm) above the wire. Ensure that there are two buds below the cut.*

2 In the spring, *when the buds grow, train the shoots out along the wires, on either side of the main stem.*

3 Then *each arm is pruned like a cordon (see cordon training, step 4). Stop growth when the arms meet those of the next plant.*

Cultivation of fruit

The detailed cultivation techniques vary somewhat and are given for each fruit (*see pp. 215–231*). There are, however, some cultivation points common to all fruit.

FEEDING

The organic method of feeding is very simple. In early spring apply two handfuls of blood, fish, and bone meal per square yard/meter around the plants. The feeding roots are at the tips of the plant's main root system rather than near the stem, so apply fertilizer in a wide band around it. In addition to this, mulch around the stem with well-rotted manure or compost, which, apart from inhibiting weed growth and conserving water, will supply all the necessary trace elements. In the unlikely event of trace element deficiency symptoms becoming apparent (*see p. 39*), spray immediately with liquid kelp fertilizer and apply kelp meal to the soil. Any special feeding requirements are given in the cultivation details (*see pp. 215–231*).

WATERING

Applying water at the right time can greatly increase the weight of a fruit crop. Water when the fruit is swelling for best results. Stop watering when the fruits color up or you could encourage fungus disease.

However, it is a mistake to put just a little water on the soil since this brings the roots nearer the surface where they are in more danger of drying out. It is essential to apply water through a hose and sprinkler, which must be left on for at least an hour at a time in dry weather.

Any special watering requirements are given in the cultivation details (*see pp. 215–231*).

THINNING

Most people are happy to grow fruit that is smaller than that on sale in the supermarket, especially if there are children in the family. But, if you want bigger fruit, you will have to thin clusters as they develop. Trees and bushes will drop fruits naturally if they are carrying more than they can support. This normally happens in midsummer so delay thinning until then. To thin, remove the central fruit from each cluster; it will probably be badly shaped anyway. How much you want to thin depends on the variety, but remember that thinning will not reduce the weight of fruit harvested—there will be fewer fruits but each one will be bigger.

ENCOURAGING GROWTH

Sometimes fruit trees of all types will fail to produce shoots along one part of the stem. For some reason

Feeding and mulching *Feeding roots are toward the outer limits of a tree, so apply fertilizer around the tree, roughly from the furthest extent of the branches to halfway back to the trunk. Mulching around the base with manure or compost will also supply nutrients.*

Thinning fruit *If the developing fruits are growing in a crowded cluster, thin by removing the central fruit known as the "crown" fruit. This allows the others to swell. Always thin after the tree has dropped its fruit naturally.*

Encouraging bud growth *To encourage growth of a particular bud on a barren length of shoot, divert the flow of growth-retarding hormone by taking a notch out of the bark above the bud you want to encourage.*

the buds simply don't grow out. This can be corrected by manipulating nature. In order that the top of the tree grows more strongly than the rest, nature has provided a growth-retarding hormone, which is sent down the tree from the top bud to retard all the others. The transport channels are just below the bark so, to prevent the retarding hormone reaching the bud you wish to encourage into growth, simply take out a tiny notch in the bark above it. The hormone then flows around the bud without affecting it. Conversely, if you want to ensure that a bud does not grow, nick underneath it to concentrate the hormone.

WEED CONTROL

With all garden fruit, it is essential to reduce the competition from weeds. Many fruit plants are shallow-rooted so hoeing should be light. The best method of weed control is mulching with manure, compost, or black plastic (*see pp. 58–59*).

PESTS AND DISEASES

There is no doubt that the most persistent and troublesome pest of fruit of all sorts are our allies, the birds. We don't want to frighten them away because of the good work they do, but they cannot be ignored. If you have room, a fruit cage is a good investment (*see below*).

Specific pests and diseases are given for each type of fruit at the end of the chapter (*see pp. 232–235*). Pests and diseases such as aphids, mildew, and botrytis are common to all garden plants, not only fruit, and are dealt with in detail in *Organic Pest and Disease Control* (*see pp. 43–53*); treatment of common fruit pests such as wasps and red spider mite are given at the end of the chapter (*see pp. 232–235*).

PROTECTING FRUIT FROM BIRDS

Always protect your fruit from birds, whatever the size of your garden. If it is large you can grow all the fruit together and put up a fruit cage.

Otherwise, small bushes and trees can be covered with netting, or individual fruits protected with transparent, perforated plastic bags.

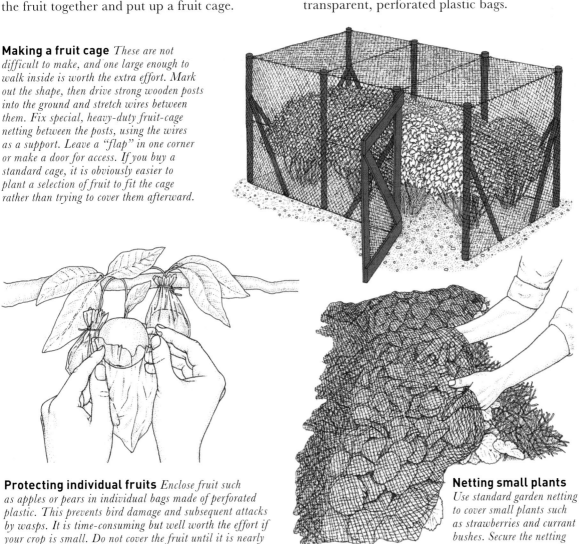

Making a fruit cage *These are not difficult to make, and one large enough to walk inside is worth the extra effort. Mark out the shape, then drive strong wooden posts into the ground and stretch wires between them. Fix special, heavy-duty fruit-cage netting between the posts, using the wires as a support. Leave a "flap" in one corner or make a door for access. If you buy a standard cage, it is obviously easier to plant a selection of fruit to fit the cage rather than trying to cover them afterward.*

Protecting individual fruits *Enclose fruit such as apples or pears in individual bags made of perforated plastic. This prevents bird damage and subsequent attacks by wasps. It is time-consuming but well worth the effort if your crop is small. Do not cover the fruit until it is nearly ripe; this is the time it is most likely to be attacked.*

Netting small plants *Use standard garden netting to cover small plants such as strawberries and currant bushes. Secure the netting with bricks.*

Tree fruit

No garden is too small for a fruit tree. With the increased use of special rootstocks, which limit the size of the tree, trees can be used as decorative, as well as productive, features. You can make use of walls by training trees as fans or espaliers. If your garden is very small, fruit trees can be grown in tubs on the patio.

▲ **CHERRIES** *Prunus sp.*
You can grow sweet cherries as fans against a south-facing wall or acid varieties on a north-facing wall. *For cultivation details, see p. 216.*

▲ **NECTARINES** *Prunus sp.*
These smooth-skinned fruits are cultivated in the same way as peaches. *For cultivation details, see p. 216.*

▲ **APRICOTS** *Prunus armeniaca*
Plenty of sun is required if a crop is to be guaranteed. In temperate areas they are best grown as fans on a south-facing wall. *For cultivation details, see p. 218.*

▲ **PEACHES** *Prunus persica*
They need well-drained soil and a sunny position. Grow the trees as fans on a south-facing wall. *For cultivation details, see p. 216.*

▲ **PLUMS** *Prunus domestica*
Fan-trained trees are hardy enough to be grown on north-facing walls, although they will fruit later than those on south- or west-facing walls. *For cultivation details, see p. 218.*

▲ **FIGS** *Ficus carica*
Figs will tolerate any type of soil as long as it is well drained yet moisture retentive. *For cultivation details, see p. 219.*

▲ **OLIVES** *Olea europaea*
Long-lived trees that are only suitable for warmer areas. The tree eventually develops a twisted, gnarled appearance that adds greatly to its decorative value. *For cultivation details, see p. 219.*

▼ **MULBERRIES** *Morus* sp.
The trees are large and slow growing but, since they are
self-pollinating, you will only need to plant one in your
garden. *For cultivation details, see p. 220.*

▼ **DESSERT APPLES** *Malus domestica*
The most popular fruit of temperate climates, apples are easy
to grow in the organic garden. They can be grown on several
different tree shapes to suit even the smallest of gardens. There
are many different varieties available; grow one that flowers
later if your garden is in a frost pocket. Some varieties are not
self-pollinating. *For cultivation details, see p. 220.*

▲ **QUINCES** *Cydonia oblonga*
These relatives of the pear need plenty of sun; grow
them against a south-facing wall in a temperate
climate. *For cultivation details, see p. 220.*

Suntan

Greensleeves

Jonared

▼ **PEARS** *Pyrus communis*
Since they flower fairly early in the year, pears should not be
planted in a frost pocket, so try to choose a sunny, sheltered
spot in the garden. *For cultivation details, see p. 221.*

▼ **COOKING APPLES** *Malus domestica*
These are usually larger and more acid tasting than
dessert apples. The branches may need supporting as
the crop can be heavy. *For cultivation details, see p. 220.*

William

Bramley

Conference

Citrus fruit

Only for warmer areas, these subtropical fruits grow on evergreen trees that need plenty of warmth and shelter. In temperate climates they can only be grown successfully in the greenhouse or sunroom because they are not frost-hardy. If your garden can provide the right conditions, they are not difficult to grow and are very rewarding. They grow best in well-drained soils; if your soil is heavy, the planting area should be raised above the level of the surrounding soil.

KUMQUATS ▼
Fortunella japonica
These dwarf evergreen trees produce good crops of miniature oranges. They can be grown outside provided the temperature will not drop lower than 15°F (-10°C). *For cultivation details, see p. 222.*

LIMES ▲
Citrus aurantiifolia
Limes are cultivated in exactly the same way as their close relatives, the lemons. They have a slightly more acid flavor. *For cultivation details, see p. 222.*

ORANGES ▼
Citrus sinensis
Like all other citrus fruits, oranges are not frost-hardy so, in temperate areas, they are best grown in the greenhouse unless your garden is particularly sheltered. *For cultivation details, see p. 223.*

LEMONS ▲
Citrus limon
They grow best on slightly heavy, acid soils. If grown outside on badly drained soil, the planting area should be raised by at least 18in (45cm). *For cultivation details, see p. 222.*

GRAPEFRUIT ▶
Citrus paradisi
Grow grapefruit in a sunny, sheltered site, on an acid soil. Ensure that the soil is well drained. *For cultivation details, see p. 223.*

Cultivating tree fruit

If your garden is small, a large fruit tree will cast a lot of shade, reducing the number of plants you can grow, so it makes sense to grow trained fruit trees on dwarfing rootstocks and make a decorative feature of all available wall and fence space. All fences and walls can be utilized, whichever direction they face, but a south-facing wall is particularly valuable, especially for the more tender types such as peaches, nectarines, or citrus fruits.

TREE FRUIT						
Fruit	Shape and planting distance		Site	Soil preference	Cropping age	See page
Cherry	Standard	15–20ft (4.5–6m)	Acid—shade Sweet—sunny	Well-drained loam	4–5 years	216
	Bush tree	10–15ft (3–4.5m)				
	Fan	18ft (5.5m)				
Nectarine	Bush tree	15ft (4.5m)	Sunny	Well drained. Not too rich	4 years	216
	Fan	12ft (3.6m)				
Apricot	Fan	15ft (4.5m)	Sunny	Well drained. Not too rich	2–3 years	218
	Dwarf pyramid	5ft (1.5m)				
Peach	Bush tree	15ft (4.5m)	Sunny	Well-drained medium loam	4 years	216
	Fan	12ft (3.6m)				
Plum	Standard	10ft (3m)	Tolerant	Heavy loam or clay	3–5 years	218
	Dwarf pyramid	6ft (1.8m)				
	Fan	12ft (3.6m)				
	Festoon	6ft (1.8m)				
Fig	Bush tree	10ft (3m)	Sunny	Any, well drained	3–4 years	219
	Fan	15ft (4.5m)				
Olive	Standard	25–36ft (7.5–12m)	Sunny	Any, well drained	5–6 years	219
Mulberry	Standard	30ft (10m)	Sunny	Any	10 years	220
	Bush tree	30ft (10m)				
Quince	Bush tree	20ft (6m)	Sunny	All well-drained deep soils	2–3 years	220
	Fan	15ft (4.5m)				
Apple	Standard	20ft (6m)	Sunny	All well-drained deep soils	2 years	220
	Bush tree	20ft (6m)				
	Dwarf pyramid	5ft (1.5m)				
	Fan	15ft (4.5m)				
	Espalier	15ft (4.5m)				
	Cordon	2ft 6in (75cm)				
	Stepover	15ft (4.5m)				
	Festoon	5ft (1.5m)				
Pear	Standard	20ft (6m)	Sunny	All well-drained deep soils	2 years	221
	Bush tree	20ft (6m)				
	Dwarf pyramid	5ft (1.5m)				
	Fan	15ft (4.5m)				
	Espalier	15ft (4.5m)				
	Cordon	2ft 6in (75cm)				
	Stepover	15ft (4.5m)				
	Festoon	5ft (1.5m)				
Kumquat	Bush tree	15ft (4.5m)	Sunny	Medium heavy	7–8 years	222
Lime	Bush tree	15ft (4.5m)	Sunny	Slightly heavy	7–8 years	222
Lemon	Bush tree	15ft (4.5m)	Sunny	Slightly heavy	7–8 years	222
Orange	Bush tree	25ft (7.5m)	Sunny	Light, sandy	7–8 years	223
Grapefruit	Bush tree	30ft (10m)	Sunny	Acid, well drained	7–8 years	223

Cherries

Sweet cherries grown as standard or bush trees grow very large. In order to avoid the problems caused by excessive shade, and to be able to protect them from birds, grow them as fans trained against a south-facing wall. They should only be grown as bush trees on the dwarfing rootstock *Gisela 5*. Acid (cooking) cherries are not as vigorous and can be grown fan-trained against north-facing walls.

VARIETIES *Stella* is the only self-pollinating sweet cherry and so is suitable for a small garden. If you have room, grow an acid cherry and a sweet cherry that flower at the same time since the acid ones pollinate the sweet ones. The flowering period of the sweet *Bigarreau Gaucher* coincides with that of the self-fertile, acid *Morello* cherry.
Rootstocks The dwarfing rootstock *Gisela 5* is by far the

best and has now replaced *Colt*. It will keep trees small and induce early cropping.
TREE SHAPES Sweet and acid cherries can be grown as standard, or bush trees, or fan-trained against a wall (*see p. 206*).
SOIL AND SITE Sweet and acid cherries do best on deep, well-drained loams. Prepare the soil by deep digging, and add organic matter before planting. The soil pH should be 6.0–7.0.
   Grow sweet cherries in sun; acid cherries do well in shade.
 PLANTING Standard and bush trees should be planted in winter as shown on pp. 82–83, at least 15–20ft (4.5–6m) apart. Fan-trained trees should be planted against a wired wall, 18ft (5.5m) apart.
MAINTENANCE
Feeding An annual mulch with well-rotted manure or compost is normally sufficient. Too much lime in the soil sometimes causes magnesium deficiency (*see p. 38*);

this can be corrected with an application of kelp meal.
Pruning Standard and bush trees are pruned very little. Allow the tree to grow naturally for a few years, then, every midsummer, remove dead, diseased, crossing, or overcrowded branches, taking them right back to the main stem. Fan-trained sweet cherries are pruned in the same way as plums (*see p. 218*), and fan-trained acid cherries like peaches (*see opposite*).
Protection Sweet cherry trees must be netted against birds.
HARVESTING AND STORING Leave the cherries on the tree as long as possible, but pick them before they split. Eat sweet cherries right away. Acid cherries should be cooked and eaten no more than a few days after picking, or stored canned, or made into jam.
PESTS AND DISEASES Cherries are affected by blackfly, winter moth, bacterial canker, and silver leaf (*see pp. 233–234*).

Peaches and nectarines

Peaches and nectarines are identical in all their cultivation requirements, the only difference is their skins—peaches have fuzzy skins, while nectarines have smooth ones. They are both ideal fruits for warmer climates, but will grow in temperate regions as fan-trained trees against a south-facing wall. Peaches are slightly more hardy than nectarines so these are a better choice for temperate regions. They can also be grown in the greenhouse (*see right*). Peaches and nectarines do not fruit until their fourth year but bear fruit for about 30 years.

VARIETIES Peaches and nectarines are self-pollinating so only one tree is needed.
Peaches Choose from *Duke of York* and *Rochester*. In colder regions grow *Harken* and *Madison*.
Nectarines Grow the peach leaf curl resistant variety *Avalon Pride* or *Nectared* for an extended season.

Rootstocks These less vigorous trees, if grown as bushes, do not require a dwarfing rootstock. To grow fan-trained trees use *St. Julien A*. Pixy will produce small trees for growing in tubs.
TREE SHAPES Free-standing bush trees should only be grown

in warm areas where the flowers will not be damaged by frosts in early spring. In temperate regions grow them fan-trained on a south-facing wall (*see p. 206*).
SOIL AND SITE Good drainage is essential so prepare the soil well. If you are growing

CULTIVATING PEACHES AND NECTARINES IN THE GREENHOUSE

Peaches and nectarines in the greenhouse are grown in the same way as those outside, against a wall or post-and-wire support. The only difference in cultivation may arise from the better growing conditions that make it necessary to keep growth and fruiting in check. During winter keep the greenhouse as cold as possible to keep the tree dormant. In early spring mulch round the tree with well-rotted manure or compost and water well. Then allow the greenhouse temperature to reach 50°F (10°C) before ventilating.
   Spray daily with clear water during the spring and summer, except at flowering time.

Hand pollination *To transfer pollen from flower to flower, dab the center of each one with a soft camel hair brush.*

When in flower, hand pollinate as there will be few insects indoors. Feed weekly in the growing season with liquid kelp fertilizer. Don't let too many fruits develop or they will be small. Allow 15 fruits per square yard/meter.

FAN-TRAINING PEACHES AND NECTARINES

Fan-training is a pruning method that produces trees that grow flat against the wall. The reflected and stored heat allows otherwise tender fruits to be grown successfully in temperate climates. Grow the trees against wires fixed to a wall, 9in (23cm) apart.

1 Immediately after planting, *cut back to a strong bud, making sure there are two buds beneath this. Leave the tree about 18in (45cm) high. The following season, three shoots will grow.*

2 In the second winter, *remove the central shoot. Prune the two remaining shoots to 18in (45cm) long and tie them to poles fixed to the wires about 20° above the horizontal.*

3 In the following summer, *select four shoots from these side-branches; two from the top, one underneath, and its extension. Tie them in and rub off any other buds that appear.*

4 In the third winter, *cut back the selected shoots, leaving them 18in (45cm) long.*

5 In the following summer, *tie in branches as they grow. Select sideshoots 4in (10cm) apart to form the fruit-bearing shoots. Rub off any unwanted buds.*

6 In the fourth winter, *reduce the growth from the main framework branches by about half. From now on, pruning is aimed at producing fruit.*

7 In the following summer, *allow the sideshoots to grow four to six leaves and form a new shoot at their base. Pinch out any other new growth.*

8 Once the fruit has been picked, *prune the fruited shoot. Tie the replacement shoot into its place. Repeat the process every year.*

standard or bush trees follow the general recommendations on p. 210. For wall-trained plants dig out a trench 2–3ft (60–90cm) wide, 10ft (3m) long and a spade deep. Dig some old rubble or broken bricks into the bottom and cover this with a layer of well-rotted manure or compost. Refill, working more organic matter into the upper levels. Peach and nectarine trees will grow on sandy soils if plenty of organic matter is added. They prefer a soil pH of 6.5–7.0 and they need a sunny position, above all, they should not be planted in a frost pocket.

PLANTING Plant standard or bush trees in winter as recommended on pp. 82–83. For fan-training use one-year-old trees, planted in winter,

against wires spaced at 9in (23cm) intervals.

MAINTENANCE

Feeding Feed as suggested on p. 210 in the years before they are old enough to fruit. Once they begin bearing, an annual mulch with well-rotted manure or compost will probably be enough. If deficiency symptoms are noticed (*see pp. 38–39*), reinstate the feeding program.

Pruning Prune free-standing trees in the spring, removing all dead, diseased, or crossing branches, and prune fan-trained trees as recommended above.

Pollination Both peaches and nectarines flower early, before the pollinating insects have appeared in temperate regions, so pollen may have to be

transferred by hand, taking it from flower to flower with a camel hair brush (*see opposite*).

Protection Protect the blossoms with woven polypropylene or fine netting (old net curtains are ideal), when frost is forecast.

HARVESTING AND STORING

The fruit is ripe when it comes off the tree easily when gently pulled and twisted. Take great care when harvesting because it bruises very easily. Peaches and nectarines will not store for more than a few days unless they are canned.

PESTS AND DISEASES Aphids (*see p. 50*). Peach leaf curl and red spider mite affect fruit grown outside (*see pp. 232–233*) and in the greenhouse; they are also affected by scale insects and mildew in the greenhouse (*see p. 257*).

Apricots

Apricots are grown in the same way as plums, although they require plenty of sun to guarantee a crop. They can be grown in temperate climates as fans against a south-facing wall.

VARIETIES All varieties are self-pollinating, although you may need to transfer pollen by hand because they flower before many pollinating insects are around. Choose *Alfred* or *Moorpark*.

Rootstocks They are now grown on either *Montclaire* or *Torinel*, both of which are semi-dwarfing.
TREE SHAPES Apricot trees can be grown as fans and dwarf pyramids in warmer areas (*see p. 206*).
SOIL AND SITE Apricots will grow in light soils if plenty of organic matter is incorporated. The pH should be about 6.0. The site should be well drained, very sunny, and sheltered from the wind.
PLANTING Apricots need well-drained soil so, unless your soil is very light, prepare by digging an area 3ft × 10ft (lm × 3m), two spades

deep, putting a layer of gravel in the bottom and refilling with soil liberally mixed with well-rotted organic matter.
MAINTENANCE Thin the fruits if the tree becomes overburdened (*see p. 210*).
HARVESTING AND STORING Pick and eat when they are soft. To dry them, pick and split them when they are still firm.
PESTS AND DISEASES General pests include birds and aphids (*see pp. 46, 50, and 232*). Red spider mite, sawfly, rust, silver leaf, and bacterial canker (*see p. 233*).

Plums

Plums are relatively easy to grow and can bear very heavy crops, although they may not be worth growing in areas that get late-spring frosts. Damsons are related to plums and are grown in exactly the same way.

VARIETIES All the varieties listed here are self-pollinating. A suitable plum variety is *Stanley*. Damson plums are not typically grown in the US.
Rootstocks Plum and damson trees can grow very large unless they are

grown on one of the two dwarfing rootstocks. *St. Julien A* is a semi-dwarfing rootstock suitable for making dwarf pyramids and fans. *Pixy* is a new dwarfing rootstock that produces small trees suitable for training against a support.

FAN-TRAINING PLUMS

Fan-trained plums grow best on south- or west-facing walls. They can be grown on north-facing walls but fruit will be produced later in the year.

Varieties for fan-training should be grafted onto *St. Julien A* or *Pixy* rootstocks. Sweet cherries and damsons should be fan-trained as below.

1 In the winter, *attach horizontal wires to the wall at 9in (23cm) intervals and plant a one-year-old tree against the wall. In the first spring, cut it back to 18in (45cm) high.*

2 In the summer, *select three strong shoots. Let these grow on, but pinch back any other branches to two leaves.*

3 The following spring, *prune the two main side branches to 18in (45cm) in length and tie them to the first horizontal wire. Remove the central stem.*

4 Every spring and summer, *tie upward-growing shoots from the side branches onto the wires, using soft string, to make a fan shape.*

5 Later in summer, *pinch out any branches growing into or away from the wall. Pinch out any other shoots not required to form the fan shape.*

6 When the fruit has been picked, *cut out any dead wood and shorten the shoots you have pinched off by half.*

TREE SHAPES Grow them as dwarf pyramids or fans on *St. Julien A* or *Pixy* rootstocks (*see p. 206*).

SOIL AND SITE Plum trees like deep loam or clay soils that are well drained. Damsons are more tolerant of shallow topsoil. The soil pH should be between 6.0–6.5. Fan-trained trees should be grown on south- or west-facing walls.

PLANTING Plant bare root trees in the fall (*see p. 83*). Plant dwarf pyramids on *St. Julien A* rootstocks 10ft (3m) apart, and 6ft (1.8m) apart if on *Pixy* stocks. Plant festooned trees 6ft (1.8m) apart and fan-trained trees 12ft (3.5m) apart against a wall or a post-and-wire support.

When tying plum trees to their supports, use a commercial tree tie with a collar to prevent chafing, as the debilitating silver leaf disease enters through wounds.

MAINTENANCE
Feeding Feed as recommended in the general cultivation techniques (*see p. 210*).
Pruning Since plums and damsons are susceptible to silver leaf disease, never prune in winter because pruning wounds will remain unhealed for a long time.
Thinning Heavy crops can lead to breakage of branches. If the crop is large, wait for the natural drop in midsummer, then thin so that the fruits are 3in (7cm) apart. Support the heavy branches with a forked prop covered in burlap to prevent chafing, or tie the branch up to the main stem (*see p. 221*).
HARVESTING AND STORING The fruit is ripe when it comes off the tree easily. Pick fruit for cooking or canning when a bloom appears on the skin. For eating fresh, fruit is best left on the tree until it is fully ripe; this is when it feels soft to the touch.
PESTS AND DISEASES General pests that attack plums include aphids and birds (*see pp. 46, 50, and 232*). Wasps can also attack the fruits (*see p. 232*). Specific pests and diseases are plum sawfly, red spider mite, rust, silver leaf, and bacterial canker (*see pp. 232–233*).

Figs

The cultivation details below apply to figs grown outside and in the greenhouse.

VARIETIES The darker-skinned *Brown Turkey* and *Brunswick* are the hardiest. *LSU Purple* and *San Piero* are recommended for warmer areas.
TREE SHAPES Figs can be grown as bush trees or fans (*see p. 206*). No pruning is needed to form the fan, simply tie the branches onto wires spaced at 9in (23cm) intervals.
SOIL AND SITE They will grow on any soil as long as it is well-drained yet moisture retentive, with a pH of 6.5–7.0. Grow against a south-facing wall as they require plenty of sun to produce fruit.
PLANTING Plant free-standing bushes 10ft (3m) apart, and trees for fan-training 15ft (4.5m) apart. To encourage fruiting, restrict root growth by digging a hole 3ft × 5ft (1m × 1.5m) and two spades deep. Cover the base of the hole with gravel and contain the sides with corrugated iron sheets or bricks. Refill with an equal mixture of topsoil and well-rotted manure or compost. This kind of preparation may appear to be overelaborate but, without it, trees will produce abundant growth at the expense of fruit.
MAINTENANCE
Watering Figs may need hand-watering during the first year.
Pruning Cut out old wood in winter and thin in summer to allow sunlight to ripen the fruits.
Frost protection Protect the shoots from frost by wrapping the plant in straw. Secure it in place with burlap.
HARVESTING AND STORING Figs should be eaten straight from the tree when they change color—the dark-skinned varieties turn deep purple and the light ones yellow. They can only be stored if dried or frozen.
PESTS AND DISEASES Pests and diseases are botrytis and birds (*see pp. 46, 52, and 232*) and canker (*see p. 235*).

Olives

Olives will grow in areas that can provide cold winters and hot summers, which is why they are grown so extensively in Mediterranean countries. African olives bear beautiful flowers but the fruit is not edible, so buy these for ornamental purposes only. European olives take five or six years to produce fruit but are extremely long-lived.

VARIETIES The European, self-pollinating varieties *Frantoio*, *Leccino*, and *Picual* are suggested.
TREE SHAPES Olives are always grown as standard trees (*see p. 206*).
SOIL AND SITE Olive trees will grow in any type of soil as long as it is well drained. Like grapevines, they are a useful crop to grow on soil that is poor or stony. The site should be in full sun.
PLANTING Container-grown, grafted trees are available and can be planted at any time of year—however, they are best planted in fall when wetter weather can be expected. If growing more than one tree plant them 25–36ft (7.5–12m) apart.
MAINTENANCE
Feeding Olives need plenty of nitrogen so they should be mulched annually with well-rotted manure or compost. If growth appears slow, apply hoof and horn fertilizer at the rate of two handfuls per square yard/meter in spring.
Pruning Prune out overcrowded or crossing branches because olives need plenty of sunlight for maximum fruit production.
HARVESTING AND STORING Pick olives by hand to avoid bruising. Gather in fall when they are green and use for pickling, or leave them on the tree until winter, when they will turn black, and press for oil.
PESTS AND DISEASES Organically grown olives have no specific pests but can be affected by the general garden pests (*see pp. 46–51*).

Mulberries

These trees are very decorative although slow-growing, taking up to 10 years before they bear fruit but then doing so for 40 years or more.

As the trees get older, the branches need the support of sturdy props beneath them.

VARIETIES Mulberries are self-pollinating, so only one tree is needed. There are three types of mulberry—red (*Morus rubra*), white (*M. alba*), and black (*M. nigra*). The black mulberry produces the best fruit—recommended varieties are *Collier* and *Wellington*.

TREE SHAPES Mulberries are grown as bush or standard trees (*see p. 206*).

SOIL AND SITE They will grow in any soil, provided it is deep, fertile, and has a pH of about 6.0–6.5. The site must be warm and sunny.

PLANTING Because of their size, they are generally grown as single specimen trees but, if you are planting more than one, they should be at least 30ft (10m) apart. Try to buy container-grown specimens because mulberries have very brittle roots that are easily damaged. Keep the area around the tree clear of grass until the tree is old enough to bear fruit.

MAINTENANCE

Pruning Prune back any overly crowded shoots to 4in (10cm) in late summer.

HARVESTING AND STORING The fruit ripens in late summer and can be picked from the tree or shaken onto sheets laid on the grass. Mulberry juice stains skin and clothes badly, so be careful when harvesting. Mulberries do not store well unless canned.

PESTS AND DISEASES They are affected by general garden pests (*see pp. 46–51*).

Quinces

These are relatives of the pear. They flower later in the year than pears, so are in little danger of frost damage.

VARIETIES Quinces are self-pollinating, so only one tree is needed. Choose from *Aromaynaya, Orange, Pineapple,* and *Smyrna*.

TREE SHAPES They can be pruned to make fans (*see p. 206*). In temperate climates, grow them as fans on a north-facing wall, like plums (*see p. 218*).

SOIL AND SITE Quinces prefer a soil with a pH between 6.0 and 6.5. Lime the soil only if soil tests show that the pH is below 6.0. Plant them in a sunny place.

PLANTING The best time to plant is in early winter, using bare root plants (*see p. 83*).

MAINTENANCE

Feeding Follow the general details given on p. 210.

Watering Follow the general details given on p. 210.

Pruning Details of pruning to shape are given on p. 218.

HARVESTING AND STORING Quinces are ripe when they become yellow and give off a strong aroma. Make jelly immediately after harvesting or store the fruits on shelves or in boxes, in a cool, moist, frost-free spot for up to three months.

PESTS AND DISEASES General pests and diseases that attack quinces include greenfly and mildew (*see pp. 46–52*). Specific pests and diseases are winter moth, woolly aphid, codling moth, sawfly, canker, fireblight, bitter pit, brown rot, and scab (*see pp. 234–235*). Wasps also damage fruit (*see p. 232*).

Apples

The most popular tree fruit of temperate climates, apples can be grown on any type of soil provided it is prepared and managed properly. It is possible to grow apples in most parts of the world with relative ease. If you live in an area where late frosts may damage blossoms, choose varieties that flower later in the year.

Though much depends on variety, rootstocks, and the prevailing conditions, trees on modern rootstocks should start to fruit in their second year and continue for about 30 years.

VARIETIES For a full crop, apple trees need to be pollinated by a different variety (*see p. 203*), so choose at least two trees that flower at the same time.

Early-flowering dessert apples Choose from *Adam's Pearmain, Norfolk Beauty, Golden Spire, Scarlet Pimpernel, Lord Lambourne, Early McIntosh, Laxton's Fortune, Spartan, Crispin, Idared*.

Late-flowering dessert apples Suitable varieties include *Merton Charm, Orleans Reinette, Ashmeads Kernel, Golden Delicious, Red Delicious, Suntan, Jonathan, Granny Smith, Cox* (self-pollinating).

Early-flowering cooking apples *Bramley's Seedling, Grenadier*.

Late-flowering cooking apples *Howgate Wonder, Royal Jubilee* are recommended.

Rootstocks *M106* is the standard rootstock and this should be used for all trees except dwarf pyramids and cordons. *M9* is a dwarfing rootstock and the trees produced will always require staking. Use it for apples grown as cordons or dwarf pyramids (*see p. 206*), but only if your soil is very fertile. The *M27* rootstock is dwarfing and suitable only for trees growing in tubs, on very fertile soil, or trained as stepover trees (*see p. 206*).

TREE SHAPES Apple trees can be grown as standards, bush trees, dwarf pyramids, fans, espalier cordons, stepovers, and festooned trees (*see p. 206*).

SOIL AND SITE Use a soil with a pH between 6.0 and 6.5. Lime the soil only if the pH is below 6.0. A sunny sheltered site is preferable.

PLANTING The best time to plant is in early winter, using bare root plants (*see pp. 82–83 for details of tree planting*). Try to get the preparation done in advance, and if the soil is wet, work from boards to avoid damaging soil structure.

MAINTENANCE

Feeding Follow the general details given on p. 210.

Watering Follow the general details given on p. 210.

Pruning Details for the various shapes are given on pp. 207–209.

HARVESTING AND STORING

Apples are fully ripe when they come easily from the tree as the fruit is pulled slightly and gently twisted. They should come off without too much effort. Always pick carefully. Place the fruit in a basket lined with a soft cloth to avoid bruising; this is important if you are going to store it.

Early varieties should be picked in the summer, just before they are fully ripe. If you like to eat them at the peak of their ripeness, pick them and leave them for a couple of days. Left on the tree to full

Supporting an apple-laden branch *Tie a length of string around the center of the branch, attaching the other end to the main trunk of the tree.*

Storing apples *Put the fruit in plastic bags and seal with a tie. Prick two pinholes for each 2lb (1kg) fruit in the bag to enable it to breathe.*

ripeness, they tend to become slightly soft and mealy.

Pick late varieties in fall or early winter, when they are fully ripe. When storing, look them over very carefully and reject any that show the slightest sign of damage or disease—these will not store well and will affect the healthy fruit. Pack one variety at a time into plastic bags and seal with a twist tie. Never mix varieties in the same bag. The fruit should be able to breathe so make pinholes in the bag. Store

them in as cool a place as possible, making sure it is frost-free. Check them regularly, removing any that show signs of disease or rotting.

PESTS AND DISEASES General pests and diseases that attack apples include greenfly and mildew (*see pp. 46–52*). Specific pests and diseases are winter moth, woolly aphid, codling moth, apple sawfly, canker, fireblight, bitter pit, brown rot, and apple scab (*see pp. 234–235*). Wasps can also be a nuisance (*see p. 232*).

Pears

Pears flower early and so may be subject to damaging frosts in temperate climates. Fruiting varies according to conditions but on average, pear trees will begin producing fruit after about two years and continue for 25–30 years.

VARIETIES They need pollinating with a different variety, so choose trees that flower at the same time.

Early-flowering varieties Choose from *Williams Bon Chrétien (Bartlett)*, *Gorham*, *Kieffer*, *Comice*, *Orient*, and *Baldwin Pear*.

Late-flowering varieties These include *Onward*, *Doyenné du Comice*, *Beurre Hardy*, *Concorde*.

Rootstocks There are only two rootstocks in common use. *Quince A* should be used on poorer soils. *Quince C* produces smaller trees that fruit earlier in their lives, and it should be used when growing pears as cordons on very fertile soils.

TREE SHAPES They can be grown as standards, bush trees, cordons, espaliers, dwarf pyramids, fans, stepovers, and festooned trees (*see p. 206*).

SOIL AND SITE Pear trees prefer a soil with a pH between 6.0 and 6.5. Lime the soil only if soil tests show that the pH is below 6.0. Plant them in a sheltered, sunny place.

PLANTING The best time to plant is in early winter, using bare root plants (*see p. 83*). Try to get the preparation done in advance and, if the soil is wet, work from boards.

MAINTENANCE

Feeding Follow the general details given on p. 210.

Watering Follow the general details given on p. 210.

Pruning Details for the various shapes are given on pp. 207–209.

HARVESTING AND STORING

Pears are ripe when they part easily from the tree if gently pulled and twisted.

Early varieties should be picked before they are ripe, when still hard and green. Put them on a shelf in a cool place and, a few days before you want to eat them, bring them indoors for final ripening. They will keep for two weeks. If kept too long, they become mushy and metallic-tasting.

Late-maturing varieties should be left on the tree longer. Pick them when they come off the tree easily and store them in the same way. If you want to keep pears longer, you will have to can or dry them. Do this before they become too ripe.

PESTS AND DISEASES General pests and diseases that attack pears include greenfly and mildew (*see pp. 46–52*). Specific pests and diseases are winter moth, woolly aphids, codling moth, fireblight, sawfly, canker, bitter pit, brown rot, and scab (*see pp. 234–235*). Wasps can also be a nuisance (*see p. 232*).

Kumquats

These are dwarf, evergreen citrus trees grown widely in the Far East. They are grown outdoors in warmer areas but can be grown in pots or large tubs in a heated greenhouse in temperate climates. Trees grown in tubs are always smaller than those grown outside.

VARIETIES Two suitable varieties are available—*Marumi* and *Nagami*.
TREE SHAPES They are always grown as bush trees (*see p. 206*).

SOIL AND SITE The ideal soil is a medium-heavy loam that drains well. Work in plenty of organic matter to improve water retention. On heavier soils, the planting site should be raised. The pH should be between 6.0 and 6.5.

They prefer an open, sunny location not overshadowed by other trees.
PLANTING Plants are available balled or container-grown so can be planted at any time of year. Plant 15ft (4.5m) apart to avoid undue competition.

MAINTENANCE
Feeding Mulch with well-rotted manure or compost.
Watering Water well when the fruit is swelling.
Pruning Cut back the current season's growth after harvesting.
HARVESTING AND STORING
Harvest when the fruits begin to turn orange. They can be eaten raw or made into marmalade.
PESTS AND DISEASES Gall wasp, little leaf, and lemon scab (*see p. 232*); red spider mite, aphids, and scale insects (*see p. 257*).

Lemons and limes

These are both subtropical fruits that will only grow outside in frost-free areas. The *Meyer* hybrid lemon, however, is slightly more hardy and will withstand temperatures as low as 15°F (-9°C), provided it is grown in a sheltered spot. Limes are more acid and contain more sugar than lemons. Both can be grown in tubs in the greenhouse.

VARIETIES
Lemon *Meyer, Ponderosa, Eureka.*
Lime *Key, Tahitian.*
TREE SHAPES Both lemon and lime trees are grown as bush trees (*see p. 206*).
SOIL AND SITE They grow best on slightly heavy soils. The beds should be raised at least 18in (45cm) above the surrounding land. Enrich the soil with plenty of well-rotted manure or compost. These trees prefer slightly acid conditions, with a pH of between 6.0 and 6.5.

The site must be very sunny and sheltered from winds if the trees are grown outside.
PLANTING Lemon and lime trees can be planted at any time of year as they are sold balled or container-grown. If they are being planted outside, spring or fall are the best times. Plant so that the grafting point is about 4un (10cm) out of the ground and, if planting more

than one, reduce competition, particularly for light, by planting at least 15ft (4.5m) apart.
MAINTENANCE
Feeding Young citrus roots are easily scorched by an excess of fertilizer, so restrict feeding to manure mulches. Alternatively, feed with one handful of blood, fish, and bone meal per square yard/meter in early spring and repeat in summer, making sure you water the fertilizer in well.
Watering Make sure the roots have plenty of water, especially in the first few years.
Pruning Lemon trees need pruning to keep them compact; cut out any straggling or inward-pointing shoots. Prune back shoots that have borne fruit.

Lime trees need thinning and any dead, diseased, or crossing wood removed.
HARVESTING AND STORING Both fruits should be cut off the trees

Storing lemons *Store them in layers of dry sand in a wooden crate or paper-lined box for up to two months.*

with pruning shears when they are ripe. Fruit is produced all year-round in favorable climates.

Store in paper-lined boxes or wooden crates, each fruit covered with a layer of dry sand. Put the boxes in a cool place. The fruit will keep this way for up to two months.
PESTS AND DISEASES Gall wasp, little leaf, and lemon scab (*see p. 232*); red spider mite, aphids, and scale insects (*see p. 257*).

CULTIVATING CITRUS FRUIT IN THE GREENHOUSE

In temperate climates, grow citrus fruit in a greenhouse. Grow the varieties recommended for outdoor use in tubs, with a diameter no less than 18in (45cm). Use the soil-based potting compost recommended on p. 254 and keep the temperature in the greenhouse at a minimum of 45°F (7°C) at all times. Water well during the growing season, but allow the plants to dry out between

waterings. In the summer, spray the foliage with water every morning. Stop spraying when the plants are in flower. Keep plants slightly drier in the winter. Feed weekly during the growing season with liquid kelp fertilizer.

Little pruning is required except to thin out crossing, overcrowded branches and remove dead or diseased wood, and to prune out the fruited shoots after harvesting.

Oranges

As they are not frost-hardy, oranges should be grown in pots in the greenhouse in temperate regions. In warmer climates they will produce a good crop when grown outside. The fruits are a good source of Vitamin C.

VARIETIES

Sweet oranges These are recommended for eating. Suitable varieties are: *Jaffa, Sanguinelli, Valencia Late, Washington, Navel.*
Sour oranges For making marmalade, use *Seville.*
TREE SHAPES Orange trees are grown as bush trees (*see p. 206*).
SOIL AND SITE The soil should be light and sandy because they hate bad drainage. To grow them on heavier soils, the planting area should be raised at least 18in (45cm) above the surrounding soil. Enrich the soil with plenty of well-rotted manure or compost. Oranges prefer slightly acid conditions, with a pH of between 6.0 and 6.5.

The site must be as sunny as possible and sheltered from wind if the trees are grown outside, so this may mean erecting or planting a windbreak.

PLANTING Orange trees are sold balled or container-grown, so they can be planted at any time of year. If they are being planted outside, spring or fall are the best times. Plant so that the grafting point is about 4in (10cm) out of the ground and, if planting more than one, plant them at least 25ft (7.5m) from each other so that they don't compete, particularly for light.

MAINTENANCE

Feeding Young citrus roots are easily scorched by an excess of fertilizer, so restrict feeding to manure mulches—if you cannot get manure, feed with one handful of blood, fish, and bone meal per square yard/meter in early spring and repeat in summer, watering the fertilizer in well.
Watering Make sure the roots have plenty of water, especially in the first few years.
Pruning Thin out by removing branches if the tree becomes overcrowded. After harvesting, prune every fruit-bearing shoot to 4in (10cm) (*see right*).
HARVESTING AND STORING Pick oranges when they are fully colored, by twisting them gently off the tree. The fruits can be left

Encouraging more fruiting spurs
When the fruit has been harvested, cut the fruit-bearing branches to 4in (10cm) long.

on the tree until you are ready to use them—they can hang there for up to six months. They can also be stored in paper-lined boxes or wooden crates, each fruit covered with dry sand. Keep the box in a cool place. They will keep this way for up to two months.
PESTS AND DISEASES Gall wasp, little leaf, and lemon scab affect oranges grown outside (*see p. 232*). Grown in the greenhouse, they can be affected by red spider mite, aphids, and scale insects (*see p. 257*).

Grapefruit

Grapefruit originates from the West Indies and is not frost-hardy. It can be grown outside in subtropical and Mediterranean-type climates, but must be greenhouse-grown in temperate climates. Like all citrus trees, It is evergreen.

VARIETIES *Red Blush, Star Ruby,* and *White Marsh* are recommended.
TREE SHAPES Grapefruit trees are grown as bush trees (*see p. 206*).
SOIL AND SITE If they are to be grown outside, good drainage is essential. Deep dig the bed, incorporating plenty of well-rotted manure or compost (*see p. 30*). On heavy soil, raise the bed 18in (45cm) above ground level. The soil should be slightly acid, with a

pH of between 6.0 and 6.5. The site should be sunny and sheltered.
PLANTING Grapefruit trees are sold balled or container-grown, so they can be planted at any time of year; spring or fall are the most favorable times if they are being planted outside. Plant so that the grafting point is about 4in (10cm) out of the ground. Avoid competition, especially for light, by planting at least 30ft (10m) from one another.

MAINTENANCE

Feeding Restrict feeding to manure mulches as young citrus roots are easily scorched by an excess of fertilizer. If you cannot get manure, feed with one handful of blood, fish, and bone meal per square yard/meter in early spring and repeat in summer. Water the fertilizer in well.

Watering Make sure the roots have plenty of water, especially in the first few years.
Pruning Thin overcrowded wood and remove weak, sappy growth in early spring.
HARVESTING AND STORING Pick grapefruit when they begin to turn yellow by twisting them gently off the tree. They can be left on the tree until you are ready to use them and they can hang there for up to six months. They can also be stored in boxes or wooden crates, each fruit covered with dry sand and put in a cool place. They will keep this way for up to two months.
PESTS AND DISEASES Gall wasp, little leaf, and lemon scab affect fruit grown outside (*see p. 232*). Grown in the greenhouse it can be affected by red spider mite, aphids, and scale insects (*see p. 257*).

Soft fruit

Soft fruits grow on bushes, stakes, or briars and are ideal subjects for the small garden. The fruits soon deteriorate after picking, so those you grow in your garden will be of superior quality to anything you buy in the supermarket. Most of the fruits illustrated are relatively easy to grow and will suit a wide range of climates and conditions.

Strawberries *Fragaria × ananassa*
One of the simplest and most rewarding of the soft fruits. They prefer a well-drained but moisture-retentive soil. *For cultivation details, see p. 225.*

Red currants *Ribes sativum*
Easy to grow and very prolific. They can be grown in very small spaces as cordons. White currants are grown using the same cultivation techniques. *For cultivation details, see p. 226.*

Black currants *Ribes nigrum*
A rich source of vitamin C, black currants will produce heavy crops in a sunny location. They require plenty of minerals so prepare the soil well. *For cultivation details, see p. 227.*

Raspberries *Rubus idaeus*
These are easy to grow in temperate climates and respond well to organic methods of growing. They can suffer from iron deficiencies. *For cultivation details, see p. 228.*

Blackberries *Rubus sp.*
These bramble fruits take up a lot of room, but are worth growing if you have the space in your garden. The newer varieties taste much better. *For cultivation details, see p. 229.*

Gooseberries *Ribes uva-crispa*
The earliest soft fruits of the season, gooseberries may not be suitable for very cold areas because they flower in early spring. *For cultivation details, see p. 229.*

Blueberries *Vaccinium sp.*
These shrubs respond well to organic culture and, as they look decorative, they can be grown in the ornamental border. They need an acid soil. *For cultivation details, see p. 230.*

Loganberries *Rubus loganobaccus*
These bramble fruits grow best in cooler climates. They need regular attention to tying in and training. *For cultivation details, see p. 229.*

Grapes *Vitis vinifera*
In temperate regions grapes grown outside are generally only suitable for wine making, though in a really sunny year they form enough sugar for dessert purposes. Dessert grapes should be grown outside in warmer climates or in the greenhouse in temperate climates. *For cultivation details, see p. 230.*

Cultivating soft fruit

The fruits in this group range from brambles and shrubs to herbaceous perennials, and the cultivation techniques vary accordingly. Cane and bramble fruits need supporting, but are well worth growing if the space is available. Bush fruits are generally grown as free-standing shrubs.

Strawberries are the only herbaceous perennials in the group. They take up little room and are attractive enough to grow in the borders if space is limited.

All soft fruits are very attractive to birds so it is essential to protect ripening fruit with netting.

SOFT FRUIT

Fruit	Shape and planting distance		Site	Soil preference	Cropping age	See page
Strawberry	Herbaceous plant	2ft (60cm)	Sunny	Any, well drained	¾–1 year	225
Red currant	Bush	5ft (1.5m)	Sunny	Heavy, moisture retentive	1–2 years	226
	Cordon	1–3ft (30–90 cm)				
White currant	Bush	5ft (1.5m)	Sunny	Heavy, moisture retentive	1–2 years	226
	Cordon	1–3ft (30–90 cm)				
Black currant	Bush	5ft (1.5m)	Tolerant	Heavy, rich	2 years	227
Raspberry	Canes on wire support	18in (45cm)	Tolerant	Heavy, rich	1 year	228
Bramble fruit	Brambles on wire support	10ft (3m)	Tolerant	Any, well drained	1–2 years	229
Gooseberry	Bush	5ft (1.5m)	Sunny	Heavy, moisture retentive	1–2 years	229
	Cordon	1–3ft (30–90 cm)				
Blueberry	Bush	6ft (1.8m)	Sunny	Acid	3–8 years	230
Grape	Vine on wire support	5ft (1.5m)	Sunny	Well drained	2 years	230

Strawberries

In the organic garden, strawberries can be grown with relative ease. They grow best in cool, moist climates, but can be grown in warmer climates if suitable varieties are used (*see below*).

VARIETIES The varieties available for sale are constantly changing as further research into this profitable commercial crop takes place. In temperate climates recommended varieties are *Pegasus, Albion, Aromel,* and a Canadian variety called *Totem.* In warmer parts of the world *Red Gauntlet* is recommended. It is self-pollinating.

SOIL AND SITE Strawberries grow best in a well-drained but moisture-retentive soil. To increase drainage, raise the growing area to form 4ft (1.2m) wide beds (*see p. 135*). The site should be sunny, avoiding areas where there is little flow

of air, because this will increase the risk of mildew.

PLANTING Buy cold-stored runners from a reputable grower who can guarantee freedom from disease. These runners will crop in their first year, with a heavier crop in the next.

Dress the soil with two handfuls of bone meal per square yard/meter. Plant 2ft (60cm) apart with 18in (45cm) between the rows. If you are planting in 4ft (1.2m) wide raised beds, plant the first row 6in (15cm) from the edge of the bed to give three rows 18in (45cm) apart. Water thoroughly after planting.

It is important to set the crown of the plant (the point where the leaves join the roots) at soil level—if set too high the plant will not establish itself and frost may pull it out of the ground. If set too low the crown will rot.

Strawberries can also be planted through black plastic

(*see below*). This helps to prevent the evaporation of water from the soil, suppresses weed growth, and prevents the runners from shooting into the soil.

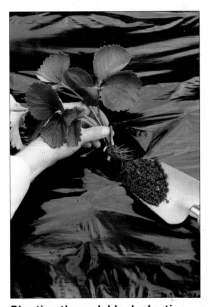

Planting through black plastic
Cover a raised bed with a sheet of black plastic. Cut slits for planting in the plastic, spacing them 18in (45cm) apart. The raised bed will protect strawberries from soil-borne diseases; the plastic suppresses weeds.

MAINTENANCE

Feeding Little fertilizer is necessary. If there is too much nitrogen in the soil, the plants will make excess leaf growth at the expense of fruit, so after the crop has been picked, sprinkle a handful of rock potash along each yard/meter run of row.

Mulching The fruits will hang on or near the ground, where they can be splashed with mud or damaged by slugs. To protect them, mulch with straw once they start to swell. Tuck the straw right under the plants to raise the fruit off the ground. Be careful, however, not to mulch too early. If the straw is put under the leaves while there is still a danger of frost, it will insulate the flowers from the rising warmth of the soil. This lowers the temperature around the developing fruit and could result in a lighter crop.

Propagating Healthy strawberry plants produce new plantlets on stems known as runners. To provide plants for forcing in the greenhouse, pin the plantlets into pots sunk into the soil beside the parent plant. Once they have rooted, they can be separated from the parent plant. Don't use them

Protecting strawberries *Surround the developing fruits with straw to raise them off the ground. This will provide protection from slug damage and prevent them from being splashed with mud.*

to restock your beds; you could spread virus disease.

Protection Strawberries are prone to bird damage when ripe. To protect them, cover the ripening fruit with netting. Cover fall-fruiting strawberries with a cloche if there is a danger of a hard frost.

HARVESTING AND STORING Pick the fruits when they are red all over, pulling off the plug, or central core, as well—leaving the plug on the plants attracts fungus diseases. Pick over the plants regularly as new fruits will ripen each day. The variety

Propagating from runners *Pin the plantlet, still attached to its runner, into a pot of compost buried near the parent plant. Use a piece of wire bent into a hairpin shape to secure the plantlet.*

Totem can be frozen and all strawberries can be made into jam. They can be stored only for a few days. Once the fruits have been picked, cut all the plants to within 1in (2.5cm) of the crown, using shears or, if you grow a lot, a rotary grass cutter. Compost the old leaves and straw. Make sure you remove any diseased leaves first.

PESTS AND DISEASES Strawberries are prone to attack by aphids, slugs, botrytis, mildew, and virus diseases (*see pp. 46–52*). They are also affected by red spider mite and birds (*see p. 232*).

Red currants and white currants

Grown against a wall or fence as cordons, they are suitable for even the smallest plot. They do best in temperate climates.

VARIETIES Red currants *Red Lake* and *Rovada*, and white currant variety *Blanka* are the best. Currants are self-pollinating so they do not need to be pollinated with another variety.

BUSH SHAPES Red and white currants can be grown as freestanding bushes or as

single, double, or triple cordons against a fence, wall, or post-and-wire support (*see p. 208*).

SOIL AND SITE Currants do best in soils with a pH of about 6.5, and prefer a sunny location. They flower in early spring so may not be suitable for very cold areas without some protection from frost.

PLANTING Though they are available in containers for planting at any time of year, currants are best planted in fall or early winter. At this time the weather is likely to be wetter and there will still be enough warmth in the soil to encourage the plants to make some roots before winter.

Red and white currants are grown on a "leg:" they differ from black currants in this respect (*see opposite*), so before planting, remove any suckers that may be present.

To encourage root growth, add two handfuls of bone meal per square yard/meter to the soil. Plant freestanding bushes at the level they grew at the garden center, setting the plants 5ft (1.5m) apart, with 6ft (1.8m) between each row. Cordons should be planted so that the "arms" are 1ft (30cm) apart—single cordons should be planted 1ft (30cm) apart, double cordons 2ft (60cm) apart, and triple cordons 3ft (90cm) apart. After planting, tie the arms so that they are at right angles to the wires, and mulch around the bushes with a thick layer of well-rotted manure or compost as a weed inhibitor.

SUPPORTING AND TRAINING

Freestanding bushes need training to produce a strong, cup-shaped bush with an open center. In the first three winters, prune back the main branches to leave half the wood made that year. Any sideshoots should be cut back to 3in (7cm). At the same time, remove any branches that are broken, dead, or diseased and any that are overcrowded or growing toward the center of the bush. After three years, prune in the summer, immediately after harvesting. Reduce all the sideshoots to five leaves and, when the main branches have grown as long as you want them, cut them back in the same way.

Train cordon-grown currants upward, rather than at an angle. Train by pruning the main arms in winter, cutting back the leading shoot to leave two-thirds of the last season's growth. In summer, prune after harvesting by cutting any sideshoots back to 3in (7cm). Any secondary shoots should be cut back to 1in (2.5cm).

MAINTENANCE

Feeding Currants require a lot of potassium, or potash, so they need extra feeding. In early spring, apply one handful of rock potash per

PLANTING CURRANT BUSHES

Black currants are grown as "stooled" plants, with the branches arising from ground level. Red and white currants are grown on a "leg," with the branches arising from a short stem.

Growing on a leg *Buy bushes with a good stem beneath the branches. Pull off any suckers arising at root level. Plant the bush at the level it grew at the nursery.*

Stooling a black currant bush *Plant the bush 2in (5cm) lower than it grew at the garden center and cut all the shoots back to ground level.*

square yard/meter. A browning of the leaf margins indicates a potash deficiency (*see p. 38*). To remedy, spray the plants with liquid kelp and feed with rock potash as recommended above.

Pruning After the initial shaping, prune in summer as above.

Protection If there is a danger of hard frost when the plants are in flower, cover the bushes with woven polypropylene or fine-meshed netting.

Currants are very susceptible to bird damage, especially when

they are in bud. Cover the bushes with garden netting as soon as the buds appear, and leave it on until the harvesting.

HARVESTING AND STORING

Pick the stalks from the bush and remove the individual currants later with a kitchen fork. They will not store while fresh, although they are suitable for freezing and canning.

PESTS AND DISEASES Currants can be attacked by aphids, birds, and mildew (*see pp. 46–52 and 232*). More specific attacks of sawfly and leaf spot (*see p. 235*) also occur.

Black currants

Black currant bushes take up a lot of room, but are worth growing because the currants are a rich source of Vitamin C.

VARIETIES *Carter's Black Champion* and *Black Naples* are two old varieties popular in some countries, but recent research has produced much better varieties that are more resistant to disease. *Ben Sarek, Ben Nevis, Noirama,* and *Ben Connan* are high-yielding newer varieties. Black currants are self-pollinating so do not need to pollinate with another variety.

BUSH SHAPES Black currants are always grown as free-standing bushes and are not really suitable to grow as cordons. They are pruned

to form "stools" (*see above*) with the majority of shoots coming from ground level or below.

SOIL AND SITE Black currants will grow in part shade, but produce heavier crops in a sunny location. The bushes like a rich soil as they are gross feeders, and so will repay good soil preparation. The soil pH should be maintained at 6.5.

PLANTING The best plants are bare root ones, planted in fall or early winter. Set them 5ft (1.5m) apart, with 6ft (1.8m) between rows.

To create a stooled plant, plant it 2in (5cm) lower than it grew at the nursery, and after planting, prune all the shoots back to ground level.

SUPPORTING AND TRAINING

Black currant bushes require no special support or training.

MAINTENANCE

Feeding Black currants have a high nitrogen requirement so apply two handfuls of blood, fish, and bone meal per square yard/meter in early spring, and mulch with well-rotted manure or compost. If growth still seems poor, give the plants further fertilizer at the same rate in early summer.

Pruning Black currants produce most fruit on wood made the previous year, so there will be no pruning and little fruit in the first year.

In the second and subsequent years cut all the fruited shoots to ground level to encourage further strong growth. This is usually done in late summer, but you can bring pruning forward slightly, to midsummer, and cut off the fruited branches with the fruit still attached. As bushes get older, you may find that fewer shoots are produced from below ground level. If this is the case, prune out the fruited wood as low as possible, just above a new young shoot. At the same time, take a few of the older branches right back to ground level, even if this means cutting out some of the new wood.

HARVESTING AND STORING
Harvest as suggested under pruning, or pick the stalks off the bush and remove individual fruits with a fork.

You can choose to eat black currants right away or store them by canning or freezing.
PESTS AND DISEASES Black currants are susceptible to attack by aphids and birds (*see pp. 46, 50, and 232*), sawfly, big bud mite, leaf spot, mildew, and reversion disease (*see p. 235*).

Raspberries

Easy to grow in cool, temperate climates, raspberries respond well to organic methods of growing. Although they take up more room than many other fruits, they will handsomely repay the use of space since they produce very heavy crops.

VARIETIES Raspberries are self-pollinating. Recent research has produced much improved varieties, so grow these if you can. Recommended varieties are *Mammoth, Anne, Caroline*, and *Latham*. For fall fruit grow *Joan J* or *Autumn Bliss*.
BUSH SHAPES Raspberries are grown as canes tied into a post-and-wire support. Fall-fruiting varieties are grown as free-standing canes.
SOIL AND SITE Raspberries prefer a deep, well-prepared soil that holds plenty of moisture. The soil pH should be 6.0 or a little below. Above pH 7.0, iron deficiency is likely to occur (*see p. 39*). They will tolerate a little shade.

PLANTING This is best done in fall and early winter, using bare root plants. Dig a trench a spade deep and at least 2ft (60cm) wide. Break up the bottom and put in a 4in (10cm) layer of well-rotted compost or manure. Mix more organic matter with the soil as you refill. Sprinkle an application of bone meal on the soil at the rate of one handful per yard/meter of trench. Set the plants a little deeper than they grew at the nursery to encourage plenty of growth from below ground and after planting, cut the canes to within 6in (15cm) of the ground. The plants should be 18in (45cm) apart with at least 6ft (1.8m) between rows.
SUPPORTING AND TRAINING
Grow raspberry canes against a post-and-wire support erected in the same way as the support for cordon apples (*see p. 204*). Tie the canes to the wires as they grow, spacing them 4in (10cm) apart.

When the canes reach the top of the support, their tips can be cut off 3in (7cm) above the top wire. Fall-fruiting varieties generally need no support, though on windy sites you may find it necessary to run a length of nylon twine down either side of the row to stop the canes from blowing around.
MAINTENANCE
Feeding Mulch with well-rotted manure or compost in late winter. A yellowing between the veins of the leaves indicates iron deficiency (*see p. 39*). To remedy this, spray with liquid kelp and give an application of kelp meal at the rate of one handful per square yard/ meter. However, the application of manure should ensure that this deficiency does not occur.
Pruning Once the fruit has been picked, cut the old canes down to ground level and tie the new ones in their place. Pull out any suckers that are spreading towards the paths. Fall-fruiting varieties bear fruit on one-year-old canes, so cut these down to ground level in late winter.
Protection Cover the canes with garden netting before the fruit colors to prevent it from being attacked by birds.
HARVESTING AND STORING
Berries for cooking can be picked a little before they are fully ripe. Leave the plug, or central core of the fruit, on the canes. Unless frozen or canned, raspberries will not store.
PESTS AND DISEASES General pests and diseases include birds, aphids, botrytis, and virus diseases (*see pp. 46–52 and 232*). More specific pests and diseases affecting raspberries are raspberry beetle, spur blight, and cane spot (*see p. 235*).

PRUNING RASPBERRY CANES

Raspberry canes will only produce fruit on one-year-old wood so fruited canes need to be cut out every year. Take the opportunity to pull out any unwanted suckers at this time of year too.

1 *When the fruit has been picked, cut all the fruited canes, and any weak ones, down to ground level.*

2 *Space the new shoots at 4in (10cm) intervals along the support. Cut out all excess canes.*

Bramble fruits

These include blackberries, loganberries, and hybrid berries. Their great value lies in their late harvesting period, following on from raspberries.

VARIETIES All the varieties are self-pollinating so only one needs to be grown.
Blackberry *Loch Ness* and *Apache* come highly recommended.
Loganberry *Variety L654* is recommended.
Hybrid berries Tayberry, Boysenberry, Youngberry.
BUSH SHAPES The brambles should always be trained on wire supports.
SOIL AND SITE Bramble fruits prefer a deep, well-prepared soil that holds plenty of moisture. The soil pH should be 6.0 or a little below. Above pH 7.0, iron deficiency is likely to occur (*see p. 39*). They will grow in a shady position. Some of the hybrid berries will grow in warmer climates if the winters are suitably cool.
PLANTING They are best planted in early winter, though they are often container-grown and so can be planted at any time of year. Dig a trench a spade deep and at least 2ft (60cm) wide. Put in a 4in (10cm) layer of well-rotted compost or manure. Mix more organic matter with the soil as you refill. Sprinkle an application of bone meal on the soil at the rate of one handful per yard/meter of trench. Allow 10ft (3m) between plants, and cut them down to 6in (15cm) after planting.

SUPPORTING AND TRAINING
Support them on wires on 6ft (1.8m) posts. The wires should start 3ft (1m) from the ground and continue at 12in (30cm) intervals to the top of the posts.

It is critical to train them onto the wires as they grow. If you leave them sprawling on the ground for too long, they become intertwined and impossible to unravel without damage.

As they fruit on one-year-old wood, it is necessary to keep the fruiting wood and the new wood separate (*see below*).
MAINTENANCE
Feeding Mulch with well-rotted manure or compost in late winter. If plants show signs of yellowing between the veins of the leaves, it is almost certainly due to iron deficiency (*see p. 39*). To remedy this problem, spray with kelp and sprinkle with kelp meal at the rate of one handful per square yard/meter. However, the application of manure should ensure that this deficiency does not occur.
Pruning After the fruit has been picked, cut all the fruited brambles down to ground level.
Protection Net the bushes before harvest time to protect the berries from bird damage.
HARVESTING AND STORING The plug should be left in, so twist them slightly when picking. Unless frozen or canned, they will not store.
PESTS AND DISEASES Bramble fruits can be attacked by aphids, botrytis, virus diseases and are very prone to bird damage (*see pp. 46–52 and 232*). They are also affected by raspberry beetle, spur blight, and cane spot (*see p. 235*).

Gooseberries

These are the earliest soft fruits of the year. They can be grown as cordons against a wall or fence and, like this, will take up no more than about 6in (15cm) of garden room so they are suitable for even the smallest plot.

VARIETIES One of the best varieties is *Jubilee* because it is resistant to mildew, as are the later *Invicta* and *Pax*. An excellent yellow variety is *Lady Sun*. All varieties of gooseberry are self-pollinating.
BUSH SHAPES Gooseberries can be grown as free-standing bushes or as single, double, or triple cordons against a fence or wall, or on a post-and-wire support (*see p. 208*).
SOIL AND SITE Gooseberries do best in soils with a pH of about 6.5 and prefer a sunny location. They flower in early spring so may not be suitable for very cold areas without some protection from frost.
PLANTING Though they are available in containers for planting at any time of year, gooseberries are best bought bare root and planted in fall or early winter.

Gooseberry bushes are grown on a "leg," a short stem below the branches (*see p. 227*), so before planting remove any suckers that may be present.

Before planting add two handfuls of bone meal per square yard/meter to the soil. Plant free-standing bushes at the level they grew at the garden center, setting the plants 5ft (1.5m) apart, with 6ft (1.8m) between each row. Cordons should be planted so that the "arms" are 12in (30cm) apart—single cordons should be planted 12in(30cm) apart, double cordons 2ft (60cm) apart and triple cordons 3ft (90cm) apart. After planting, mulch around the bushes with a thick layer of well-rotted manure or compost as a weed inhibitor—gooseberries are difficult and painful to weed!
SUPPORTING AND TRAINING
Gooseberries are supported and trained in the same way as red and white currants (*see p. 227*).

Training bramble fruits *Train all the branches in the first year to one side of the support. As the new shoots grow, train them to the other side. This will keep the one-year-old fruiting branches away from the new wood.*

MAINTENANCE
Feeding Gooseberries need a lot of potassium, or potash, so they require extra feeding. In early spring apply one handful of rock potash per square yard/meter. A browning of the leaf margins indicates a potash deficiency (*see p. 38*). To remedy this, spray the plants with liquid kelp and apply rock potash as above.
Pruning Prune free-standing bushes immediately after harvesting. Reduce sideshoots to five leaves and, when the main branches have filled their allotted space, cut them back in exactly the same way. At the same time, completely remove any main branches that are dead, diseased, or overcrowded.

Prune cordon-grown gooseberries after harvesting by cutting any sideshoots back to 3in (7cm). Any secondary branches should be cut back to 1in (2.5cm).
Thinning If the crop of goose-berries is heavy, start picking before they are fully ripe. This allows the remaining berries to swell to their proper size. Use the unripe berries for cooking.
Frost protection If there is a danger of a hard frost, cover the bushes with woven polypropylene or fine netting.

Harvesting gooseberries *This is made easier if the bushes are grown as upright cordons.*

HARVESTING AND STORING Pick gooseberries for cooking before they are fully ripe. Gooseberries will not store when they are fresh but are suitable for freezing and canning.
PESTS AND DISEASES Gooseberries can be attacked by aphids, birds, and mildew (*see pp. 46–52 and 232*). More specific pests and diseases include sawfly and leaf spot (*see p. 235*).

Blueberries

The best edible blueberries are High Bush blueberries. They take between three and eight years to bear fruit; however, once they do, the bushes crop very heavily for many years.

VARIETIES High Bush blueberries are not self-pollinating, so two or more varieties are necessary to ensure good pollination. Recommended varieties include *Bluecrop, Duke, Herbert, Sunshine Blue*, and *Berkeley*.
BUSH SHAPES They are always grown as free-standing bushes.
SOIL AND SITE Blueberries must have an acid soil—a pH of 5.0–5.5 is ideal. If your soil is alkaline, grow them in a raised bed (*see p. 37*) in a sunny spot.
PLANTING Plant bushes in the fall or early winter, setting them 6ft (1.8m) apart. They should be planted slightly deeper than they were grown at the garden center. Incorporate two handfuls of bone meal per square yard/meter into the soil, and mulch with a thick layer of well-rotted manure, compost, or peat.
MAINTENANCE
Feeding Mulch with well-rotted manure or compost every year, and in late winter apply blood, fish, and bone meal at two handfuls per square yard/meter.
Pruning In the first few years the tips of the branches should be removed in fall. As the bush gets larger, any old or weak growths should be pruned out. Ensure the free passage of light and air by pruning out any branches that are less than 6in (15cm) apart.
Protection The bushes should be netted to protect against bird damage as the fruits ripen.
HARVESTING AND STORING Blueberries are fully ripe about 10 days after they turn blue. Use immediately as they do not store well.
PESTS AND DISEASES They are prone to attack by birds (*see pp. 46 and 232*).

Grapes

In temperate regions grapes grown outside are generally only suitable for wine making. In Mediterranean and semi-tropical climates, vines grown outside will produce dessert quality fruit.

VARIETIES In temperate climates grow *Madeline Angevine, Muller Thurgau, Siegerrebe,* or *Brandt.* In warmer regions grow *Chardonnay, Solaris,* and *New York Muscat.* All varieties are self-pollinating.
SOIL AND SITE Grapevines will thrive on poor soil provided it is well drained and contains plenty of organic matter. The soil pH should be 6.5–7.0 and they prefer a sunny location.
PLANTING Plant in the fall or early winter, setting plants 5ft (1.5m) apart. After planting, mulch with well-rotted manure or compost.
MAINTENANCE
Feeding Feed annually with a mulch of well-rotted compost or manure. If growth seems poor, feed with blood, fish, and bone meal at the rate of two handfuls per square yard/meter.
Pruning Prune out the fruited vines as shown right.
Thinning Thin dessert grapes using nail-scissors or special grape-thinning scissors. Remove any berries that are misshapen or diseased, allowing the others to become pea-sized. Then begin removing berries judiciously to enable the others to swell. Thinning is unnecessary if your grapes are for wine making.
HARVESTING AND STORING When the stems turn brown the fruit is ready for picking. Cut off the bunches carefully using secateurs. To store grapes, lay the bunches on a tray and keep in a cool, shady place. They will keep for about a month.
PESTS AND DISEASES Grape are prone to attacks by wasps, birds, mildew, and botrytis (*see pp. 46–52 and 232*). In the greenhouse they may be affected by red spider mite, vine weevils, and scale insects (*see p. 257*).

TRAINING A GRAPEVINE OUTSIDE

Vines can be grown outside against a post-and-wire support or a south-facing wall. The method of training against a post-and-wire support is shown below. To grow against a wall, simply space out the shoots to form a decorative shape.

Making the support *Before planting vines, make a post-and-wire support by erecting a row of 4ft (1.2m) posts. Run wires between them; the top wire should be 4ft (1.2m) from the ground, the bottom one 18in (45cm) from the ground, with a wire strung in between them. Put a 6ft (1.8m) post at each planting point.*

1 Immediately after planting, *cut the main shoot back to leave three strong buds.*

2 In the first summer, *three shoots will grow up. These should be tied onto the stake. In the fall, pinch back the growing point of the main stem.*

3 In the second winter, *tie the two strongest shoots to the bottom wire, one on either side of the stake. Prune them back to 2ft 6in (75cm). Prune the central shoot back to leave three buds.*

4 In the second summer, *the central shoot will again produce three shoots and these should be tied to the stake. Pinch back any sideshoots, which may develop to three leaves.*

Over the summer, the shoots that have been tied in horizontally will produce sideshoots—these will bear the fruit and should be tied to the wire above. As they grow longer, tie them into the top wire and pinch off their tips. Pinch back any secondary shoots to one leaf. In the first fruiting year only four bunches of fruit should be allowed to develop, but in subsequent years allow one bunch per shoot to grow. Cut out the fruited shoots after harvesting.

5 The following season, *tie two shoots from the central stake to the wires, cut back the middle shoot and start the process again.*

CULTIVATING GRAPES IN THE GREENHOUSE

In colder areas, dessert grapes can be grown in the greenhouse. *Muscat of Alexandria* needs some heat but *Black Hamburgh* can be grown in an unheated house.
Planting Plant in late fall. Dig a wide, deep hole, put in a 12in (30cm) layer of gravel and cover with turf. Plant the vine on top.
Training Shoots can be trained horizontally along the wall, 3ft (1m) from the ground. Fruit-bearing branches from these are trained upward.

Alternatively, plant 3ft (1m) apart in the border and train the shoots up to the ridge on wires set 12in (30cm) away from the glass. After planting, remove a third of the previous year's

growth. In the first year, pinch back sideshoots to five leaves.

After leaf fall, prune the main shoot to leave half the previous year's wood. Prune all sideshoots to three buds to form fruiting spurs. In subsequent summers, allow only two shoots to grow from each spur, and stop the weakest of the two after three leaves. When an embryo bunch of grapes forms on the other shoot, allow it to make three more leaves and then pinch off the tip. Repeat the winter pruning as soon as possible after leaves have fallen.
Maintenance In early winter, untie the vines and lay them on the border to prevent the top spurs from growing faster than the lower ones. Put the vines back on the wires when spring growth starts. Keep the

temperature at 70°F (20°C) and spray to increase humidity. When the vines flower, stop spraying and tap the wires to dislodge pollen. Water and feed weekly.

Ensuring a good crop *Remove misshapen or overcrowded berries. The supporting wires should be at least 12in (30cm) from the glass to prevent scorching.*

Fruit pests and diseases

Fruit is attacked by a number of general garden pests and diseases such as aphids, birds, botrytis, and mildew; and also some more specialized pests that attack only certain species of fruit. Advice on how to deal with general pests and diseases can be found in *Organic Pest and Disease Control* (*see pp. 43–53*), although any details specific to fruit are given below.

General pests and diseases

Some pests and diseases will affect any plant, whether it is in the fruit garden, vegetable garden, or in an ornamental border. Many will be kept under control automatically if organic measures, such as companion planting, are employed. Control measures specific to fruit, however, are given below.

BIRDS

These are one of the most troublesome pests of the fruit garden. They are particularly fond of soft fruits, although they peck holes in hard fruits, which are then attacked by wasps. They also eat fruit buds, greatly reducing your crop.
WHAT TO DO The only real protection from bird attack is to use netting, since birds soon get used to any deterrent like silver foil or scarecrows. Cover the fruit with netting, individual plastic bags, or, better still, build a fruit cage (*see p. 211*).

WASPS

These insects attack fruit as it is ripening, and will damage both the tree and soft fruits. As they tend to attack after there has been an initial blemish, like a bird peck, try to protect the fruit from damage in the first place (*see left*).

WHAT TO DO One method of control is to waylay the wasps before they get to the fruit by setting a beer trap. Half-fill a jar with stale beer, cider, or anything else sweet. Cover the top with a piece of paper or plastic with a smallish hole in it. The wasps get into the jar, attracted by the smell, but once inside, they can't get out and they drown.

RED SPIDER MITE

These tiny mites will be a problem in very dry years. They cannot be seen with the naked eye, but the webs they form are visible. They suck the plant's sap, and affected leaves take on a characteristic mottled and yellowed appearance, eventually falling from the plant.

WHAT TO DO Since they thrive in dry conditions, avoid attacks by spraying regularly with water. If the attack is particularly bad, spray the plant with insecticidal soap. See also greenhouse pests (*p. 257*).

Citrus fruit

The pests and diseases given below attack fruit grown outside. In the greenhouse, fruit may be affected by more general ailments such as red spider mite, scale insects, and molds (*see above and p. 257*).

LEMON SCAB

A fungus disease that causes distortion of the fruits, making irregular corky ridges on the skin.
WHAT TO DO Spray with copper fungicide when half the petals have fallen.

LITTLE LEAF

This problem is caused by a zinc deficiency. The leaves become mottled and crinkled and the fruit may be deformed.
WHAT TO DO Ensure that the soil contains the full complement of trace elements by applying a dressing of kelp meal to the soil, or mulching around the tree with well-rotted compost or manure.

CITRUS GALL WASP

This wasp burrows into new spring growth to lay its eggs. When hatched, the larvae burrow within the shoot, causing round swellings, or galls, to appear.
WHAT TO DO There is no effective control. The only cure is to cut out all visible galls in the summer and burn them.

Soft tree fruit

This group contains all the tree fruits that have soft flesh surrounding a central stone, or pit. They are easily damaged by birds and wasps and are very prone to fungus diseases.

PLUM SAWFLY

The caterpillars of this pest make holes in the fruit, rendering them inedible and causing them to drop from the tree.

WHAT TO DO Since the pupae live in the soil beneath the tree, regular hoeing will expose them to insectivorous birds. If an attack has occurred, pick up and dispose of all infected fruits to prevent adults from overwintering.

BLACKFLY

This aphid attacks cherries in particular, though it is not generally a serious problem in the organic garden. It does, however, produce a sticky honeydew that attracts the growth of sooty mold.
WHAT TO DO Ensure your garden contains the plants that attract hoverflies, because their larvae eat aphids (*see p. 45*). If attacks persist, spray with insecticidal soap (*see p. 53*) in the evening to cover the pests but avoid insect predators.

BACTERIAL CANKER

This is a very serious and widespread disease of plums. The first signs are brown marks on the leaves. The leaf tissue then falls away, leaving what looks like caterpillar damage on the leaves. The branches then start to seep a sticky substance. The following spring, buds on infected branches fail to open or produce only small, yellow leaves.

WHAT TO DO All infected wood should be cut away and burned. Spray the leaves with copper fungicide (*see p. 53*) in midsummer and then twice more, leaving a month between each spraying.

PEACH LEAF CURL

A fungus disease that attacks all the *Prunus* species. It causes red blisters on the leaves that eventually swell up. Spores are then produced, turning the leaf surface white. The leaves fall early and the vigor of the tree is affected.
WHAT TO DO Remove infected leaves as soon as you see them, but expect an infestation every year. To control it, spray with copper fungicide (*see p. 53*) in midwinter and repeat every two weeks for at least four days. Spray again in the fall before the leaves fall. Protect fan-trained trees from rain, which carries the spores.

SILVER LEAF

Many fruit trees suffer from this disease, but plums are the most susceptible, the variety *Victoria* especially. The leaves take on a silvery hue and may then turn brown. There is a progressive die-back of shoots and small purple, brown, or white fungi appear on the dead wood. If you remove an infected branch, a brown or purple stain will be seen on the wood.
WHAT TO DO Cut back all dead growth to at least 6in (15cm) past the affected point. As the fungus enters through open wounds, pruning should be done during the growing season when cuts heal quickly. As soon as the symptoms are seen, insert pellets of the parasitic fungus (*Trichoderma viride*) into 2in (5cm) holes in the trunk.

PLUM RUST

This fungus disease causes yellow spots to appear on the upper surface of leaves and brown or orange pustules on the lower surface.

WHAT TO DO The disease occurs only in weak plants so feed those affected with blood, fish, and bone meal at the rate of two handfuls per square yard/meter and mulch with well-rotted manure or compost. Hand water if the soil around the tree is dry.

Hard tree fruit

These fruits, which include apples and pears, are prone to attack by many pests and diseases, but organic methods and good husbandry will generally reduce problems to a minimum.

CODLING MOTH

The female moths lay their eggs on developing apples and, as soon as the grubs hatch, they enter the fruit. They are virtually impossible to see and the first sign is often a maggot inside the apple.

WHAT TO DO Control by hanging pheromone traps in the trees. These are triangular plastic boxes containing a sheet of sticky paper. In the center of the sheet is a capsule containing the pheromone—the substance the female moth excretes at mating time to attract the male moth. The moths fly into the trap, stick to the paper, and the female's eggs remain unfertilized. One trap for every five trees reduces the number of fertile eggs laid by about 80 percent.

APPLE SAWFLY

Before burrowing into fruit, the sawfly larvae feed on the surface, causing a ribbonlike scar. The affected apples fail to ripen and fall from the tree in the summer.
WHAT TO DO The only really effective measure is to pick and destroy infected fruits as soon as you see any scarring. Also pick up and destroy any fallen fruits.

BITTER PIT

Small, sunken areas appear in the fruit, with brown flesh immediately below the pits. Bitter pit appears during storage but may develop while the fruit is on the tree and is caused by a calcium deficiency and an imbalance of potassium, or magnesium in the soil.
WHAT TO DO There is no effective treatment, but watering during dry periods and mulching with manure will help avoid it.

BROWN ROT

A fungus that turns fruit brown and makes the flesh decay. The fruit becomes covered with patches of white fungus spores and finally shrivels up, often falling off. Brown rot also attacks fruit in storage.
WHAT TO DO There is no totally effective control. Remove infected fruit and keep the soil around the trees clean. Check fruit for damage regularly while in storage.

APPLE APHIDS

The rosy apple aphid and the rosy leaf-curling aphid feed on shoots and leaves, causing them to turn yellow or bright red and distort. The green apple aphid clusters around shoot tips and sucks the sap, causing stunting of growth.
WHAT TO DO Spray the tree with insecticidal soap or soft soap when it is at the leaf cluster stage and again when the aphids are seen. Grow the plants that attract hoverflies (*see p. 45*).

WOOLLY APHIDS

These insects suck sap from the shoots. They live in colonies and cover themselves with a white waxy coating, which makes them difficult to attack with sprays.

WHAT TO DO Paint small infestations of woolly aphids with denatured alcohol, or simply scrape them off. Spray large areas with insecticidal soap (*see p. 53*) after the petals fall, using a coarse, high-pressure spray. If this doesn't work, you may have to cut out the infestation.

PEAR SUCKER

These pests live in the blossom buds and cover the foliage with honeydew, which attracts the fungus disease, sooty mold. Attacks generally start in early spring and continue through the summer.
WHAT TO DO Control them with insecticidal soap (*see p. 53*), applied three weeks after the petals have fallen.

WINTER MOTH

The female moths are wingless so they have to crawl up the tree to lay their eggs between fall and spring. The caterpillars hatch in the spring and feed until early summer, making holes in the leaves. They then make their way down into the soil for the winter.
WHAT TO DO The most effective control is to tie a greaseband around the tree trunk during the egg-laying period. This prevents females from crawling up the tree to lay eggs.

APPLE SCAB

A fungus that appears as dark spots on leaves and fruit. It spreads to form large, unsightly patches.
WHAT TO DO Pick off spotty leaves and burn them. Sweep up all the fallen leaves because fungus spores overwinter on them.

FIREBLIGHT

A bacterial disease that causes branches to wilt from the top and the leaves to turn brown. It generally enters the tree through cuts or damage on the branches and it can pass from one tree to another.
WHAT TO DO Prune out and burn any obvious signs of the disease, ensuring that the cut is made well into healthy wood. Always disinfect shears after pruning to avoid spreading the disease. Badly affected plants must be pulled up and burnt.

CANKER

It starts as sunken, discolored patches on the bark, which soon extend. In the summer, white pustules appear on the sunken patches and in the winter small red fruiting bodies develop. If the fungus encircles a shoot, the shoot dies.

WHAT TO DO Diseased patches, shoots, and branches must be cut out with a knife or chisel and burned immediately. It is very important to cut right back to clean wood and then disinfect all tools.

Soft fruit

All low-growing cane and bush fruits are classified as soft fruits. General garden pests and diseases affect many varieties of soft fruit. Birds are especially fond of them, particularly when the weather is hot and there is no other source of liquid. Soft fruits also have a number of specific pests and diseases.

RASPBERRY BEETLE

The larvae of this beetle feed on the ripening fruit, and are often first noticed when malformed fruits are seen. When they have finished feeding, the larvae fall into the soil and turn into pupae.

WHAT TO DO Hoe the soil to bring the pupae to the surface, where birds will eat them. Spraying with pyrethrum may also be necessary. Spray raspberries when the first fruits turn pink, and hybrid berries immediately after flowering. Blackberries should be sprayed when their flowers first open. Unfortunately, this is when bees will be most active and pyrethrum kills bees, so spray in the evenings when the bees are in their hives.

SAWFLY

The small, brown, spotted caterpillars of this pest attack leaves and can defoliate a plant within hours.
WHAT TO DO Birds, especially robins, will eat sawfly larvae, but they cannot control them totally. As soon as you see the first caterpillar, spray the bush with an insecticide such as pyrethrum.

BIG BUD MITE

This gall mite attacks buds of black currants, causing them to swell. It also carries a virus disease (*see below*). The mites attack buds in early summer, and migrate to other buds the following spring.
WHAT TO DO Check the bushes in late winter and early spring. Remove and burn any big buds.

REVERSION

A virus disease carried by the big bud mite. It is hard to recognize—mature leaves are narrower than usual and have less than five pairs of veins on the main lobe. Flower buds become bright magenta in color. The bushes lose their vigor and the yield is reduced.
WHAT TO DO There is no cure. Dig up affected bushes and burn them.

SPUR BLIGHT

This fungus disease forms silver patches and fruiting bodies on raspberry canes and the briars of hybrid berries. The affected buds will eventually die.
WHAT TO DO Meticulous pruning of overcrowded canes should prevent infection. If the disease occurs, spray with copper fungicide when the buds first open and again when the flowers are showing white at the tips.

LEAF SPOT

Brown spots appear on leaves in the spring; these spread and the leaf eventually falls off. This affects the vigor and reduces the yield.
WHAT TO DO Pick off any affected leaves and burn them. If the disease persists, spray with copper fungicide at ten-day intervals.

THE HERB GARDEN

Herbs should always be included in the organic garden, for both practical and aesthetic reasons. They are generally not difficult to grow and most are extremely decorative plants that help attract useful predators to the garden, as well as those insects—such as bees—which are needed for pollination in the fruit garden (*see p. 203*). They can be planted around shrubs as a ground cover to aid weed control, in mixed borders, or on their own in a traditional herb garden (*see opposite*). Some of the attractive low-growing species—such as thyme, rosemary, and parsley—are suitable for growing in tubs, window boxes, and hanging baskets (*see Container Gardening, pp. 126–231*).

No matter where you choose to grow them, an assortment of herbs will add color and fragrance to the garden.

Most of the herbs I have suggested can be used in the kitchen to add subtle flavors to your food. Some can be made into herbal teas or potpourri. Others may be used in homemade cosmetics or as a means of dyeing fabric. Comfrey is an especially useful herb since it provides a fast-growing mulching material and can be made into high potash liquid manure (*see p. 244*). I have suggested a basic selection of herbs, but there are hundreds of different kinds with various culinary and decorative attributes, so you will certainly want to experiment with others.

Planning an herb garden

It is worth planning a planting scheme on paper before you begin choosing and planting your herbs. In traditional herb gardens, the plants are arranged in formal patterns, with each herb or group of herbs enclosed by a low hedgelike box (*Buxus sempervirens*) or lavender (*Lavandula* sp.). The main reason for these often intricate, traditional designs is that most herbs are annuals or perennials, which die down completely in the winter, so you need to make the area look interesting all year-round. Of course, herbs can also be grown very successfully in the flower garden and were one of the main constituents of the "real" old cottage gardens (*see p. 88*).

Herbs like the variegated sages and the thymes make superb ground cover plants, swamping weeds, and providing a splash of color as well as attracting pollinating insects. It also pays to grow some of the "cultivated" forms of herbs, especially for the flower garden. There are, for example, several varieties of giant chives with large, dramatic flowers. There are also golden and variegated balms and some highly attractive colored hops, all of which are as useful in the kitchen as their more commonly grown counterparts.

If you are opting for a traditional herb garden, remember to make the plants accessible by putting in pathways or stepping stones so that each plant can be reached without stepping off the path. Herbs will be harvested more regularly than most other plants, so good access is vital. Locate the herb garden in the sunniest part of the garden. Most herbs originate from the Mediterranean, so they thrive in warm sunshine. The few that prefer a little shade can be planted in the shade of one of the large sun lovers.

SOIL PREPARATION FOR HERBS

Ideally, the soil in which herbs are grown should be well drained and light though, with good preparation, they will grow well in heavier soils. Double dig the area (*see p. 264*), breaking up the subsoil and working in plenty of well-rotted manure or compost, or one of the alternatives (*see pp. 18–34*). Since most herbs like a soil pH of between 7.0 and 7.5, spent mushroom compost is ideal (*see p. 30*).

The one thing most herbs cannot stand is bad drainage so, if your soil is wet and heavy and cannot be improved by deep digging or the inclusion of coarse sand and organic matter, it is best to build a raised bed (*see p. 37*). If you can, use hard-wearing brick or stone to raise the sides, although wood can also be used. Old railroad ties are ideal and they will raise the bed by about 12in (30cm), which is all that is needed.

If you are going to plant container-grown plants in the spring or summer, rake in two handfuls of blood, fish, and bone meal per square yard/meter about two weeks before planting. Use a similar quantity of bone meal alone before planting herbs in the fall and winter.

SOWING AND PLANTING HERBS

The first essential is to ensure the soil is completely free of weeds. If there is so much as a sprig of ground elder root or a sprout of couch grass, it will thrive unnoticed among the sprawling herbs. Then the only option is to remove the plants and thoroughly clean the soil.

If you decide to grow your herbs in a special herb garden, delay planting for a year. Dig the area thoroughly, removing any trace of a weed, then cover the whole area with black plastic sheeting, dug into the ground all around to prevent it from blowing away, and leave it for a year.

Before sowing or planting, consider the potential height and spread of each plant, as well as its rate of growth and how much sun it prefers. Some, such as lovage, grow to enormous proportions and are only suitable for the back of a large herb garden. Plants like borage need a great deal of sun, while mint, for example, will thrive in semi-shade; both are fast spreading. Any special planting requirements are described in the individual entries on pp. 241–245, and the maximum height of each herb is given also.

MAINTAINING AN HERB GARDEN

Feeding A mulch of well-rotted manure or compost applied over the top of the whole garden will maintain fertility. Spread a layer about 2–3in (5–7.5cm) thick in mid or late winter, but guard against slugs (*see p. 50*).

Watering Some watering may be necessary in dry weather. Use a sprinkler for at least two hours to ensure that the water permeates through to the lower levels.

Weeding During the early stages of cultivation, it is important to remove weeds by hand. When the plants become established, they will spread and inhibit weeds themselves.

Pruning Some herbs, like lavender and thyme, must be trimmed back after flowering to keep them compact and within bounds. Regular harvesting will keep most herbs in check, but they will all respond well to being cut back from time to time.

Thinning Some herbs need to be watched carefully and self-sown seedlings need to be removed at an early stage. Plants like borage, mint, and especially feverfew can completely take over if their seedlings are allowed to grow unchecked.

Propagation Perennial herbs can be dug up and divided (*see p. 273*). The ideal time for this is the fall and early winter, though it can also be done in early spring. Propagate the shrubby herbs, like rosemary, bay, and lavender, from softwood cuttings in early summer (*see p. 274*).

▲ **An informal herb garden**
Thyme, mint, chives, sage, and rosemary can be grown for their color and scent as well as their culinary uses.

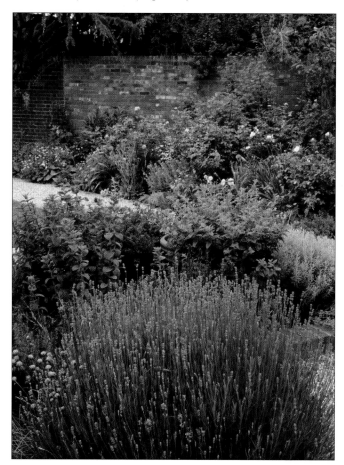

▶ **Herbs in a cottage garden**
Herbs form an integral part of this traditional walled garden. Lavender softens the edge of the border, ready to release its scent when visitors brush past.

An herb collection

Herbs are easy to grow, decorative, and useful plants. They can be made into potpourri and used fresh, dried, or frozen to add flavor to food. Plant them in the borders, in a special herb garden, or in any odd space you have. This is a basic collection of 19 herbs, but there are many more you could include. Cultivation details are given on pp. 240–245.

CHIVES *Allium schoenoprasum*

Fast growing, reaches 8in (20cm). Lilac flowers. *For cultivation details, see p. 242 and* Perennials, *p. 115.*

BORAGE *Borago officinalis*

Easy to grow, reaches 2ft 6in (75cm). Attracts bees. *For cultivation details, see p. 241 and* Annuals, *p. 116.*

BALM *Melissa officinalis*

Robust and aromatic, reaches 3ft (90cm). Attracts bees. *For cultivation details, see p. 242 and* Perennials, *p. 115.*

CHERVIL *Anthriscus cerefolium*

Fast growing, reaches 2ft (60cm). Prefers shade. *For cultivation details, see p. 241 and* Annuals, *p. 116.*

SPEARMINT *Mentha spicata*

Fast growing, reaches 3ft (90cm) Prefers semi-shade. *For cultivation details, see p. 242 and* Perennials, *p. 115.*

DILL *Anethum graveolens*

Fast growing, reaches 2ft 6in (75cm) in warm conditions. *For cultivation details, see p. 241 and* Annuals, *p. 116.*

WINTER SAVORY *Satureia montana*

Evergreen shrub, reaches 12in (30cm). Attracts bees. *For cultivation details, see p. 242 and* Perennials, *p. 115.*

SWEET BASIL *Ocimum basilicum*

Reaches 2ft (60cm), grown as annual in temperate areas. *For cultivation details, see p. 241 and* Annuals, *p. 116.*

SORREL *Rumex acetosa*

Broad leaved, reaches 18in (45cm). Prefers semi-shade. *For cultivation details, see p. 243 and* Perennials, *p. 115.*

Plant type — Tree · Shrub · Perennial · Annual · Biennial · Bulb · Climbing plants | **Sun preference** — Sun · Partial shade · Shade · Tolerant | **Soil preference** — Acid · Alkaline · Tolerant

FRENCH TARRAGON
Artemisia dracunculus

Aromatic, reaches 2–3ft (60–90cm). Subtle flavor.
For cultivation details, see p. 243 and Perennials, *p. 115.*

LEMON THYME
Thymus citriodorus

Evergreen shrub, reaches 8in (20cm). Attracts bees.
For cultivation details, see p. 244 and Shrubs, *p. 112.*

FENNEL *Foeniculum vulgare*

Fast growing, reaches 5ft (1.5m). Decorative flowers.
For cultivation details, see p. 243 and Perennials, *p. 115.*

SAGE *Salvia officinalis*

Hardy shrub, reaches 2ft (60cm). Decorative and aromatic.
For cultivation details, see p. 245 and Shrubs, *p. 112.*

LOVAGE *Levisticum officinale*

Very tall, reaches 8ft (2.5m). Attractive seedheads.
For cultivation details, see p. 243 and Perennials, *p. 115.*

ROSEMARY *Rosmarinus officinalis*

Aromatic evergreen, reaches 3ft (90cm). Attracts insects.
For cultivation details, see p. 245 and Shrubs, *p. 112.*

POT MARJORAM *Origanum onites*

Reaches 15in (35cm). Other types also grown. *For cultivation details, see p. 244 and* Perennials, *p. 115.*

JUNIPER *Juniperus communis*

Tall conifer, reaches 10ft (3m). Blue-black berries.
For cultivation details, see p. 245 and Shrubs, *p. 112.*

HORSERADISH *Armoracia rusticana*

Fast growing, reaches 2ft (60cm). Hot-flavored tap root.
For cultivation details, see p. 244 and Perennials, *p. 115.*

BAY *Laurus nobilis*

Frost tender, reaches 20ft (6m). Prefers semi-shade.
For cultivation details, see p. 245 and Shrubs, *p. 112.*

Cultivating herbs

The range of plants you grow will depend on personal priorities. You may base your selection on culinary value, decorative qualities, or a combination of these and other factors. However, you must also consider the practicalities of your choice. A young specimen of fennel, for instance, may seem an attractive option, but remember it will grow into a bushy plant about 5ft (1.5m) tall. If you wish to grow sensitive species, like bay, in a temperate area, they must be planted in pots and brought into a frost-free greenhouse during the winter. So, before you buy your seeds or young plants, ensure you can provide the space and conditions needed to grow them successfully.

Attracting pollinating insects
The decorative lilac-pink flowers of thyme attract bees and other insects that are necessary for the pollination of border plants.

HARVESTING AND STORING HERBS

Many of the herbs in this chapter can be preserved by drying. This enables them to be used throughout the year and can sometimes actually improve the flavor. To get the best results, pick leaves for drying before the plant flowers. Most of the herbs are dried very simply, in the way described below. If a different method is required, this is explained under the relevant herb entry.

1 *The leaves of many herbs, including thyme* (shown here), *can be harvested fresh throughout the growing season. For drying purposes, though, cut them before the plant comes into flower, and only take young, healthy leaves. Do not harvest more stems than you have room to dry immediately, and avoid handling the individual leaves.*

2 *Tie the stems in small bunches and hang them in a dry, airy place. Do not tie large bunches together as this will slow down the drying process by restricting air circulation. Any damage to the leaves causes essential oils to be lost and has a detrimental effect on the aroma and flavor of the herbs, so be very careful when handling them. Crumble the dried leaves into an airtight jar.*

3 *If you want to save the seeds, harvest the stems just as the seeds ripen and hang them upside down in small bunches in a dry, airy spot. Place a cloth or bowl beneath the hanging plants to catch the seeds as they fall. Apart from the seeds used in cooking—such as lovage* (shown here)—*remember to save those of annual herbs for sowing the following year.*

Borage

This hardy annual will freely seed itself each year. The arching sprays of deep-blue flowers make borage worth growing in the border for its decorative value alone, but it is also an excellent bee attractor.

SOIL AND SITE Borage prefers a sunny, open location and will not do well in shade. It is tolerant of a wide range of soil conditions.
SOWING Sow seeds in the open ground in mid-spring, and thin to 15in (35cm) apart. The herb will die down in the winter after seeding itself, and the seedlings will grow the following year. Remove any seedlings that start to grow where they are not wanted.
MAINTENANCE This herb needs no further encouragement to grow well, but it will need regular trimming to keep it in check.
HARVESTING AND STORING Pick young leaves during the summer. They freeze successfully but do not dry well. The flowers can be crystallized by painting them with egg-white and then dipping them in superfine (caster) sugar.

Chervil

This self-seeding hardy annual is not a very attractive herb, looking rather like a weedy version of parsley, but it is one of the most useful in the kitchen. It has a spicy, aniseed flavor.

SOIL AND SITE It is essential that you give chervil a shaded position in moist soil, or it will run to seed as soon as the sun shines.
SOWING Sow seeds in early or mid-spring, 9in (23cm) apart. Either allow them to reseed themselves, thinning to 9in (23cm), or let one or two plants run to seed. Harvest the seeds, then resow in late summer or early fall. These late sowings will have to be covered with cloches (see p. 140) to protect them against the cold in all but the mildest areas.
MAINTENANCE Keep the plants well-watered in dry weather and pick off flowers as they form to delay seeding until the last flush of flowering.
HARVESTING AND STORING Take fresh leaves from the outside of the plants to encourage continued production from the centers. The leaves can be frozen or dried (see facing page).

Dill

This attractive, hardy annual may sometimes seed itself but, in cold areas, it is worth saving the seed for resowing. Its feathery leaves and delicate yellow flowers make dill a suitable plant for the border, and it is also a widely used culinary herb.

SOIL AND SITE A well-drained soil and sunny location will suit dill best.
SOWING AND PLANTING Sow seeds in short rows 12in (30cm) apart, outside, in mid-spring, and thin the plants to 12in (30cm) apart. Sow once if you only require the seeds but, for leaves, collect them each month until midsummer. If you buy plants or grow them in pots, plant them 12in (30cm) apart. Do not sow dill near fennel (see p. 43) because the two varieties may cross-pollinate.
MAINTENANCE Keep plants free from weeds and well watered in dry weather.
HARVESTING AND STORING Pick fresh leaves as they are required. The leaves and the seeds can be dried and stored as described on the facing page.

Basil

Basil is grown as a perennial in warm climates, and an annual in areas where it is liable to get killed by frost. There are two types: sweet and bush. Sweet basil is taller, and has larger leaves and a better flavor.

SOIL AND SITE Plant basil in a sunny, sheltered place in the best possible soil.
SOWING AND PLANTING Sow in small pots inside, in early spring. Harden off in a cold frame (see p. 256) and plant 12in (30cm) apart when all danger of frost has passed.
MAINTENANCE Keep the plants well-watered at all times and pinch off the flower buds as they appear, to maintain the rate of growth.
HARVESTING AND STORING Harvest the fresh leaves throughout the summer. Leaves can be dried in the sun and stored in airtight jars, but will not be as flavorful as when fresh. They can also be frozen.

Parsley

There are several varieties of this popular herb: the crisp type (*Petroselinum crispum*) or the plain-leaved "French" parsley are generally grown. They are biennials, but should be grown as annuals to prevent seeding at the end of the first year. The plants grow up to a maximum height of about 12in (30cm).

SOIL AND SITE Parsley prefers some shade and a soil that is enriched with well-rotted manure or compost.
SOWING Sow an early crop inside in late winter, and transfer to the open ground in mid-spring, planting seedlings 6in (15cm) apart. Alternatively, directly sow outside in mid-spring and again in midsummer, for a continuous supply. You can also sow another midsummer crop in pots for growing inside during the winter. The seeds take a long time to germinate, so be prepared to wait for signs of growth. Remove the crops at the end of the season.
MAINTENANCE There is little to do except remove weeds and water during dry weather.
HARVESTING AND STORING Cut the leaves as and when they are needed, but do not completely defoliate plants, to allow them to regrow. Leaves can be dried quickly in a hot oven or frozen in ice cubes.

Chives

This well-known and much valued hardy perennial herb makes an attractive border edging because of its distinctive globular flowers. The fresh leaves are usually chopped over potato or egg dishes or in soft cheeses. The bulbs can also be pickled in wine vinegar. There are several different forms that have great decorative merit.

SOIL AND SITE Chives have no specific light requirements, but prefer moist soil conditions.
SOWING AND PLANTING Sow seeds outside 12in (30cm) apart in early spring. Alternatively, divide established plants and plant divisions 12in (30cm) apart in spring or fall.
MAINTENANCE Dig up the clumps every three years in early or mid-fall, divide them with a knife and replant them in fresh soil as described for all perennials (*see p. 273*). If you want to keep the plants in the same place, dig them up, heel them into a spare piece of land (*see p. 113*), turn over the soil—incorporating well-rotted manure or compost—and replant.
HARVESTING AND STORING The plants thrive on being cut back, so cut off the leaves with scissors to leave about ½in (1cm). They can be frozen into ice cubes, but do not dry well.

Balm

This perennial herb has a pleasant lemon flavor and can be planted in the flower border to attract bees to the garden. Decorative variegated and yellow varieties are available.

SOIL AND SITE Balm prefers a water-retentive soil enriched with organic matter. Plant it in a sunny or semi-shaded place, as the leaves tend to blanch in deep shade.
SOWING AND PLANTING Sow seeds outside in mid- or late spring, 18in (45cm) apart, or divide established plants and plant at the same distances.

MAINTENANCE Keep plants trimmed back to maintain the bushiness and retain the color of variegated and yellow varieties. Dig and divide established plants every three years (*see p. 273*).
HARVESTING AND STORING Cut fresh leaves throughout the summer. Balm leaves do not dry well, but they can be frozen in plastic bags or in ice cubes.

Mint

There are several types of mint, but apple mint and spearmint are best for cooking. Apple mint is perhaps preferable as it has some resistance to mint-rust disease. Mint is a hardy perennial and easy to grow, though it can also be invasive.

SOIL AND SITE Mint will grow very well in practically any soil, but prefers a semi-shaded area.
PLANTING Plant root cuttings taken in fall (*see p. 274*). Mint

STORING MINT

As an alternative to potting mint, you can store the herb to ensure a fresh winter supply.

1 *Dig up a clump of mint and carefully remove a few sprigs with roots. Replant the remainder.*

2 *Put a layer of moist compost in a wooden box. Lay the sprigs in the box and cover them with more compost.*

can be very invasive, so plant it in a bucket or plastic tub sunk in the ground with the rim of the bucket above the soil level to prevent shoots from rooting in over the edge. Plant it 2ft (60cm) away from other herbs.
MAINTENANCE Mint needs little encouragement to grow. Water in dry weather and pick regularly to keep the plants in check.
HARVESTING AND STORING Pick freely throughout the spring and summer. At the end of the season, dig up a few roots and put them in pots in the greenhouse to ensure a supply of fresh mint during winter. This makes drying unnecessary. The leaves freeze well in ice cubes or can be stored in moist compost (*see left*).

Savory

There are two types: summer savory is a droopy annual, while winter savory is a more erect perennial evergreen shrub. Both can be grown in the herb garden or the border, where they will attract bees.

SOIL AND SITE Both types prefer a sunny location and a well-drained soil rich in organic matter.
SOWING AND PLANTING Sow summer savory direct outside in mid- or late spring, 6in (15cm) apart. Sow plenty, because the yield of each plant is not high. Increase the winter variety by taking cuttings (*see* Softwood cuttings, *p. 274*) during the summer, or by sowing seeds outside in late summer. Space the plants 18in (45cm) apart.
MAINTENANCE Summer savory requires little attention except weeding and watering. Winter savory can become leggy, so keep pinching back—removing the top growth to encourage shoots at the base of the plant. In really cold weather, protect plants against frost by covering with cloches (*see p. 140*). Replace savory plants every three to five years.

HARVESTING AND STORING

Pick leaves from summer savory throughout the season for immediate use and, for drying, just as the plant starts to flower. You can pick winter savory leaves fresh throughout the year.

Sorrel

There are two types of sorrel: the broad-leaved type shown on p. 238, and the French variety. The latter has smaller leaves and is slightly lower growing than broad-leaved sorrel. Both are hardy perennials. Sorrel has a sharp taste, so use it sparingly.

SOIL AND SITE Sorrel prefers partial shade and a moist soil enriched with plenty of organic matter.

SOWING AND PLANTING The herb can be raised from seed but takes a long time to mature, so you may prefer to obtain an established root. Plant seeds or roots outside in the fall about 12in (30cm) apart.

MAINTENANCE Remove the flower heads as soon as they appear to delay seeding until the final flush. Keep the plants weed free and make sure they are never short of water. Sorrel tends to deteriorate after awhile, so dig it up, divide and replant the outer young offsets every three years (*see p. 273*).

HARVESTING AND STORING Pick fresh leaves throughout the season. The plants can be picked over thoroughly and they will soon regenerate. Dry the leaves as shown

Drying sorrel *Lay fresh leaves flat on a wire cake tray. To hasten the drying process, ensure they are well spaced so air can circulate freely around each leaf.*

below, and store them in airtight jars. They do not freeze well unless you make them into a purée first.

Tarragon

There are two types of tarragon: French (shown on p. 239) and Russian. Both are hardy perennials, though the Russian variety is hardier and can withstand lower temperatures. Tarragon is a very useful culinary herb—the French variety has a particularly strong flavor.

SOIL AND SITE A sunny, sheltered location and good drainage are essential.

SOWING AND PLANTING French tarragon cannot be grown from seed, so buy young plants and space them 18in (45cm) apart. Mature plants can be divided in the spring (*see p. 273*). Russian tarragon can easily be raised from seed sown 2ft (60cm) apart in the spring.

MAINTENANCE Weed and water as required. In the winter, French tarragon in particular will need protecting from frost, so mulch with a light layer of straw or bracken. Dig, divide, and replant both types of tarragon every four years to retain vigor because the flavor of the leaves deteriorates as the plant matures.

HARVESTING AND STORING Pick fresh leaves throughout the season. The leaves cut in the spring can be dried, though this will cause them to lose their delicate aroma (*see p. 240*).

Fennel

Not to be confused with Florence fennel, which is grown for its swollen stem bases (*see p. 181*), this is a vigorous hardy perennial herb. Fennel is a tall, stately plant with finely divided, feathery green leaves and bright-yellow flowers that will enhance the flower borders. A red-leaved variety is also available. The leaves and seeds both have a pleasant aniseed taste.

SOIL AND SITE Fennel requires a fertile soil and plenty of sunshine.

SOWING AND PLANTING Sow seeds 2ft (60cm) apart, in the fall or spring. Alternatively, plant young plants or divided clumps in mid-spring or fall, 2ft (60cm) apart.

MAINTENANCE Keep the plants trimmed down to provide a succession of young leaves, but allow some flowering heads to provide seeds. Keep fennel away from coriander, caraway, and dill to avoid cross-pollination. Dig, divide, and replant established plants every three years (*see p. 273*).

HARVESTING AND STORING Harvest fresh leaves as required. They can also be dried but tend to lose much of their flavor. Hang the plants up to dry the flower heads and collect the seeds as described on p. 240.

Lovage

A shrubby, hardy perennial that dies down each year, lovage grows extremely tall and needs a lot of space, so is therefore best suited to the back of a large herb garden. It can also be used in the borders, since its foliage, large seedheads, and clusters of yellow flowers are very attractive. All parts of the plant have a strong flavor, so experiment with the herb carefully.

SOIL AND SITE Lovage will tolerate partial shade, but does better in a sunny location. It needs a moist soil with plenty of organic matter dug in.

SOWING AND PLANTING Sow seeds in spring or plant divided clumps in early spring or fall. You will probably only need one plant but, if you do plant more than one, set the plants 3ft (90cm) apart. Lovage dies down almost completely each winter.

MAINTENANCE This herb needs no further encouragement to grow vigorously. It will reach full size in approximately four years. Dig, divide, and replant established plants (*see p. 273*).

HARVESTING AND STORING Harvest the fresh leaves throughout the season. They can be dried as described on p. 240.

Marjoram

Wild and pot marjoram are both hardy perennials, but sweet marjoram—the most flavorful and aromatic of the three—is hardy only in warm areas and must be grown as a half-hardy annual elsewhere. All can be used plentifully in the kitchen.

SOIL AND SITE All types of marjoram grow best in a sunny site. They prefer a well-drained soil but dislike dryness at the roots, so work in plenty of well-rotted organic matter before planting.
SOWING AND PLANTING Plant young plants or divided clumps of wild and pot marjoram about 12in (30cm) apart. In temperate climates, sow sweet marjoram inside in early spring and plant 8in (20cm) apart after all danger of frost has passed. In warmer areas, treat it like wild and pot marjoram, which can be sown directly outside in the spring.
MAINTENANCE Pinch off regularly to ensure bushy, compact plants. Keep the plants weed free and water if necessary. Pot marjoram can be potted at the end of the summer and brought inside where it will continue to grow. Dig, divide, and replant the perennials every three years (*see p. 273*).
HARVESTING AND STORING Pick fresh leaves from early summer onward. Sweet marjoram dries well and its flavor will strengthen with drying (*see p. 240*). However, with a supply of fresh leaves all summer and more from potted plants in the winter, you may not consider it worthwhile. All types will also freeze well.

Horseradish

This vigorous hardy perennial is grown for its hot-flavored root. The name of the herb derives from "coarse radish."

SOIL AND SITE Horseradish likes a rich soil and a sunny or semi-shaded position. If you want a large crop,

the best way is to grow plants in a raised bed on a concrete path, raising the soil about 2ft (60cm) high (*see p. 37*). That way you can be sure of containing the roots. Horseradish is a tap root, which means it is capable of reproducing from any small piece of the root left in the ground. It is very persistent if not kept in check.
PLANTING Buy some roots, take cuttings about 6in (15cm) long, and plant them vertically 12in (30cm) apart in early spring.
MAINTENANCE This herb needs no encouragement to grow rapidly.
HARVESTING AND STORING Dig up the whole plant each year to prevent it from overrunning the garden. Store the roots in boxes of damp sand or peat in a shed until needed. Save some for replanting in spring.

Comfrey

This prolific perennial herb is a useful crop to cultivate as compost material. The foliage is very rich in potassium and contains some trace elements. The best variety is *Symphytum officinale* "Bocking 14."

SOIL AND SITE Comfrey prefers a soil rich in organic matter, a shady location, and damp conditions.
SOWING AND PLANTING Comfrey can be grown from seed but takes a long time to mature. It is better to buy an established plant and remove offsets from the outside of the root each fall. Plant these 3ft (90cm) apart.
MAINTENANCE This herb needs no further encouragement to take off. Pull, divide, and replant clumps every three years (*see p. 273*).
HARVESTING AND STORING Cut the leaves with shears as required. To make a liquid manure high in potash, steep leaves of the Russian variety in a bucket and dilute the resulting liquid by about 10:1. The leaves which can grow up to 12in (30cm) long—and the pretty, bell-shaped flowers can also be used for dyeing; they produce a yellow or orange color.

Thyme

There are several low- and high-growing varieties of thyme that make decorative garden plants and will attract pollinating insects. They can be used as edging for borders or as ground cover. Common and lemon thyme are the two most generally used in the kitchen.

SOIL AND SITE Thyme likes a sunny location and well-drained soil. It prefers a soil pH of about 7.0, so add lime to neutralize acid soil if necessary (*see p. 36*).
SOWING AND PLANTING Common thyme can easily be raised from seed sown in mid-spring outside, and both types from cuttings taken during summer, or by division (*see pp. 273–274*). Thyme is often bought in pots, which can be planted at any time. Sow or plant about 12in (30cm) apart. The plants will spread considerably, so plant them further apart if you are prepared to wait for ground cover a little longer.
MAINTENANCE Pinch off regularly to prevent plants from becoming leggy (*see below*) and cut them back hard after flowering.
HARVESTING AND STORING Pick the leaves fresh throughout the season, though this is one of the few herbs whose leaves have more flavor dry than fresh. Cut the sprigs before flowering and dry them in an airy site, as described on p. 240.

Pinching off thyme *You can encourage bushy growth and keep the plants compact by regularly pinching the growing tips between your index finger and thumb.*

Sage

This is a hardy shrub that makes an attractive addition to the borders. It has pretty, velvety-gray and blue flowers. Several variegated forms and flowering cultivars are worth growing for their decorative qualities alone, but sage is also widely used as a culinary herb.

SOIL AND SITE Sage likes a sunny position and a well-drained soil, so dig in plenty of organic matter (*see p. 20*). Add sand to heavy soils to further improve drainage.
SOWING AND PLANTING Sage can be grown from seed sown in spring, but often does not breed true. Alternatively, you can buy sage plants in containers or as bare root shrubs. These should be planted 2ft (60cm) apart. It is also easy to propagate sage by layering (*see below and p. 275*).
Plants raised in this way can be potted or replanted in the spring. A third option is to take softwood cuttings in early summer.
MAINTENANCE Pinch back shoots as they grow to keep the plant compact. If shoots do get leggy, they can be layered as described below and left in place.
HARVESTING AND STORING Pick young fresh leaves throughout the summer. These can be dried in an airy spot (*see p. 240*), though they must be picked before flowering or the flavor will be impaired.

Layering sage *Weigh down some shoots into the soil. When new roots develop at the point of contact, cut the shoots away from the parent plant.*

Rosemary

There are several named varieties of this attractive evergreen shrub. It makes a fine plant for the border, where its aromatic blue flowers attract insects.

SOIL AND SITE Rosemary prefers a sunny location and well-drained soil enriched with organic matter. Lighten heavy soils by incorporating coarse sand (*see p. 16*).
PLANTING Plant container-grown plants at any time, setting them 2–3ft (60–90cm) apart. You can grow them from cuttings taken in early summer (*see p. 274*). Rosemary can also be used for hedging, in which case the individual plants should be spaced closer together, with 18in (45cm) between them.
MAINTENANCE Trim back the plants after flowering or the bushes will become leggy and will sprawl. Once they do, it is best to replace them.
HARVESTING AND STORING This evergreen plant will provide fresh leaves all year-round, so there is really no point in preserving them. However, if you don't want to waste the prunings, dry them in an airy place and crumble them into airtight jars (*see p. 240*).

Juniper

This shrubby conifer has silvery-gray foliage which is aromatic when crushed. It needs plenty of room in the garden, and both male and female plants are needed to produce berries. Juniper makes a good background for other plants and can be kept in check by clipping.
SOIL AND SITE A sunny location will give the berries a fuller flavor. The plant likes a soil pH of about 7.0, so add lime if necessary (*see p. 36*). A well-manured soil ensures rapid establishment.
SOWING AND PLANTING Sow seeds outside in late winter or plant young plants or softwood cuttings (*see p. 274*) in early summer.
MAINTENANCE Make sure the plants are weeded and fed with blood, fish, and bone meal in late winter. Clip them in late summer if necessary.
HARVESTING AND STORING Pick the berries when they are fully ripe, plump, and black. They can be frozen or dried on open trays at room temperature. It is important to dry them very slowly. When they are shriveled and have lost their moisture, store them in airtight jars.

Bay

Bay is a frost-tender tree, so can only be grown in the soil in warm areas. Elsewhere, grow it in a tub and bring it inside in winter. Bay resembles laurel, which is poisonous to eat, but it can be identified by its characteristic pungent smell, while laurel is practically odorless.

SOIL AND SITE Bay prefers a dry, semi-shaded location. If you grow plants in tubs, use the soil-based compost recommended on p. 252.
PLANTING You can buy trees in containers or plant softwood cuttings taken in early summer (*see p. 274*). One plant is all that is needed.
MAINTENANCE Make sure the trees have adequate water at all times. Bay trees can be left to grow naturally or clipped into various shapes. If you choose to train your trees, regularly pinch off the tips of shoots that grow out of place during the summer to maintain the shape of the head.
   Plants growing in tubs must be watered regularly. Let the top of the compost dry out before rewatering and never let the pots become waterlogged. Feed once a month during the summer with liquid manure. In areas affected by frost, bring the tubs in for the winter or, if you leave them outside, wrap the container in burlap and cover the top with a sheet of woven polypropylene.
HARVESTING AND STORING Pick fresh leaves during the summer. They can be dried in the sun and stored in airtight jars.

GREENHOUSE GARDENING

A GREENHOUSE is a very useful addition to any garden. The major advantage of owning one is that it enables you to sow and harvest crops months earlier than would otherwise be possible in temperate or cold areas. The growing season is therefore considerably extended, which makes it possible to increase annual yields substantially. Indeed, with careful planning, certain crops can be harvested continuously, and many frost-tender plants can be "overwintered"—kept in the greenhouse during the winter months to protect them from the cold. A greenhouse therefore turns the cultivation of plants into a year-round activity.

The warmth and light provided by the greenhouse also make it possible for you to raise a great many plants from seed. Their growth will be much stronger and healthier than any you manage to raise on a very sunny windowsill in the house, where no more than 50 percent of available light will actually reach the plants. By starting off young plants in the best possible environment, you can ensure that the seedlings are in peak condition when you plant them outside. Growing from seed allows you to choose any crop or variety you wish, rather than relying solely on the range of comparatively expensive young plants offered by a nursery. Provided you buy seed that has not been "dressed" with a fungicide, you can also be certain that your crops are completely untainted by chemicals.

A further benefit of greenhouse gardening is the opportunity of cultivating tender plants that can normally be grown outside only in subtropical or tropical conditions. This applies to many vegetable and fruit crops (*see pp. 132–197 and 202–231*) as well as exotic decorative plants. Even if you garden in a warm climate, the relatively high temperature provided by a greenhouse increases the range of plants you can grow. In addition, the quality and yield of some crops, such as tomatoes and eggplants, which can be grown outside in temperate climates, will improve if they are cultivated in the greenhouse where they are protected from adverse weather conditions.

Always allow for a greenhouse in your plan (*see pp. 72–73*) if you possibly can. The increased choice, quality, and quantity of the plants you can grow in a greenhouse more than repays the initial cost, and the space taken up could not be put to better use. Remember that it needs a sunny position and try to position it fairly close to the house, to make the connection of heating, water, and electricity supplies as easy as possible.

Choosing a greenhouse

Greenhouses come in an assortment of shapes, sizes, and materials. Of course, the appearance of the structure is important, but practicality should be the first consideration. There are many factors that will affect your choice, and it is difficult to lay down strict guidelines. For example, sunrooms (*see opposite*) are becoming increasingly popular. Despite the fact that they do not admit as much light as conventional greenhouses, and are therefore less efficient, they take up less space and are generally cheaper and more convenient to heat. Each person's priorities are different, so check the advantages and disadvantages of each greenhouse carefully before deciding which to buy.

SIZE
Even a tiny greenhouse can accommodate a large quantity of plants and produce, especially if you use it in conjunction with a cold frame or even with cloches (*see pp. 254 and 140*). Buy the biggest you can afford, or consider one designed to take additional sections at a later date because, in my experience, a greenhouse of any size will always be full. If you cannot heat it all, a large greenhouse can easily be divided.

GREENHOUSE SHAPES

There are many different shapes of greenhouses available, ranging from the traditional rectangular structure to a modern, multi-faceted dome. You must balance the aesthetic and practical advantages and disadvantages of each.

Whichever type you prefer, always ensure that the height to the eaves is sufficient to make working in the greenhouse comfortable, and that the design of the structure will not restrict the range of plants you wish to grow.

Traditional *The standard rectangular "barn" shape has four vertical sides and a span roof with a central ridge. It is a very popular and practical design and enables you to make the best possible use of the available space. The walls may be glass or timbered to staging level.*

Circular *Round or lantern-shaped greenhouses usually have six, nine, or twelve sides and are one of the most attractive designs. The working space inside is usually fairly limited, but they are very useful for small gardens.*

Sunrooms *Sunrooms, or "lean-to" greenhouses, also serve as an additional room in the house. Their location makes heating and regular plant care convenient, but means that light levels are reduced because light can only enter from three sides.*

MATERIALS

Greenhouse frames are usually made of aluminium or wood. Aluminium houses let in more light because the glazing bars can be thinner. This is important if you garden in a comparatively cold area where light levels are low in the early spring. Wooden houses are perhaps slightly cheaper to heat, because the wood itself is warmer, and they certainly look more attractive. However, the wood must be painted regularly to protect it against decay—unless you choose cedar, which is particularly weather-resistant. Never use creosote as a greenhouse preservative because it gives off fumes that are toxic to plants.

Although glass is the most commonly used material for the walls and roof, greenhouses can also be made from plastic sheeting stretched over metal hoops or a greenhouse-shaped frame. This is considerably cheaper than using glass, even though the plastic has to be replaced every couple of years.

VENTILATION

In order to maintain the best possible growing conditions, it is vital that the temperature inside the greenhouse can be accurately controlled. This is achieved by regulating the passage of air through vents in the roof or sides of the structure. Ensure that any house you choose has an adequate number of vents. A 6×8ft (2×2.5m) greenhouse should have at least two roof vents, and there should be proportionally more in larger houses. Plastic

greenhouses can be difficult to ventilate. The plastic generates a great deal of condensation, and it is impractical to install adjustable ventilation panels. Permanent ventilation has to be installed instead: plastic greenhouses up to about 10×25ft (3×8m) should have an open-mesh panel in the door; larger ones should have a mesh "skirt" running along the base of each side. This reduces condensation and allows the free passage of air in and out of the greenhouse. However, it also makes it impossible to control the temperature, so plastic greenhouses can only be used for crops that need no extra heating.

Using alternative materials *Plastic greenhouses have excellent light transmission qualities. They are usually reserved for crops that need no supplementary heating, but are valuable as "walk-in cloches" (see p.140). Although comparatively cheap, the plastic sheeting must be replaced regularly.*

THE GREENHOUSE

Whatever type of greenhouse you have, it will provide you with the space and environment to extend your gardening activities. Certain features will be included in the greenhouse you buy and others can be added, together with basic equipment, to enable you to get the best from it.

Shading Special compounds can be painted onto the outside of the glass in the summer.

Ventilation Panels in the roof and walls control greenhouse temperatures.

Insulation Sheets of insulated plastic can be used to help prevent heat loss.

Capillary mat Plants can be watered automatically using absorbent matting.

Blinds These protect against sun scorch in hot weather.

A permanent water supply Keep a tank of water inside the greenhouse, under the staging if space is limited. Refill it after watering each day, so the water is always at greenhouse temperature.

Measuring temperature A maximum/minimum thermometer has two small markers that are forced up or down by the movement of the mercury and record the highest and lowest temperatures reached during a specific period. The thermometer is reset so a daily record can be maintained. The difference between the two extremes should be kept as minimal as possible.

Propagator Seeds can be germinated in a specially heated container.

Watering can Use a rose attachment when watering delicate seedlings.

Greenhouse borders Many crops, such as lettuce, can be grown to maturity in the greenhouse borders.

Raising seedlings After germination, seedlings are grown in trays and pots on the greenhouse staging.

Storage space The space below the staging is used to store greenhouse equipment.

Hot bed Fresh straw horse manure is used as an organic means of heating the soil around plants growing in the borders.

Staging Many greenhouse plants are cultivated on waist-high benches made from wood or aluminium. These raise the plants up nearer to the light, ensuring healthy growth.

Heating A variety of permanent and portable systems are available.

Potting bench Use a portable bench for messy jobs such as repotting.

Growing bags A range of plants can be grown in self-contained beds.

MAKING YOUR OWN STAGING

Ready-made staging is often included in the price of a greenhouse, or it can be bought separately from most manufacturers. A cheap and easy alternative is to make your own.

1 *Using 3 × 2in (7.5 × 5cm) lumber, make a series of rectangular frames for the "legs." Cut the wood to convenient lengths and join them with steel bolts, as shown here.*

2 *Space the "legs" about 3ft (1m) apart and bolt long wooden rails to the back and front of each to secure them. The staging will have to support a lot of weight, so it is important to ensure the basic framework is strong.*

3 *Fix a sheet of corrugated metal or aluminium onto the base and cover this with a layer of sand, which can be kept moist, to supply the plants with water. Alternatively, make a lighter top with ⅛in (3mm) marine grade plywood and cover this with a sheet of capillary matting (see p. 255).*

WORK SURFACES

In large commercial greenhouses, the high light levels mean that plants can be grown satisfactorily on the floor. But in a small greenhouse, and especially one that has a wooden or brick wall around the base, plants must be lifted up toward the light to avoid leggy growth. The raised surfaces on which many greenhouse plants are grown are collectively known as "staging." This consists of aluminium or wood benches, about 3ft (1m) high, with a maximum width of 3ft (1m) (*see above*).

Heating a greenhouse

The amount of heat you are prepared to use in the greenhouse will determine the range of plants you can grow in it. Even in an unheated greenhouse, yields will always be considerably earlier and therefore often heavier than from plants grown outside. However, in temperate climates, frost-tender plants can only be kept in a "cold" greenhouse from four to six weeks before the last frost is expected.

If you decide to provide just enough heat to keep frost at bay, the greenhouse becomes much more of an asset. Half-hardy perennials like fuchsias and geraniums can be housed over the winter, and tender plants can be planted much earlier than would otherwise be possible.

You can, theoretically, grow tropical plants in even the coldest area—as long as you provide enough heat. However, in practice, this is likely to be prohibitively expensive.

CONTROLLING TEMPERATURES

When heating your greenhouse, it is vital to keep a check on the temperature. The important statistics to know are the minimum temperature at night and the maximum reached during the day. To grow plants well, the variation between the two figures should be no more than about 50°F (10°C). However, if left to its own devices, the daily temperature variation in a closed greenhouse can be up to 95°F (35°C) in the spring. Such a fluctuation can be disastrous for young seedlings, so use a maximum/minimum thermometer to record the daily extremes of temperature, and try—by careful ventilation (*see p. 247*) and heating adjustment—to even out the differences as much as possible.

Reducing heating costs

Unless you specialize in growing temperature-sensitive plants, it is not normally necessary to heat the greenhouse to high temperatures for more than a few months of the year. Even then, you will want to keep your costs as low as you can. Locate the house in a bright place so it can

METHODS OF HEATING

Connecting your greenhouse heating to a main supply is initially expensive but more economical in the long run than using portable heaters. Most modern heaters, whether permanent or portable, are controlled by thermostat so the temperature can be kept at a constant level.

Solid fuel
Various forms of solid fuel can be used to heat water pipes in the greenhouse. Coal, the most commonly used material, is cheap and efficient. However, it requires a considerable capital outlay for the boiler and the necessary piping. Frequent refueling is also necessary.

Gas
Heating with gas is more expensive than using solid fuel, but very convenient. It can either be bought in portable propane or butane gas cylinders or piped to the greenhouse via the normal household supply. Either way is efficient, since gas can be controlled with a thermostat and constant refueling is not necessary. However, it requires a fairly large capital outlay and can emit fumes harmful to plants.

Oil and paraffin
The cost of heating with oil is liable to fluctuate frequently. A small paraffin heater is lower in cost but controlling the thermostat is difficult and heaters can emit fumes harmful to plants. As with solid fuel, portable paraffin heaters require frequent refueling. The wick must be adjusted according to the weather conditions and trimmed regularly to avoid the emission of harmful fumes.

Electricity
Using electricity is now one of the cheapest options, and certainly the most convenient. The cost is not high and temperature control is very accurate (and therefore cost-effective). Portable fan or convection heaters keep the air in the greenhouse circulating well. Make sure the initial wiring of a permanent system is professionally installed because special waterproofing of the equipment is essential.

benefit from as much free solar heat as possible and, if you can also provide shelter from strong winds, do so. Inside the greenhouse, insulate to prevent heat loss and ensure you are heating the minimum area required.

USING A PROPAGATOR
A propagator helps reduce heating costs by restricting the area to which heat has to be supplied. Propagators are enclosed cases that contain some form of built-in heating element and are used for germinating seeds at the start of the season. You can buy them or make your own (*see below*). A small container will accommodate all the seeds required by most gardens, and a steady temperature of 65–70°F (18–21°C) can be provided to ensure rapid germination.

HEATING THE SOIL
Heating the roots of plants reduces the need to heat the air around them. Plants that grow in pots on the staging are usually heated from below, as heating is generally located low down, around the greenhouse walls, or on the floor. However, those plants that grow in the borders do not receive the benefit of the rising warm air. A simple way to overcome this is to install an electric soil-heating cable, which will warm the root areas directly (*see below*). Alternatively, you can make a hot bed (*see p. 253*).

Using a homemade propagator *This simple propagator is very efficient and cheap to run. The wooden case has been lined with heavy plastic and filled with expanded styrofoam granules to retain heat. It has a clear acrylic lid for maximum light transmission. One way of heating the propagator is with boiling water* (left). *Every morning and evening, the water is poured into a small can that stands inside a larger one in the center of the case. Alternatively, you can use an electric heating cable* (above). *This is installed in serpentine fashion between layers of styrofoam granules and connected to the main supply through a hole in the box. Electric cables can also be used to heat the soil in the greenhouse borders.*

USING PLASTIC INSIDE THE GREENHOUSE

Once the seedlings raised in the propagator are big enough to transfer to wider spacings in the trays, you need more room, though not usually the whole greenhouse. If you can manage with part of it, divide the greenhouse with a curtain of plastic sheeting so that you only need to heat a small area.

The roof and sides can be lined with plastic sheeting too, to keep in the heat. The best material to use is insulated packaging, which consists of thousands of air-filled bubbles, so it acts as a double insulator.

Plastic sheeting of any kind reduces the amount of light admitted to the greenhouse considerably. Unfortunately, the insulation it provides is needed at the time of year when the light levels are most critical. Young seedlings need all the light they can get, and in the early spring the levels are low. One way to overcome this problem is with a "thermal screen" (see below) that can be drawn at night to retain the heat when it is most needed, and pulled back to admit light during the day.

Insulating the greenhouse *You can cut heating costs by covering the inside of the greenhouse with insulated packaging, which is cheap and easy to use. Fix it to the greenhouse frame with staples or special clips, so that about 1in (2.5cm) of air is trapped between the plastic and the glass. Provided it is fitted correctly, insulated plastic insulation can cut heat loss by between 40 and 50 percent.*

MAKING A THERMAL SCREEN

Dividing a heated greenhouse with a plastic screen that can be moved back and forth enables you to provide maximum sunlight during the day and save money by cutting heat loss at night.

1 *Run a length of wire along either side of the greenhouse, about 12in (30cm) from the sides, and at the height of the eaves. The wire will have to bear the weight of the screen, so make sure it is attached securely to the frame of the greenhouse.*

2 *Measure the length and width of the greenhouse and cut a large sheet of plastic to the same size. Cut some thin pieces of wood slightly narrower than the greenhouse. Fix these across the plastic at regular intervals, using glue or tacks, and position the sheet so it rests on the wires.*

3 *Pull the thermal screen toward the door at night and push it back again first thing in the morning—as soon after sunrise as possible, to avoid wasting valuable daylight hours.*

Caring for greenhouse plants

Plants grown in the greenhouse have different requirements from those cultivated outside and will need much more attention. As well as providing adequate ventilation and heating (*see pp. 247 and 249*), you must feed and water regularly, decide on the most suitable growing medium, provide the necessary humidity, and keep the house clean (*see p. 255*) in order to discourage pests and diseases.

Choosing potting composts

A number of organic potting or seed composts are commercially available, either peat-free or peat mixed with animal manure, worm-worked material or kelp. It is difficult to advise on commercial composts because they vary greatly. Trial and error is the only possible way to evaluate them so, once you have found a compost that suits you and your plants, I recommend you stick with it.

MAKING PEAT-FREE POTTING COMPOSTS

As an alternative to commercial composts, it is very possible to make your own. I have grown perfectly good plants in peat-reduced as well as peat-free composts. To minimize the use of peat, mix it 50:50 with green compost and add 1oz (30g) of Dolomite lime (*see p. 36*) to every 2 gallons (9 liters) to balance out the acidity of the peat.

Remember that both contain little or no nutrients, so you must add the trace as well as the major elements. I find a combination of pelleted chicken manure mixed into the compost, with kelp liquid feed applied when required, does an admirable job.

Moisten the compost prior to sowing with a half-strength solution and use it in the same dilution at the seedling stage. After potting the young plants, change to full strength.

Alternatively you can make a worm-worked compost mixed with peat, or for peat-free use leaf mold mixed with vermiculite.

MAKING SOIL-BASED POTTING COMPOSTS

Many gardeners prefer to use a soil-based compost and there are certainly some advantages. Soil retains moisture longer than peat and is much easier to rewet if it does dry out. Most good garden soils also contain a certain quantity of trace elements. Use soil-based compost for plants grown in containers outside—where they tend to get forgotten and perhaps not watered as much as they need. Some plants, like chrysanthemums and fuchsias, seem to prefer the stability of loam-based composts. The problem is that not all garden soil is good enough. The loam must be fibrous and crumbly to be useful and this type is only obtained from freshly cultivated grassland or from stacked turf—so supplies are not always easy to come by. However, it is possible to make your own (*see below*).

For sowing, mix two parts of loam made from stacked turf (*see below*) with two parts of sphagnum peat and one part of coarse sand. To each 2 gallon (9 liter) bucketful, add 2oz (60g) of bone meal and 1oz (30g) of garden lime.

For potting, use seven parts of loam to three parts sphagnum peat and two of coarse sand. Add 1oz (30g) of garden lime and 5oz (150g) of blood, fish, and bone meal to every bucketful.

Repotting plants

When the roots of a plant completely fill its pot, the plant must be repotted into a slightly larger container. Do this in the spring or summer—never in the winter, when the plant is dormant. Plants should not be moved into pots very much larger than the one they are in because this simply surrounds the roots with a mass of cold, wet compost and is not conducive to root growth.

There is an easy way of repotting plants that prevents any damage to the root ball (*see opposite*). Water repotted plants and then leave them so the roots spread outward in search of water.

MAKING LOAM FOR POTTING COMPOST

Making a fibrous loam for soil-based potting compost is very simple. Use the space between and around rows of raspberries, soft-fruit bushes, or even apple trees. Sow this ground with grass and use it as a path for at least a year. Then strip off the grass with a 1in (2.5cm) layer of soil and stack it, grass side down, for a year. Replace the soil you remove with the once-used compost you throw out after the greenhouse crops have finished, and then resow it immediately with

grass. The process takes three years in all, so you need three plots to provide a succession.

I have never encountered any problems with my loam other than weeds, which are easily pulled by hand when they are very small. However, as a safeguard against soil-borne pests and diseases, you may choose to sterilize your loam. This can be done with an electric sterilizer or by heating in an ordinary oven to a temperature of 212°F (100°C) for 15 minutes.

MAKING A PLANT MOLD

The most convenient way of repotting plants is to pack fresh compost around the discarded pot, forming a mold into which the root ball of the plant will fit, without risk of being damaged.

1 *Put some compost into the new pot, to bring the top of the two pots level when the new one is placed inside. Remove the plant from its pot and place the empty pot in the center of the new one.*

2 *Fill the gap between the two pots with compost. Firm it down and remove the inner pot, leaving a mold. Drop the plant into the new pot, tap it on the bench to settle it, and water well.*

PLANT CONTAINERS

Many of the seedlings raised in the greenhouse are planted out in the garden, but others may be potted on into clay or plastic pots. Clay pots are porous and therefore "breathe" through the sides, giving a circulation of air around the roots. However, they also absorb moisture from the compost, so plants grown in clay pots may need more watering, and they tend to harbor more disease because they are difficult to clean thoroughly (*see p. 255*). I prefer to use clay pots for soil-based composts and plastic for peat-based and peat-free, because they dry out more quickly than soil. (*See also* Propagation, pp. 268–277).

MAKING A HOT BED

A hot bed heats the roots of plants by surrounding them with a horse manure mixture. It is a cheap, organic alternative to undersoil cable heating (*see p. 250*).

1 *Break up the border soil and stack a 9in (23cm) layer of fresh straw horse manure. Cover this with a 2in (5cm) layer of soil and a dusting of lime.*

2 *Add two more layers of manure, with a second layer of soil and lime between. The lime has the effect of neutralizing the acid manure.*

3 *Make a series of holes, and fill them with soil-based potting compost (see opposite). Cover the whole bed with a layer of soil.*

4 *Transplant young plants into the compost-filled holes. The manure warms the roots and gets the plants off to a good start.*

Growing plants in greenhouse borders

Provided the soil is well prepared, with plenty of organic matter added (*see p. 20*), the greenhouse border can be used to good effect.

There is a risk of encouraging the build-up of soil-borne pests and diseases if you grow the same crop year after year—tomatoes, for example, are especially at risk from root rot. However, there are several ways in which you can avoid this. One is to grow varieties that have inbred resistance to disease. Another is to dig out the border soil each year and replace it with fresh soil from the garden. This involves a lot of hard work, so you may prefer to wait until trouble strikes, which might not be for several years. Then, simply grow a different crop in the borders and plant your tomatoes in growing bags on the other side of the house (*see right*).

Homemade growing bags *A cheap alternative to buying commercially prepared growing bags is to fill old compost bags with worm-worked compost or animal manure. Tape up the end of the bag and cut holes in the top.*

THE COLD FRAME

A cold frame is an important piece of equipment, especially if you use the greenhouse to raise seedlings for planting outside.

If plants that have been raised in the warm, humid conditions of the greenhouse are put straight out in the open ground, their rate of growth will be considerably reduced. This is especially true in colder climates in the early spring. The plants need to be acclimatized gradually to lower temperatures and increased exposure, a process called "hardening off." The best way to do this is with a cold frame.

Most frames are comprised of a wooden, metal, or brick box with a glass lid. The simplest—which you can build yourself—is a wooden box with a sheet of rigid plastic over the top. For a large garden, one with larger glass panes supported on old railroad ties is a possibility. However, because all the plants in the cold frame must be at the same stage of hardening off, it may be more convenient to have two small frames than one large one.

Frames can also be used during the spring in colder climates to grow early vegetables of all kinds and crops such as melons. They also come in useful in the winter for growing vegetables that mature in spring, like lettuce.

Choosing a cold frame

The frame you choose must be deep enough to accommodate the range of plants you wish to grow and let in plenty of light. Various designs are available in wood, metal, and plastic.

Using the cold frame

1 *A week or so before they are due to be replanted, bring greenhouse seedlings outside and put them into a closed cold frame. Leave it closed for the first 24 hours. During the second day, open the top slightly to begin acclimatizing the plants but close it again at night.*

2 *Gradually increase the opening until the top is off completely during the day but is still almost closed at night. Then start opening the frame more at night until the top is removed completely. The plants are then fully acclimatized and ready to be planted outside.*

Feeding greenhouse plants

The base fertilizer contained in all composts will be used up by the plants within about eight weeks. This is because there is less soil life than outside to create and release nutrients (*see p. 38*), and because constant watering tends to wash away any nutrients that are present more quickly. Greenhouse plants must therefore be provided with additional food. Use either homemade animal-manure tea (*see p. 42*) or a commercial liquid kelp or animal-manure feed (*see p. 41*). I find kelp ideal for most purposes because it contains the full range of nutrients needed for healthy plant growth.

Intervals between feeds will vary according to the crop; these are covered under the separate entries (*see The Vegetable Garden, pp. 146–197 and The Fruit Garden, pp. 216–231*). Always be sure to use fertilizers at the recommended strength and frequency; overfeeding can do more damage to plants than underfeeding. Generally, plants that are expected to grow and produce fruit at the same time—like tomatoes and cucumbers—are more demanding than most pot plants. At the height of the growing season, these plants will need to be fed every time you water them.

Watering greenhouse plants

Plants that are grown inside rely on you for food and water, so you must be committed to giving them constant attention. In the summer the plants will need a lot of water, so install a hose that reaches inside the greenhouse and water them straight from the tap.

In the early spring, however, the water from the tap is likely to be much too cold for tender young seedlings. To avoid damaging the plants, fill the can after watering and leave it in the greenhouse so that the water has warmed to greenhouse temperature by watering time the next day. Better still, keep a tank inside the greenhouse and top it off with tap water as soon as the watering is finished.

Delicate young plants and seedlings must be sprayed with water using a fine mist to avoid damaging them. Use a hose with a plastic or brass nozzle or a can with a spout long enough to reach to the back of the bench. Always water in the morning rather than later in the day. Watering "little and often" is not a good idea; most greenhouse plants do better if they are given a thorough soaking and then left for a while before the next watering.

AUTOMATIC WATERING

An automatic watering system will save you a lot of time. There are many types available but, in my

▲ **Watering with capillary matting**
Stand potted plants on the mat and place one end in a container of water. The water is gradually drawn out to moisten the whole mat and the plants take it up as required.

◄ **Watering with a trickle irrigation system**
The main hose leading from the overhead tank rests flat on the staging. From it, lengths of narrow-gauge tubing, spaced at regular intervals, are fixed into each pot with staples. The system can also be used to water plants grown in the border soil.

experience, the simplest is just as efficient as the most expensive.

For pot plants, put a sheet of plastic over the staging area and cover it with a length of absorbent material known as a "capillary mat" (*see right*). If the mat is kept moist, the plants can absorb water whenever they need it.

Alternatively, install a trickle irrigation line to water the plants individually. These are available from garden centers and consist of a series of nozzles fed through tubes leading from a water tank above the staging. The tank must be refilled regularly or connected to the main supply through a valve and a ball cock. Trickle irrigation nozzles let a drop of water through at a slow but regular intervals, and can be adjusted to suit the requirements of the plants. They can be used for any greenhouse plants.

Maintaining a greenhouse

The environment inside the greenhouse must be routinely maintained to ensure the best possible growing conditions at all times. Controlling temperature and ventilation levels is very important (*see pp. 247 and 249*) but other factors must also be considered.

KEEPING THE GREENHOUSE CLEAN
By keeping the greenhouse spotlessly clean, you will discourage pests and diseases that might otherwise thrive in the warm, humid environment. Make sure you remove any plant debris in which pests and diseases may hide and, at the end of the season, wash the house thoroughly with warm, soapy water, brushing it into every corner. If you empty the house for the winter, leave it open for the frost to help sterilize it. Always keep the glass clean, as dirty panes reduce the amount of light available to the plants.

Before reusing pots or seed trays, wash them thoroughly in boiling water to kill any disease spores or insect eggs that may be lurking. Plastic pots and trays are much easier to clean.

PROVIDING HUMIDITY
Most plants grown under glass require a moist, humid atmosphere. This is achieved by wetting the paths, the staging, and often the plants themselves, early in the morning, a process known as "damping down." Sometimes it may be necessary to repeat this process in the afternoon, but leaves should only be moistened in shaded houses or on dull days to prevent sun-scorching. Use a fine mist sprayer when dampening foliage.

Shading greenhouse plants

In the early spring, you will need all the light you can get to produce strong, bushy plants but, in the summer the greenhouse must actually be shaded to reduce high light levels, which would otherwise scorch the plants and produce unacceptably high temperatures. The best method is to use roller blinds, which are simply pulled up or let down as required. A cheaper alternative is to paint the side of the house with a special shading material (*see opposite page*). Use one of the commercial shading paints as they are designed to stay on in wet weather but wipe off easily with a dry cloth when no longer needed. Homemade shading is often washed off by rain and has to be replaced regularly, or else it is almost impossible to remove at the end of the season.

Painting on shading materials *The cheapest way to shade greenhouse plants is by coating the exterior glass with a special white compound that reflects light. This can usually be mixed to various concentrations so you can provide light or heavy shading. The local climate and the nature of the plants you are growing will determine the appropriate strength of the shading.*

Using roller blinds *Slatted wooden blinds can be expensive but provide a permanent and controllable means of shading. They are best fitted on the outside of the greenhouse, as interior blinds are less effective at keeping down temperatures. Fabric or plastic blinds are cheaper, but liable to blow away in strong winds. Remove the blinds each winter and store them indoors.*

Deciding what to grow

To make the best use of your greenhouse, you should keep it full for the major part of the year—if not all year-round. To do this you must first decide on the range of plants you would like to raise and how much heat you are prepared to supply (*see p. 249*), bearing in mind the cost of heating the house. If you wish to cultivate exotic species, for instance, it is perfectly possible to do so but considerably more expensive than just using the house "cold" or slightly heated to overwinter frost-tender plants.

The greenhouse is particularly useful for raising fruit and vegetable plants for setting outside in the spring. The propagation of these is covered in *The Vegetable Garden* (*see pp. 132–201*) and *The Fruit Garden* (*see pp. 202–235*). Greenhouse plants are susceptible to the same range of pests and diseases (*see opposite*).

VEGETABLES

You can use the greenhouse to raise early crops of a range of vegetables, in exactly the way described for growing under cloches (*see p. 140*). It is generally possible to sow or plant a week or two earlier if the house is heated (*see below*). However, there is little point in starting too soon since light levels are low in midwinter and this will have a marked effect on growth. In any case, the cost of heating will make growing the vegetables uneconomic.

Of course, if you decide to heat the greenhouse for raising seedlings, and there is excess space, it is sensible to fill the borders with early vegetables. Some, like radishes and lettuce, can even be grown in pots. Grow them as described for cloches (*see p. 140*) but start them off in midwinter, or as soon as the heating is available.

Most vegetables are grown in unheated or slightly heated houses during the spring and summer and, in this way, early yields can be produced economically.

FRUIT

In cold areas the greenhouse can be used to produce high-quality, inexpensive fruit (*see pp. 202–231*) which could not otherwise be grown. Most permanent fruit plants occupy little space, being confined to a wall or to the end or roof of the house. Some, like grape vines, may exclude light, but only during the summer—when it is likely that the glass would be shaded anyway. A vine or a peach is certainly worth considering in most houses as the fruits will be far superior to those produced outside.

DECORATIVE PLANTS

Many flowering and foliage plants can be cheaply raised from seed and used either as houseplants or to decorate the greenhouse itself. In cold climates you can grow tropical plants that you would not otherwise be able to grow in the garden or bring on bedding plants for planting outside (*see* The Ornamental Garden, *pp. 74–125*). The range of possible plants is almost limitless and they will require no heat once the danger of heavy frosts has passed. Grow your plants in the peat-free compost fed with kelp, in worm-worked sowing and potting compost, or in the soil-based medium, depending on your preference (*see p. 252*). Feed them all with liquid kelp or animal manure while they are growing rapidly.

Greenhouse pests and diseases

Greenhouse pests can build up rapidly because the warmth and humidity that are necessary for healthy plant growth are also ideal for pests and diseases. Try to prevent attacks by vigilance and scrupulous cleanliness (*see p. 255*), removing any damaged plant material as soon as you see it. The following are general pests and diseases that attack a range of plants in the greenhouse. Specific problems are discussed in the relevant chapters (*see pp. 198–201 and 232–235*).

TREATING COMMON GREENHOUSE PROBLEMS

VINE WEEVILS
These small grubs, which have white bodies and brown heads, invade potting compost and eat the roots of many plants. Severely affected plants may keel over. **WHAT TO DO** Use nematodes or knock off all the compost and repot, ensuring all larvae have been removed.

APHIDS
These small green or black flies are one of the most common and troublesome of all garden pests (*see also p. 50*). Aphids weaken a wide range of plants by sucking the sap from their stems. They also transmit virus diseases (*see right*), and the sticky honeydew they secrete can attract sooty mold (*see p. 52*), which spoils the appearance of the host plant. **WHAT TO DO** There are certain flowers you can plant to attract hoverflies, which will eat the pests (*see Companion planting, p. 46*). Spray with pyrethrum or insecticidal soap in severe cases (*see p. 53*). Introduce their natural predator *Aphidius colemani*.

WHITEFLIES
Serious and persistent greenhouse pests, these small white flies weaken plants by sucking sap and are often found on the undersides of leaves (*see also p. 50*). **WHAT TO DO** The flies can be controlled with the parasitic wasp *Encarsia formosa* (*see Biological pest control, p. 52*). Alternatively, hang a grease-coated yellow card in the greenhouse. This attracts the flies and they stick to it. As a last resort, spray with insecticidal soap (*see p. 53*) at five-day intervals; do not spray if you have already introduced the *Encarsia* parasite.

LEAF MINERS
This pest burrows into leaves, making characteristic yellow tunnels that are clearly visible. **WHAT TO DO** Remove and destroy affected leaves as soon as you see them or squash the grubs by squeezing the leaf.

RED SPIDER MITES
Although invisible to the naked eye, these tiny pale green or red mites cover plants with webs and cause a fine mottling on leaves. **WHAT TO DO** They are only a problem in a dry atmosphere, so increase the humidity as a safeguard (*see p. 255*). If they persist, they can be controlled by encouraging the parasitic mite *Phytoseiulus persimilis* (*see Biological pest control, p. 52*). Deal with small infestations by spraying with insecticidal soap (*see p. 53*) three times at six-day intervals: the last spray must be at least a day prior to introducing *Phytoseiulus*.

SCALE INSECTS
These are small, disclike insects that cling tenaciously to leaves and stems, sucking sap and secreting honeydew. Affected plants are weakened and turn yellow, and their leaves drop. **WHAT TO DO** Introduce the natural predator *Metaphycus helvolus* as soon as you see them or scrape off the insects with a piece of wood (*see p. 52*).

BOTRYTIS
Also known as gray mold, this is a common fungus disease showing as a dirty white or gray-brown mold on leaves and stems. It affects plants both in the greenhouse and the garden (*see also p. 52*). **WHAT TO DO** It thrives in low temperatures and poor ventilation, so increase both. Remove and burn infected material immediately since it will not recover.

DAMPING OFF
Another fungus disease affecting seedlings, damping off shows as a blackened area at the base of the stem. Affected plants will topple over and die. **WHAT TO DO** Sow seeds more thinly, water less, and increase the temperature in the greenhouse. Sometimes, the disease is carried in the soil, which will need to be sterilized by heating to kill it. Watering with copper fungicide (*see p. 53*) will help prevent its spread.

MILDEW
Mildew is a white, powdery coating that forms on leaves, causing puckering and distortion (*see also p. 52*). **WHAT TO DO** Remove affected leaves immediately since they will not recover and will spread the disease to the rest of the crop. Mildew is more likely to attack when soil is dry, so make sure plants never go short of water. Spray with copper fungicide or dispersible sulfur in severe cases (*see p. 53*).

BLIGHT
Brown marks on leaves, and sometimes fruit, may well be caused by blight. These marks are likely to spread and can later turn black. **WHAT TO DO** Remove infected leaves immediately and, if the disease persists, spray with copper fungicide (*see p. 53*).

VIRUS DISEASES
Affecting tomatoes, cucumbers, and many other plants, virus diseases cause a variety of symptoms, among them yellow mottling of the leaves and a "ferny" appearance in young leaves. The leaves also wilt badly and appear to recover in the morning only to wilt again during the day. Affected plants lose vigor and the crop will be poor. Virus diseases are spread by insects, garden tools, or by hand. **WHAT TO DO** There is no cure, so dig up and burn all affected plants, and do not use them for propagation. If the disease strikes tomatoes, grow them in growing bags the following year or buy plants grafted onto the resistant KNVF rootstock.

LEAF MOLD
Thriving in poor ventilation and overcrowded conditions, leaf mold causes yellow spots and a brown mold to appear on leaves. **WHAT TO DO** Space plants further apart to give them more air and adjust greenhouse ventilation if necessary (*see p. 247*) if the condition persists.

BASIC TECHNIQUES

THE BASIC TECHNIQUES of practical organic gardening draw much from traditional methods. The spade, for example, which has been with us since Roman times, remains the very best tool for digging; gardeners have been controlling weeds with the hoe ever since men started to cultivate the soil, and it is still the most effective and beneficial method of weed control in the garden.

It would, however, be foolish to ignore some of the results of modern research and technology. It may be manufactured, and it is certainly not organic in origin, but I would not like to be without plastic sheeting in the garden. Neither would I choose to revert to tying with old-fashioned hemp string if it had to last more than one season; I would rather use long-lasting nylon twine.

So, the organic techniques of today should combine the best of modern technology with tried and tested traditional methods, without us having to sacrifice our valued organic standards. We owe a lot to the research carried out for commercial growers, but it would be ridiculous to copy their methods blindly because their requirements are very different.

Gardening is like many other types of activity, in that you need to have a basic core of information, perhaps gleaned from more experienced "old hands" or from books such as this, and, of course, the correct tools for the particular tasks you are undertaking. If you are new to gardening in general, or organic gardening in particular, you will almost certainly find that other gardeners are only too pleased to share their knowledge with you.

Choosing the right tools

If you are new to gardening, you might easily spend hundreds of dollars on a complete set of tools, or, by choosing the bare essentials, buy just what you need for relatively little money. Bear in mind, however, that buying anything but the best is not really a bargain. Cheap tools just don't last and, far worse than that, they make the work more difficult. So, if your budget is tight, buy slowly, one tool at a time, but buy the best quality you can afford. And, with all tools, but the fork

and the spade in particular, do not buy anything that is too large for you. You can do a lot more, much quicker, with a smaller fork that does not tire you out than with a larger one that you find difficult or awkward to use.

I have listed some of the more common tools below. Naturally there are many more that are useful, and many that are not. Beware of the "gimmicks" claimed to be indispensable: you can usually manage just as well without them.

Fork The digging fork is second only to the spade in usefulness in the garden, and invaluable for loosening the soil without inverting it. I have listed it first simply because, if you have no equipment at all, then you can use the fork in place of the spade for most digging jobs (and it will double as a rake, too). Buy a fork that is made of forged steel, fitted with a wooden or metal handle. Never buy a pressed steel fork, since it will bend and distort as soon as you put it under pressure.

Spade You will probably use a spade more than any other tool, so it is worth buying a really good one. Stainless steel spades are undoubtedly the best: soil, no matter how sticky, simply falls off the polished surface, making digging much easier. If you cannot afford stainless steel, buy a strong, forged steel spade and always keep it clean. Once this type of spade is broken in (when the blade becomes sharp and the corners rounded) digging is much easier. Buy the size to suit you.

LARGE TOOLS

Rakes Once again, forged steel rakes are the best. Those consisting of a metal strip with what look like nails driven through it tend to be awkward to use, as do rakes with more than about 12 teeth, unless you are very strong.

A spring-tine, or lawn, rake is useful for removing dead thatch from lawns in the spring and fall and for raking in grass seeds after sowing.

Hoes Ideally, you should have two hoes—a Dutch, or push, hoe and a swan-necked, or draw, hoe. Make sure the handles are long enough for you to work almost upright without straining your back.

With the Dutch hoe, you push it backward and forward while walking backward, thus avoiding treading the weeds back into the soil again. Use the swan-necked hoe for hoeing weeds that have grown too large to hoe any other way, for earthing-up vegetables, and making rows for sowing seeds.

A small "onion" hoe is ideal for working between closely planted items and particularly useful on deep beds. A wheel hoe is a great time saver and it is invaluable on larger vegetable plots, though you will have to space your plants to allow for its width (see p. 57). You would rarely use a wheel hoe in the ornamental garden because there is less space between plants.

Hollow-tined fork This is a useful tool for conditioning the lawn in the spring. It consists of a frame, attached to which are two or more tubes. When pushed into the lawn, a number of cores of soil are removed. You can fill these holes with gravel, sand, or compost to improve drainage or water retention.

Shovel A shovel is not simply a large spade: the blade is angled in a very different way in order to make shoveling much quicker and easier. Its main use is for mixing compost or shifting a lot of soil in a new garden. Buy a builder's shovel with a metal handle and, if you ever use it with concrete, wash off every bit of cement. In this way it should last you a lifetime

Rake

Spring-tine rake

Hollow-tined fork

Dutch hoe

Draw hoe

Onion hoe

Shovel

HAND TOOLS

Hand fork A small hand fork is not as useful as a trowel, but many gardeners use one for weeding and for smoothing over border soil to good effect.

Trowel Trowels are used extensively in the ornamental garden for planting and, to a lesser extent, in the vegetable garden. As with the spade, buy a stainless-steel one.

Hand fork

Trowel

CUTTING TOOLS

Knives A pocket knife is just about the most used tool in the garden. Buy one that fits comfortably into your pocket and make sure that you keep it sharp. Use a small silicon carbide sharpening stone to sharpen the edge of the blade regularly, especially if you use it for cutting string, or anything similar, which tends to blunt the knife blade extremely quickly.

If you are going to do any budding, you need a special knife with a notch at the bottom of the blade.

Pruning saw This is a useful tool for cutting branches too large for secateurs or shears to handle. The saw is slightly curved with a narrow blade to allow you to cut in restricted spaces.

Edging knife This is a half-moon-shaped tool for cutting out lawn edges. If you are the type of gardener who demands absolute precision, then it is essential. Personally, I have never used anything other than a spade for this job and the edges of my lawn look fine to me.

Pruning saw

Pocket knife

Budding knife

Edging knife

CUTTING TOOLS
(continued)

Secateurs There are two types of secateurs: the anvil type and the "parrot-bill" type. In my opinion they are both perfectly good for most pruning jobs and choice is largely a matter of personal preference. It is important, however, to ensure that you only use them on the size of wood they are designed for. Cutting branches that are too thick will damage them, and probably the branch being cut. For large fruit trees, you need a pair of long-handled pruners.

Shears You need two pairs of shears—a short-handled pair for cutting hedges, and a long-handled pair for trimming the lawn edges. Neat edges make a lot of difference to the look of a lawn and it is not easy with short-handled shears. It is worth buying expensive shears that will keep a good, sharp edge.

Anvil secateurs

Parrot-bill secateurs

Long-handled shears

Shears

WATERING EQUIPMENT

Watering can Buy the largest watering can you are able to carry comfortably, but remember that it will be a lot heavier when full of water. If you have a greenhouse, make sure the can has a long handle and spout so that you can water plants at the back of the staging. A fine nozzle for watering seedlings is essential.

Hose Watering the garden needs to be thorough, so a hose is an essential piece of equipment. Buy the more expensive type that does not easily kink.

Ideally you should store your hose on a reel—preferably a through-feed type, which allows you to unroll just enough hose for your needs.

You may also find a seep hose useful. This slowly drips water along its length and you can leave it permanently in position underneath plastic mulches and simply turn it on whenever necessary (*see p.58*).

Sprinkler A sprinkler is essential because you can never get enough water on the garden if you have to stand and hold a hose.

Choose one with a fine spray pattern and one that has the sprinkler head mounted on a tall stand so that it is held well above the ground. In some areas, a license is needed for both the hose and the sprinkler.

Sprayer Although, as an organic gardener, you should always consider spraying a last resort, from time to time it will be necessary. If you buy a sprayer that breaks up the solution into small droplets and deposits it evenly, you need fewer chemicals.

Watering can

Hose

Seep hose

Sprayer

Sprinkler

HOMEMADE TOOLS

Sieve A sieve with a $1/16$in (1.5mm) mesh is necessary for sprinkling a fine layer of compost over seeds after sowing. It is not expensive to make your own sieve; all you need to do is nail a piece of plastic mesh onto a square or circular frame.

Planting board A planting board is simple to make and it is invaluable for the accurate spacing of plants. It should be about 10ft (3m) long, made from 3×1in (8×2.5cm) wood with a sawcut every 3in (8cm). Mark each 12in (30cm) division with an appropriate number of nails. If you grow vegetables on deep beds (*see p. 136*), make a 4ft (1.25m) board as well. Mark this board with 6in (15cm) divisions.

Garden line Used for marking lines for drawing seed rows and marking off areas of soil for digging. It consists of two sticks, or pegs, and a length of thick nylon string. Always make at least two garden lines.

Dibber Used to transplant seedlings, you can make your own using a broken spade or fork handle. Cut it to 12in (30cm) and shave the end to a point.

Sieve

Garden line

Planting board

Dibber

HOMEMADE TOOLS *(continued)*

Tool cleaner Cut a piece of wood to a spade shape and use it regularly when digging to remove any dirt sticking to the blade. It makes all the difference, especially when working heavy soil. Use it to clean all your tools before putting them away at the end of the day.

Firming board A firming board is a 1/2in (1cm) thick piece of wood cut slightly smaller than your seed trays with a handle screwed to one side. It is invaluable for leveling off compost when filling the trays and for firming down compost evenly prior to sowing. Make one to fit each tray size.

Tool cleaner

Firming board

CONTAINERS

Buckets Buy plastic rather than metal buckets; they are lighter to carry when full and last longer. All the "bucketful" measurements given in the book are based on a 2 gallon (9 liter) bucket.

Wheelbarrow The best type is a builder's wheelbarrow—which is often cheaper to buy from a home improvement store than a garden center. Choose the type with a pneumatic tire—it makes all the difference when wheeling a heavy wheelbarrow over rough ground. If you ever use it with concrete, make sure you wash off every bit of cement afterward.

Wheelbarrow

Bucket

Choosing garden equipment

Power tools can be a great help to the gardener, saving many hours of repetitive and exhausting work. They can, however, be expensive.

If equipment, such as a lawn mower or hedge trimmer, is likely to be used on a regular basis, then its purchase is easily justified. If, however, you have only an occasional need for equipment, such as a rotary cultivator, then, unless you have an enormous garden, it is better to rent it. Make sure when renting equipment that it comes with full instructions, with all safety features fitted, and that it is fully operational.

Mowers There are two main types: a cylinder mower and a rotary grass cutter. A cylinder mower will generally produce a better finish than a rotary mower. Choose one with as many blades on the cylinder as possible.

Rotary mowers perform well if you have areas of tall grass. You can use them on closer-cut lawns but they will not give a very fine finish.

You can buy gas- or electric-powered mowers. Some gasoline engines even have electric starters. Electric mowers are cheap to buy and easy to use, but you will need to drag a length of cord behind you, which can be a real disadvantage in a large garden. They are very safe to use since the machines are double insulated. It is advisable, though, to fit a device that instantly cuts off the power if you

Cylinder mower

Rotary mower

accidentally cut through the cord or if there is any other kind of electrical issue.

Rotary cultivator A rotary cultivator is invaluable in a very large garden: you can make a very fine seedbed in half the time it takes to dig one by hand, and it is extremely useful for incorporating green manure, compost and other organic matter into the soil. However, you must hand dig at least part of your garden every year because constant rotary cultivating can "glaze" the soil, creating an impermeable layer; most machines cultivate down to about 6in (15cm) and rarely deeper than about 9in (23cm).

There are various types of rotary cultivator. Those that are driven through their wheels and have the blades at the back of the machine are easiest to use and the most controllable. Unfortunately, they also tend to be expensive.

Wheel-driven cultivator

Much cheaper are the models that are driven forward solely by the rotor blades. This type can be difficult to control, particularly on hard ground, because it may tend to get away from you. However, once you learn to push the rear skid into the ground instead of pulling back on the handles when it accelerates, it is not hard to use.

Blade-driven cultivator

String trimmer

Hedge trimmer

String trimmer A fairly recent development is the nylon-line trimmer. A short length of strong nylon line turns at high speed and cuts grass without danger of anything more substantial being damaged. This enables you to use them right up to walls or trees. String trimmers are available with gas engines, electrically driven, or with rechargeable batteries.

Hedge trimmer This is useful if you have a large area of hedging to keep under control. Once you become accustomed to it, it can do almost as good a job as hand shears—but not quite. Hedge trimmers are available as models with rechargeable batteries, electrically driven, or with gas engines.

Shredder

Shredder This is an electrically- or gasoline-driven machine capable of shredding woody material extremely finely. It takes all the prunings from the garden that would otherwise only be burned. The resulting material is excellent for mulching and is a cheap alternative to chipped or composted bark (*see p. 59*). The machines are expensive but useful.

Cultivation techniques

If you have difficult soil, either in a new garden or in your existing plot, and poor drainage seems to be responsible, then there is much you can do to alleviate the problem. You can improve dramatically the condition of your soil by adopting the correct cultivation techniques and by the addition of plenty of organic matter and free-draining material. Soil management for the five main soil types is described in more detail in *The Soil* (*see pp. 15–17*).

Improving drainage

Badly drained soil can be a problem. But gardeners are often unrealistic about the subject of drainage. There is a great deal you can do to improve the soil drainage by digging and incorporating organic matter and sand. In some areas it is also possible to install a drainage system. However, there is no point in digging out and laying an elaborate system of drainage pipes unless you have somewhere to drain the water to. It is sometimes suggested that you dig a soakaway in one corner of the garden. This is a hole filled with gravel or other drainage material that will, in theory, absorb excess water from your land. In fact, a soakaway can only take so much water and, once it is full, you are back to square one again.

The only possible way that a drainage system can be effective is if you are lucky enough to have a drainage ditch near the garden into which water can be drained and subsequently removed. It is sometimes possible to obtain permission from local authorities to run your drainage system into the public storm drains, but make sure you inquire *before* you start laying your drains.

INSTALLING A DRAINAGE SYSTEM

If you have an outlet for the water, a herringbone system of drains is ideal (*see right*). The distance between the "arms" of the system will vary according to the soil—constantly wet soil needs the arms closer together than soil that has only a mild problem. On an average, 8–10ft (2.5–3m) between arms is ideal.

Fill the arms with twiggy material or, better yet, earthenware or perforated plastic pipes, available from agricultural supply companies, then cover them with soil. Plastic pipes are no cheaper than the earthenware ones, but they are much easier to lay—just roll them out into the trenches. On land that lies very wet, this kind of effort will be amply rewarded. However, in reality, it is rarely necessary to go to these lengths.

Herringbone pattern drains *Dig a series of trenches, about 18in (45cm) deep, that slope gently toward the outlet. Put a 6in (15cm) layer of stones or twiggy material in the bottom of each, then refill the remaining 12in (30cm) with soil. Better still, lay tile drains (short lengths of pipe) on a bed of gravel to form a continuous run. Cover the pipes with about 4in (10cm) of gravel and then refill the trench with soil. The water seeps in through the spaces left between the pipes.*

COMPACTED AND HEAVY SOIL

The most common reason for badly drained soil is that there is an impervious layer of compacted soil beneath the surface. This is often caused during the building of a house. Immediately after construction, the builder covers compacted soil with extra soil, unfortunately often subsoil, which is guaranteed to cause wet conditions. You can usually solve the problem by digging to break up the compacted layer.

Sometimes the impervious layer is caused by constant plowing to the same depth, so if you have a new house built on land that was farmed, dig deeply to investigate any hard layer of soil that might be present.

If, however, the problem is simply one of heavy soil, you can generally overcome this simply by using the correct cultivation methods without resorting to complicated drainage systems. Dig deeply, incorporating gravel and lots of organic matter, to raise the areas that will be cultivated. It is difficult to be precise because each piece of land requires slightly different amounts, but one or two bucketfuls each of gravel and organic matter per square yard/meter should be sufficient. Improvement will take some time to bring about, but just growing plants on heavy soil helps improve drainage by opening up the soil (*see pp. 15–16*).

In the ornamental garden, if you raise the flower borders, your lawn will be at risk of constant dampness. To counter this, put down a 6in (15cm) layer of ash or gravel below the topsoil before sowing or laying turf for a new lawn.

Digging

Hand digging is the main method of cultivating the soil: it breaks up compacted land, introduces air, and allows water to drain away and roots to penetrate. It also enables you to work organic matter into the lower levels, increasing the depth of the topsoil. Prepare all new ground by double

digging, then single dig every year in the fall for heavy soils and in spring for light soils (*see next page*).

DIGGING HEAVY SOILS

It is best if you dig heavy soils in the fall, before the worst of the winter rains makes cultivation difficult. Choose your timing carefully, when the soil is neither too dry and hard nor too wet and sticky. If necessary, cover an area of soil with heavy plastic to keep it dry.

When digging heavy soils in the winter, throw the spadefuls forward, leaving them rough and unbroken for the winter. This leaves the maximum amount of soil surface exposed to the drying winds and to the frosts. By the spring, the weather will have broken the surface down to a fine tillage that you will only have to rake to make suitable for sowing. Leaving the soil rough over winter also allows heavy rains and frost to kill weeds and pests, as well as making them more accessible to birds and other predators.

DIGGING LIGHT SOILS

Sandy and chalky soils will crumble to a fine tillage more readily than heavy soils. The problem with light soils is that they drain easily, causing leaching of the nutrients. To minimize this, keep the ground covered for the winter by sowing a green-manure crop in the fall and digging it in a short time before sowing.

BASIC RULES OF DIGGING

Digging can cause severe back strain or it can be a healthy, invigorating, and enjoyable exercise—it all depends on using your common sense.

- Never dig when the soil is wet enough to stick to your boots—you risk spoiling its structure.
- Start by using a spade and fork that are the correct size for you. You gain nothing by using oversized tools, which simply tire you quickly and slow you down.
- Never take spadefuls that are too big to handle comfortably. By taking smaller amounts, and not straining yourself, you can dig more for longer.
- Always take your time: there is no point in rushing. Adopt a rhythmic and methodical approach to digging, being conscious all the time of avoiding strain. As soon as you feel you have had enough or you begin to find it difficult to straighten up—stop! It is at this stage that you are likely to hurt yourself. Above all, don't try to do all the digging at once. Leave plenty of time so that you can do it in stages.
- Finally, keep your tools in good, clean condition. Carry a scraper in your pocket and use it regularly to clean soil from your tools. When you finish, clean the tools thoroughly and rub them over with an oily cloth to prevent rust.

DOUBLE AND SINGLE DIGGING

You should double dig all new ornamental borders before planting to work organic matter to the lower levels of soil. The vegetable plot also benefits from initial double digging and, subsequently, you should double dig at intervals of about five years, depending on soil type.

The best way to achieve this is by digging a least one-fifth of your land each year, on a rotation basis.

With single digging it is only necessary to dig one spade deep and incorporate one layer of manure; and so there is no need to mark out trenches as carefully as for double digging.

Double digging

1 Mark out the plot to be dug by setting up lines down either side. If it is a wide plot, divide it down the middle as well. Cut two 2ft (60cm) stakes to mark the width of the trenches. Make each trench exactly the same size so you refill each one with the same amount of soil as you have taken out.

2 Mark out the first 2ft (60cm) trench with the stakes and dig out all the soil to the depth of the spade, putting it in a wheelbarrow. Take it to the other end of the plot, so it can be used to refill the last trench. If you are digging a wide plot divided into two halves, put the soil at the start of the other half.

3 Clean out the clumps of soil from the bottom of the trench and then "fork" the soil to the depth of the fork. This is the subsoil and should not be inverted. Simply loosen it by digging it up and throwing it back in as it came out.

4 Put a 2–3in (5–8cm) layer of organic matter in the bottom of the trench. Then, leaving one stake in the corner of the trench you have dug out, mark out the second trench, to the same size, with the other stake.

5 Start digging out the new trench to the same depth, but throw the soil forward to cover the organic matter in the first trench. Spread another layer of organic matter in the first trench and cover it with the remaining soil from the second trench. This will raise the bed.

6 Keep working down the plot in this way and, when you get to the last trench, refill it with the soil you removed from the first trench. Cover the entire area with another layer of organic matter. It will soon be washed into the bed by the rain.

Single digging

1 Dig out the first trench one spade deep, taking no more than 4in (10cm) "bites." Throw all the soil behind you, spreading it out more or less evenly over the surface of the bed.

2 Spread a layer of manure over the soil about 1 yard/meter behind you; there should be enough to fill up to three trenches with a 2–3in (5–8cm) layer of manure. Then, scrape some forward into the bottom of the first trench.

3 Dig a second trench, throwing the soil forward to cover the organic matter in the first trench. Continue the process until all the organic matter has been covered. Then spread another layer further down the plot and continue.

REMOVING WEEDS

Whenever you are digging, you should put any perennial weeds in a bucket and then burn them or throw them away. Annual weeds can go in the bottom of the trenches to add to the organic content of the soil. It is sometimes suggested that you can scrape annual weeds off the soil surface with a spade before starting to dig. In my experience, however, there are always a few perennials mixed with them and they can be difficult to recognize without their foliage. Thus, it is best to remove them by hand as you dig.

Raking

The soil must be raked level before you can start sowing. This is a technique that can be learned only through experience. There are a few basic rules. First, choose a rake that suits your body size; a large-headed rake in the hands of a small person will be difficult to control.

Second, try not to lunge forward with the rake, pulling back soil from some way away; it will result in a wavy, uneven surface. Instead, reach forward no more than about 12in (30cm) and keep the head of the rake nearly parallel to the surface of the soil.

Finally, take time to step back now and then, squat down and squint across the soil surface, looking for any high and low spots in the soil.

Hoeing

This is the principal organic method of weed control. There really is no need to resort to chemicals to keep your garden weed free.

Always hoe *before* it is necessary to do so. If you have perennial weeds, for example, cutting off their shoots below ground level, so depriving them of light, eventually starves them into submission. Annual weeds are not so much of a problem. Hoe them out when they are very small—no larger than about ¹⁄₂in (13mm)—and certainly don't let them flower or seed.

Choose a hot, sunny day for hoeing. That way the weeds will lie on the surface where their roots will soon become dried out and die, returning their organic matter to the soil. If hot days are too infrequent, try to rake off as much of the weed as you can, then use a Dutch hoe to pull the root. Walk backward to avoid walking on the hoed weeds and effectively transplanting them (*see also* Organic Weed Control, *p. 57*).

Mulching

This is a technique that involves covering the surface of the soil—either with organic matter to condition the soil, or with plastic sheeting or paper to inhibit weed growth. Mulching with well-rotted manure or compost in the spring is more important than most

people realize. In an organic garden, the regular addition of bulky organic matter is essential. A 2–3in (5–7.5cm) layer helps to retain moisture in the soil by preventing evaporation, and it can also help to control weeds, (*see p. 58*). The compost or manure adds vital nutrients and will eventually be incorporated into the soil by the action of the weather and soil organisms. In addition, it will help to prevent "capping"—the formation of a crust on the soil surface that stops rain from entering and restricts the natural air flow.

MULCHING WITH ORGANIC MATERIAL TO CONDITION THE SOIL

You can use any organic material. Manure is ideal, but it must be well rotted or it can scorch young shoots; even well-rotted manure should be kept away from direct contact with foliage.

Coir can be used as a soil conditioner, but is quite expensive, while composted bark is even more costly. Grass cuttings are the most convenient, but look rather conspicuous until they have rotted down to a dark brown color. Never put grass cuttings on too thickly or they will rot down into a slimy mass.

Peat has often been used as a soil conditioner, but should not be the organic gardener's first choice due to the environmental damage caused by extracting it.

You will find more information about the nutrient values of organic materials in *Soil Improvement* (*see pp. 18–34*). All organic mulches, with the exception of bark, improve conditions for slugs and other soil pests, so take steps to prevent them (*see pp. 49–50*).

MULCHING WITH POLYETHYLENE, PAPER, OR GRAVEL

Polyethylene mulches add nothing to the soil and paper only a very small amount. They are, however, perfect weed controllers and minimize water loss through evaporation. They have the added advantage of keeping low-growing fruits clean by preventing soil splashing.

Either lay these materials between rows of crops, holding them down at the edges with stones or with piles of soil, or cover the ground completely, burying the edges in a shallow trench, and plant through slits in the material. Areas over about 4ft (1.2m) wide must have a process for providing water; so lay a length of seep hose on the ground before laying the polyethylene.

In the ornamental garden, you could consider a permanent mulch of gravel. It will have excellent water retention and inhibit weed growth and, in the right setting, it looks extremely attractive. It adds nothing to the soil and you should not use it where regular surface dressing with organic matter is needed.

Watering plants

All plants require adequate supplies of water, and there are always occasions when it is necessary to water artificially. However, watering is not simply a matter of pouring water on to the soil. This can, in fact, do more harm than good.

First, never add water in small amounts. It is essential to apply enough to get right down to the root zone where it is needed. Otherwise, roots will come to the surface in search of the water, and there they will be even more vulnerable to the effects of heat and lack of moisture.

Second, although large quantities of water are required, you must apply it carefully. Water applied in the form of large droplets or with great force will cause the soil "crumbs" to break down and form a hard surface crust. This prevents further water from entering the soil and it also inhibits the free interchange of air and gases, with disastrous effects. On a seedbed, this crust can actually stop the tender young seedlings from pushing through the soil to the surface. To prevent this from occurring, apply water through a sprinkler with a fine spray pattern of small droplets. When watering seed trays, use a watering can fitted with a fine nozzle. Start pouring the water to one side of the tray or pot, then pass the can over the seedlings, keeping the angle of the nozzle constant throughout. When you have finished, do not raise the can until it is clear of the tray or pot.

The size of droplets is not as important where the soil is covered with grass, so lawn sprinklers are not generally made with such attention to optimum droplet size. Consequently, if you want to buy only one sprinkler, buy one with a fine spray; it will be perfectly suitable for the lawn as well as the seedbeds.

WHEN TO WATER

It is not necessary to keep the soil moist all the time—water when the soil is dry, but before the plants begin to suffer—and, provided you use a fine sprinkler, you can water at any time of day. However, timing is important. For example, watering when fruits or vegetables are swelling will greatly increase their overall weight. Once fruits, in particular, begin to color, though, extra water could invite a fungus attack, especially from botrytis (see p. 52).

HOW MUCH WATER TO GIVE

It is, of course, not difficult to overwater, especially with plants in pots. Try to strike a balance between an aerated soil or compost and one with sufficient moisture. A cold, wet, airless compost will not do anything to encourage plant growth. If you are watering in the ornamental or vegetable garden, leave the sprinkler on for at least an hour each time.

WATERING NEW PLANTS

When you have just put in a plant, encourage it to search for water, thus increasing its root system. Water it thoroughly immediately after planting, then leave it to its own devices for a while, almost allowing the soil to dry out, before watering the plant again.

Supporting plants

Plants need supporting for a variety of reasons. New trees and shrubs, for example, must have their roots firmly anchored to stop them from moving in the soil and breaking young roots. Trained fruit trees must be tied in at regular intervals, and so you need a framework to fix them to. Some naturally climbing plants need an artificial support or can be allowed to grow through trees and shrubs, while climbing vegetables must be provided with a framework. Tall herbaceous plants may also need support to stop them from flopping over in the borders.

TREE STAKES

Newly planted young trees must be supported with a stake no more than one-third the length of the stem. If the tree is bare rooted, a single stake driven into the planting hole before planting is enough. Make sure that the stake is thicker than the tree and that you drive it into the soil to a depth of at least 18in (45cm). Container-grown trees are best supported with a stake on either side of the root ball, with a crossbar nailed to them (see pp. 82–83).

As the stakes will not be permanent, there is no need to treat them with preservative and they should be left in the ground until they rot. In both cases, fix the tree to the stake with a plastic tree-tie, nailed to the stake to prevent slippage.

SUPPORTING TRAINED TREES

Trained fruit trees and bushes—cordons, fans, and espaliers—will need support throughout their lives. Because the support is permanent, use pressure-treated lumber or metal stakes. Use 8ft (2.5m) stakes, 3in (7.5cm) in diameter, or 2in (5cm) angle irons, and drive them at least 18in (45cm) into the ground, about 10ft (3m) apart. The end stakes need angled struts secured to the lower half. Galvanized wires are then fixed horizontally between the posts at various intervals; the distance depends on the method of training (*see pp. 206–209*).

Start by straining the top wire and work downward, since there is more leverage at the top of the stake. If you work the other way around, you will slacken the wires already in place. If you have a lot to do, it is worth hiring a professional. Fix the wires to the stakes with staples or simply twist them around. Trees should not be tied directly to the wires because the wires will rub against the bark. Instead, tie stakes to the wires and the plants to the stakes. It is also possible to train fruit trees along wires by a wall or fence (*see also pp. 206–209*).

SUPPORTING HERBACEOUS PLANTS
Many herbaceous plants, such as poppies, have weak stems and need to be supported. The best technique is to install the support before the plant starts to grow too tall, and allow it to grow through. There are special wire frames for this purpose or you could use old wide-mesh wire netting or even thin twigs bent over at the top. Tall herbaceous plants, such as delphiniums and dahlias, will need the support of single stakes or posts. Tie them in regularly with soft string as they grow.

Alternatively, you can support climbers on a wooden archway, or "pergola," or on a single pillar of stout, pressure-treated lumber. You must drive the stakes at least 18in (45cm) into the ground, so buy lumber of an adequate length. Tie the plants to the uprights loosely, using soft string (*see p. 114*).

SUPPORTING VEGETABLES
In the vegetable garden, the main methods of support are stakes, strings, and netting.

The best way to support beans is with a double row of 8ft (2.5m) bamboo canes pushed about 12in (30cm) into the ground. Set them 12in (30cm) apart in the row, making two rows with 2ft (60cm) between them. Tie the canes so that they meet in the middle of the row and tie a cross cane in the V at the top to provide support and rigidity. A cheaper way is to set two strong 2×2in (5×5cm) posts about 8ft (2.5m) tall at least 18in (45cm) into the ground, one at each end of the row. Then run a wire or strong nylon twine from post to post at the top and another about 12in (30cm) from the ground. Next, tie vertical strands of nylon twine at 12in (30cm) intervals from wire to wire.

You can also train beans, cucumbers, and melons onto "cane" wigwams. You need four 8ft (2.5m) canes. Put them in the ground to form a 36in (90cm) square and then tie them together at the top. Plant at the base of the canes and tie in cucumbers or melons at regular intervals; beans will wind themselves around the canes naturally.

SUPPORTING PLANTS AGAINST WALLS

Climbing plants can be trained up a wooden or plastic trellis fixed to the wall and supported on wooden battens; ensure that there is a space between the trellis and the wall to allow for tying. Alternatively, you can use galvanized wires tied to vine eyes and spaced horizontally at 12in (30cm) intervals. For twining climbers, such as clematis or honeysuckle (*Lonicera* sp.), attach vertical wires, also about 12in (30cm) apart to form a mesh pattern. Train fruit trees by fixing the wires at the required heights and the canes to the wires to prevent chafing.

Wooden or plastic trellis *This can be screwed to wooden battens fixed onto the wall, so a gap is left to enable the plants to be tied in. The trellis itself is more decorative than a wire support.*

Vine eyes and wall ties
These are used to secure wire supports to a brick or stone wall and ensure that there is a gap between the wall and the wire. Vine eyes are small, flat steel tags with a hole at one end; wall ties are nails with a "tie" at one end. Both can be knocked into the wall very easily and do not damage the mortar. Use brass eyes if the mortar is crumbly.

Horizontal wires
These can be fixed to the wall about every 12in (30cm) to help support climbing plants; tie the shoots into them as they grow. Twining plants may need a few vertical wires as well. Fix these at the same spacings to make a wide mesh.

PROPAGATION TECHNIQUES

THE MODERN TREND is toward "convenience gardening," and a whole industry has developed to service this market. Instead of raising plants from seed and cuttings, for example, we are generally encouraged to buy young plants from the garden center or nursery—all we have to do is plant them.

For the organic gardener, however, there are some very good reasons why this "convenience" method is not good enough. First and foremost, if you are interested enough to adopt an organic approach to gardening, it is likely that you will want to do the whole thing from start to finish. Second, it can be difficult to find plants that have been raised organically—very few commercial growers can guarantee that their produce has been raised in organic compost without the "benefit" of chemical sprays or fertilizers. So, as an organic gardener you have no alternative but to raise all your plants yourself.

By following a few simple rules and taking sensible precautions, your success rate with home-raised seed, even using the minimum of equipment, will be gratifying; and by using other methods of propagation, such as division, cuttings, layering, budding, and grafting, you can make sure of a constant and inexpensive supply of organically raised plants for the entire garden.

Growing from seed

The best way to ensure that everything in your garden has been cultivated organically is to grow as much as possible from seed. Either sow directly into your garden, or start seeds in the greenhouse. Prepare the soil well for sowing outside and use a good compost if you are sowing in containers (*see p. 252*).

Sowing outside

The cheapest method of raising plants is by sowing seeds directly into prepared soil. This is the method you should adopt for most vegetables, hardy annuals, and many herbaceous perennials. You can raise some trees this way but, since you need only a few, it is better to sow them in pots or boxes and plant them later.

SOIL PREPARATION

Normal, organic methods of soil preparation will produce a good, workable structure. Rake the soil down to make it level and then sprinkle fertilizer over the top at the recommended rate. A firm bed is usually required so, if your soil has been recently cultivated, compress it by walking over the surface with your weight on your heels. Next, rake the soil down to a fine tillage. Never do this when the soil is wet enough to stick to your boots; you risk destroying the soil structure.

On deep beds, this consolidation is unnecessary and, really, you should never tread on the beds. Instead, leave them for three or four weeks after digging so the soil has a chance to settle.

WHEN TO SOW

The correct time to sow seeds varies from one plant to another and is normally shown on the back of the seed packet. I have given sowing times for different plants throughout the book where relevant. There is, however, no point in sowing too early. As a general rule, seeds sown in soil with a temperature below 45°F (7°C) will not germinate until the soil warms up. Seeds sown in mid-spring will often germinate at the same time as, or even before, seeds sown in cold, wet soil. There are, of course, exceptions to this rule. Some alpine seeds, for example, and some trees require a period of freezing weather before they will germinate.

By sowing seeds under cloches you can start sowing outside in early spring. Place the cloches in position two weeks or so before sowing in order to warm the soil up (*see p. 140*).

ENCOURAGING SEEDS TO GERMINATE

Some seeds have extremely hard coats. They germinate more successfully if you soak them overnight in water. Very hard seeds can first be filed with a nail file to assist the entry of the water into the seed coat.

Other seeds, such as beets, have a natural germination inhibitor within the seed coat to ensure premature germination does not take place. To speed up germination, remove the inhibitor by washing the seeds under the cold tap or by soaking them in water overnight.

DEPTH AND DISTANCE TO SOW

There is no doubt that the main cause of seeds failing to germinate is that they are sown too deeply. Seeds have a reserve of food that will enable the shoot to reach the surface and find the light. Until it does this, it cannot manufacture any more food. So, if the seed's reserve runs out before the shoot reaches the surface, the seedling will never appear. Of course, it is nonsense to suggest sowing seeds ¼in (6mm) deep or less, since it is impossible to be that accurate when working with soil. I suggest making "shallow" rows, which means making a furrow as shallow as you can.

It is also important to space the seeds and rows correctly to avoid overcrowding. Some seeds can be thinned and transplanted later, others, such as those of root crops, will "fork" if transplanted. Recommended sowing distances are given in the book where relevant, but they will also be listed on the back of seed packets.

SOWING TECHNIQUES

Always aim to sow seed thinly. With the vast majority of seed varieties, between 60 and 90 percent of your seeds will germinate and, if they come up too thickly, they tend to compete for the available light, becoming

THE STALE SEEDBED

If the soil is prepared and in a condition for seeds to germinate, the weed seeds that are almost certainly lying there will soon be springing into life, too. Being native, they will germinate faster and grow quicker than most cultivated varieties. It is essential, therefore, to eliminate this competition before sowing.

The simple remedy is to cultivate the seedbed a few weeks before you need it. Let weed seeds that are lying dormant germinate, then hoe them out immediately before sowing. This way only seeds that appear later will cause problems, and these will not only be fewer in number but also lagging behind the cultivated varieties you have sown and will be easy to recognize.

thin and straggly in the process. Some gardeners become adept at sowing straight from the packet, but I find it much more accurate to hold the seeds in the palm of my hand and sow a pinch at a time.

Some seeds are large enough to sow singly or in "stations" (placing groups of two or three seeds at the required distances, then thinning if more than one seed germinates at any station). With deep beds you should adopt a block-sowing technique (see p. 136).
Sowing in dry soil If your soil is very dry, water the rows before sowing. Use a watering can, more or less fill up the row, allow the water to drain, then sow as directed. Never sow and then water afterward, since this leads to "capping," where the soil forms a crust on top that can prevent the entry of further water or even prevent young

DRAWING SEED ROWS

There are two different types of seed rows: narrow rows and wide bands. Both types should be as shallow as possible and of a uniform depth.

Rake your soil to a fine tillage and tread down the soil firmly. Set up a tight planting line (see p. 260), then make a furrow as described below.

Drawing a narrow row *This is the most commonly used seed row. Put one corner of a draw hoe in the ground and pull it toward you gently. Alternatively, many gardeners find it easier to draw a regular row using a short stick.*

Making a narrow seed row with a broom or rake handle *If you find it difficult to draw a row using a hoe, place a broom handle or rake handle along the planting line and press it into the soil with your foot.*

Drawing a wide band *Put your hoe flat on the ground and pull it toward you. Make sure the furrow is of a uniform depth. Wide bands are used in deep-bed cultivation when sowing vegetable crops that are thinned selectively.*

seedlings breaking through to the light.

Covering after sowing Cover all seeds by running the back of your rake down the center of the row. Then, lightly tap down the soil with the back of the rake to ensure that the seed is in close contact with the soil.

Labeling rows of seeds Always use a commercial plant label to mark the row clearly with the name of the plants. It is not good enough just to stick the seed packet on to a cane, because it always seems to blow away or becomes unreadable after heavy rain.

Pre-germinating seeds Sometimes it is an advantage to pre-germinate seeds inside and sow them outside only after they have started to grow. Examples of plants that benefit from this are parsnips, which take so long to germinate in the early spring that they often rot in the soil, and lettuce, which will not germinate in soil temperatures over 68°F (20°C), a temperature often reached in summer even in colder areas.

Sow the seeds onto a piece of moistened tissue in the bottom of a plastic container. If the seeds need heat to germinate, place the container in a warm place, perhaps near the clothes dryer, until the first roots show through, and then sow as soon as possible. Do not let the roots grow longer than about ⅛in (3mm). If you cannot sow the seeds immediately, put the container in the refrigerator (not in the freezer), where they can be kept for a few days.

You must sow the seeds without damaging the fragile roots. With large seeds this is not too difficult, since you can pick up each individual seed with tweezers. With small seeds, however, you need to fluid sow them. Suspend them in a special alginate gel or wallpaper paste and "sow" the mixture in a seed row (*see p. 140*). If your soil is dry, break the normal rule and water over the top immediately after sowing; otherwise the gel may set too hard and trap the seeds under the soil.

SOWING ALPINES AND TREES

Seeds of many alpine plants and trees require a cold period before they will germinate, so you must sow them outside. Since these seeds are often very small, and not used in large quantities, it is a good idea to sow them in pots. Fill the pots with compost made from equal parts of peat, soil, and coarse sand for alpines or peat and coarse sand for trees, and sow the seeds thinly on top. Cover with a small quantity of coarse sand or grit.

Do not use a can for watering but, instead, stand the pot up to its rim in a bowl of water. Leave it there until you see that the top of the compost has darkened slightly, then remove it. The seeds will then be drawn down slightly into the compost. Put the pots outside in a shaded spot and cover them with a piece of wire netting as protection against birds and mice.

Sowing inside

By sowing seeds in trays or pots inside you can start much earlier in the year. Vegetables can be sown in midwinter and planted out under cloches in early spring. This way, you will have your first crop in late spring. A greenhouse is ideal for this purpose, because it is easier to control the environment to give the seeds the best possible start, but you could put them on a windowsill indoors. Check the recommended sowing temperature before you begin and ensure that you can provide it by starting the seeds off either in a heated propagator in the greenhouse or a warm cupboard.

Fill a pot or tray with moist seed compost (*see p. 252*) and firm it up lightly. Peat-free composts require very little firming, so don't overdo it; merely push your fingers into the compost. Then level the top of the compost and firm up the soil, with a firming board (*see p. 261*) if you are using a tray, or with the bottom of another pot.

When you are sowing in containers, it is very important to moisten compost thoroughly before sowing. Spread some compost onto your work bench, make a well in the center and pour some water into it. Gradually work the water into the compost by rubbing it through your hands. Fill the container, then water again, since watering after sowing tends to wash the seeds into one spot, or even right out of the pot! Allow the compost to drain for a few minutes and then sow the seeds as described below.

Cover all except very small seeds, such as those of begonias or lobelias, with their own depth of vermiculite. Then cover the pot or tray with a piece of opaque plastic and put it in a warm place. The furnace room can be useful, but check the temperature first to ensure that it is suitable for the seeds you are sowing: the shelf directly above the hot water heater may very well be too hot. Check the seeds every day and, as soon as the first one germinates and pushes to the surface, remove the whole container to a light place. Do not put the container in direct sunlight, and cover the seedlings with a sheet of newspaper if there is any chance of the sun scorching them.

If you are growing your seedlings on the windowsill, the fact that the light always comes from one direction only may make them long and spindly. You can reduce this effect to a minimum by making a "light box" out of a cardboard box, lined with kitchen foil to reflect available light all around the plants. If you use the light box in the winter, you should bring it into the warmth of the center of the room at night. You can cover the box with plastic at night, but remember to remove the cover in the morning, since it will greatly reduce the amount of light reaching your seedlings.

POTS AND CONTAINERS

Wood and clay are the traditional materials used for raising and growing on plants. However, the plastic and styrofoam containers now available are much cheaper and in some respects, give improved results.

Although there are commercial trays and pots available (*see below*), in fact you can use any shallow container for sowing seed, from styrofoam meat trays to margarine tubs or even the foil containers used for take-out food. Plastic yogurt containers, styrofoam coffee cups, and cut-off plastic bottles are ideal for sowing large seeds or for cuttings. Remember, though, if you use any of these items, they must be thoroughly cleaned before use and they must have adequate drainage holes in the bottom.

Pots These are available in clay or plastic. Clay pots have two main advantages over plastic ones. They are porous and therefore "breathe" allowing the free flow of air around the plant's root ball and thus reducing the risk of overwatering. Conversely, of course, the compost will dry out faster, so the plants may need watering more often. Clay pots are also heavier than plastic. This is important if you are growing tall, leafy plants that can become top heavy. The disadvantages of clay pots are that their porous nature makes them more likely to harbor disease, and more difficult to clean and sterilize, and that they are considerably more expensive than plastic.

Plants in plastic pots require less frequent watering than those in clay pots. This can be an advantage, particularly if you are using peat-free compost which dries quicker than a soil-based one.

I recommend using clay pots and soil-based compost for plants such as alpines, which need very good drainage, and plastic pots and peat-free compost for most other plants.

Seed trays These are shallow trays, generally about 2–3in (5–7cm) deep and either 15 × 9in (35 × 20cm) or 7 × 4in (15 × 10cm). Traditional seed trays are made of thin wood.

The disadvantage of wood is that, because it is porous, it is difficult to clean and can harbor disease. Plastic seeds trays, on the other hand, are very easy to sterilize with boiling water and are much cheaper.

Module trays Module trays are particularly useful as they are divided into smaller, individual cells for sowing into. They can be made from plastic or styrofoam. The plastic trays are light and cheap, with the styrofoam trays having an excellent heat retaining capacity. Seed is sown in the individual cells, and then, when it has germinated and developed a root system, the seedling and compost can be pushed out with the presser board and planted or repotted. Because the roots are never disturbed, this eliminates growth check that sometimes follows transplanting. These module trays are particularly suitable for multiple sowing (*see p. 139*).

Peat-free blocks You can buy compressed coir discs that sit in 1½in (4cm) propagation coir pots. Once sat in water these discs reconstitute enough to nicely fill the pot. I like to stand the pots in a small seed tray, which keeps them in place and stops them from falling over. Sow directly into the coir and transplant before too much root shows.

SOWING IN SEED TRAYS

Raising seed in trays inside means that vegetables and flowers can be started earlier in the year, without the risk of frost damage. Do not sow plants that fork when transplanted, such as long root vegetables, in seed trays; they have to be sown directly into the soil.

1 *Fill the seed tray with moistened sowing compost. Remove the excess by running the side of a firming board across the top.*

2 *Press the sowing compost into the edges of the tray with your fingers. Then consolidate it by pressing it down lightly with the firming board.*

3 *Pour some seed into your palm, then cup your hand slightly to form a channel in the side. Tap your hand with your finger to move the seeds along the channel; sow seeds around the edge of the tray, then work into the center.*

4 *Cover the seeds with their own depth of vermiculite or seed compost. Vermiculite can be sprinkled over the seeds by hand. If using compost, shake it over the seeds using a fine sieve.*

The best way to sow

Sowing very small seeds *Put a small amount of silver sand into the seed packet to act as a spreading agent. Put the seed and silver sand mixture into your hand and sow as shown above. These seeds do not need to be covered.*

Sowing large seeds *Large seeds, such as beans or cucumbers, for example, should be sown two to a pot. Make holes in the compost using a small stick, or dibber, and put the seeds in them on their sides. If both of the seeds germinate, carefully remove the weakest one (see next page).*

Thinning and transplanting seedlings

When seeds have germinated and are large enough to handle, they will need to be thinned to prevent overcrowding. Seeds that have been sown outside can be transplanted and thinned at the same time. You cannot, however, transplant all seedlings. Root crops will probably fork if seedlings are transplanted but most ornamentals and leaf vegetables can be moved.

SEEDLINGS GROWN OUTSIDE

Before either thinning out or transplanting, water the rows well. To thin seedlings, simply pull up unwanted seedlings, leaving the remaining plants at the required distance from each other. Put the thinnings into a seed tray and take them to the compost heap. Left on the ground, the bruised stems attract pests.

If you need thinnings for transplanting, then you must take more care when handling the seedlings. Thin to leave one row of seedlings at the required spacing, then transplant the rest in new rows as recommended.

CONTAINER-GROWN SEEDLINGS

Container-sown seedlings need to be thinned, or transplanted, into a larger seed tray or pot when they are large enough to handle (*see below*). Before they are planted out, seedlings grown in the greenhouse must be acclimatized to the colder conditions. Do this by placing them first into a closed, unheated cold frame. Then gradually open up the frame a little during the day and, finally, a little at night as well, until you leave it completely open (*see* Greenhouse Gardening, *pp. 246–257*).

THINNING AND TRANSPLANTING

Whether grown outside in seedbeds or in the greenhouse in seed trays, seedlings need to be thinned to prevent overcrowding. If you are thinning for transplanting, handle the seedlings by their leaves and not their stems because they bruise easily and could succumb to fungus attack. Transplanting from seed trays or pots into another container is known as "pricking out."

Transplanting outside

1 *Water the row of seedlings the day before you want to move them. Firm up the soil at the base of the plants that are to remain by straddling the stems with two fingers and pressing the soil down.*

2 *Remove the remaining seedlings either by placing your fingers under them and lifting carefully or by using a trowel, leaving as much root as possible on the plant. Then lay them in a seed tray.*

3 *Transplant the seedlings to new rows, using a planting board to calculate the spacing. Water the seedlings using a watering can with a fine nozzle.*

Pricking out

1 *Fill a larger seed tray with peat-free compost. Water the seedlings thoroughly, then lift them out carefully by pushing a small dibber under the roots, handling the seedlings by the leaves only. Never touch the stems.*

2 *Use a small dibber to make holes in the new compost. Put the seedlings in the holes and firm the compost. After filling the new tray, water it well and put it in a light place out of direct sunlight.*

Thinning pot-grown seedlings

When growing two large seeds in the same pot, remove the weaker seedling when one reaches 2–3in (5–7cm), and leave the other to continue growing. Firm down the roots of the seedling that is to remain while you remove the weaker one.

SAVING SEED

Seed can be expensive to buy so it is wise to save it, if you can, from season to season. Always open seed packets in a dry place and take out only as much as you need. Then reseal the packets, put them into a dry, airtight container, and keep them in a cool but frost-free place. Most should then last to at least the following season.

It is also possible to "harvest" your own seeds from many plants, both vegetables and ornamentals. Don't save the seeds of F1 hybrids because they will not grow true to type and the resulting plants will not resemble the parents.

Allow seeds to mature and ripen on the plants and remove the seed pods just before they fall. Great vigilance is necessary but, with a little practice, it soon becomes easy. If you find this difficult, when the pods are almost mature, place a paper bag over them to catch seeds as they ripen. Alternatively, cut the whole flowering stem and hang it in an airy spot upside down over a sheet or bowl to catch the seeds as they fall.

Other methods of propagation

Growing plants from seed is the most common method of propagation, but it is by no means the only one. Some plants will not produce their exact replicas from seed. Often, flower colors and sometimes even flower shapes will be different, so alternative, vegetative techniques of propagation are required. Of these, division is the simplest method but, for plants that you cannot divide, layering, cuttings, budding, and grafting are methods that will ensure that the new plants are exactly the same as the parent.

Propagation by division

Division is a method used to increase perennials. It is perhaps the simplest and most effective method of propagation and it produces good, sizable plants very quickly. Indeed, many perennials begin to lose vigor after a few years and will benefit greatly from being removed from the soil and divided.

For most perennials, this should be done in the fall. Cut back the old flower stems and lift the whole clump using a fork. Divide it in half and remove the young shoots from the outside of the clump (see below). The center of the clump is the older, less vigorous, part of the plant and you should discard it.

DIVIDING PLANTS WITH FLESHY ROOTS

Some plants, such as plantain lilies (Hosta sp.), have fleshy roots and should be treated differently. These are best dug up for division in the spring, just before they start into growth. Then you will be able to see new buds and have an idea of where to cut. Each new piece should have at least one good bud. Cut through the root with a sharp spade or a large knife and replant the parts as soon as possible.

DIVIDING PERENNIALS

Perennial plants that form spreading clumps should be divided every few years to perpetuate the existing stocks and prevent overcrowding.

Small clumps can be divided by hand or with a trowel. Larger clumps or very old clumps, however, have to be pried apart using garden forks.

1 Pull the entire plant out of the border and divide it in half. If it has a large matted root system, stick two garden forks back to back into the center of the clump and force it apart.

2 Remove the young shoots from the outer side of the clump by breaking or cutting them off.

3 Cut all the leaves right back to within 1in (2.5cm) of the roots and replant immediately, or pot them in potting compost and put the pots in a shady area until you can replant them.

Taking cuttings

Most plants can be propagated by taking cuttings without too much difficulty. There are many different types of cuttings recommended for various plants, but I just take "hardwood" cuttings in fall, when the wood is ripe, and "softwood" cuttings in summer, when the shoot is still growing. Most root using one of these methods, while half-hardy perennials require slight modification of the basic technique.

SOFTWOOD CUTTINGS

This method can be used to increase any shrubs. Softwood cuttings can be taken any time during

TAKING SOFTWOOD CUTTINGS

Take cuttings of soft, new plant growth, selecting healthy shoots about 4in (10cm) long. This method is suitable for most shrubs. Use the same method for conifer cuttings, but tear the leaves away from the shoots because the stems need to be bruised before they will root.

1 *Fill a tray with a peat-free propagation compost. Trim cutting back by half, just below a leaf joint.*

2 *Carefully trim away all the side leaves, then dip the cutting in copper fungicide solution.*

3 *Organic rooting powder is now available. Dip the end of the cutting into the powder and gently shake off the excess. Then put the cutting in the seed tray. Space cuttings in rows 1in (2.5cm) apart each way.*

4 *Water using a copper fungicide solution. Wrap the tray in light plastic sheeting so that the sheeting touches the tops of the cuttings and is sealed under the tray. Put the tray into a softwood cuttings frame.*

Taking clematis cuttings

Take a cutting that is at least 12in (30cm) long. Make two cuts, the first one immediately above a leaf joint and the second about 1¹/₂in (4cm) below it (see below). Dip the cutting in copper fungicide and insert it into the compost up to the leaves.

TAKING CUTTINGS OF HALF-HARDY PERENNIALS

These are best taken in late summer or in early spring when the tubers produce new shoots. They root more readily than shrubs, but need a temperature of 55–60°F (13–15°C) at the roots.

1 *Take a cutting that has at least three leaves and a new shoot. Then carefully cut away all the lower leaves.*

2 *Trim the stem of the cutting just below the lowest leaf joint. Then dip the stem in organic rooting powder; tap off the excess powder.*

3 *Put the cutting in a pot filled with peat-free compost. Make a hole with a small dibber, insert the cutting, and firm down the compost by pushing the dibber into the compost and pressing sideways toward the cutting.*

4 *Bend a piece of wire to form an arch over the cutting and place it in the pot. Cover with a plastic bag. Alternatively, put the pot in a plastic bag, blow up the bag with air, and seal the top.*

Making a softwood cuttings box *Make two wooden frames about 6in (15cm) deep and both exactly the same size. Make a lid for the first box from a sheet of corrugated plastic and use an onion sack as shading. Hold it in place with a thick rubber band, nailed on to one side and hooked to a nail on the other side. As the plants grow, the other frame can be set on top, and a new lid of sacking, weighted down at the front with a batten and nailed to the back, can be hung over the top.*

the summer, but the best time is early in the season. You need a small amount of equipment, but this should cost you next to nothing, and the success rate should be about 80 percent.

In order to maximize not only the percentage rooting of your cuttings but also the speed the cuttings will root, most gardeners like to use an organic rooting powder. Since they contain no synthesized hormones, they are very safe to use in an organic garden and may make the difference between cuttings rooting or not.

Once the cuttings are potted and in a cold frame or home-made softwood cuttings box (*see above*), providing the right amount of light is vital. The cuttings will be feeding through their leaves, so they need a certain amount of sunshine. Too much, on the other hand, will cause wilting. I use old onion nets, but a piece of greenhouse shade netting will do just as well. If the weather is likely to be very sunny during the day, cover the frame with two pieces of shading material. If it is only fairly sunny, use one piece. If it is dull, remove the shade altogether. Doing this makes all the difference between success and failure.

HARDWOOD CUTTINGS

This method is used to increase deciduous shrubs such as black currants and gooseberries in the fruit garden, and many ornamental shrubs such as dogwoods (*Cornus* sp.), mock orange (*Philadelphus* sp.), and Japanese rose (*Kerria* sp.) in the fall. It is worthwhile trying this with most deciduous shrubs because it is simple and cheap and the plants will not suffer from the small amount of pruning required.

TAKING HARDWOOD CUTTINGS

Hardwood cuttings should be taken in the fall, just after the plants have lost their leaves, although some, such as gooseberries, can be taken earlier in the season. Hardwood cuttings take some time to establish, but are worth the effort to increase a favorite or valuable shrub.

1 *Cut off a length of stem about 8–9in (20–23cm) long using a sharp knife or secateurs. Trim it below the lowest bud and cut off the soft top growth by trimming just above a bud.*

2 *Make a narrow trench and line the bottom with sharp sand. Place the cuttings in the trench, leaving 3in (7.5cm) of the top out of the ground. Refill the trench, press in the cuttings, and leave them for one year.*

3 *The following winter, plant them approximately 6–9in (15–23cm) apart in rows in a corner of the garden. Leave them for another year, then transplant them to their permanent position in the garden.*

Propagation by layering

This method of increasing plants involves putting part of the plant into the ground and leaving it attached to the parent until it has developed a root system sufficient to support itself. There are three different ways: tip layering, normal layering, and serpentine layering.

TIP LAYERING

Use this method mainly for plants that root readily, particularly the bramble fruits—blackberries, loganberries, and other hybrid berries. In late summer, pull down as many shoots as you need and make a hole in the soil where the tip of the shoot rests. Place the tip in the hole and pin it in position using a forked stick. Cover the tip with soil and leave it until the leaves of the parent plant fall. You can then cut the layer from the parent, lift it and transplant the new plant to its permanent position.

NORMAL LAYERING

This method involves burying part of the shoot with the tip exposed, and leaving it to root. Layering is usually carried out in early spring for shrubs and early summer for climbers. It is suitable for plants that root less readily, such as rhododendron, clematis, abelia, some viburnum, magnolia, witch hazel (*Hamamelis* sp.), Mexican orange blossom (*Choisya* sp.), camellia, and azalea. You may be able to cut the layer away from the parent plant by the following fall, but some plants need longer to root. Rhododendrons, for example, can take two, even three years. You can tell when the layer has rooted by its more vigorous appearance.

SERPENTINE LAYERING

This method of propagation is suitable for certain types of climber, particularly clematis. Follow the instructions given for normal layering (*see below*), but alternately bury and expose parts of each stem, making many more plants from each. Wound the stem by slitting it underneath and place that part underground. Then repeat the process further along the stem, making sure that there is at least one bud between the layers to provide the new shoot. The layers will produce shoots along the stem and, when the shoots start showing signs of growing, you can separate them from the parent plant and split them up to provide several new plants.

Grafting and budding

These are two similar techniques used to put new varieties on to existing plants, particularly fruit trees, and certain ornamental plants. They can be used either to change a variety, to put a variety onto a rootstock, or to put another variety onto a fruit tree to provide a pollinator.

Grafting is generally used to change a variety of an apple or pear tree completely, or to put a pollinator onto an existing tree. There is a risk with the latter because, if you don't use a new variety with the same vigor as the first tree, the

NORMAL LAYERING

By burying part of a shoot underground and leaving it to root, a new plant can be formed.

1 *Make a hole with one straight side by putting a spade or a trowel into the ground and pulling the soil toward you.*

2 *Carefully put the end of the shoot in the hole so that the tip is about 6in (15cm) out of the ground. Take care to avoid snapping the stem.*

3 *Pin the shoot into the ground with a forked stick or a wire pin, cover it with soil, and put a large stone over the layer. This keeps the layer in the ground and conserves moisture in dry weather.*

4 *Very often, this is all you need to do, but sometimes it is better if you damage the stem of the plant to encourage it to root. You can achieve this simply by twisting the stem fairly vigorously or by cutting a slit in the underside.*

CLEFT GRAFTING

Use this method to graft a new variety onto an existing tree in late winter or early spring.

1 *In midwinter, prepare the limb where you will site the graft by cutting back two branches just above a fork.*

2 *In late winter or early spring, just as the tree is starting its new growth, split each of the cut ends by driving a billhook into each one with a hammer.*

3 *Prepare four lengths of stem (known as scions) from the required variety. Each scion should be of one-year-old growth and about 4–6in (10–15cm) long. Cut the base of each one to form a wedge shape.*

4 *Insert scions into each cut end, making sure the cambium layers (the layers just beneath the bark) correspond. Tie in the scions using raffia or string and cover the wounds with grafting wax.*

more vigorous variety may dominate. Cleft grafting is normally used to graft a new variety onto an existing tree; use the whip-and-tongue method if you want to graft a variety onto a rootstock. The latter technique is also used to graft varieties onto ornamental plants that do not respond to budding.

Grafting should be done in late winter or early spring, just as the tree is beginning its new growth, although the "limb" for grafting should be prepared in midwinter.

Budding is a modified form of grafting and a slightly easier method. It is most commonly used to put new varieties onto rootstocks. It involves making cuts in the bark of the tree or rootstock and inserting one or more buds from another variety into them. It should be done in early to midsummer, when the sap is running well and the bark will separate freely from the tree. It is generally possible to buy rootstocks from any nursery where they do their own budding. And, as they are sold bare root, plant them in the winter before you need them.

WHIP-AND-TONGUE GRAFTING

Use this method to graft a variety onto a rootstock. Several ornamental plants can also be grafted using this method.

1 Trim the rootstock back and, with a sharp knife, make a long slanting cut in the top part of the stem to leave a long wedge shape.

2 Using a one-year-old scion (see left), cut the end to form a corresponding wedge.

3 Make two more cuts, one upward in the rootstock and one downward in the scion, to form two "tongues" that will fit together.

4 Fit the scion into the rootstock, making sure that the cambium layers correspond. Tie the graft with raffia and cover the wound with grafting wax.

BUDDING ONTO A ROOTSTOCK

Budding is a form of grafting used to put new varieties onto rootstocks and is a relatively simple technique to carry out.

1 In summer, cut a length of stem from the variety you want to bud. Leaving the leaf stalks on the cutting, remove all the leaves. (If you are budding a rose, remove the thorns first.) Immerse the whole stem in a bowl of water until it is needed.

2 With a sharp knife, cut a T-shaped slit in the bark of the rootstock and peel back the bark very slightly.

3 Remove a bud from the prepared stem—insert a sharp knife into the stem below the bud and pull it upward, keeping the knife just under the bud.

4 Examine the base of the bud carefully and you will see a sliver of wood in the center. Remove it with your fingernail.

5 Slide the bud into the T-shaped slit using the leaf stalk as a handle. When the bud is secure, cut away any excess bark to ensure a perfect fit and tie the bud onto the tree using raffia or a special rubber tie.

6 When the bud shows signs of having taken, carefully cut the raffia away; rubber ties can be left to rot. In the fall, prune off the growth on the rootstock above the new shoot, and tie the shoot to the stub.

THE GARDENING YEAR

Gardening is far from being an exact science, and the gardener who makes rules and sticks to them rigidly is bound to suffer disappointment and frustration. For there are almost always alternative methods to follow to reach desirable gardening goals, although new gardeners can't be expected to find much comfort in this truth. Of more concern to them, as well as to more experienced gardeners, are the existence of different regions with varying climatic conditions and soil types. These all affect plant growth, the kinds of plants that can be grown, and the timing of gardening duties.

In the US, there are many different climatic regions, as the map below shows. The gardening year is, in fact, more a state of mind than a reality in much of the country where frigid winters, often with long-lasting snow cover, stop outdoor gardening.

Assistance in coping with the regional aspects of gardening can come from several sources. Other gardeners in the area can be helpful, as can the Cooperative Extension Service, an organization of university-trained horticultural specialists with offices in nearly every county. New gardeners can also benefit from a guide such as the Calendar that follows. The Calendar is divided into seasons: spring, from March to the end of May; summer, from June to the end of August; autumn, from September to the end of November; and winter from December to the end of February.

CLIMATIC REGIONS OF THE US

Region 1 Cool dry summers, often foggy. Heavy rainfall in winter.

Region 2 Drier and warmer than Region 1 in summer. Lowest temperature 10° to 20°F.

Region 3 Hot, dry summers and mild winters. Lowest temperature 22° to 24°F. Winter rainfall 8–10in.

Region 4 Conditions vary with altitude in this mountainous region.

Region 5 Coastal summers are cool and dry, with higher temperature inland. Rainfall 10in in valleys, 30in in mountains.

Region 6 Warm summers, with cool winters. Winter temperature 10° to 15°F. Highest rainfall in spring and winter.

Region 7 Warm summers with winter temperatures of 0° to 15°F. Rainfall 10–20in.

Region 8 A semi-arid region with hot summers and cold winters. Winter temperature -10° to 0°F.

Region 9 Hot summer days, frost at night. Cold winters.

Region 10 Very hot. Rainfall 3–10in.

Region 11 Very hot summer days. Some areas get very cold in the winter, with frost.

Region 12 Rainfall and temperature vary with elevation and exposure.

Region 13 Rainfall and temperature vary with elevation and exposure, but temperatures about 7°F hotter than Region 12.

Region 14 Rainfall and temperature vary with elevation and exposure. Warmer than both Regions 12 and 13.

Region 15 Warm summers with very cold winters.

Region 16 Summers warmer than Region 15. Rainfall 12–22in.

Region 17 Hot and dry despite 12–22in rainfall due to excessive evaporation.

Region 18 Humid summers with cold, dry winters.

Region 19 Hot winds in summer. Winter temperatures subject to sudden variations.

Region 20 Transition zone. Warm and dry to the west, humid to the east.

Region 21 Annual rainfalls up to 20–30in. Cold winters with drying winds.

Region 22 Flat prairie country with cold, drying winds in winter. Rainfall 30–40in.

Region 23 West of region has cold winters with drying winds. East of region is warmer and more humid due to proximity to water.

Region 24 Very humid atmosphere. Rainfall of 30–40in, spreads throughout the year.

Region 25 Warm summers and moderate winters. Rainfall 40–50in, but still a risk of drought in summer.

Region 26 Long summer days, with cool nights. Winter brings heavy snowfalls.

Region 27 Heavy winter snows in colder areas. Rainfall 30–50in, falling throughout the year.

Region 28 A warmer zone than Region 27. Drought may occur at the end of summer. Winters moderate.

Region 29 Warm summers. High rainfall of 45–60in.

Region 30 Hot summers and short winters. Heavy rains in the winter.

Region 31 Warm summers. Annual frosts may cause damage. Rainfall 50in.

Region 32 Only slight temperature variations throughout the year. No killing frosts. Rainfall 50–60in.

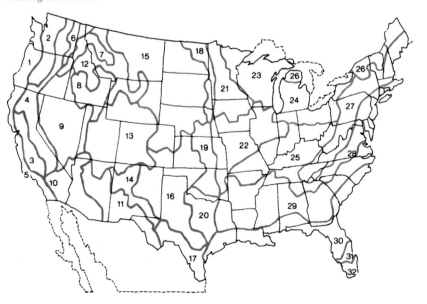

Spring

THROUGHOUT SPRING:
• **Heavy soils** Rake soil for sowing.
• **Light soils** Dig in overwintered green-manure cover crops in enough time to allow soil to settle before sowing.
• Start hoeing regularly from now on.
• Mulch between plants to control weeds and help water retention.
• Water regularly in dry weather, particularly newly planted items.
• Check the worm compost; put it outside again if you overwintered it inside. If it was left outside and the worms have died over the winter, replace them and start filling it.
• Start spraying with insecticides or fungicides as necessary but never on open flowers.
• Construct a pond.
• Carry out grafting.

	Early Spring	Mid-spring	Late Spring
THE ORNAMENTAL GARDEN **Throughout spring:** • Hoe between ornamental plants. • Lightly loosen the soil to prepare it for planting annuals. • Mulch empty areas with organic matter.	• Rake the lawn with a spring-tine rake. • Start mowing lawn when the grass is growing well. • Sow new seed lawns and resow patches. • Lay turf lawns. • Feed lawns and borders with blood, fish, and bone meal. • Lift and divide perennials. • Prune hybrid bush roses, cutting away any frost damage. • Finish planting bare root deciduous trees, shrubs, and hedges. • Start outside sowing of hardy annuals and many shrubs and climbers. • Start planting summer-flowering bulbs and perennials if ground is not frozen or waterlogged. • Start planting sweet peas. • Take softwood cuttings of heathers and layer shrubs.	• Plant bare root evergreen trees, shrubs, and hedges. • Prune shrubs that flower on one-year-old wood immediately after flowering. • Prune shrubs that flower on wood made in the same season. • Prune heathers as they finish flowering. • Plant floating, submerged oxygenating and marsh plants in and around the pond. • Finish planting sweet peas. • Continue to plant perennials, and to dig up and divide crowded clumps. • Continue to sow herbs and thin those sown in early spring. • Take cuttings of half-hardy perennials overwintered inside. • Plant tubs and hanging baskets for spring and summer color. • Start spraying roses if black spot has been a problem.	• Finish planting bare root evergreen plants. • Support tall perennials. • Trim ground cover after flowering. • When all danger of frost has passed, plant out half-hardy annuals and perennials. • If half-hardy annuals in seed trays look yellow, feed them with liquid kelp fertilizer. • If space is needed, dig and heel in spring-flowering bulbs. • Start clipping fast-growing hedges. • Prune early flowering climbers. • Start tying in climbers. • Plant deep-water aquatic plants. • Sow hardy perennials and biennials in a seedbed. • Continue sowing herbs. • Start taking softwood cuttings. • Look out for caterpillars on roses and other ornamentals. • Control aphids.
THE VEGETABLE GARDEN **Throughout spring:** • Cover emerging potato shoots with garden fabric if frost is likely. • Start successional sowing in early to mid-spring.	• Feed spring cabbages with dried blood or kelp meal. • Start sowing peas and beets outside under cloches, and green beans under cloches or in the greenhouse. • Sow leeks, Brussels sprouts, and cabbages in a stale seedbed. • Start sowing chard outside. • Plant sea kale, shallots, garlic, onion sets, potatoes, and Jerusalem artichokes. • Plant out peas and early spinach sown in the greenhouse in late winter.	• Plant asparagus crowns. • Sow sweet corn outside under sheets of polyethylene, and in the greenhouse in pots. • Sow main crop Florence fennel, peas, okra, turnips, kohlrabi, salsify and scorzonera, carrots, beets, cauliflower, broccoli, kale, and Swiss chard outside. • Plant out globe artichokes, green beans, and onions sown inside, and finish planting potatoes. • Set up canes for runner beans. • Plant eggplant and peppers under cloches.	• Finish planting squash and fruiting vegetables under cloches. • Mound soil around potatoes. • Plant out leeks. • At the end of spring, if soil and weather conditions permit, transplant celery, sweet corn, green and runner beans, fruiting vegetables, and celeriac. • Pinch off tops of broad beans if affected by blackfly. • Place carpet pad around newly planted cabbages to protect against cabbage root fly. • Erect carrot fly barriers around carrots.
THE FRUIT GARDEN **Throughout spring:** • Protect blossoms of early flowering trees from frost with garden fabric. • Finish winter pruning and planting of fruit trees. • Prune fan-trained cherry and plum trees. • Start training branches of bramble fruits. • Feed and mulch fruit trees and bushes. • If apple and pear scab or gooseberry mildew have been a problem, spray at biweekly intervals.	• Feed red currants and white currants with rock potash and black currants with blood, fish, and bone meal. • Check netting on fruit bushes. • If you have protected figs for the winter, remove the straw and sacking, untie the branches, and retrain them. • Graft apples, pears, and plums. • Hand-pollinate blossoms covered with fabric.	• During the day, take off some of the cloches protecting strawberries, to allow pollinating insects to get to the flowers. • Continue hand-pollinating blossoms.	• Water fruit bushes and trees. • Mulch under strawberry plants with straw to keep the fruits off the ground, and cover with netting to protect from birds. • Start tying in and pinching off wall-trained fruit. • Pull up unwanted shoots of raspberries that are growing into the paths. • Thin gooseberries to form large dessert fruits; use thinnings for cooking. • Put out codling moth traps. • Leave blossoms uncovered in daytime to allow insect pollination.
IN THE GREENHOUSE **Throughout spring:** • Ventilate the greenhouse on sunny days but close it at night. • Keep the atmosphere fairly dry.	• Sow the last of the ornamental half-hardy annuals. • Start sowing herbs. • Take cuttings of overwintered half-hardy perennials. • Sow peppers, eggplants, and cucumbers for growing in a cold greenhouse, and tomatoes for planting under cloches. • Sow okra and leeks. • Tie up rods of vines that were taken down for the winter. • Mulch around peaches.	• Start shading as necessary and increase ventilation. • Sow cucumbers for planting under cloches. • Sow leeks, runner beans, okra, squash, and celeriac for planting outside. • Plant tomatoes in an unheated greenhouse in growing bags or in prepared soil in the borders. • Plant eggplants and pepper seedlings in an unheated greenhouse.	• Start summer pruning grapevines. • Feed tomatoes and remove sideshoots. • Continue shading the greenhouse on very sunny days and increase ventilation.

Summer

THROUGHOUT SUMMER:
• Water the garden in dry weather but don't water ripe fruit.
• Continue hoeing; many weeds will now be seeding so this is very important. Cut down perennial weeds near your garden.

• Continue to mulch to control weeds and help with moisture retention.
• Start a new compost bin if the first is full and not yet ready for use.
• Cover bare ground with compost as it becomes available.
• Sow vacant ground with mustard or phacelia green-manure cover crop.

• Top off the worm compost regularly as the worms work very fast now; water if necessary.
• Watch continually for signs of pests and diseases and treat immediately.
• This is the best season to take softwood cuttings and for budding.
• Start layering.

	Early Summer	Midsummer	Late Summer
THE ORNAMENTAL GARDEN **Throughout summer:** • Mow lawn regularly, but not if the weather turns very dry, and remove rosetted weeds. • Top off pond and soak marsh garden in dry weather. • Deadhead perennials, shrubs, and roses to prolong flowering. • Tie in long-stemmed perennials. • Tie in climbers. • Save seeds of spring-flowering plants for use next year.	• Remove rose suckers. • Cut back early flowering perennials. • Continue to dig up and heel-in spring-flowering bulbs. • In cold areas, start to plant half-hardy perennials and annuals. • Plant deep-water aquatic plants. • Transplant to nursery rows seedlings of perennials and biennials sown in early spring. • Continue sowing biennials. • Continue propagating climbers by layering.	• Trim fast-growing hedges regularly. • Cut back herbaceous plants that have finished flowering—shred woody stems before composting—leaving a few to produce seed for next year. • Transplant biennials and perennials raised from seed into nursery rows. • Plant autumn-flowering bulbs. • Harvest herbs for drying before they come into full bloom.	• Lightly prune conifers. • Prune shrubs that have finished flowering. • Deadhead annuals. • Cut down gladioli, leaving some foliage to build up food for next year's corms. • Continue transplanting perennials and biennials. • Plant spring-flowering bulbs. • Save seeds from perennials as they ripen. • Start layering rhododendrons. • Take cuttings of half-hardy perennials. • Pot some bulbs for flowering in the house; leave them outside. • Store dried herbs and collect seeds. • Set earwig traps; if they are still troublesome, smear light grease below the affected blooms. • Take softwood cuttings of alpines, heathers, and perennial herbs such as sage and rosemary.
THE VEGETABLE GARDEN **Throughout summer:** • Check all vegetable netting. • Continue successional sowing until late summer.	• In colder areas, start planting out tender vegetables such as sweet corn, outdoor tomatoes, green beans, and zucchini. • Transplant autumn and winter cole plants and protect new plants from cabbage root fly. • Finish transplanting leeks sown inside or in a seedbed. • Support asparagus ferns with stakes in exposed areas. • Harvest and store shallots. • Tie cucumbers to stakes if growing them up tripod frames. • If growing sweet corn under plastic, cut slits to allow the leaves through. • Plant out sweet corn raised in the greenhouse. • Sow chicory outside. • Earth up main crop potatoes. • Harvest early potatoes.	• Put straw under bush tomatoes to keep the fruit clean and prevent from rotting. • Start late sowings of vegetables such as turnips and carrots for maturing outside; use early varieties. • Sow Swiss chard. • Draw soil away from onions to speed up ripening. • Earth up main crop potatoes again. • Spray potatoes against blight at two-week intervals from now until you dig them.	• Sow spring cabbages in a stale seedbed. • Sow quick-maturing varieties of lettuce for a late crop. • Save some seeds of broad beans for use next year. • Harvest some zucchini; leave some to form squashes, putting them on bricks to ripen for storing. • Start pulling and storing onions.
THE FRUIT GARDEN **Throughout summer:** • Check all the fruit netting in the garden. • Tie in bramble fruit and wall-trained fruit. • Spray aphids with insecticidal soap, if necessary. • Watch for sawfly larvae attacks on gooseberries; spray bushes with a biological nematode as soon as they are seen. • If apple or pear scab or mildew has been a problem, continue spraying at two-week intervals.	• Protect cherries against birds and pick fruit when ripe. • Start summer pruning trained soft fruit to encourage fruiting branches. • Continue tying in and pinching off wall-trained trees. • Feed black currants if necessary. • Pin down strawberry runners if you want them for forcing, or cut them off.	• After tree fruit has dropped naturally, thin fruit clusters. • Harvest and prune black currants at the same time. • Harvest summer-fruiting raspberries, cut out fruited canes and weak new growth. Tie in new canes. • Harvest strawberries and cut old leaves down. Remove and compost leaves and straw. Dig up unwanted runners. • Start summer pruning soft fruit and trained pear trees. • Support heavily laden branches of tree fruit. • Towards the end of the period, tip layer bramble fruit.	• Summer prune all trained forms of apples and pears. • Summer prune black currants if not pruned already. • Tie in branches of decorative trees. • Prune plum and Asian plum trees. • Pick early apples for eating. • Continue summer pruning bush fruit. • Harvest bramble fruits, then cut back fruited branches. • Pot rooted strawberry runners and leave them outside. • Plant new strawberry beds. • Continue spraying against pear and apple scab and mildew.
IN THE GREENHOUSE **Throughout summer:** • Feed all fruiting vegetables grown under glass at weekly intervals. • Spray down regularly.	• Paint shading onto greenhouse or let down blinds for the summer and increase ventilation. • Start pinching off, training, and feeding fruiting vegetables. • Remove tomato side shoots. • Summer prune vines.	• Make sure the greenhouse is in a good state of repair; renew cracked panes of glass, and paint frame as necessary. • Continue feeding and removing side shoots from tomatoes and cucumbers and start harvesting.	• Take fuchsia and geranium cuttings and sow cyclamen. • Start sowing winter lettuce in seed trays. • Maintain continual day and night ventilation.

Autumn

THROUGHOUT AUTUMN:
• **Heavy soils** Start digging soil, working in manure or compost as soon as land becomes vacant. Keep off all wet soil; cover an area with plastic so that you can cultivate it when the rest is wet.
• **Light soils** Sow green-manure crops to cover vacant land for winter.
• Dig in spring-sown green-manure crops.

• There will be an enormous amount of compost at this time. If bins are full, use some of the material as sheet compost.
• Start collecting leaves and compost them for leaf mold separately, or with the shredded prunings.
• Clean out debris under hedges.
• If you have ordered bare root ornamental or fruit trees and bushes, cover a piece of ground with plastic to prevent the soil from freezing. They can then be planted

temporarily if the rest is frozen.
• Take the mower in for servicing.
LATE AUTUMN:
• Check all tree ties and stakes; renew or repair as necessary.
• Mulch around trees and bushes.
• Make sure compost bins are covered.
• Pull up all garden stakes and poles, clean and store for next year.
• Insulate all outside water pipes.
• Carry out any "hard" landscaping provided ground is not frozen.

	Early Autumn	Mid-autumn	Late Autumn
THE ORNAMENTAL GARDEN **Throughout autumn:** • Remember to water borders if the weather is very dry. • Send for catalogs from specialty nurseries, and order plants. • Start preparing empty borders for autumn planting. • Lightly fork over any vacant ground in the borders and mulch with compost or manure.	• Do not cut the lawn if the weather turns very dry. • If sowing a new lawn, prepare the soil and sow now. • Finish planting spring-flowering bulbs other than tulips. • Continue to tie in stems of tall-growing autumn-flowering perennials. • Prune climbing and rambling roses and weeping standards. • Prepare trenches for planting new hedges. • Continue trimming coniferous trees and hedges.	• Stop mowing the lawn. • Lay turf lawns. • Cover the pond with netting. • Dig up, divide, and replant perennials, if they are old, crowded, or restricting shrubs. • Dig up and store half-hardy perennials and bulbs. • Dig up gladioli, remove the old corms, and store new ones. • Replant tubs and hanging baskets for winter/spring. • Dig up and compost annuals; replant with biennials. • Start planting bare root evergreen trees, shrubs, and hedging plants. • Plant lilies. • Finish planting tulips. • Plant hardy perennials, alpines, and heathers. • Sow sweet peas in cold frame. • Start taking hardwood cuttings. • Pot mint roots for winter.	• Start planting bare root deciduous trees, shrubs, and hedging and continue planting conifers. If ground is frozen or waterlogged, heel them in. • Dig a few perennials such as primulas and Christmas roses (*Helleborus niger*) for forcing in the greenhouse. • Remove fallen leaves from the rock garden and cover woolly-leaved alpines with glass. • Continue planting perennials if soil is not frozen or waterlogged. • Continue to take hardwood cuttings.
THE VEGETABLE GARDEN **Throughout autumn:** • Keep leaves and vegetable debris cleaned up to prevent spread of disease.	• Start digging and storing root vegetables, except those that need frost to improve flavor. • At the end of the season, protect fruiting vegetables with cloches. • Earth up celery, celeriac, and leeks. • Transplant spring cabbages. • Lift and store main crop onions. • Dig up and store potatoes; burn the foliage if there has been any sign of blight. • As runner beans finish, cut off the tops and compost them. Save some seed for next year. • Remove any caterpillars on cabbages.	• Plant winter lettuce. • Transplant spring cabbages. • Cut down peas and beans; leave the roots in the soil. • Earth up celery, leeks, and celeriac. • Harvest chicory and store roots. • Dig up and store root vegetables except those that need frost. • Force chicory roots inside, and sea kale and rhubarb outside. • Remove all stumps of cole plants as they are harvested. • Cut down Jerusalem artichokes. • Blanch endives. • Cut down asparagus foliage and mulch bed. Mulch rhubarb when leaves have died down.	• Secure bird netting over cabbages. • Start sowing broad beans outside. • Continue forcing crops in a warm place. • Protect cauliflowers from frost by bending leaves over the heads. • Firm the stems of tall cole plants to prevent them from rocking. • Remove yellowing leaves of cole plants and compost them. • Take up all stakes, clean them, and store for use next year. • Finish earthing up celery. • Dig up and store a few parsnips and Hamburg parsley in case the ground freezes.
THE FRUIT GARDEN **Throughout autumn:** • Continue to tie in new shoots of bramble fruits. • Check all tree ties and stakes; replace as necessary. • Cut out damaged or diseased wood.	• Send for catalogs from specialty nurseries; order plants. • Complete summer pruning of all trained trees. • Mulch under autumn-fruiting strawberries with straw and cover with bird netting. Toward the end of the season, protect them with cloches. • Continue planting straw-berry beds. • Pick blackberries and cut fruited shoots back. • Take hardwood cuttings of currants and gooseberries. • Cut off and burn mildewed tips of fruit trees and bushes. • Check apple, pear, and quince trees for canker.	• Prepare planting areas for next month. • Put greasebands around apple and cherry trees. • Pick and store late apples, pears, and quinces. • Winter prune currants and gooseberries after leaves fall. • Cut back foliage of autumn-fruiting strawberries after harvesting and remove straw mulch; compost everything.	• Plant bare root trees and bushes and rootstocks for budding next spring. It is also the best time to plant container-grown trees and bushes. • If the soil is frozen when trees arrive, cover the roots with coir or peat substitute and burlap, or heel the trees in. • Start winter pruning of bush and standard trees and formative pruning of trained trees. • Cover soft fruit bushes with bird netting. • Finish storing tree fruit. • Inspect fruit in storage; remove any showing signs of deterioration. • Check fruit cage netting and repair if necessary.
IN THE GREENHOUSE **Throughout autumn:** • Reduce ventilation and spraying down.	• Continue sowing winter lettuce. • Check that your heaters are working.	• Sow short-day lettuce in a cold greenhouse or cold frame. • Check all plants; remove foliage or shoots that have been attacked by fungus disease. • Start closing the cold frame and greenhouse at night; start heating if necessary.	• Transplant short-day lettuces. • Plant vines, peaches, and nectarines. • If the greenhouse is heated and large enough, bring the worm compost inside and the worms will keep going through the winter.

Winter

THROUGHOUT WINTER:
• **Heavy soils** Continue digging. Keep off the soil as much as possible, working from boards if necessary. Always keep off the soil if it is wet—cover some land with plastic sheeting so that you can continue cultivating when the rest is wet.
• Dig new deep beds and manure existing ones.

• **Light soils** Spread manure or compost over ground that is not sown with green manure.
• When the ground is frozen, try to keep off the soil and especially off the grass.
• If you have not already done so, check stakes and ties of all ornamental and fruit trees; renew and repair as necessary.
• Protect roots of all plants in containers by wrapping the tubs or pots with burlap.
• Repair tools and machinery.

• Make any new tools.
• Send for seed and bulb catalogs and plan next year's planting.
• Repaint woodwork such as fences and gates. NEVER use creosote near plants.
MIDWINTER:
• Sterilize pots and seed trays with boiling water ready for sowing in late winter.
LATE WINTER:
• Start cleft and whip-and-tongue grafting.

	Early Winter	Midwinter	Late Winter
THE ORNAMENTAL GARDEN **Throughout winter:** • Mulch between plants in borders. • Winter prune trees. • Plant bare root trees, shrubs, and bushes when soil conditions are suitable. • If there have been any frosts, check all newly planted shrubs to see if they have uprooted. If they have, firm them back into the ground. • Examine stored dahlia tubers: soak in warm water any that are shriveled; if any show signs of rot, cut out the affected parts and dust the tuber with sulfur. • Close the cold frame to protect sweet pea seedlings in very cold or wet weather.	• Replace worn areas of lawn with turf. • Lay turf lawns if ground is not frozen. • Start winter pruning trees and shrubs. • Trim heathers with shears after flowering. • Sow alpines and tree seeds that need exposure to frost and leave them outside. • Put container-grown, frost-tender plants, such as bay trees, in the greenhouse or leave outside and cover with garden fabric to protect from frost. • Bulbs that have been potted and covered outside should be brought into the house as soon as some of the buds are about 2in (5cm) high.	• Finish sowing alpines and trees.	• Spike badly drained areas of lawn with a hollow-tined fork and brush peat or sand into the holes. • Start feeding the borders and lawn in late winter/early spring. • Start pruning late-flowering climbers. • Dig and divide mint and propagate from runners.
THE VEGETABLE GARDEN **Throughout winter:** • Pot chicory roots and sea kale and keep in a warm place for forcing every three to four weeks. • Test soil pH and add lime if necessary. • Continue digging and manuring. • Examine stored vegetables; remove any that show signs of deterioration.	• Dig up and replant rhubarb.	• Continue sowing broad beans. • Cover some soil with cloches to warm it up so it is ready for sowing outside in a few weeks. • Set up potato tubers to sprout if planting under plastic. • Plant rhubarb if the soil is not waterlogged or frozen. Cover an established plant for early shoots.	• Feed spring cabbages with dried blood or kelp meal. • Start sowing early vegetable varieties under cloches and hardy varieties outside. • Start planting early potatoes under plastic. • Set up more potato tubers. • Plant Jerusalem artichokes, shallots, and garlic. • Start planting out under cloches early sowings made in the greenhouse.
THE FRUIT GARDEN **Throughout winter:** • Winter prune apple, pear, and quince trees; cut out and burn shoots showing signs of canker. • Plant bare root trees and bushes when weather conditions are suitable. • Inspect fruit in storage; remove any showing signs of deterioration. • Prune newly planted fruit trees and bushes.	• Cut back branches ready for grafting in the spring. • In cold areas, protect fig shoots by tying them together and covering with straw and burlap.		• Feed and mulch fruit trees and bushes. • Protect blossoms of early flowering wall-trained fruit from frost by covering with sheets of garden fabric; hand-pollinate flowers. • Start training in new shoots of bramble fruits. • Prune autumn-fruiting raspberries. • Put potted strawberry runners into the greenhouse for forcing, or cover some plants with cloches. • If peach leaf curl has been a problem in the past, start spraying now.
IN THE GREENHOUSE **Throughout winter:** • Ventilate whenever possible on sunny days. • Keep atmosphere dry. • Check maximum/minimum thermometer regularly and adjust heating as necessary.	• Take down greenhouse vines and lay them on the greenhouse borders. • Wash down the greenhouse.	• Start heating the greenhouse if sowing early crops now. • Mid to late winter: start sowing globe artichokes, peppers, cucumbers, onions, radishes, carrots, turnips, summer cabbages, and spinach in a heated greenhouse.	• Start sowing seeds of flowering pot plants. • Start sowing half-hardy annuals in late winter/early spring. • Start sowing celery, tomatoes, eggplants, melons, peas, sweet corn, and early spinach. • Start sowing tomatoes for growing under glass. • Tie up rods of greenhouse vines taken down for the winter as soon as they start new growth.

USEFUL ADDRESSES

Burpee Gardening
900 Park Ave.
Warminster, PA 18974
www.burpee.com
Seed (request untreated), plants, biological controls, organic pest controls, netting, cold frames. Catalog.

Cape Cod Worm Farm
30 Center Ave.
Buzzards Bay, MA 02532
www.capecodwormfarm.com
Red worms, worm castings.

Gardens Alive!
5100 Schenley Pl.
Lawrenceburg, IN 47025
www.gardensalive.com
Dedicated to biological control of garden pests.

Gardener's Supply Co.
128 Intervale Rd.
Burlington, VT 05401
www.gardeners.com
Tools and supplies, including organic pesticides. Catalog.

Gurney Seed and Nursery Co.
P.O. Box 4178
Greendale, IN 47025
www.gurneys.com
Seeds, plants, supplies. Catalog.

Johnny's Selected Seed
955 Benton Ave.
Albion, ME 04910
www.johnnyseeds.com
Vegetable seeds, including heirloom varieties, untreated except for corn and flower seeds. Tools, supplies, and organic pest controls. Catalog.

George W. Park Seed Co.
1 Parkton Ave.
Greenwood, SC 29647
www.parkseed.com
Seeds, supplies, including fluorescent lamps, cold frames. Catalog.

Paradise Water Gardens
15 May St.
Whitman, MA 02382
www.paradisewatergardens.com
Water garden plants and supplies. Catalog.

Plants of the Southwest
3095 Aqua Fria Rd.
Santa Fe, NM 87507
www.plantsofthesouthwest.com
Seeds, including ancient American vegetables and wildflowers, and regional books. Catalog.

Roses of Today and Yesterday
802 Brown's Valley Rd.
Watsonville, CA 95076
www.rosesofyesterday.com
Disease-resistant shrub roses, old and modern rose bushes. Catalog.

Stark Brothers
P.O Box 1800
Louisiana, MO 63353
www.starkbros.com
Fruit plants of all types, some developed in-house. Catalog.

Cooperative Extension Service
www.csrees.usda.gov/Extension/
Government-funded organization associated with the US Dept. of Agriculture.

National Gardening Organization
www.gardening.org
Non-profit organization promoting gardening. Monthly magazine emphasizes food gardening without chemicals. Catalog.

Seed Savers Exchange
Director: Amy Goldman
www.seedsavers.org
Organization dedicated to preserving heirloom food seeds of the US and Canada. Catalog.

Organic Gardening
www.organicgardening.com
Monthly organic gardening magazine.

Canadian Organic Growers
National Office
323 Chapel St.
Ottawa, ON K1N 7Z2
www.cog.ca

City Farmer
Box 74567, Kitsilano RPO
Vancouver, BC V6K 4P4
www.cityfarmer.org
Online resources for urban gardeners, including information on many organic options.

Forest Stewardship Council Canada
70 The Esplanade, Suite 400
Toronto, ON M5E 1R2
www.fsccanada.org

Pesticide Action Network North America
49 Powell St., Suite 500
San Francisco, CA 94102
www.panna.org
Promotes safer alternatives to pesticides, the production of healthy food, and sustainable farming.

Salt Spring Seeds
Box 444, Ganges P.O.
Salt Spring Island, BC V8K 2W1
www.saltspringseeds.com
Supplier of heritage and heirloom organic seeds.

Veseys
P.O. Box 9000
Charlottetown, PE C1A 8K6
www.veseys.com
Supplier of certified organic seeds and other gardening supplies.

Worm Composting Canada
www.wormcomposting.ca
Information about vermicomposting, and online retailer of vermicomposting supplies.

INDEX

Page numbers in **bold** refer to illustrations and captions

Acknowledgments

Author's acknowledgments The material in this book is the result of 10 years of trials and observation. This represents a great deal of work in growing plants and recording, collating, and evaluating information. My thanks are due to my colleagues who did much of the work with skill, patience, and dedication. To Carol Woods, Sue Jeal, and Rod Biggs, the other three-quarters of the growing team at Barnsdale, I owe a major debt of gratitude.

My thanks are also due to the many manufacturers, growers, and merchants who make up the British gardening industry for their unstinting support in supplying both materials and information.

Photographer Dave King was forced to break the habit of a lifetime and set out at dawn for my remote residence to take all the on-site photographs. The quality of his work needs no acclaim from me. It speaks for itself.

The editorial and design team of Jemima Dunne, Neville Graham, Sophie Mitchell, Tim Hammond, Derek Coombes, and Joanna Martin, deserve not only my sincere thanks but a medal for fortitude and diplomacy. They have suffered grueling hours plus my impatience and bad temper with commendable patience and humor.

My grateful thanks to a team of real professionals.

Geoff Hamilton, Barnsdale, 1987

Dorling Kindersley would like to thank: Vic Chambers and Tony Wallace without whom we would never have finished the book; Henrietta Winthrop for production; James Allen and Jonathan Hilton for editorial help; Tina Vaughan and Philip Lord for design help; Fred and Cathy Gill for proofreading; Richard and Hilary Bird for the index; Chris Cope for the black and white prints; Elizabeth Robinson for collecting the seaweed (kelp); Mr Grant at Whitkirk Produce Co. for the wool shoddy; Mr Don at Young's Brewery for the spent hops; Fulham Palace Road Garden Centre for plants and soil conditioners; Mrs Tree for reference photographs; Susan Watt for the mulberries; Mary Daniell and David Burnie for collecting weeds; Jim Keesing at the Royal Botanical Gardens, Kew; Dr Loveland at Rothamsted Experimental Station; Mrs Bench at Herb Nursery, Thistleton; Avon Bulbs; Hilliers of Winchester; Blooms of Bressingham; Hyam and Cockertons; and everyone at Barnsdale.

Illustrators
David Ashby
Vanessa Luff
Andrew Macdonald
John Woodcock
Brian Sayers

Photography
Andreas Einsiedel – *Still-life photography*
Dave King – *Step-by-step photography*
All other photography © DK Images except:

Key:
T = top   R = right
B = bottom   L = left
C = center

p6 (L) Andrew Butler; *p7* Karl Buhler/ Elizabeth Whiting and Associates; *p37 (L)* Clive Boursnell/DK Images, *(C)* Peter Anderson/ DK Images, *(R)* Alan Briere/DK images; *p45 (B)* Heather Angel; *p70* Alamy Images/ Red Cover; *p71 (L)* Photolibrary/Clay Perry, *p76 (R)* Marianne Majerus Garden Images/ Marianne Majerus, Chestnut Farm; *p80 (T)* Stephen Hamilton, *p84 (CL)* Alamy Images/ Arco Images GmbH, *(CR)* Garden World Images/Jenny Lilly, *(BR)* Natural Visions/ Heather Angel; *p91 (T)* Alamy Images/Dave Zubraski; *p127 (TR)* Getty Images/GAP Photos; *p130 (BC)* Mark Winwood/DK Images; *p133 (T)* Andrew Butler; *p141 (B)* Peter Anderson/DK Images; *p176* Andrew Butler; *p237 (L)* Photolibrary/David Sellman.

For further information about DK Images see www.dkimages.com

3 1901 04987 3328